W9-CLJ-456

ALUMNI
BOOK
FUND

PEACE BY PIECES—

United Nations Agencies and Their Roles:

a reader and selective bibliography

edited by
ROBERT N. WELLS, JR.

The Scarecrow Press, Inc.
Metuchen, N.J., & London
1991

British Library Cataloguing-in-Publication data available

Library of Congress Cataloging-in-Publication Data

Peace by pieces : United Nations agencies and their roles : a reader
and selective bibliography / edited by Robert N. Wells, Jr.
     p.   cm.
   Includes index.
   ISBN 0-8108-2510-4 (alk. paper)
   1. International agencies. 2. United Nations. I. Wells,
Robert N.
JX1995.P38   1991
341.23--dc20   91-39751

To Pat, Cynthia,
Gretchen and Christopher

COPYRIGHT ACKNOWLEDGMENTS

International Peace, by permission of the author and *Foreign Policy*.

Wilhelm H. Lampe, "The 'New' International Maritime Organization and its Place in Development of International Maritime Law," is reprinted from the *Journal of Maritime Law and Commerce*, 14, July 1983, 305-309, Anderson Publishing Company, Cincinnati, OH, by permission of the author and the Anderson Publishing Co.

George A. Codding, Jr., "Financing Development Assistance in the ITU," is reprinted from *Telecommunications Policy*, 13, March 1989, 13-24, by permission of the author and Butterworth-Heinemann Ltd., Guildford, Surrey, UK.

Ron Sanders, "An Assessment of UNCTAD's Effectiveness as an Instrument to Promote the Interests of the Third World," is reprinted from *The Round Table*, 311, July 1989, 272-287, London, UK, by permission of the author and *The Round Table*.

Ursula Wasserman, "The Universal Postal Union," is reprinted from *The Journal of World Trade Law*, 7, no. 2 (1973), 241-246, Geneva, Switzerland, by permission of the author and *The Journal of World Trade Law*.

Kathryn Sikkink, "Codes of Conduct for Transnational Corporations: The Case of the WHO/UNICEF Code," is reprinted from *International Organization*, 40, Autumn 1986, 815-840, MIT Press, Cambridge, MA, copyright 1986 by The World Peace Foundation and the Massachusetts Institute of Technology, by permission of the author and MIT Press.

Michael K. Kirk, "WIPO's Involvement in International Developments," is reprinted from the *Albany Law Review*, 50, Spring 1986, 601-610, Albany Law School, Albany, NY, by permission of the author and the *Albany Law Review*.

Arpad Bogsch, "The World Intellectual Property Organization: Its Recent Past and its Future Plans," is reprinted from the *Bulletin of the Copyright Society of the U.S.A.* 26, 1979, 194-201, by permission of the author and the *Bulletin of the Copyright Society of the U.S.A.*

John A. Leese, "World Meteorological Organization — Demonstrated Accomplishments and Strong Plans for the Future in Applying Space Technology," is reprinted from *The Journal of Space Law*, 14, 1986, 140-147, by permission of the author and *The Journal of Space Law*.

Eugene W. Bierly, "The World Climate Program: Collaboration and Communication on a Global Scale," is reprinted from the ANNALS, AAPSS, 495, January 1988, 107-116, by permission of the author and Sage Publications, Inc., copyright 1988.

CONTENTS

Contents

UNITED NATIONS AGENCIES

FAO	Food and Agriculture Organization
GATT	General Agreement on Tariffs and Trade
IAEA	International Atomic Energy Agency
IBRD	International Bank of Reconstruction and Development (World Bank)
ICAO	International Civil Aviation Organization
IFAD	International Fund for Agricultural Development
ILO	International Labor Organization
IMF	International Monetary Fund
IMO	International Maritime Organization
ITU	International Telecommunications Union
UNCTAD	United Nations Conference on Trade and Development
UNDP	United Nations Development Program
UNESCO	United Nations Educational, Scientific and Cultural Organization
UNICEF	United Nations Children's Fund
UNIDO	United Nations Industrial Development Organization
UPU	Universal Postal Union
WFC	World Food Council
WFP	World Food Program
WHO	World Health Organization
WIPO	World Intellectual Property Organization
WMO	World Meteorological Organization

PREFACE

The U.N. Specialized Agencies do not receive the notoriety that the U.N. Security Council or General Assembly do. Their economic, scientific and technical functions have often been referred to as "low politics" in comparison with the "high politics" practiced by the political organs of the United Nations. Most of the students entering my course on international organization cannot identify more than one or two of the agencies or their functions. People invariably confuse UNICEF with UNESCO. The World Bank (IBRD) and WHO are easily recognized but not necessarily as U.N. Specialized Agencies. In fact, when asked to identify the principal components of the United Nations family, it is not uncommon for individuals to omit mention of the specialized agencies all together.

Yet the specialized agencies have a long and distinguished record of international service. The ITU, WMO and UPO were among the first international organizations established in the nineteenth century. Because of their presence the world has been able to embark on programs of health improvement and disease eradication, famine relief and food security, illiteracy reduction and the improvement of workers' rights and working conditions. The agencies have received numerous international awards for their service, including three Nobel Peace prizes. Together with the United Nations Development Program (UNDP), the specialized agencies have been the major providers of technical assistance to the developing countries.

However, one more book on the specialized agencies will not, in all probability, push them into the foreground of United Nations activities. My goal is more modest, to bring together a selection of articles on the several agencies which examine them at work rather than merely describing their organization and functions. At the beginning of each chapter I have summarized the agency organization and primary activities of each for the reader. The selections on the various agencies were chosen to examine them in their policy and rule-making roles and the agencies' extensive involvement in development assistance; e.g. the World Bank and poverty, WHO and UNICEF and a code of conduct on breast milk substitutes.

Since 1960, when the former colonial states received their independence and joined the United Nations, the functions of the U.N. Specialized Agencies have greatly expanded. Today these agencies provide much of the scientific and technical expertise for the United Nations Development Program (UNDP), the United Nations agency most concerned with economic and social development. For most of the agencies, development assistance in conjunction with the UNDP is their primary function. The third world has recognized their importance and it has lobbied to gain a larger role in the functioning of the specialized agencies.

Another phenomenon since the expansion of the U.N. and the specialized agencies is the emergence of politicization. Historically the specialized agencies have avoided political questions, leaving such matters to the U.N. political organizations. However, political issues have spilled over to the agendas of many of the agencies and jeopardized their normal functioning. In particular, UNESCO, ILO, FAO, and WHO have experienced varying levels of politicization. In the cases of ILO and UNESCO it led to the withdrawal of the United States, the two organizations' largest contributor. Victor-Yves Ghebali provides a detailed analysis of politicization and its causes in Chapter II.

A secondary goal of this study was to bring together, under one cover, an examination of all the specialized agencies, large and small. General studies of the United Nations provide limited coverage to the specialized agencies. This study will provide the student of international organization a comprehensive coverage of the seventeen agencies and an extensive bibliography for further reference.

I wish to thank the authors and publishers who kindly consented to allow me to include their articles in this study. Thanks to Innis Claude and Harold Jacobson who first sparked my interest in the United Nations. My student research assistants, Stephen Todd and Tracy Williams, provided invaluable assistance in assembling this work. Sheila Murphy and Sherry Towne were ever available to provide editorial assistance, manuscript typing, and assembling bibliographies. Laurie Olmstead and Bonnie Enslow prepared the entire manuscript for the publisher. I cannot thank them enough. I would like to acknowledge my gratitude to St. Lawrence University for their generous financial support and encouragement. To my students, a special thanks. Over a period of twenty-five years they have provided me with the inspiration to pursue my interest in the specialized agencies and edit this book of readings.

Robert N. Wells, Jr.
Munsil Professor of Government
St. Lawrence University
1991

Chapter I

Introduction

The UN's Specialized Agencies: Adaptation and Role Changes in an Altered International Environment

When the subject of the United Nations is introduced, most individuals respond by mentioning such organs as the UN General Assembly, Security Council, World Court or UN Peacekeeping activities. Given the fact that the United Nations' primary function is international peace and security, it is quite natural to associate the United Nations with its political and security functions and the agencies which perform those roles. There is, however, another United Nations which is lesser known but equally important to the promotion of international peace and cooperation. I refer to the economic, social and development activities of the United Nations and the agencies which undertake these tasks. These agencies are commonly referred to as the specialized agencies.

They are independent international agencies which are linked to the United Nations system by treaty or international agreement and coordinate their work with the UN through the United Nations Economic and Social Council (ECOSOC). The specialized agencies are the principal providers of technical assistance for the United Nations Development Program (UNDP), the UN's lead agency in development assistance to third world countries. In that four-fifths of the UN budget is concerned with economic and social development and technical assistance, the specialized agencies perform a very important development assistance role. Although the specialized agencies have other functions

1

and responsibilities, their primary focus has been technical assistance and expertise since the inception of the United Nations Development Program in 1965.

Three of the seventeen agencies examined in this book function similar to the other specialized agencies but have a somewhat different political and legal status. The International Atomic Energy Agency (IAEA) is an independent intergovernmental organization under United Nations aegis. Because of its special responsibility in the area of international safeguarding of nuclear materials, the IAEA reports directly to the UN Security Council. In all other matters the IAEA functions similar to a specialized agency and coordinates its program activity with ECOSOC and the UNDP. The 1947 Charter of Havana provided for an International Trade Organization (ITO). The ITO Charter was never ratified and the provisional secretariat of the proposed ITO was given responsibility to administer the General Agreement on Tariffs and Trade (GATT) which was approved in 1947. Since that time GATT has played a significant role in substantially reducing tariff and non-tariff barriers to international trade.

In 1964, the General Assembly, at the urging of the third world and socialist countries, established the United Nations Conference on Trade and Development (UNCTAD) as a United Nations Agency responsible to the General Assembly. The creation of UNCTAD was an effort to provide developing countries with an organization which would provide them a greater say in world trade and development programs. UNCTAD was to become the Third World's lobby in the United Nations.

The Specialized Agencies: An Overview

Several of the specialized agencies are very old and precede both the League of Nations and the United Nations. The Universal Postal Union (1875), the World Meteorological Organization (1873) and the International Telecommunications Union, formerly known as the International Telegraphic Union (1865), are the oldest continuous specialized agencies. These organizations also share the distinction of being among the first international organizations. All three came into being in the second half of the nineteenth century to enlist international cooperation in the fields of communication, weather forecasting and mail service. Some characteristics of these early agencies were information sharing, functional cooperation among the states in the scientific and technical fields of interest, international standard setting and the drafting of international instruments (treaties) to regulate the field. Another important feature of these early organizations was the principle of sovereign equality among the members and open membership upon application.

Almost another half century passed until another specialized agency emerged. The International Labor Organization (ILO) was created by the Allied Powers at the Versailles Peace Conference and its charter was affixed to the Versailles Treaty (1919). One of the prime motivations for the founding of the ILO was a strong desire to promote international labor cooperation and improve labor standards. With the rise of bolshevism in the Soviet Union and Europe, the capitalist states were concerned with the inroads that communism might make with the working class. The unique tripartite membership of the ILO and its system of international labor conventions (treaties) and recommendations were the response to the perceived bolshevik threat. The ILO is also important in the history of international organization as its first Director General, Albert Thomas, set the standard for leadership and executive direction of an international agency.

It was not until the waning years of World War II that the next group of specialized agencies was created. In almost every instance the new agencies were established to cope with a pressing issue arising out of the war or its aftermath, or in response to circumstances which were viewed as contributing factors to the breakdown of the international political and economic system in the period between the two world wars. Seven new agencies were established between 1944 and 1948 (see table 1).

At Bretton Woods in 1944 the International Monetary Fund (IMF) and the International Bank for Reconstruction and Development, "World Bank," (IBRD) were created to insure a stable currency system, provide loans for

Table 1: United Nations Specialized Agencies

Agency	Founded as S.A.	Membership	Budget
FAO	1945	158	492 Million Swiss Francs (biennial 1988-89)
GATT	1947	99	$64.9 Million (annual 1989)
IAEA	1957	113	$150 Million (annual 1989)
IBRD	1944	151	$171.4 Billion (1989 capital)
ICAO	1947	160	$33.7 Million (annual 1989)
IFAD	1977	143	$36.3 Million (annual 1989)
ILO	1919	150	$357 Million (biennial 1988-89)
IMO	1958	133	$21.6 Million (biennial 1988-89)
IMF	1944	151	$6.5 Billion[1] (1989 capital)
ITU	1865	166	115 Million Swiss Francs (annual 1990)
UNCTAD	1964	168	$77 Million (biennial 1988-89)
UNESCO	1945	158	$350.4 Million (biennial 1988-89)
UNIDO	1985	151	154.3 Million Swiss Francs (biennial 1988-89)
UPU	1875	169	24.5 Million Swiss Francs (annual 1988)
WHO	1948	167	$653.7 Million (biennial 1990-91)
WIPO	1974	124	107.1 Million Swiss Francs (biennial 1988-89)
WMO	1873	161	170 Million Swiss Francs (triennial 1988-91)

[1]Standby and extended lending authority source: *United Nations Handbook*, New Zealand Ministry of External Relations and Trade, 1989.

development and reconstruction and promote international trade. The fear of postwar famine and world wide food shortages prompted the founding of the Food and Agriculture Organization (FAO). Largely through British and French influence, the United Nations Educational, Scientific and Cultural Organization (UNESCO) was established in 1945. It would prove to be one of the UN's most creative, yet controversial, agencies. The World Health Organization was founded in 1948 in response to the need for international cooperation in disease control and the great disparity in health conditions among the world's peoples. A unique feature of WHO is its regionalized organization and its long record of extensive medical and scientific cooperation among countries of differing political persuasions. Together with the ILO, WHO, UNESCO and FAO comprise what is known as the "big four" of the United Nations Specialized Agencies. Big in this instance refers to the size of their budgets, program activities, number of personnel, role in technical assistance and influence within the United Nations system. One additional agency was created in the immediate post World War II period, the International Civil Aviation Organization, 1947 (ICAO). The war had spurred on the development of aviation and in the post 1945 world, the dramatic growth of international civil aviation dictated the need for regulation and standard setting for civilian aircraft and airports.

In 1970, the secretariats of the Paris and Berne Unions were joined and a new specialized agency, the World Intellectual Property Organization (WIPO) was established four years later. The Paris Union provides international legal protection to industrial property and the Berne Union provides international protection to literary and artistic works. Since that time additional international treaties have been ratified to give legal protection to additional areas of international property.

Two additional specialized agencies were created in 1977 and 1985. The International Fund for Agricultural Development (IFAD) was established in response to the serious food shortages and famine conditions in Africa and Asia beginning in the early 1970s. IFAD focuses on the development of long term food security, research on the development of new food plants and varieties and the improvement of the economic condition of small rural farms. IFAD has a distinctive funding arrangement to meet its budgetary needs. One-third of its funding is derived from developed countries, one-third from developing countries and a final third from OPEC countries.

The   United   Nations   Industrial   Development Organization (UNIDO) is the most recent specialized agency. In 1966 UNIDO was established as an autonomous organization within the UN Secretariat. Twenty years later it became a specialized agency.   The transformation of UNIDO from an organ of the UN Secretariat to a specialized agency was substantially aided by the "Lima Declaration and Plan of Action" which called for the strengthening of UNIDO in order to assist developing countries in the most efficient manner.   The achievement of specialized agency status by UNIDO was a major objective of those countries supporting "A New International Economic Order" and the increase of industrial output in the developing countries.

A Changing Role for the Specialized Agencies

Historically the specialized agencies have functioned out of the limelight of international politics.   Matters such as transportation, energy, communication, education, health and food have not been at the forefront of international relations until quite recently.   Indeed some scholars have contended that the apolitical manner by which the specialized agencies dealt with such matters would elicit international cooperation and gradually erode sovereignty and nationalist tendencies of states. Beginning with the cold war and then following with decolonization and post colonial independence, the separation of political and apolitical international activity became blurred.   Some of the earliest cold war verbal battles were fought out in the UNESCO General Conference.   The ILO became politicized by the presence of communist dominated worker and management delegations at the International Labor Conference.   The Soviet Union and Eastern bloc countries refused to join many of the specialized agencies because they would need to reveal vital statistics about their currency, resources, food production and health statistics.

With the entrance of former colonies into the United

Nations in the 1960s the organization was overwhelmed with requests for economic aid and technical assistance. The United Nations Congo Operation, 1960-1964, nearly bankrupted the organization and created one of the most serious political and financial crises the UN has experienced. In 1965, the United Nations Development Program (UNDP) was instituted by combining two existing programs; UN Program of Extended Technical Assistance and the UN Special Fund. The voluntary funding for the UNDP was substantially increased and the UN Specialized Agencies became the key providers of technical assistance for the UNDP. In fact, many of the budgets of the specialized agencies were doubled by the infusion of UNDP funds. With some notable exceptions, e.g. GATT, IMF, the principal function of the specialized agencies moved from standard setting, rule making, public safety and research, to technical assistance and human development in the third world. It was not a role that all agencies readily adjusted to immediately.

The record of the specialized agencies in the post 1945 period has been impressive. The WHO has eliminated small-pox and is actively pursuing programs to eradicate malaria, AIDS, river blindness and other tropical diseases. UNESCO's literacy campaign has reduced illiteracy by 50% over the past two decades. In conjunction with UNICEF (United Nations Childrens Fund), UNESCO has embarked upon a program to provide teachers, curriculum materials and schools for children of the third world. The World Bank has made a major commitment to agriculture, "Green Revolution," and to the poor of the developing countries by sponsoring the "basic human needs" program. The WMO's programs on weather forecasting (World Weather Watch) and climatology have provided valuable scientific data to predict long term climatic trends, including floods, drought and famine.

The ILO has championed worker safety, human rights and technical training. Its Freedom of Association Committee has played a prominent role in supporting the development of worker associations and unions through its complaint and oversight system. GATT has been instrumental in the lowering of industrial tariffs by 80% or more over the past four decades. The elimination of tariff and non-tariff barriers through GATT negotiations has contributed to an unprecedented expansion of world trade. The IAEA has played an instrumental role in the development of nuclear power for fuel, medicine and food preservatives. Its "safeguards" system provides for the orderly expansion of peaceful nuclear development for the supply of energy. A most important responsibility of IAEA is the supervision of the Nuclear Non-Proliferation Treaty.

Politics and Confrontation

During the past two decades political questions have emerged within the specialized agencies which have disrupted their normal working environment. Within the United Nations, politics and diplomacy have been historically the responsiblity of the General Assembly, Security Council and the Secretariat. For the most part these specialized agencies have focused on technical, scientific, educational and health issues. That is not to say that politics and political maneuvering do not occur in the specialized agencies, but the resolution of political questions has not been their purpose.

How did this change come about and why? One reason was the numerical growth in the membership of the agencies in response to the creation of new states after 1960. A second was the formation of UNCTAD in 1964 and the establishment within UNCTAD of a third world caucusing group known as "The Group of 77." One of the goals of this group was to bring the agenda of the developing countries to all the forums within the UN System. Thirdly, after 1967, the Arab-Israeli dispute and the PLO drive for recognition forced these issues into the United Nations including the specialized agencies. In addition to these matters, two other circumstances contributed to politicization of the specialized agencies: Apartheid in South Africa and the decision by the Soviet Union and other socialist states to join the specialized agencies in 1955 after initially withholding their membership after World War II.

Of the seventeen agencies examined in this study, those which have been most affected by political questions are UNESCO, ILO, WHO and FAO. Additionally, the United States withdrew from active participation in the IAEA for six months between September 1982 and February 1983 over the vote of the IAEA General Conference to deny credentials to the Israeli delegation. In fact, the Arab-Israeli question has been the greatest source of politicization. However, there were others. In UNESCO the United States and its western allies objected to what was alleged to be an anti-western bias. The most inflamatory issue was UNESCO's attempt to establish a "New World Information Order" which the developed capitalist states viewed as an attempt to muzzle the western press and manage the news emanating from the third world. On December 31, 1984 the United States withdrew from UNESCO after appropriate formal notification, followed by Singapore and the United Kingdom. In addition to politicization, the United States also raised other issues as a cause for its departure from UNESCO: administrative mismanagement, budgetary irregularities, pro-Soviet bias and attacks on the world's free press.

The issues in the ILO were more long standing and ideological. Under the leadership of President George Meaney of the AFL/CIO the United States government was under constant pressure to reform the ILO and reduce Soviet influence. The AFL/CIO objected to government control of management and labor delegations from Socialist states as a violation of the ILO tripartite principle. The appointment of a Soviet national as an Assistant Director-General of the ILO and a vote by the International Labor Conference to give the PLO observer status in the ILO were the last straws. Under severe labor pressure, the United States withdrew from the ILO in November 1977, after appropriate notice. In the case of the ILO and UNESCO, U.S. withdrawal meant a reduction of 25% of their budgets. Two and one-half years later (February 1980), the United States rejoined the ILO when the organization agreed to United States proposals for reform.

Within the WHO the contentious issues were observer status for the PLO and condemnation of Israel for its treatment of Palestinians within Israeli occupied territories. Acting on a report of medical experts, the World Health Assembly criticized Israel for its violations of the Geneva Conventions as they related to the treatment of civilians in occupied territory. In addition, the Reagan Administration was highly critical of the WHO/UNICEF Code of Conduct on

Breast Milk Substitutes. They viewed it as anti-capitalist and as an attack on western free enterprise.

Beyond withdrawal, beginning in 1980, another response of the United States to politicization was to impose financial and managerial constraints on the specialized agencies. Withholding or delaying payment of dues, unilateral reduction of assessed obligations, legislative prohibitions on the spending of U.S. contributions and United States initiated audits of agency budgets and programs are prime examples. ILO and UNESCO were the primary targets of these financial initiatives.

In 1985 Senator Nancy Kassebaum (R-Kansas) introduced an amendment to the Foreign Relations Authorization Bill to reduce U.S. assessed contributions to the United Nations and its specialized agencies from 25 to 20 percent in an effort to apply pressure for structural and financial reform in the UN. Although the amendment was later softened to allow more discretion in evaluating budget and program reform, the message was clear that the U.S. and its allies were willing to use their financial leverage to make the UN and its specialized agencies more responsive and more responsible.

Summary

The specialized agencies play a significant role in the United Nations system. These agencies perform the lion's share of the technical assistance and human development functions of the UN. They work hand in hand with ECOSOC and UNDP in the UN's program of action to assist developing countries. They are also important international actors in developing global cooperation in a broad range of areas of state interest: trade, monetary stability, development assistance, food security, minimum standards of health and education.

Unfortunately of late, politics, cold war rhetoric and north-south differences have preoccupied their agendas and disrupted their normal workings. It appears that these issues are abating and the specialized agencies may now preoccupy themselves with issues germane to their function. In the remaining chapters of this book the several authors will describe the various specialized agencies, their work and the distinctive functions which they perform within the UN system. Without their expertise and professionalism it would be difficult for the UN to carry out its economic and social development goals.

BIBLIOGRAPHY

Bennett, A. Leroy. *International Organization: Principles and Issues*. 4th ed. Englewood Cliffs, NJ: Prentice-Hall. 1988.

Imber, Mark. *The USA, ILO, UNESCO, and IAEA: Politicization and Withdrawal in the Specialized Agencies*. New York, NY: St. Martin's Press. 1989.

Plano, Jack C., & Riggs, Robert E. *Forging World Order: The Politics of International Organization*. New York, NY: Macmillan. 1967.

"Symposium on the Role of the United States in Specialized International Organizations," Hearings before the Committee on Government Affairs, United States Senate, 95th Congress, 1st Session, June 15, 1977. Washington, D.C.: Government Printing Office, 1977.

United Nations Handbook. New Zealand Ministry of External Relations and Trade. Wellington: Government Printer. 1989.

United States Department of State, "United States Participation in the United Nations," Report by the President to the Congress (annual).

Williams, Douglas. *The Specialized Agencies and the United Nations*. London: Hurst. 1987.

Chapter II

Politicization

The Politicisation of UN Specialised Agencies: A Preliminary Analysis

Victor-Yves Ghebali

In his first annual report on the work of the United Nations (1982), the Secretary-General, Xavier Perez de Cuellar, expressed his concern about the crisis which the multilateral approach to international relations is experiencing, and the related erosion of the authority and prestige of international institutions.[1] In the context of this crisis, which has prevailed since the early 1970s, the Specialised Agencies — whose efficiency formerly was praised in contrast to the impotence of the United Nations — are experiencing a loss of credibility and are being taken to task. The central question of continuing sponsorship and commitment on the part of the Western member countries is generally linked to the vague and ambiguous notion of 'politicisation.' This article attempts to analyse the nature of this phenomenon, arguing that it is essentially a manifestation of organisational dysfunction and its effects.[2] Before doing so, however, it would be helpful to review the global systemic evolution of the UN system of specialised agencies. For the purpose of this exercise, the term 'specialised agency' will be used in its broadest sense to cover all kinds of functional organs as well as institutions forming part of the UN system, and will not be restricted to those entities falling within the scope of Article 57 of the United Nations Charter.

12

The Overall Systemic Evolution of the Specialised Agencies

The United Nations system is now 40 years old. During the four decades since its creation, it has evolved into an increasingly complex amalgam and has witnessed the growing autonomy of its component units. Today, it is both cumbersome and fragmented; its components often give the impression of competing with one another and co-ordination has become an almost impossible task.[3] With regard to the specialised agencies, there are three elements of this evolutionary process to consider: changes in membership, structure and management.

The specialised agencies have achieved near universality — something which the League of Nations failed to attain — with membership being a normal state of affairs in the post-war period and withdrawals rarely occurring. In numerical terms, universality has meant a tripling of the number of member states. In qualitative terms, however, this has not been accomplished without corresponding cost — notably the end of homogeneity of membership which, until then, had been characteristic of international organisations and which had allowed them to operate more or less harmoniously. The massive influx of new members to international organisations (former colonial territories and East European countries, groups dissatisfied with the *status quo*) overturned the existing political majority. Transformed into a decided minority within the very institutions which they had created and which bore the imprint of their liberal philosophies, the Western founding members increasingly found themselves on the defensive, if not in outright 'opposition.'[4]

The heterogeneity of member states, as expressed in their commitment to differing goals and strategies, constitutes a very definite phase in the systemic evolution of international organisations. The specialised agencies are torn between those who see themselves as custodians of their constitutional values and those who call for fundamental structural changes together with a reorientation of their purposes and principles. As a result, these agencies have been transformed into arenas where confrontation has become a common occurrence. Their operation has become

increasingly dependent on consensus-building, a process
whose outcome, by virtue of its ambiguity, is constantly called
into question and subject to redefinition.

In an environment both qualitatively and quantitative-
ly more complex than ever before, the interdependence of
national interests, as well as the interdependence of the
sectors of international co-operation have altered the process
by which member states participate in the international
system. Apart from a few special or exceptional cases ('pariah
states' and the superpowers), the individual member state
cannot conduct its policies in total isolation, as in the past;
instead it must increasingly work within the broader
framework of group diplomacy.[5] Decisions of any importance
are therefore the products of the intra- and inter-group
consensus. While group diplomacy certainly enhances the
negotiating power of individual states, and gives greater
political foundation to the decision-making process, it has the
inherent disadvantage of being both cumbersome and slow.

The variety of structures prevalent in international
organisations, the expansion of their agendas, and the
increasingly specialised and political nature of the issues
under consideration have added to the problem of coordinating policy at a national level within the member states
themselves. Because of the political issues at stake, foreign
ministries can no longer disregard the proceedings of
specialised agencies. Conversely, the increasingly technical
content of modern political issues has spurred the technical
ministries to become involved in the wider dimensions of
multilateral policy-making. The larger the country, the
greater the complexity and difficulty inherent in co-ordinating
positions at domestic level, which in turn leads to a situation
in which the same country speaks with different 'voices' in
different fora, even though the issues are the same.[6]

By the same token, the increase in the work
undertaken by the international bodies, together with the
attendant need for continuous and direct information about
their activities, has affected the process by which member
states are represented. Before 1945 permanent missions
were a mechanism generally restricted to a small number of
countries. This mechanism has now been adopted by all
member states and, in certain cases (such as the EEC), it has

become institutionalised. Although the permanent missions obviously vary with regard to the resources and importance of the countries represented, they generally play a role which is far from negligible in the United Nations system.[7]

While the nation-state still remains the basic unit within the international system, the notion of what constitutes a member of this system has changed. During the 1970s entities which were not recognised as subjects of international law (such as Namibia) were nevertheless admitted to full or associate membership of international organisations.[8] Another extreme case within the UN system was the official recognition accorded to national liberation movements. Most of these, in particular those supported by the OAU and the Arab League, enjoy formal observer status and, in some cases (*e.g.*, within the ILO), they also receive a certain amount of technical assistance.

It should also be noted that non-governmental organisations (NGOs) are now officially associated with the work of intergovernmental organisations and are accorded formal consultative status, which enables them to express their own points of view and to take useful initiatives. The proliferation of NGOs and the ever expanding range of their interests illustrate the permanence of the private association phenomenon. Its principal merit is to highlight the aspirations of individuals in an age when the dogma of state supremacy seems to have become all-pervasive.[9]

As far as organisational structure is concerned, the evolution of the UN system since 1945 seems to confirm the existence of a sociological 'law' whereby no organisation functions exactly the way its founders had planned. This would seem to apply to all intergovernmental organisations. Behind the formal constitutional structure ('organigramme') there have evolved informal structures ('sociogramme') which operate in accordance with their own rules. There are four developments to observe in this respect.

Firstly, it is striking to note that executive bodies, which were originally intended to operate with a limited and selective membership, have increasingly grown in size. In many cases, their enlargement (promoted in deference to the abstract principle of sovereign equality of states) now entails the participation of one-third of the membership of the

plenary organs.[10] Whatever the political intent of enlargement, it would appear that wider representation in the
executive bodies adversely affects their efficiency and the
very relevance of their decisions. Thus, the composition of the
UNESCO Executive Board passed from 18 members in 1946
to 51 in 1980;[11] similarly, the ILO Governing Body, originally
composed of 24 members in 1919, will comprise 108 members
with the adoption of the forthcoming 'reform structure.'[12]

Secondly, there has been the continuous expansion of
the plenary organ's agenda. This expansion is the result of
the overwhelming pressure of the developing countries, who
regard the plenary assemblies as being the only fully
democratic organs of universal institutions. As will be seen
later, this trend is one of the main features of the so-called
politicisation process. In any event, the field of intergovernmental co-operation is increasingly widening. Since the
Second World War, new fields (*e.g.*, environment, human
settlements, disaster relief, control of multinational
corporations and direct-broadcasting satellites) have become
regular agenda items. Promotion of the idea of a 'common
heritage of mankind' and the claims for a 'new international
economic order' have no doubt accelerated this same trend.

Thirdly, reference can be made to the operations of
subsidiary organs. These show two trends. The first relates
to committees established by the executive or plenary bodies
to help cope with specialised questions and with the
increasing volume of work. These subsidiary entities have
functioned as laboratories for collective decision-making. In
the ILO, for instance, any consensus reached at this level is
rarely questioned in the plenary sessions, where it is usually
formally adopted without further debate. The second trend
concerns those organs, designated as a particular
'programme,' 'fund,' 'project,' *etc.*, which have been created not
so much to assist the main bodies as to perform more
ambitious and autonomous tasks; these are generally
financed from extra-budgetary resources on the basis of
voluntary contributions.

Fourthly, it is useful to note the various ways in which
the international secretariat has evolved.[13] The number of
employees has increased tremendously, fully justifying the
expression 'international bureaucracy.' This phenomenon

explains the need for an overall personnel policy, covering recruitment, promotion, staff administration and so on. The international staff are, for the most part, unionised and, on occasion, some have not hesitated to resort to strike action. In some organisations, such as the WHO and UNESCO, 'ombudsmen' have been appointed to promote good relations between staff and higher echelons of management.[14] Moreover, due to the proliferation of technical assistance programmes, a new category of international civil servant has come on the scene, consisting notably of the field experts and consultants recruited for short, specified periods of service. In some cases (such as the ILO), the number of personnel belonging to this category equals or even exceeds the number of career professional staff based at headquarters. This decentralisation of structure and of functions has generally resulted from the expansion of technical assistance programmes.

The primacy often given to the criterion of 'equitable geographic representation' has had a certain negative effect on the performance of the international civil service. Member states are now entitled to well-defined quotas for employment of their respective nationals within the organisations to which they belong.[15] On the basis of what actually constitutes an abusive interpretation of the principle of sovereign equality, member states expect, as a matter of right, a certain level of 'equitable representation' within the international secretariat, and tend increasingly to intervene in the secretariat's consideration of their national candidates for recruitment.

Finally, the role of the heads of international organisations seems to have broadened while at the same time they have lost much of their autonomy. The typical secretary-general or director-general (depending on the constitutional designation), remains the key element in the operation of the organisation, but the increased number of functions attributed to him has to be seen against a backdrop of member state divisiveness. Under these conditions the options open to the international executive are quite limited; broadly speaking, he can either adopt a neutral position and avoid taking any radical initiatives, or he can act along the lines most acceptable to the majority of member states. In

either case, his room for maneuver is limited. The high
degree of personal initiative enjoyed in the past by such
striking individuals as Albert Thomas (ILO), Gunnar Myrdal
(UN/EEC) and Dag Hammarskjöld (UN) would be out of the
question today.

As far as international administration and management are concerned, important changes have also taken place.
The complexity of modern intergovernmental co-operation has
led to increasing involvement on the part of the international
organisations in the process of planning and programming
work on the basis of more well-defined and rational priorities.
In general, their activities depend on work programmes,
which tend to reflect a global approach rather than disparate
emphasis on individual projects. An advantage to be derived
from this new approach is that budgets are given an
enhanced transparency and, therefore, programme evaluation
is, in principle, facilitated.   Since the mid-1960s, the
organisations comprising the UN system have also abandoned
long-term 'rolling plans' in favour of 'fixed horizon' medium-
term plans, usually of six years duration (three successive
biennial budgets).[16]

The continuing growth of the international organisation
budgets, in absolute as well as real terms, should also be
noted. The international secretariats are now responsible for
considerable amounts of funding, derived from the regular
budgets and voluntary contributions. The need for rational
management and full accountability gradually led to the
adoption of biennial programme budgets in the early 1970s.
The financing of such universal membership organisations
remains, however, highly controversial.   Third World
countries, whose contributions are set at the minimum level
of assessment, argue in favour of increased expenditure in
support of development assistance. The Western countries
(who are the major contributors) oppose budget growth and,
depending on the circumstances, abstain from voting or even
vote against budgets deemed to be excessively high. Since the
beginning of the Reagan Administration, the most important
contributors (including the United States) have consistently
argued in favour of 'zero net budget growth in real terms.'
The argument underlying the American position is that the
international organisations should be able to operate more

effectively if they are not automatically assured of donor support. It is felt by the US and others that the previous high rates of budget growth worked more to the advantage of the burgeoning international bureaucracies than to that of field operations. All of these transformations can be set against the background of the natural evolution of the international system over four decades. They should also be considered as the by-product, to a large extent, of the numerous upheavals which characterised the 1970s, including emerging claims for a New International Economic Order (NIEO). Those upheavals accelerated the normal course of evolution, with politicisation being the most direct and prominent product of that acceleration.

'Politicisation' Defined

International organisation constitutes a channel of communication between the political units (member states), interacting in both co-operative and conflictual situations.[17] Consequently, all intergovernmental institutions — whether Specialised Agencies or not — are exposed to politics. They were created as a result of political agreements, and their resolutions and work inevitably reflects, in one way or another, the prevailing political climate. When seen in this light, politicisation is hardly anything new. As a concept it must be examined in the light of the goals of the founders of the UN system in the closing days of the Second World War.[18]

The idea of specialised agencies derived partly from the experience of the League of Nations and from ideas propounded by the so-called 'functional' approach. For the purpose of this paper there is no need to expand on this approach; it should suffice to recall that one of its underlying premises is that politics can be separated from 'non-political' co-operation within certain types of international organisations.   In other words, the functional approach postulates that the specialised agencies can perform their technical tasks as purely co-operative institutions and in complete isolation from political turmoil.[19]

The assumption, or possibly myth, of separability

prevailed for more than two decades. Then constituting the majority, the Western states and, in particular, the United States, used the specialised agencies for their own political purposes. This was particularly the case during the Korean War. By the early 1970s, with the development of a new approach postulating that international problem-solving required a holistic or ecological approach, the shoe was on the other foot. The concept of interdependence, both of nation-states and of the sectors of international co-operation, undermined the separability argument.[20] Furthermore, the multiplication of actors on the international scene, which resulted from the decolonisation process in the 1960s, also undermined one of the other traditional precepts of international organisation stability — the homogeneity of member states, hitherto assimilated to the principle of universality. Western in origin, the notion of politicisation serves to transpose these two seemingly irreconcilable phenomena: on the one hand, the interdependence of international issues and, on the other, the clashing diversity of nation-states. Politicisation has always existed, but what is new today is that it operates systematically in favour of the new, non-Western majority of nation-states.

Whether semantically correct or not, the notion of politicisation is far from meaningless. It implies serious dysfunction which impairs the operation of the complex UN system of specialised agencies. This dysfunction is particularly evident in delegates' speeches, in the work programmes and within the decision-making mechanisms of the agencies. For the purpose of the present analysis, six types of dysfunction will be considered.

The first type is dysfunction through 'extraneity.' In this case, politicisation derives from the systematic insertion of extraneous issues into agendas, debates and work programmes. This is exemplified by the intrusion of the Middle East question into the debates of virtually all the agencies since 1973.[21] The same holds true for the disarmament issue (usually raised by the Soviet bloc countries) within the work programmes of organisations such as UNESCO, the ILO, and the UN Committee on Peaceful Uses of Outer Space.[22]

In both cases this constitutes a serious impairment of

the workings of the Specialised Agencies. On the one hand, the Specialised Agencies are obliged to spend a disproportionate amount of time and effort on sensitive political issues, which more correctly fall within the mandate of the United Nations, at the expense of their own well-defined activities. On the other hand, as exemplified by the disarmament issue, this overloading of work programmes produces overlapping and considerable duplication of effort, as well as intensifying (rather than resolving) the controversy.

The second type of dysfunction can be tied to the erosion of liberal principles embodied in the charters of the various Specialised Agencies, particularly those of the ILO, the IBRD, the IMF and UNESCO. From the Western standpoint there is an undeniable undermining of the constitutional purposes and functions of the charters which is exemplified by efforts to promote the NIEO. The NIEO implies state supremacy as distinct from traditional liberal emphasis on individual and private enterprise. Another emanation of the 'statist approach' (an expression currently used by the US Department of State), is to be found in various international codes of conduct dealing with transfer of technology (the UNCTAD/TOT code), marketing of breast-milk substitutions (WHO), and transnational corporations (UN).[23] A similar philosophy is reflected in the New World Information and Communication Order (NWICO), advocated within UNESCO in favour of a 'free and *balanced* flow of information.'[24] The issue of so-called 'solidarity rights,' which again implicates UNESCO, is also relevant. In this particular instance, UNESCO is being accused by the United States of having ignored the spirit of the Universal Declaration of Human Rights (which permeates its constitution), in favour of vague and ambiguous notions (since there is little difference between 'peoples' and 'states') which cannot even be enforced by legal sanctions.[25]

The third type of dysfunction may be called 'hyper-confrontation.' In this type of dysfunction, politicisation is seen as leading to changes in the rules of the game in parliamentary diplomacy. On the one hand, constructive debates are losing ground to polemics and ill-disguised propaganda.[26] In this respect, the plenary meetings of the

Specialised Agencies tend to resemble those of the UN General Assembly.[27]   On the other hand, outright confrontation tends to prevail over any spirit of compromise within the decision-making process; the majority voting process (characterised by the West as 'automatic') imposes resolutions which are unacceptable to the minority, whose viewpoints are, in some instances, totally ignored.   Two particular cases illustrate this situation.   The first, which occurred in the UN Committee on Peaceful Uses of Outer Space, produced UNGA resolution 37/92 (10 December 1982) which laid out the principles governing the utilisation by states of earth satellites for the purpose of direct broadcasting.   The second example is provided by UNCTAD's consideration of a system for South-South preferences when, in the absence of a consensus, the Group of 77 excluded Israel and Turkey by putting the matter to a vote (November 1983).

The fourth type is dysfunction through 'nomomania,' a term derived from the Greek *nomos* (law), meant to describe the abusive practice of forcing through resolutions of normative content.   With each perception of fresh inequities in North-South relations, the developing countries have tended to seek a remedy by voting a further resolution.   Since 1974, normative resolutions of this kind have spread as outgrowths of claims for an NIEO.   They are characterised by a one-sided statement of problems and their solutions, generally propounded within a global framework.   At best, they constitute an exercise in rhetoric.   Qualified by numerous reservations on the part of the developed countries, they contribute little to solving the pressing problems at hand.   The time and effort given to lengthy and hortatory preambles are in inverse proportion to their practical value. Moreover, 'nomomania' fosters misunderstanding between the protagonists and heightens the frustration and tension. Whilst the developing countries could be criticised for proposing unrealistic solutions, the developed countries are by no means free of blame; they know that these draft resolutions are worthless but do not bother to work towards something more constructive.   Instead, they choose to follow the line of least resistance by abstaining or mildly endorsing them and then expressing their reservations in the closing debates.

The fifth type of dysfunction takes the form of condemnation and excommunication. The condemnation and near-expulsion of member states through the resolutions enacted by the voting majority constitute, without doubt, the most disturbing aspect of politicisation. In accordance with a somewhat double standard, certain states (but never others) are singled out for this kind of treatment. The Western states object to such practices with a rare display of determination.

Governed by the rule of law, the liberal democracies attach considerable weight to the principle whereby the accused is considered innocent until proven guilty in accordance with a detailed investigation and clearly established procedures. In contrast to this, the condemnatory resolutions so frequently adopted by the Specialised Agencies display a rather summary conception of justice: they call certain member states to account for political considerations and without due process of law. Such states find themselves condemned by plenary meetings in which the majority serve as prosecution, judge and jury.[28] Since the 1973 war, Israel — following the precedents of South Africa, Portugal and Chile — has become the major scapegoat in resolutions passed by the various organisations, beginning with the ILO.[29]

It is also in deference to the principle of universality that the Western states object to any attempt aimed at excluding a member state or depriving it of its constitutional entitlements. Once again, the treatment accorded to Israel provides concrete examples; for some time it was not included in any of UNESCO's regions, and a similar situation is now arising within the ILO.[30] In recent years, proposals to exclude Israel have been advocated unsuccessfully within the Universal Postal Union (UPU), the International Telecommunications Union (ITU), and the International Atomic Energy Agency (IAEA). It should be noted that Israel benefits from an official declaration by Secretary of State George Schultz (dated 16 October 1982), which indicates that a decision within any international organisation to exclude Israel will be followed by the suspension of United States participation or the withholding of the US budgetary contribution.[31]

The final type of dysfunction occurs through

administrative mismanagement and budgetary excesses. The
budgetary aspects of this problem are that the Western
states, which happen to be the most important contributors,
are increasingly called upon to finance programmes which are
of less and less interest to them. Perhaps it should be
recognised, drawing upon a recent report of the Council of
Europe relating to UNESCO matters, that 'the time has long
passed when the major states could both pay and give the
orders.'[32] The level of budgetary growth is, in any case, a
cause of additional political conflict within the international
organisations. According to one American ambassador, the
United States pays into the UN budget an amount which
exceeds the total value of contributions paid by 149 other
member states.[33] The warnings and calls by the Reagan
Administration directly to the international secretariats have
had a pronounced moderating effect. According to American
estimates, the following rates of budgetary growth within the
major agencies of the UN system have, in real terms, been
less during the 1984-85 biennium than in previous years:
UNESCO (5.5 per cent), IAEA (2.25 per cent), ILO (1.92 per
cent), UN (0.7 per cent), FAO (0.5 per cent), IMO (0 per cent),
and WHO (-0.31 per cent).[34]

The above-quoted report of the Council of Europe also
states that

> when they reach a certain volume, the criticisms which
> can be levelled at the internal structure of any state or
> inter-state organisation indicate either that the states
> which established the organisation have failed in their
> subsequent political commitment to it or that the staff
> appointed to administer it are not fully up to the
> task.[35]

The international secretariats have not escaped from
politicisation, as is poignantly shown in the cases of UNCTAD
and, above all, UNESCO. Two major complaints are levelled
at UNESCO. The first concerns implementation and
evaluation of programmes; member states are simply not
given adequate information about its operations.[36] The
second derives from the burgeoning secretariat's increasing
involvement in policy-making — a process whereby authority

seems to be passing from the intergovernmental bodies (Executive Board and General Conference) to the Secretariat.[37]

The Western Response to Politicisation

Western reactions to this phenomenon are of particular interest because they emanate from a group of countries which constitute both a minority of voters and a crushing majority of financial contributors. These reactions can be categorised under two headings: withdrawal and reform. Several Western countries (United Kingdom, Federal Republic of Germany, Netherlands and Japan) expressed their intention to leave UNESCO, should no serious reforms be implemented.[38] So far, however, actual withdrawal has only been effected by the United States. As both leader of the Western world and contributor of a quarter of the UN system's budgetary resources, the US Government decided to withdraw from the ILO (1977) and from UNESCO (1985) for reasons of foreign and domestic policy.

The ILO Crisis

The American-induced ILO crisis was played out in two acts, spread over the ten year period, 1970-1980.[39] A dispute first arose over the appointment of a Soviet national, in July 1970, to the post of Assistant Director-General. This appointment was considered unacceptable by the Americans. They argued that this individual, who had been proposed by his government, would not be able to enjoy even a minimum of the independence expected of authentic international civil servants. They also felt that the appointment had been made without adequate prior consultations, contrary to assurances allegedly given by Director-General Jenks (a point which he later contested). Despite the merits of these responses, and pushed by the AFL-CIO leadership as well as a by no means unimportant group of American employers, the United States Senate decided on 24 August 1970 to suspend the second installment of the US financial contribution due that year. President Nixon did not want to oppose this decision. He even let it be known, through official channels, that the

United States would withdraw from the ILO if politicisation trends and the growth of Soviet influence persisted. The Administration did not, however, make good its threat. It preferred to have the US remain within the Organisation and extricated itself from a position difficult to justify in law by discharging its financial arrears in 1972. The first American-induced crisis thus ended after two years, but not without having created serious problems, particularly as regards financial matters.

Improvements of relations between the United States and the ILO in 1972 did not last long, given new stresses arising from renewal of the Middle East crisis in 1973, the ensuing petroleum crisis, and demands by the developing countries for an NIEO. The condemnation of Israel for practicing racial discrimination and for violating trade union rights in the Occupied Territories (1974), the admission to observer status of the PLO (1975), and the pressure exercised by the influential president of the AFL-CIO, George Meany, in favour of American withdrawal all contributed to the Ford Administration's decision to give formal notice of withdrawal on 5 November 1975.

Secretary of State Kissinger's communication to the ILO Director-General reiterated four complaints.[40] Firstly, the United States deplored the erosion of tripartism caused by government encroachment on the independence of workers and employers. Secondly, the US deplored the use by the International Labour Conference of double standards in matters of human rights, particularly with regard to trade union freedom and forced labour, the selective condemnation or exemption of certain groups of member states by virtue of their political systems undermined ILO credibility as well as respect for human rights. Thirdly, and most importantly, the United States denounced resolutions condemning particular member states on the basis of political criteria without due process of law; such resolutions were in flagrant disregard of established ILO procedures for examining complaints alleging violation of trade union freedoms. Finally, the United States categorically condemned the 'growing politicisation' which had caused the ILO to divert its attention from its social mandate and to become increasingly involved in matters more properly within the competence of the United Nations.

The Administration would have preferred not to have left the ILO, an organisation with which the United States had particularly strong historical ties. It was hoped that the American concerns would be taken into account, which would have enabled the Administration to reconsider its decision to withdraw. But, in the interim period before the notification took legal effect, the situation took a turn for the worse. In 1976, the Governing Body, which had originally refused to admit the PLO to the World Conference on Employment, reversed its decision under pressure from the Arab and African member states.[41] The following year, sharp exchanges during the International Labour Conference debates served to heighten tensions. Under these conditions, and in deference to persistent pressure from the AFL-CIO, President Carter confirmed the decision of the preceding Administration. The US withdrawal from the ILO became effective on 5 November 1977.

The American departure had considerable reper-cussions on the day-to-day operations of the Organisation. The Director-General, Francis Blanchard, initiated immediate and unprecedented Draconian cuts.[42] These took the form of cancelling or reducing the frequency of meetings, slowing down the process of decentralisation, suspending publications, cutting down on research, and abolishing more than a hundred positions accompanied by a freeze on virtually all recruitment.[43] The ILO withstood the test, but the crisis, aggravated by the radical fall in the dollar/Swiss franc exchange rate, left marks still visible today, particularly on the ILO's staffing.

After realising that the 'empty chair policy' had not worked, and following a change in the high-level leadership of the American trade unions, the United States rejoined the ILO on 18 February 1980. It is interesting to note that the Reagan Administration, even though more inclined than its predecessors to take an offensive line, has not come into conflict with the ILO. On the contrary, those within the Administration currently responsible for US multilateral policies seem to have given the ILO a clean bill of health.[44]

As a matter of fact, it is now the Eastern countries which are greatly dissatisfied with politicisation within the ILO. It is rather ironic to note that their complaints are

being expressed not so differently from Western grievances
current in other UN fora. In a collective letter addressed to
Director-General Blanchard on 23 November 1984, seven
East European members (the USSR, the Ukraine,
Byelorussia, Bulgaria, Hungary, the German Democratic
Republic and Czechoslovakia) and Mongolia denounced 'the
use of the Organisation for purposes contrary to its
Constitution,' use of the ILO forum 'to foster a hostile attitude
towards the socialist countries,' 'the blatant misuse of the
ILO's supervisory bodies for ill-intentioned political purposes,'
and even 'undermining' the principle of universality.[45] This
East European assault on the ILO constitutes the former's
angry reaction to the 1984 report of the commission of
enquiry (established in full accordance with Article 26 of the
ILO's Constitution), which concluded that Poland had
violated its legal obligations in the field of freedom of
association.[46]

The UNESCO Crisis

As in the case of the ILO, the UNESCO crisis goes back
to the 1970s. However, the events leading up to it were more
dramatic: condemnation   of   Israel   for   conducting
archaeological excavations in Jerusalem, followed by
UNESCO's suspension of all technical assistance and the non-
inclusion of Israel in UNESCO's regional structures. By way
of reprisal the Western countries, particularly the Europeans,
boycotted UNESCO's activities, whilst the United States
suspended payment of its contributions. The first phase of
the crisis ended in 1976 with Israel's admission to UNESCO's
European region.
Reagan Administration policies and the brash
behaviour of UNESCO Director-General M'Bow subsequently
served to precipitate a fresh and more serious phase of the
crisis. In June 1982, the Reagan Administration expressed
the five basic principles which it intended to promote with
regard to American participation in the work of international
organisations. These included restoration of US leadership,
active promotion of liberal principles (including free
enterprise as opposed to statist doctrines), increasing the
number of US nationals employed by the international

secretariats, reducing the number of international conferences and meetings, and promoting zero budget growth in real terms.[47] On the basis of these aims the Department of State's Bureau of International Organisation Affairs proceeded to a systematic review of some ninety-six international institutions of which the US is a member. Five of these institutions seemed to pose problems: the ILO, the ITU, the IAEA, UNEP and UNESCO. The Reagan Administration embarked on a series of consultations with the executive heads, and appeared to have succeeded in all cases but one. Consequently, in June 1983, the Administration decided to examine in depth the pros and cons of continued US participation in UNESCO. This exercise lasted six months and entailed consultations with some 500 people from the public and private sectors. The career diplomats seem to have counselled against withdrawal, but an influential group of political appointees swung the balance in the opposite direction.[48] The decision to withdraw was endorsed by President Reagan and transmitted to UNESCO by the Secretary of State on 28 December 1983. The test of the formal notification mentioned three basic complaints: politicisation, abuse of democratic principles and bad management.[49]

Director-General M'Bow tried to refute, point-by-point, the American charges. Politicisation, he recalled, had always existed in UNESCO, particularly in the Korean War era (1950-1953) when it had worked to the advantage of the United States. With respect to the budget, he argued that UNESCO had a well-managed and sound system which enabled him to regularly refund to member states large sums earned by the Organisation as the result of currency fluctuations. UNESCO had not departed from its constitutional mandate, he argued; it had only endeavoured to respond to the wishes of the overwhelming majority of its members.[50]

These arguments had little effect. The United States formally withdrew from UNESCO on 31 December 1984[51] — a move which was also intended to be a clear warning to the other elements of the UN system, such as UNCTAD, the UN Committee on the Peaceful Uses of Outer Space, the International Fund for Agricultural Development (IFAD) and even the General Agreement on Tariffs and Trade (GATT).[52]

The threat of withdrawal is an extreme reaction and one which can serve to destabilise the entire system of international institutions. It essentially has a financial and psychological impact, but it is by no means the sole recourse open to the Western members, who can also apply pressure for internal reform. At the present time, such reform efforts are underway within UNCTAD, UNESCO and the ILO.

Towards Reform: UNCTAD, UNESCO and the ILO

In January 1984, during the course of an OECD working group considering North-South economic issues, the United States' representative expressed his country's intention of having UNCTAD put back on the track, or otherwise to withdraw from participation. The reasons given were UNCTAD's ineffectiveness, poor management and intense politicking.[53] According to the American view (which was not fully shared by the Europeans for whom the real issue is to end the deadlock in the North-South dialogue), reforms would entail the following measures: a clear definition of UNCTAD's mandate, in order to prevent it from venturing into monetary and financial questions such as Third World indebtedness; the attribution of purely deliberative powers to UNCTAD's various organs; decision-making exclusively by consensus; the rationalisation of programme activities and institution of a greater degree of visibility and accountability in their implementation; the reform of the Secretariat, starting with a UN Joint Inspection Unit evaluation and replacement of the current UNCTAD Secretary-General by a Third World individual more acceptable to the developed countries;[54] and imposing limits on the use of resolutions. The US position paper argued that:

> It is essential for Group B countries to begin to take a firmer, more forthright and less patronizing attitude in negotiating with the developing countries. As long as we continue to accept radical and non-serious proposals as bases for negotiation, the more the serious and moderate elements will continue to be shunted aside.... When Group B does not react forthrightly to such

proposals, it does not prevent confrontation; rather it ensures it by preventing an honest meeting of the minds.... Uncritical acceptance of all proposals followed by negotiation that leads to artificial results, can and should be regarded by the developing countries as a sign that the developed countries do not take them seriously.[55]

In the case of UNESCO, the American notification of withdrawal has had a beneficial effect by stimulating member states' awareness of the problems and by unleashing a preliminary process of reform. Following a recommendation of the Executive Board in May 1984, a Temporary Committee was established to examine UNESCO's operation. It submitted a report containing 116 recommendations. These can be summarised under four main headings:

(1)   the strengthening of the authority of the two main UNESCO bodies, especially with regard to decisions concerning the general orientation of the Organisation and approval of its work programmes;[56]

(2)   the widest possible use of consensus (a procedure which the committee did not, however, wish to codify), particularly with respect to adoption of work programmes and the budget;[57]

(3)   the initiation of a decentralisation process which, among other things, would promote a greater degree of mobility between headquarters staff and those based in the field;[58] and

(4)   the rationalisation of UNESCO programmes, including improved evaluation techniques, avoiding duplication of activities undertaken by other agencies of the UN system, revision of existing guidelines for publications and documentation, and the improvement of operational activities.[59]

The ILO reform process[60] (or 'reform structure') is quite different from the other examples because it started

over twenty years ago. It pre-dates 'politicisation,' although
this undoubtedly interfered with subsequent reform efforts.
And, in contrast with the case of UNESCO, this process has
reached an advanced stage. Since 1983, the International
Labour Conference has been seized with a series of draft
amendments to the Constitution and to the standing orders of
the Governing Body and the Conference. Political opposition
to some elements of what is considered to be an indivisible
package continues to obstruct reform and still prevents the
formal adoption of these amendments.[61]

The ILO 'reform structure' emphasises three categories
of rather complex problems: election to the three groups of
the Governing Body (governments, employers and workers);
redistribution of powers between the Governing Body and the
International Labour Conference; and, what is of direct
relevance to the present article, the treatment of resolutions
dealing with items not on the agenda of the Conference and
which are of a condemnatory nature.

It was in 1974 that the United States, concerned with
the increased tensions generated by Conference debates,
proposed an amendment to deal with draft resolutions
extraneous to subjects on the agreed agenda. The prevailing
practice allowed delegations to use the Conference as a sort of
political tribunal. Article 17 of the Conference standing
orders empowered the Director-General to suspend
distribution of any draft resolution of this type, which had not
been submitted at least fifteen days before the opening of the
Conference, pending a unanimous decision by the Governing
Body. In actual practice, however, the Director-General and
the officers of the Governing Body refrained from exercising
this authority. A consensus was finally reached in favour of
'filtering' politically condemnatory draft resolutions. The new
Article 17 will establish a two-phase procedure entailing the
intervention of a small special committee composed of
Conference officers and three members from each of the three
constituent groups of the ILO. Without anticipating the full
impact of such a procedure, it seems reasonable, nevertheless,
to expect that it could have a moderating effect on
'politicisation through condemnation.' It could also serve as a
general model for other specialised agencies to consider.

Conclusion

While it is evident that politicisation adversely affects Western interests, it does not follow that Third World and East European members are able to reap real benefits from it. This is because international co-operation cannot be reduced to a simple zero-sum game. The international system is composed of actors with a very high degree of interdependence who are not in a position either to eliminate each other or even to gain a decisive victory. Thus, politicisation appears to be a purely negative phenomenon. Its persistence could even lead to a situation detrimental to the very idea of international co-operation through international organisation — the prospect of 'A World without the United Nations' which has been envisaged in a book published under the auspices of the Heritage Foundation.[62] The time has surely come for the UN system to devise and implement acceptable, imaginative adjustments between what has been referred to as the 'organigramme' and 'sociogramme' of international organisations. It is necessary to take into account the existence of a new political majority as well as to safeguard the vital interests of the present minority. Such safeguards could, *inter alia*, involve a redefinition of constitutional mandates, the use of consensus in all substantive decision-making (including budgets), and self-restraint in budgetary and bureaucratic expansion.

FOOTNOTES

1. See UN Doc. A/37/1, 7 September 1982. On the present stage of international organisation, see Robert E. Cox, 'The Crisis of World Order and the Problem of International Organizations,' *International Journal* 25, no. 2 (Spring 1980) and Marie-Claude Smouts, 'La crise des organisations internationales,' *Etudes* (February 1983), 165-173.

2. Academic analysis on politicisation is not frequent. See, however, Gene M. Lyons, David A. Baldwin and Donald W. McNemar, 'The Politicization Issue in the UN Specialized Agencies,' in David A. Kay (ed.), *The Changing United Nations: Options for the United States* (New York: Praeger,

34 Peace by Pieces

1977), 81-92. See also, Manuela Tortora, *Institution Specialisèe et Organisation Mondiale: Etude des Relations de l'OIT Avec la SDN et l'ONU* (Brussels: Bruylant, 1980), 412-438.

3. On the problem of co-ordination, see Evan Luard, *International Agencies: The Emerging Framework of Interdependence* (London: Macmillan, 1978), chapter 17, and Andre Lewin, 'La Coordination au Sein des Nation Unies: Mission Impossible?', *Annuaire Francais de Droit International* 29 (1983), 10-22. On the general evolution of Specialised Agencies, see Jeffrey Harrod, 'Problems of the United Nations Specialised Agencies at the Quarter Century,' *Yearbook of World Affairs* (London: Stevens & Sons, 1974), 187-203 and Evan Luard, 'Functionalism Revisited: The UN Family in the 1980s,' *International Affairs* 59, no. 4 (Autumn 1983), 677-692.

4. This is especially the case of the United States. See, in this connection, Daniel P. Moynihan, 'The United States in Opposition,' *Commentary* 59 (March 1975), 31-44.

5. For the special case of EEC member states, see Marlis G. Steinert, 'Un Exemple de Diplomatie de Groupe: les Activitès de la CEE à Genève,' *Relations Internationales*, no. 32 (Winter 1982), 543-560.

6. On the question of the dual interests of foreign affairs and technical ministries, see Raymond Ferretti, *La Coordination de l'action des Organisations Internationales au Niveau Europèen* (Brussels: Burylant, 1984), 137ff.

7. See Michael Virally, Pierre Gerbet, Jean J.A. Salmon and Victor-Yves Ghebali, *Les Missions Permanente Auprès des Organisations Internationales*, Vol. 1 (Brussels: Bruylant, 1971). Useful information can also be found in Vols. 2, 3 and 4.

8. See Ebere Osieke, 'Admission to Membership in International Organizations: The Case of Namibia,' *British Yearbook of International Law* 51 (1980), 189-229.

9. See, for instance, Pei-heng Chiang, *Non-Governmental Organizations at the United Nations: Identity, Role and Functions* (New York: Praeger, 1981).

10. See, for instance, Bengt Broms, *The Doctrine of Equalilty of States as Applied in International Organizations*, unpublished PhD thesis, University of Helsinki, 1959.

11. See UNESCO Doc. 22 C/33, 24 October 1983.

12. See *Provisional Records of the 1983 International Labour Conference*, no. 38, 21-24.

13. Recent analyses on international secretariats are to be found in Lewis B. Kilbourne, *Organizational and Political Conflict Within the United Nations Secretariat* (Ann Arbor, MI: University Microfilms International, 1980); Norman A. Graham and Robert S. Jordan (eds.), *The International Civil Service: Changing Role and Concepts* (New York: Pergamon Press, 1980) and Robert I. McLaren, *Civil Servants and Public Policy: A Comparative Study of International Secretariats* (Waterloo, Canada: Wilfrid Laurier University Press, 1980).

14. See Warner J. Feld and Lewis B. Kilbourne, 'The UN Bureaucracy: Growth and Diversity,' *Revue Internationale des Sciences Administratives* 43, no. 4, (1977), 321-333; Paul C. Szasz, 'Unions of International Officials: Past, Present and Future,' *New York University Journal of International Law and Politics* 14, no. 2, (Summer 1982), 807-839, and Jean-Marie Becet, 'A propos de l'ombudsmanie: le Mèdiateur et les Organisations Internationales,' *Human Rights Review* 10, no. 1, (1977), 117-139.

15. For the UN quotas, see UN General Assembly Resolution 35/210 of 4 February 1971. See also Henri Reymond, 'The Representation of Nationalities in the Secretariat of the United Nations,' *Revue Internationale des Sciences Administratives* 49, no. 4, (1983), 349-360.

16. For the special case of the ILO, see Franz von Mutius, 'Planning for Stagnation or Innovation?', in Joseph H. Kaiser (ed.), *Planning VI* (Baden-Baden: Nomosverlagsgesellschaft, 1972), 137-156. Long and medium-terms plans adopted within the ILO since 1970 are to be found in Docs. GB. 180/FA/6/4, GB/185/FA/1316, GB. 192/PFA/16/1 and GB.212/PFA/4/1.

17. For a development of this idea in the East-West context, see Franklin Griffiths, 'Cooperation as a Form of Conflict,' *The Atlantic Community Quarterly* 12, no. 4, (Winter 1974/75), 481-499.

18. On the origins of the concept of 'specialised agencies,' see Manuela Tortora, *op. cit.*, 174-192. See, also, George A. Codding, 'The Relationship of the League of

Nations and the United Nations with the Independent
Agencies: A Comparison,' *Annals of International Studies* 1
(1970), 65-87.
    19. Besides the classic works of David Mitrany, Ernest
B. Haas and James P. Sewell, see A.J.R. Groom and Paul
Taylor (eds.), *Functionalism: Theory and Practice in
International Relations* (London: University of London Press,
1975). See also Andrew W. Green, 'Mitrany Reread with the
Help of Haas and Sewell,' *Journal of Common Market Studies*
8, no. 1, (September 1969), 50-69; Peter Wolf, 'International
Organization and Attitude Change: A Re-examination of the
Functionalist Approach,' *International Organization* 27, no. 3,
(Summer 1973), 347-371 and Mark F. Imber, 'Re-Reading
Mitrany: A Pragmatic Assessment of Sovereignty,' *British
Review of International Studies* 10, no. 2, (April 1984), 103-
123. For an early treatment, see Pitman B. Potter, 'Note on
the Distinction between Political and Technical Questions,'
Political Science Quarterly 50, no. 2, (June 1935), 264-271.
    20. The notion of 'interdependence' is far from being
new. It can be found for instance in the works of early
specialists such as Pitman B. Potter, 'Progress in
International Cooperation,' *Political Science Quarterly* 50, no.
3, (September 1935), 390.
    21. Before the intrusion of the Middle East question, the
problems of apartheid and of Portugal's African colonies were
the most prominent instances of politicisation in the 1960s.
    22. See the American protest in the framework of the
Committee on the Peaceful Uses of Outer Space, Doc. EUR-
405, 14 June 1984 and *Daily Bulletin of the US Mission in
Geneva* no. 61, (29 March, 1984), 1.
    23. For a useful overall description of proposed
international codes, see ILO Doc. GB.228/MNE/3/1, November
1984.
    24. On the NWICO issue, see Victor-Yves Ghebali, 'La
Problématique du Nouvel Ordre Mondial de l'information,'
Défense Nationale 34, (December 1978), 25-39.
    25. See Victor-Yves Ghebali, 'L'UNESCO et le Probléme
de la Formulation d'un Droit à la Communication,' *Aspects du
Droit des Medias: II* (Fribourg: Editions Universitaires,
1984), 245-257.
    26. See, for instance, the debates of the 59th (1974)

International Labour Conference concerning Israel and of the
22nd General Conference of UNESCO (1983) where American
policy in Grenada, Lebanon and Central America was heavily
attacked by many Third World and Eastern countries.
27. See Gregory Newell's declaration on the American
unwillingness to 'see the 96 UN agencies become 96 general
assemblies, discussing political issues that are the
responsibility of the UN General Assembly.' Doc. Eur-206,
Daily Bulletin of the US Mission in Geneva no. 45, (March
1984).
28. See the speech of the Israeli delegate at the 59th
session of the ILO in *Record of Proceedings* (1974), 418.
29. Israel has been condemned twice within the ILO: in
1974 and in 1980. Draft condemnatory resolutions failed to
pass, however, in 1971, 1973, 1978 and 1983. On the
politicisation of the ILO, see David Tajgman, 'Political
Resolutions in the International Labour Organization: The
Experience since 1964,' *Industrial Relations* 36, no. 3, (1981),
499-529.
30. See Richard Hoggart, 'UNESCO in Crisis: The
Israel Resolution,' *New Universities Quarterly* 30, no. 1,
(1975), 15-23: Gordan Lang, 'UNESCO and Israel,' *Harvard
International Law Journal* 16, (1975), 676-682 and Josette
Beer-Gabel, 'La participation d'Israël aux activités régionales
de l'UNESCO: autopsie d'une crise,' *International Problems*,
Jerusalem 18, (1979), 66-88. For the ILO case, see Doc. GB.
225/20/21.
31. See Doc. EUR-1, *Daily Bulletin of the US Mission in
Geneva* no. 196, (18 October 1982), 1.
32. *Report on the Activities of Unesco and Co-operation
with the Council of Europe*, Rapporteur, Mr. Beix
(Parliamentary Assembly of the Council of Europe Doc. 5274,
20 September 1984), 29.
33. Declaration of Ambassador Alan Keyes, *Daily
Bulletin of the US Mission in Geneva* no. 193, (15 October
1984), 5.
34. See the declaration made by the American delegate
at the 22nd General Conference of UNESCO, Doc. 22 C/VR.9
(provisional), 29.
35. *Report of the Activities of Unesco and Co-operation
with the Council of Europe, op. cit.*, 32.

36. See the declaration made by Ambassador Jean Gerard before the US Congress (8 March 1984), Doc. EUR-512 (9 March 1984).

37. *Ibid.* For more details, see *Improvements Needed in UNESCO's Management, Personnel, Financial and Budgeting Practices, Report to the Committee on Foreign Affairs and Committee on Science and Technology, House of Representatives, by the Comptroller of the United States* (Washington, DC: General Accounting Office, 1984), Doc. GAO/NSIAD-85-32.

38. On the official British position, see UNESCO Doc. 119 EX/30, (19 April 1984).

39. See Gregory T. Kruglak, *The Politics of United States Decision-Making in United Nations Specialised Agenices: The Case of the International Labor Organization, 1970-1972* (Washington, DC: University Press of America, 1980) and Walter Galemon, *The International Labor Organization: An American View* (Madison, WI: The University of Wisconsin Press, 1981).

40. See Doc. GB. 198/22/11.

41. See Doc. GB. 200/PV, pp. IV/8-10.

42. See *Report II to the 1979 International Labor Conference*, 85. See also Docs. GB. 204/PFA/12/23 and GB. 204/PV (rev.), III/1-8.

43. See Docs. GB. 205/PFA/6/3; GB. 205/PFA/6/4; GB. 205/PFA/6/16 and GB. 208/PFA/9/12.

44. See Mr. Newell's press conference of 23 January 1984 in Jerusalem. See also, *Sustaining US Participation in the International Labor Organization Requires New Approaches. Report to the Chairman, Committee on Labor and Human Resources, United States Senate, by the Comptroller General of the United States* (Washington, DC: General Accounting Office, 1984), Doc. GAO/NSIAD-84-85.

45. See *ILO-Press*, no. 47-84, (4 December 1984), 1-2.

46. For the text of the Commission of Enquiry report on Poland, see *ILO Official Bulletin* 57, (1984), series B, special supplement.

47. See *Daily Bulletin of the US Mission in Geneva* no. 22 supplement, (20 June 1983).

48. See *The Guardian*, (23 January 1984).

49. See UNESCO Doc. 119/EX/14.

50. *Ibid.*, Annex II.

51. See Victor-Yves Ghebali, 'Les Etats-Unis et l'UNESCO: Analyse d'une Crise,' *Défense Nationale 40* (May 1984), 45-66. See also Evi Underhill, UNESCO and the American Challenge,' *Journal of International Trade Law* 18, no. 5, (September-October 1984), 381-395; Gordon Crovitz, 'The Decline and Fall of UNESCO,' *Encounter* 63, no. 5, (December 1984), 9-18; Brian Hocking, 'Words and Deeds: Why America left UNESCO,' *The World Today* 41, no. 4, (April 1985), 75-78 and various Authors, 'The US Decision to Withdraw from UNESCO,' *Journal of Communication* 34, no. 4, (Autumn 1984), 81-179.

52. On GATT, see *Daily Bulletin of the US Mission in Geneva*, no. 223, (28 November 1982), 7-8.

53. See *Daily Bulletin of the US Mission in Geneva*, no. 180, (25 September 1984), 1-4.

54. Since then, Mr. Alister McIntyre (Grenada) has replaced Mr. Gamani Corea (Sri Lanka) as Secretary-General.

55. Undated position paper entitled, 'US Paper on North/South Dialogue and UNCTAD' (private source).

56. UNESCO Doc. 120 EX/3 (3 October 1984) Recommendations A.1 to A.19 and B.1 to B.17.

57. *Ibid.*, Recommendations C.1 to C.8.

58. *Ibid.*, Recommendations D.1 to D.8.

59. *Ibid.*, Recommendations E(1).1 to E(1).13; E(2).1 to E(2).5; E(3).1 to E(3).9; E(4).1 to E(4).4 and E(5).1 to E(5).4.

60. For a more detailed treatment, see Victor-Yves Ghebali, 'Vers la Réforme de l'OIT,' *Annuaire Francais de Droit International* 30 (1984).

61. The deadlock is essentially caused by the problems of Israel's eligibility for the purpose of election in the Governing Body and the long-standing issue of the representation of Eastern countries' employers in the same Body.

62. Burton Yale Pines (ed.), *A World without a UN: What Would Happen if the United Nations Shut Down* (Washington, DC: The Heritage Foundation, 1984).

Chapter III

Food and Agriculture Organization (FAO)

The Food and Agriculture Organization (FAO) was the first United Nations specialized agency established following the Second World War, and it is currently one of the largest. In October 1945, the FAO began its appointed task of fighting hunger and co-ordinating programs for development in agriculture, forestry and fisheries. There are 158 member nations, and the FAO conference meets every two years. The staff consists of 2,970 employees at the Rome headquarters and 2,830 in the field. The budget is financed by contributions from member countries, and in 1988-1989 it totaled US$492 million. The FAO's main task is to raise levels of nutrition and living standards by improving the efficiency of the production and distribution of various commodities. In order to do so, emphasis is placed upon analysis and distribution of information, advisement of member states on planning and policy, provision of technical advice and assistance, and promotion of co-operation among member states. The FAO helps developing countries to build institutions and to promote and improve educational and training facilities which, in turn, improve food security, raise rural incomes, and increase rural productivity. This growth, particularly in the developing countries, contributes to the expansion of the world economy and the improvement of living standards. The FAO also provides emergency food assistance in response to natural or man-made disasters through its World Food Program (WFP).

Who Governs the Rome Food Agencies?

Ross B. Talbot and H. Wayne Moyer

Four international organizations based in Rome are concerned with food and nutrition worldwide: FAO, WFC, WFP and IFAD. This article analyses their power structure, considering first the constitution and history of each organization, as background to the central question: Who governs? The effectiveness of each organization is also weighed, and the options for the power structure towards the close of the century are examined. The authors conclude that the four-organization structure has brought some positive results, and that it is optimal for balancing the interests of competing factions. It provides the various political blocs (OECD, OPEC, Third World, etc.) with multiple channels to pursue their varied interests.

The purpose of this article is to analyse the structure of power in the four world food organizations headquartered in Rome, specifically the Food and Agriculture Organization (FAO), World Food Council (WFC), the World Food Programme (WFP) and the International Fund for Agricultural Development (IFAD).

Our basic premises are: (1) this is a world of nation states, each claiming to be sovereign; (2) a nation state joins and participates in an international organization (IO) in pursuit of its own perceived national interests; (3) in order to achieve this objective, the state will usually form a coalition with other states which have closely identical interests; (4) policy outcomes within the IO will be determined through the negotiations carried on within and between these political coalitions, with the secretariat of the IO functioning as a semiautonomous and self-interested intermediary.

Political scientists have engaged in countless arguments over the definition of power, but we will arbitrarily use the one advanced by Thomas Hobbes: Power is the present means to achieve some future apparent good. The means will primarily be wealth (money, resources, technology) and votes; in an IO each member state has one vote (although Orwellian logic generally prevails — that is, some nation states are more, or less, equal than others).

The humanitarian factor must also enter into these calculations; we will eagerly and seriously engage in a war on hunger, under certain circumstances. Starvation and famine are cultural taboos within rich nations; however, malnutrition is less of a social-psychological inhibition to rich nations in their relations with developing nations. Nevertheless, there is an obverse side to this value proposition. Food is obviously a basic human need, but too much food enters into the political calculations of food-surplus nations with at least as much potency as does too little. This complicates policy making for wealthy, and (usually) food-surplus, nations. Their capabilities for supplying food to needy nations are evident, but the motives for doing so are complex. Food aid is politically more feasible when farm surpluses are a burden to the national economy. However, when the wealthy nation enters a period of rising food prices, the concern for meeting human needs in poor nations commands much less political

force. Then political realism takes a commanding role;
domestic economic interests (that is, stable food prices) must
be served first.

Although we will have to examine this matter super-
ficially, it must at least be noted that power always has a
historical dimension. The structure of world power is
continuously in a state of flux and change, and these
international organizations are both a historic and a
contemporary result of this struggle for power among nations.
The FAO became an international organization in the 1943-
45 period. It was a creature of the Allied Powers,
predominantly the USA, the UK and Canada, with the
exclusion (by its own choice) of the USSR. Third World
nations, excluding Latin America, were nearly all colonies at
that time. FAO's members originally numbered 34; today
there are 158, and the distribution of power has been
significantly altered.

The World Food Programme is a product of the 1960-63
period; sponsored by the US government, abetted by the FAO,
supported by Canada and Australia, and somewhat
reluctantly agreed to by the new and suspicious developing
nations. Today, the European Economic Community has
become a major contributor and Third World nations have
acquired a power status nearing equality within the WFP.
Both the World Food Council and the International Fund for
Agricultural Development were the creations of the World
Food Conference, which was held in Rome in November 1974
at a time when a worldwide food shortage seemed to be on the
immediate horizon. But their configurations of power differ
decidedly from each other, and from those of FAO and WFP.
The World Food Council is primarily a policy innovator, a
minor broker in superpower politics, with the USA, USSR
and China as continuing members. IFAD has a unique
configuration: OECD (Organization of Economic Cooperation
and Development), OPEC (Organization of Petroleum
Exporting Countries) and the Group of 77 (Third World
nations). Process follows structure by and large and, as we
will indicate, this means that the issue of 'who governs?' must
often be answered differently over time. Using the FAO as an
example, the structure of power within that IO changed
during the 1945-85 period, and as a result the answer needs

to be modified at particular points in time.

An International Triangle (Quadrangle) Model

We will speak to the question of 'who governs?' in turn, for each international organization. However, we were unable to formulate a single model which would explain both structure and process for all four organizations. Conceptually, an international triangle of power works fairly well for FAO and WFP. One side of the power triangle would be the OECD member states (i.e., the nations of Western Europe and North America, plus Japan, Australia and New Zealand) who are, by far, the principal funding actors; a second side would be the Third World nations, somewhat loosely organized into a political coalition called the Group of 77, who are the principal recipients of this funding; with a third side being the secretariats (the bureaucracy) of FAO and WFP, which have the crucial roles of policy innovator and mediator for promoting mutually acceptable agreements between those who fund and those who receive.[1] But the triangle-of-power concept has to be restructured into a quadrangle in order to explain the workings of IFAD; OECD, OPEC, Group of 77, and the IFAD bureaucracy. And for the World Food Council, the USSR and the Eastern Europe bloc have to be included, and OPEC becomes a part (unrealistically, in economic terms) of the Group of 77.

These schematic arrangements are useful in explaining how the world food organizations function. There is, to some extent, a commonality of interest. OECD nations (the North) have political, economic and cultural interests in assisting developing nations (the South) to emerge from conditions of poverty; the developing nations, obviously, have the desire to do so, but claim that a prerequisite is abundant development assistance. On the other hand, this agreement on goals and objectives often does not translate into an agreement on means and methods. North and South need each other, but the latter's demands are insatiable, while the former believes that the resources available for redistribution are limited. The respective international bureaucracies function as a kind of influential prime mover, inclining towards finding policies and means to meet the demands of the South, but understanding the limitations of their power to make a claim on the wealth of the North. Moreover, these bureaucracies have vested interests of their own. The result is compromise; incremental change which is presumed to be an optional arrangement by the major political actors at that particular moment. Also, none of these power configurations takes sufficiently into account three other important considerations. One is the influence on the world food agencies of the United Nations itself and some of the other IOs — specifically, the United Nations Development Program (UNDP), the World Bank and the regional banks, and, to a lesser extent, such organizations as the World Health Organization (WHO) and the International Labour Organization (ILO). Secondly, the non-governmental organizations (NGOs), such as CARE, Catholic Relief Service and Church World Service, are secondary actors, but not without influence, in the policy making of each of the world food organizations. They are effectively organized, politically and functionally, in North America, Western Europe and Australia, and are closely associated with an international structure in Geneva — The International Council of Voluntary Agencies. Thirdly, in each international organization there is a director-general (or an executive director or president), who is certainly first and foremost in the bureaucratic hierarchy; jealous of his or her authority, suspicious of competitors, authoritarian (in varying degrees) in leadership style, although dependent on the imaginative insights, analytical expertise, personal and corporate loyalty, and administrative skills of the IO's professional and technical staff. Moreover, problems of organizational competitiveness and jurisdiction, always prevalent and occasionally of some magnitude, exist within and between the bureaucracies of these world food agencies.

In any respect, we could not develop a singe model which describes the behaviour of all of these agencies, and the two variations we have offered are not without their defects, which we will later elaborate.

A Descriptive Explanation

We will attempt an answer for each of the world food agencies to our central questions: Who governs? Our presentation cannot be comprehensive but we will provide an overview based on the following outline. First, there will be a brief look at the constitutional-political basis of power of each IO. Those who study IOs tend to overlook the constitutional basis from which the agency must proceed; if this legal framework is abused or violated it is quite likely that serious political conflict will ensue, and little will be accomplished until those constitutional issues are resolved. Second, we will explain the budgetary-financial basis of each organization. An IO does not have the power to tax; even less does it have the power of the sword (ie, exacting and enforcing penalties on the negligent or recalcitrant member state). But the questions of 'Who pays? Who receives?' always generate fundamental political and economic issues, the answers to which tell us much about who gets what, when and how. Third, we will sketch out the policy-making process, and do so by briefly explaining, where applicable, the internal power relationships which occur at the various stages of the policy cycle. We will use a frequently employed, five-state policy cycle: agenda building, formulation, legitimation, implementation and evaluation.[2]

What eventuates, in terms of policy decisions and their implementation, is what a reasonably knowledgeable person would suspect, based on the power models we discussed earlier. That is, the policy process in the international organization is one of compromise and mutual accommodation, resulting usually in incremental change. Conflicts of interest and ideology do occur, of course, and the competing demands are decided on in an environment in which the principal actors must search for a consensus. One of the definitions of power offered by Keohane and Nye — 'The ability of an actor to get others to do something they otherwise would not do (at an acceptable cost to the actor)'[3] — has come to have a special meaning in these IOs. The Third World nations have the votes, but not the resources; conversely, the have-nations have their own interests in maintaining a forum for continuing international cooperation which would not be served by withdrawal or persistent 'stonewalling.' The power of the actors (member states and bureaucracies) is so limited that, confronted with interests

both common and conflicting, there is really no visible
alternative other than a search for a mutually-acceptable
consensus.

Who Governs the Food and Agriculture Organization?

The Food and Agriculture Organization of the United
Nations was created in 1945 as one of the autonomous
specialized agencies of the United Nations system whose
purpose was to promote cooperation among nations and
encourage action on common problems, thus contributing to
world peace. FAO actually predated the formal establishment of the United Nations, and was given a broad mandate
under its constitution. It had four purposes.

- Raising levels of nutrition and standards of living
  under the jurisdiction of the member governments.
- Securing improvements in the efficiency of production
  and distribution of food and agricultural products.
- Bettering the conditions of rural populations.
- Contributing to an expanding world economy and striv-
  ing to assure freedom from hunger.[4]

The organization which emerged reflected a compromise
between those who wanted a strong action-oriented agency to
foster agricultural development and those who wanted a more
limited fact-gathering and advisory agency.[5]

FAO was established with an organizational structure
fairly common for intergovernmental organizations. The
supreme governing body is the Conference which holds
regular sessions biennially and elects the Director-General
and FAO Secretariat. The Conference also decides the scale
of member contributions to FAO. Assessments have generally
been made in accordance with the UN formula, with members
contributing a percentage of the FAO budget proportionate to
the relative size of GNP.

Another function of the Conference is to elect member
countries to the Council which meets between conferences
and serves as a second-level governing body. The membership of the Council has grown to 49 members. The USA has
always been a member. Much of the substantive work

discussed by the Conference and Council is carried out by committees.   There are seven standing committees dealing with programme, finance, constitutional and legal issues, commodities, agriculture, forestry and fisheries.   The Conference and Council also carry on their work through a number of *ad hoc* bodies such as the Committee on World Food Security and Commission on Fertilizers.

FAO has grown very significantly since its inception. Its budget in the 1946-47 biennium was $8.4 million. For the 1986-87 biennium, total funding was $1.1 billion.   (If calculated in constant dollars, the increase would, of course, be considerably less dramatic).   In FAO's early years, prior to decolonization, FAO was dominated by the Western industrial powers who took a rather restricted view of what the organization could accomplish.   Primary emphasis was given to making technical studies, collecting and publishing statistics, conducting conferences, establishing technical commissions and dispatching occasional field study missions. In this period, the FAO budget grew slowly.

Independence for the former colonies led to a significant increase in the membership of FAO in the 1950s and 1960s and a shift in the voting balance to give the developing nations a significant majority in the Conference.   New pressures were generated on FAO to change its focus from information gathering and dissemination to field activities in support of Third World agricultural development.   An active field programme was developed by FAO, funded by extra-budgetary resources contributed primarily by UN agencies and national governments.   However, the transition proceeded slowly.   Change was resisted by the FAO bureaucracy and resistance developed, and continues, among the industrial nations to FAO becoming primarily a development agency.

The early 1970s saw the development of a world food crisis caused by global drought occurring in the context of Third World population explosion.   FAO was severely criticized for not anticipating the crisis and for not having done enough to stimulate Third World agricultural development and thus limit the effects of the famine. The general dissatisfaction with FAO was an important factor leading to the 1974 Rome World Food Conference, which was held under UN rather than FAO auspices.[6] New international food organizations, independent of FAO, were established to accomplish missions which it was thought were not well carried out by FAO.

The Rome World Food Conference galvanized change in FAO. The sense of crisis forged a new consensus of OECD and Group of 77 countries, which led to the election of a dynamic Director-General, Edouard Saouma, committed to Third World agricultural development and widespread support for such reforms as the development of an extensive system of country representatives, the establishment of a Technical Cooperation Programme with quick grants for short-term development needs, increased support for agricultural investment, and a considered effort to shift personnel resources from headquarters to the field. The crisis atmosphere facilitated mutual adjustment along with a rapid growth of FAO's budget and extra-budgetary resources.

As the world food crisis receded in the late 1970s, the consensus between OECD and the Group of 77 weakened and FAO's budget growth and innovations slowed down perceptibly. The USA, concerned about an increasing balance of payments deficit, among other reasons, began to exert cost containment pressures. Since 1983, FAO has operated with almost a no-growth budget.

The FAO policy process is a cumbersome one with a strong tendency towards incrementalism, as one would expect from an organization with 158 member governments and 6,600 staff. The programme of work is put together in the various divisions of FAO and the Director-General makes the final determination of priorities after consultation with the staff and member countries. Director-General Saouma has a decisive style and dominates the policy process. He has to walk a very fine line between meeting the demands of the Group of 77 countries for expanding FAO programmes without offending the OECD countries, which still provide the bulk of the funding. The Conference, in practice, is unwieldy and does not play a major role in planning or determining priorities. Its major function appears to be to ratify the decisions reached by the Director-General and staff. The Council is more involved than the conference in FAO substantive matters, primarily as a sounding board for new proposals but still tends to defer to the Director-General and the Secretariat.

FAO is severely constrained in its policy autonomy in that its resources are primarily technical rather than financial. Unlike the World Bank and IFAD, FAO cannot carry out development projects, but can only provide technical support. Hence, FAO activities must remain very closely tied to the projects funded by the major lending agencies. FAO's dependence on extra-budgetary funding provides the regular assessed budget.[7] The remainder comes from a variety of grants and trust funds provided by international organizations and countries, and FAO must do what the donors want, if it is to retain access to this funding.

The Director-General gains support to legitimize his policies in a number of ways. He can use his discretionary authority to distribute Technical Cooperation Programme funds to gain support from Third World governments. He also has power to make staff appointments and can exert significant leverage on member governments by adroit use of his patronage power, at some cost, arguably, to the general technical competence of the FAO staff. He maintains influence internally through control of promotions and by placing 'his own people' in important positions.

FAO can implement its policies only to the extent that it has the support of the nations where it operates. Our sense is that FAO has gained a freer hand to function in Third World countries as the perceived need for agricultural development has increased. A more serious problem is the sensitivity of many governments to criticism. Hence, FAO has been slow to develop meaningful evaluations and in communicating the results of those evaluations it has made. Since the World Food Conference, FAO has developed a more rigorous evaluation process, though these assessments are still not generally available to outsiders.

Another obstacle to effective implementation is that FAO programmes need to be coordinated with the activities of other international organizations and of national governments. This was very difficult before the Rome World Food Conference when most of FAO's personnel were headquarters-based. Director-General Saouma has alleviated this problem somewhat with his system of 74 country

representatives, who now serve 98 countries. These country
representatives, under the direct control of the Director-
General, are responsible for seeing that FAO intentions are
carried out, and in coordinating FAO activities with those of
host governments and other international organizations.
    FAO has shown itself effective in adjusting to shifting
international priorities. It responded well to the call of the
Rome World Food Conference for an increased emphasis on
agricultural production and investment and for the
development of an agricultural early-warning system. It has
also moved to extend its efforts to the peasant farmer by
sponsoring the 1979 World Conference on Agrarian Reform
and Rural Development (WCARRD), and by emphasizing
small farmers in its recent programmes of work and budget.
It has also given emphasis in recent years to food production
in Africa, the region with the most serious problems.
However, it is not possible to measure correctly the increased
commitment to Africa and to agricultural reform by analysing
FAO budget figures. The percent of the FAO budge for Africa
only increased from 29.9% in 1978-79 to 30.7% in 1986-87.[8]
One can surmise that the political balance is so delicate that
it is difficult to make any significant policy changes in the
absence of real budgetary growth.

Who Governs the World Food Council?

    The World Food Council is a product of the World Food
Conference of 1974. Resolution XXII, which was later ratified
by the UN's Economic and Social Council, and then the
General Assembly, designated the WFC as the highest
political institution in the UN system dealing with world food
policies and problems. It is not an operating agency, '...but
rather a forum and mechanism for initiating ideas and for
reviewing the work of other international organizations with
operating programs.'[9]
    The construction of the 36-member Council gives some
political leverage to the Group of 77, whose members occupy
25 of the Council seats. But the Council has no funds for
projects or programmes, only ideas and proposals. Its
operating budget amounts to less than $2 million, sufficient to
pay for an almost miniscule bureaucracy, consultants and

internal programming.

The Council exists because, in the minds of many of the delegates at the World Food Conference, the Food and Agriculture Organization failed to fulfill its principal mission — that is, to foresee and, presumably, to prevent the world food crisis of 1972-74. This is likely an unfair and misdirected charge, but the FAO has suffered from, and has become embittered by, this perceived failure. The relationship between the two organizations, particularly at the highest levels, has generally been one of studied, brooding and mutual incompatibility.

The Council's Executive Director and (to a lesser extent) its elected President have provided the Council with dynamic and imaginative leadership. Its annual agenda has been dictated to a minor extent by desires made explicit at a previous Council session, but much more often Council proposals concerning 'what should be done' to alleviate world food problems are the brainchild of the Executive Director, his staff and their consultants. Searching for and exposing ways and means to improve food production, enhance world food security, and increase the flow of food aid constitute the Counsil's central objectives. The annual formulations of proposed strategies and programmes are contained in a set of documents drafted by the WFC bureaucracy, which heretofore have first been considered at the Preparatory Meeting, and then ratified (largely without revision) by the Council at its annual session, usually held in June each year in a different continent. The Group of 77, through the device of the Preparatory Meeting, has endeavoured to gain control of the Council's agenda in order to modify the secretariat's proposals in their favour, but the Executive Director has managed to maintain control. Indeed, in 1986 the Preparatory Meeting was simply abolished.

The Council is not an implementing agency, and has no formal mechanism for evaluating the activities and programmes of the other world food agencies. In establishing the council, the World Food Conference envisaged high-level, policy-discussing annual meetings, composed not only of ministers of agriculture but also with some representation of those from finance, planning and development. But in 1975-76 the world food crisis began to slip from its status as high

politics on the world scene, down to a kind of middle-level
position as the crisis receded. Gradually, there developed the
realization that the world food problem, at its core and
conscience, was actually one of poverty. A massive
redistribution, from rich to poor nations, would likely have to
take place if this condition was to be attacked in a serious,
concerted manner. The political environment simply did not
(and does not) exist for that kind of revolutionary policy
making to take place.

The World Food Council does not and cannot govern; it
endeavours to pursuade (to use a prominent and current
example) the Third World nations to formulate and
implement a national food strategy which will, over extended
time, enable that food-deficit nation to become food self-
reliant. And simultaneously the Executive Director and his
staff have persisted in their efforts to persuade the OECD
nations that they, in turn, must support — financially and
through non-protectionist trade policies — those Third World
nations who are endeavouring to implement a national food
strategy.

Not only does the World Food Council seek to be
creative and innovative, but it must also be concerned with
searching for the means whereby ideas can be transformed
into effective policies and programmes. Over the past decade
much has been heard of the concept of political will: that the
international community could overcome the scourge of
poverty — and the problems of food, shelter, ignorance and
illness which follow in its wake — if the OECD and Group of
77 states displayed the political will to do so. Ideally, perhaps
this is so, but the peroration has been essentially self-
denying. This world, we would argue, is composed of many
interdependent nation states, but they do not perceive of
themselves as constituting a world community. From those
according to their ability to those according to their need is
not the dominant theme in world politics. The World Food
Council endeavours to function as a policy innovator and
political broker between those who have and those who have
not. In that pursuit the Council has been successful to the
extent that a North-South dialogue continues on major issues
relating to agriculture and food, and many of these issues
have been either initiated or enlightened by the endeavours of

the Council.

Who Governs the World Food Programme?

Viewed constitutionally, the World Food Programme is a voluntary agency built upon a FAO Conference resolution passed in November 1961, and subsequent UN General Assembly resolutions enacted in 1961, 1965 and 1975.[10] The economic reality was that the origin of the WFP came about because of the growing burden of over-bountiful farm surpluses, especially in the USA. The political reality was two-fold: (1) the FAO bureaucracy had devised a programme whereby surplus agricultural commodities of rich nations could be utilized in Third World countries for rural development projects, welfare programmes, and food-disaster emergencies; (2) the Kennedy administration — more explicitly, the Food For Peace director George McGovern — seized the opportunity presented by the FAO scheme and proposed the establishment of a World Food Programme, financed predominantly by US agricultural commodities and dollars.

Over time the WFP has become a unique type of voluntary agency. In essence, it is financed primarily (80-90%) by OECD nations who contribute food, cash and services for the support of WFP-sponsored development and disaster relief projects. Every two years a pledging conference is held in New York. In 1963, the pledges were valued at $100 million. By the end of 1985, just over one billion dollars had been pledged for the 1985-86 biennium, although this amount was some 25% short of the established target of $1.3 billion.

This fund of food, cash and services is spent on both development and emergency projects in Third World nations. Development projects are broadly of two types — primarily for agricultural and rural development (e.g., land rehabilitation, soil conversion, irrigation), and to a lesser extent for human resource development (nutritional support for mothers, their infants and primary school children). In 1985, resources provided to development projects were valued at $642 million. During the 1980s, emergency food commitments (disaster induced by humans, drought, natural catastrophes) have been on the increase, and in 1985 their cost came to over $225 million.

Because the funding is voluntary, the policy-making process must be two-sided. Funding must first be volunteered, essentially by OECD countries; the expenditures are completely within Third World countries. Herein lies the international iron triangle, with the WFP bureaucracy occupying a prominent corner through its influence in the determinations of the project cycle. That is, projects are initiated and formulated by a Third World nation, sometimes with the assistance of the WFP Field Representative in the least-developed nations. The legitimation stage takes place in the Committee on Food Aid Policy and Programmes (CFA). In a sense, CFA performs a legislative function. Its 30 members — composed of OECD and Group of 77 members, in approximately equal numbers — discuss each project, and occasionally will influence the WFP staff to modify the terms of a project proposal. Small projects, costing WFP less than $1.5 million, may be approved by the Executive Director, then reported and justified to CFA. Since adequate food resources are available, projects are rarely denied, at either the formulation or legitimation stage. (Funds, however, are usually in short supply.) The implementation of an approved project is primarily the responsibility of the recipient Third World nation, although the WFP is gradually becoming more involved in the transportation and distribution functions within the recipient nations. The WFP has been a pioneer agency in the use of project evaluations, which must be reported periodically to CFA, and a final evaluation report is required after a project has been completed.

The answer to the question of who governs the WFP must therefore be somewhat complex. On the input side, the OECD nations have to make the major financial commitment, although agricultural surpluses in North America, Western Europe and Australia have meant that the opportunity costs of food aid have been quite low in recent years. On the output (project) side, the WFP staff and the proposing/recipient Third World nations play the dominant roles. Internally, emergency project proposals have to be approved by FAO's Director-General. Importantly, too, catastrophic events — such as Kampuchea, the Sahel, and the Ethiopian food crises — are an exogenous variable which mandate a positive decision. The WFP staff desires to be viewed as primarily a rural development agency, but Third World disasters (human-made and natural) impose an increasing and recurring responsibility. In 1985, for example, regular WFP assistance to Ethiopia cost over $211 million for 14 development projects and almost $70 million for 20 emergency operations.

As mentioned earlier, this triangular power configuration has to be modified, at least marginally, because of the desires and influence of the NGOs and other UN specialized organizations. But, in general terms and discounting the exceptions to the rule, we believe that the triangular model has significant descriptive power.

Who Governs the International Fund for Agricultural Development?

The World Food Conference's Resolution XIII states that 'an International Fund for Agricultural Development should be established immediately to finance agricultural development projects primarily for food production in the developing countries.' Implicit, too, in this resolve was that IFAD's projects should be aimed predominantly at the rural peasantry who live in conditions of abject poverty. The concurrence of the UN General Assembly soon followed, and the UN Secretary-General proceeded to initiate a search for voluntary pledges to finance IFAD's operations. Funding has constantly been one of its principal concerns. Probably no international organization has been accorded as positive, indeed enthusiastic, a public press as has IFAD, but none has been plagued by so many obstacles in the search for funds, at its inception and especially during the negotiations for replenishment.

Resolution XIII also set forth, in somewhat vague terms, the constitutional structure of IFAD: a Governing Board representing 'contributing developed countries [ie, OECD], contributing developing countries [ie, OPEC], and potential recipient countries [ie, Third World nations].' Moreover, this representation was to be selected so as to ensure 'regional balance' and an 'equitable distribution.' After some difficult negotiations, a set of Articles of

Agreement was drafted, and opened for signature by willing
nation states. But a serious controversy between OECD and
OPEC member states over funding was resolved only after
difficult negotiations, and IFAD could not commence
operation until 30 November 1977.[11] The Articles specified
the establishment of a Governing Council (all signatory
countries) and a tripartite Executive Board with each part
having one-third of the 1,800 votes. According to Section 6(b),
'...decisions of the Executive Board shall be taken by a
majority of three fifths of the votes cast [except for voting for
suspensions or amendments], provided that such majority is
more than half of the total number of votes of all members of
the Executive Board.'

The realities of power within IFAD are quite different,
however, from the constitutional requirements. Some 141
nations are now voluntary members of IFAD, and constitute
its Governing Council. The Council meets annually; its
authority is decidedly limited, but the Council formally elects
a President (the first was from Saudi Arabia, the second from
Algeria), who in turn selects a Vice President (thus far, an
American). However, political power actually lies with an
Executive Board of 18 members: six in Category I (OECD), six
in Category II (OPEC), and six in Category III (Group of 77).
Initially nearly all of IFAD's small bureaucracy were on
secondment from other international or national aid agencies,
although this is much less the situation today. The
reputation of this bureaucracy has been consistently high:
dynamic, experienced, resourceful, innovative.

IFAD's conundrum has been how to secure funding for
projects which would increase food production in developing
countries, and would also '...improve the nutritional level of
the poorest populations in the poorest food deficit
countries...[and] in other developing countries.'[12] In its
origin as an idea, IFAD was probably the brainchild of the
Secretary-General of the World Food Conference — Saved
Ahmed Marei, the Egyptian Minister of Agriculture. The idea
proved attractive to at least some members of OPEC,
primarily because that organization was incurring sharp and
increasing criticism from non-oil-producing Third World
countries who had been subjected to a sixfold increase in oil
prices. The OECD countries, and principally the USA, were

opposed to the creation of new international organizations, but they were attracted to the idea of securing OPEC's financial contributions to aid food production in the Third World countries. In a nutshell, an 'equitable' contribution meant 50-50 to the OECD members, but the OPEC equity could be defined as no more than a 60-40 ratio, with OPEC on the lesser side. Finally, by late 1977, a compromise was agreed to: a 58-42 ratio, with the total pledged fund for 1978-81 amounting to just over $1 billion (actually $1021 million, with category III nations pledging $19 million). The contribution of the USA was $200 million.

IFAD's financial troubles began with the first replenishment, which was to be for the 1981-84 period. The target figure of $1.1 billion was arrived at without much difficult negotiation, with approximately the same ratios prevailing. But the USA arbitrarily cut its funding from $200 million to $180 million, and soon fell behind in its payments because of Congress's refusal to appropriate any funds, even in annual increments. However, other OECD countries finally agreed to fill in the deficit in the Category I pledge. On the Category II (OPEC) side, the Iranian revolution turned that nation into a non-contributor; then Libya defaulted, as did Iraq after the Iran-Iraq war began.

The second replenishment, for 1985-87, was even more complicated. Indeed, our sketch does little justice to its complexities. A dramatic reduction in oil prices put all OPEC contributions at risk, and President Reagan and the US Congress vied for honours in setting up replenishment obstacles for the US contribution. Tentatively, an agreement was arrived at in January 1986 for a second replenishment of just over $500 million (Category I, $300 million; Category II, $200 million; Category III, $24 million) although it seems unlikely that those amounts will actually be pledged, and if so that the pledges will be honoured.

Despite this severe handicap, IFAD's record is noteworthy. In some eight years, IFAD has financed 177 projects in 87 developing countries at a total cost of almost $9.1 billion, of which IFAD's share has been $2.1 billion. For example, even in the African nations some 47% of the project costs were incurred by the recipient government, while 28% were co-financed (primarily, by the World Bank and regional banks).

The politics involved in IFAD's policy cycle are complicated. Our description and explanation are somewhat superficial, but hopefully sufficient to answer: who governs IFAD? The agenda of IFAD is clearly stated in its constitutional documents; for example, *Lending Policies and Criteria* (December 1978, Article 27) specifies that projects and programmes must '...normally...provide proportionately large benefits to the poorest segments of the population when compared with other groups.' Because IFAD has a remarkably small bureaucracy (84 professionals and 106 support staff, as of February 1986) the matter of identification and formulation of project proposals which are in accord with IFAD purposes and criteria has been a particularly difficult matter. Through the use of technical assistance grants and special programming missions IFAD has largely succeeded in influencing this process in a manner which enables the organization to function in accord with its objectives, at least in the view of IFAD's secretariat.

It is difficult to generalize about the legitimation stage. The Governing Council has almost no role; the Executive Board is influential in moulding and modifying project proposals, but to what extent and in what matter we are uncertain. Executive Board sessions are closed; minutes are kept, but (we are told) they are recorded only in terms of decisions, not verbatim. However, we do not desire to leave the impression that the IFAD President and staff govern. The Executive Board must primarily be a reacting institution, but interviews with some members of IFAD's Secretariat caused us to believe that, on occasion, the Board's reactions have been critical, influential and demanding.

At the implementation stage, the limitations (in numbers) of the IFAD management staff again become apparent. Our impression, based heavily on a few interviews and a reading of IFAD's annual reports, is that the bureaucracy has been gradually gaining effective control over its implementation process. More accurately, the principal responsibility for implementation lies with the recipient Third World nation; IFAD's responsibility is '...to ensure timely and effective implementation of its projects,'[13] which it seems to be accomplishing. The IFAD staff has been especially active and innovative in the evaluation stage, again within the confines and constraints imposed by a shortage of professional staff. Robert Berg has recently commended IFAD: '...they set up monitoring authorities at the project level and strengthen evaluation at the ministerial levels [of the recipient country].'[14]   And the UN's Joint Inspection Unit, in a 1985 report, noted that '...IFAD has continued to establish and strengthen monitoring and evaluation as a central element of its programme.'[15]

What does all of this mean in terms of IFAD as an organization of power? The current situation has evolved into a kind of political enigma. There is strong ideological support for IFAD, particularly from liberals in OECD states, although IFAD is not without conservative support. On the other hand, IFAD continues to face serious funding difficulties. Nearly all of the media's adverse criticism has been directed at the Reagan Administration because of its obstinacy towards the funding of IFAD. But most of the other OECD nations (and notably the major contributors to IFAD) and all the members of OPEC seem to be permitting the USA to receive the opprobrium for niggardliness which they would incur, too, if put into a situation where they would be committed to increase their financial commitment to IFAD. More will be said on this matter below.

The Rome Food Agencies, Towards 2000

We conclude with a brief foray into the hazardous field of forecasting. What do we guess the structure of power in the world food agencies will look like by the year 2000? We see four possible alternatives.

Unification

In a recent article, John Gerard Ruggie observed that '...it was not international bureaucrats but national governments that established...no fewer than four international agencies dealing with food and agriculture alone.'[16]   Political scientists have a kind of abiding passion for advising against overlap and duplication in the structure and functions of governments, and the Rome food agencies, at

least deductively, seem to be a logical target for
reorganization and consolidation.

For over a decade there has been an unorganized but
articulate anti-World Food Council contingent; some of them
are quartered within the Food and Agriculture Organization,
but by no means all of the dissenters are there. Based on a
recommendation of the 11th session of the World Food
Council (Paris, June 1985), an 'advisory group' of three was
set up to investigate what the future role of the World Food
Council should be. Their preliminary report has now been
released, and the terse summary of their nine
recommendations would be that the Council should be
strengthened in its authority, funding and independence.[17]
This report will not silence WFC's detractors, but our surmise
is that the end result will be a marginally stronger Council.

Then there is the school of disbelievers concerning the
IFAD. That is: Why do we need an IFAD when we already
have an IDA (International Development Association — the
soft-window, concessional arm of the World Bank) and three
regional banks? There is no intrinsic need for a duplicative
specialized agency; besides, the pie of development assistance
is shrinking so a competitive structure is not only
unnecessary but divisive and damaging, or at least inefficient.
(So the Anti-IFAD argument goes.)

There has never been much discussion regarding the
abolition of the World Food Programme, at least to our
knowledge, but there is concern (and notably so within the
WFP) as to its increasing involvement in worldwide disaster
relief. There is also some discussion about the future of the
Committee on World Food Security, which was established by
the World Food Conference to monitor and recommend
regarding those concerns; it meets annually in Rome, and
reports to FAO and the UN General Assembly.

There will be no unification of world food agencies by
2000; at least that is our forecast, and primarily for two
reasons — one negative, one positive. On the negative side,
the Food and Agriculture Organization is still suspect
throughout much of the world food policy network. In our
judgement, a considerable amount of the criticism of FAO has
been unfair and misdirected. Nevertheless, its image has
been blemished; it is improving, but the FAO continues to be

viewed as a 'bureaucracy' in the pejorative sense of the term — overstaffed, overpaid, unimaginative, not at the cutting edge of current agricultural science and technology. On the positive side, the other three world food agencies (with the World Food Council as somewhat problematical) have proven themselves. There are those who are opposed to food aid, multilateral and bilateral, and their disincentive arguments constitute a valid concern. But these criticisms have been heard and the necessary preventive measures factored into WFP policies. IFAD has yet to prove that its policies and programmes will enable those in rural poverty to improve their degraded condition, at least in substantial numbers, but there is considerable evidence that IFAD has a positive image within the world food policy network. To be sure, its funding problems are immediate and impairing, but they do not appear to be unresolvable.

Major Expansion of Authority

This is an unlikely alternative. Neither the World Food Council nor FAO will be permitted by the OECD, or even by the Group of 77, to become a World Food Authority. Lord Boyd-Orr's vision will continue to be unrealized. The World Food Programme will not be transformed into the world disaster agency; there are too many other international disaster agencies who would engage themselves with ardour and vehemence in that kind of turf fight. Besides, this would require a considerable reconstitution of the WFP as an institution; there is more to disaster relief than the supply of food, important as that is. Likewise, the World Bank's IDA is not going to be dissolved into an IFAD, although a considerable increase in oil prices would renew the appetites of OECD members towards finding ways to direct substantial amounts of those 'undeserving' profits into development assistance. In this kind of thinking, IFAD is not without growth potential, although one is sorely pressed to think of ways that would convince OPEC that the unpleasant is the necessary.

Dissolution

Cynics (or are they realists?) often conjecture that

international bureaucracies, like those of the national variety, are rarely abolished and seldom tend to fade away. There are possibilities here, although we see the probabilities as quite high that no one of these world food agencies will be abolished. Our reasons can fairly well be extracted from the discussion concerning unification. If the World Food Council were to be abolished, who would assume its persuading, mobilizing, coordinating responsibilities?[18] The FAO would be the logical, but politically unviable, choice, although this prediction might be disapproved, depending on the outcome of the election of a Director-General in 1987. In the best of all possible worlds, food aid should become an anachronism, but that is a 21st century dream. Besides, the WFP is politically useful as a multilateral agency, performing functions that OECD surplus-producing nations would find to be awkward, perhaps embarrassing, and possibly counterproductive, if they had to be carried out exclusively within a bilateral framework. The USA's PL 480 programme and, to a lesser extent, the European Community's food aid programme, are vulnerable to the charges of self-serving, subtle bribery and undue influence, as viewed by Third World recipients. IFAD is a candidate for dissolution, but not realistically; the late 1980s may not be the heyday period for liberals, but we see IFAD as institutionally invulnerable because of its special rural-poor focus which the International Development Association does not have. However, IFAD's funding arrangements will continue to be the subject of hard negotiating.

Incremental Change

There will necessarily be policy changes, but we do not see them to be of a dramatic nature. Likewise, since their decision-making processes have not changed much in the last decade they are not likely to change much in the future. At its 1986 session in Rome, the World Food Council reverted, at least in part, to the format and agenda for which it was originally designed: a policy-innovation kind of arrangement orchestrated by the Council's Executive Director and his staff, at which ministers of agriculture, and a few of their money- and planning-oriented counterparts, would talk over what they are, might be, and could be doing. The final report constituted a kind of 'sense of the meeting,' experiential in content, rather than a politicized set of conclusions and recommendations. Whether these high-level, time-conscious political administrators will accept this format as both utilitarian and perception-broadening, and not just another cacophony of rhetoric, remains to be seen.

In this increasingly interdependent world there is a vital need for a Food and Agriculture Organization. And in several policy areas — food quality standards, plant and animal genetics, seed identification and preservation, the use and sale of pesticides, fungicides and rodenticides, among others — we believe that FAO's power and responsibility will be gradually increased.

The World Food Programme is now adjusting to its recent increases in authority, which were granted following the deliberations of the Joint UN/FAO Task Force on WFP Relationship Problems. WFP management 'won' more autonomy from FAO in internal matters involving personnel, finances and auditing. But that power struggle seems now to have been resolved, and WFP still does not have the status of an independent specialized agency. However, WFP will likely have incremental increases in its authority over the next few years — such as funding of programmes (rather than only projects), and multi-year funding.

Just how the funding difficulties of IFAD will be resolved (meaning alleviated; funding is never finally resolved) is unclear. The two principal actors in this matter seem to be the USA and Saudi Arabia. In our judgement, the USA — in its own interests and those of Third World nations — should retreat from two wrong-headed positions: that funding for IFAD must be niggardly and defensive, and that IFAD's staff needs are now being adequately served. We have no grandiose numbers in mind; perhaps a return to the original $1+ billion for a three-year period and a doubling of the management staff. But IFAD has earned its right to be treated with respect, and to adequate funding.

To conclude, our own intelligent perspective comes out of a kind of American Lockian tradition: 'Men [and women] are not angels and angels do not govern men' — 'ambition must be made to counteract ambition' — '...experience has taught mankind the necessity of auxiliary precautions.'[19] Within that kind of a philosophical outlook, we view the international food organizations as useful and, to a considerable extent, necessary instruments to be used in the pursuit of justice and equity, for rich as well as poor nations. By and large, these organizations have functioned effectively, with some positive results. We view the four-organization structure as optimal in terms of balancing the interest of the competing factions, while at the same time facilitating some constructive action. That is, the present arrangement provides the various political blocs (OECD, OPEC, Third World, etc.) with multiple channels to pursue their varied interests. How these Rome food agencies are governed — by whom, for whom, in what manner, and with what results — are political matters of enduring consequence.

FOOTNOTES

1. For an elaborate theoretical analysis of this proposition, see Robert O. Keohane, *After Hegemony: Cooperation and Discord in the World Political Economy* (Princeton, NJ: Princeton University Press, 1984), especially chapters 4-6.

2. Standard sources are: James E. Anderson, *Public Policy-Making* 3rd ed (New York: Holt, Rinehart and Winston, 1984) and Charles O. Jones, *An Introduction to the Study of Public Policy* 3rd ed (Monterey, CA: Brooks-Cole Publishing Company, 1983).

3. Robert O. Keohane and Joseph S. Nye, *Power and Interdependence: Politics in Transition* (Boston: Little, Brown, 1977).

4. See Ralph W. Phillips, *FAO, Its Origins, Formation and Evolution*, 1945-1981 (Rome: FAO, 1981), 9.

5. Select Committee on Nutrition and Human Needs, US Senate, Staff Report, *The United States, FAO and World Food Politics: U.S. Relations with an International Food Organization*, (Washington, DC: US Government Printing Office, 1976), 70.

6. Important, too, was the fact that the USSR was (and is) not a member of FAO.

7. Martin Kriesberg, *International Organizations and*

Agricultural Development, Foreign Agricultural Report 131, (US Department of Agriculture, November 1984), 48.

8. Wayne Moyer, 'FAO is a Structure of Power: the Reality of its Limitations,' paper delivered at the annual meeting of the Midwest Political Science Association (April 1986).

9. Kriesberg, *op cit*, Ref 7, 121.

10. World Food Programme, *World Food Programme Basic Documents* 4th ed (Rome: WFP, September 1978), 55.

11. See the *Agreement Establishing the International Fund for Agricultural Development* (Rome: IFAD, 30 November 1977) and *Lending Policies and Criteria* (Rome: IFAD, December 1978).

12. *Articles of Agreement*, Article 7, section 1, [d], [i and ii].

13. International Fund for Agricultural Development, *Annual Report - 1984* (Rome: IFAD, May 1985), 37.

14. Robert J. Berg, 'Donor Evaluations: What is and What Could Be,' a paper prepared for the International Conference on the Role of Evaluation in National Agricultural Research Systems, held in Singapore, 7-9 July 1986, 25.

15. A report of the UN's Joint Inspection Unit, October 1985, 24.

16. John Gerard Ruggie, 'The United States and the United Nations: Toward a New Realism,' *International Organization* 39, no. 2, (Spring 1985), 353.

17. At the 1986 meeting of the World Food Council in Rome, a document issued for review and discussion was based on one section of the report of the advisory group: 'Recommendations and Suggestions For the Future,' WFC/1986/5 (14 March 1986).

18. A person who refereed this paper responded to our question as follows: 'No one. Would that leave a vacuum of the sort nature would abhor?'

19. John Locke, *Federalist Papers*, 10 and 51.

Chapter IV

The General Agreement on Tariffs and Trade (GATT)

The General Agreement on Tariffs and Trade (GATT) was established in 1948 as a multilateral treaty designed to "liberalize world trade and place it on a secure basis, thereby contributing to economic growth and development and to the welfare of the world's peoples." The GATT is based largely on the draft International Trade Organization (ITO) charter, which was never successfully ratified. Though ITO would have been a United Nations specialized agency, GATT is not, as it was erected without a great deal of institutional arrangement to temporarily take the place of ITO. After ITO failed to be ratified, GATT remained as the only international instrument laying down trade rules accepted by nations responsible for most of the world's trade. There are currently ninety-seven contracting parties plus one provisional acceptance and twenty-eight countries which apply GATT rules in practice. This accounts for more than four-fifths of world trade volume. The Secretariat consists of four hundred employees at the Geneva headquarters. The budget is financed by contributions from members based on share of total trade, and in 1989 it amounted to 64.8 million Swiss francs. GATT activities are based upon four fundamental principles. First, trade must be non-discriminatory. All contracting parties are bound to grant to each other treatment as favorable as they give to any country (i.e. Most Favored Nation principle). Second, protection should be given to domestic industry through customs tariffs. Third, a stable and predictable basis for trade is provided by the binding of tariff levels negotiated by contracting parties. Fourth is the principle of consultation, conciliation and settlement of differences. The main programs and activities of GATT serve as a code of rules and a forum in which countries can deal with problems and differences. GATT provides a framework for negotiations on tariff barriers, consultations on specific trade problems affecting specific products or countries, and periodic major multilateral trade negotiations. The last of these three activities is probably the most widely known, and there have been seven such "rounds" of negotiation. The most prominent of these are: the Dillon Round (1960-1961), the Kennedy Round (1964-1967), the Tokyo Round (1973-1979), and the Uruguay Round (1986-). Since the Second World War, world trade volume has increased tenfold due, in large part, to the success of GATT. The Uruguay Round, being negotiated at Punta del Este, has the objectives of further liberalization and expansion of world trade, strengthening the role of GATT, and making GATT more responsive and flexible to changes in the market and the balance of world economic power. This last objective refers, in large part, to the realization that Japan and Western Europe now exercise greater effective influence in the world economy, relative to the United States, than the current system of GATT is designed to accommodate.

Negotiations on GATT Reform and Political Incentives

Joachim Zietz

The Uruguay Round of multilateral trade negotiations, under the auspices of the General Agreement on Tariffs and Trade (GATT), is addressing a number of unresolved issues from previous GATT rounds. Prominent among them are the 'special cases' of agriculture and textiles, non-tariff interventions in the market process and the elaboration of Article XIX, the GATT's main escape clause, in a new 'safeguards' code. Negotiations on each of these topics are complex and potentially divisive. Against this background, the task of securing agreement on a more liberal trading environment appears formidable. Nevertheless, progress would be possible — and without compromising the institution of the GATT or good economics — as long as the constraints facing governments are given sufficient attention.

This article explores some of the implications of taking seriously the incentives to political action, both to secure agreements in multilateral trade negotiations and to avoid undesirable surprises when it comes to their implementation. Ways of improving the chances of achieving agreements are discussed first. In the second section, some suggestions are developed on how to avoid problems in the implementation of agreements, problems arising from a lack of incentive for governments to comply. These are illustrated by three issues which are playing a central role in the Uruguay Round negotiations, namely the provisions of Article XIX, 'voluntary' export-restraint agreements and subsidies to production.

WAYS OF SECURING NEW TRADE AGREEMENTS

There can be little hope of achieving agreements in multilateral trade negotiations unless (i) the participating countries are treated fairly and (ii) the influence of domestic pressure groups opposed to structural adjustment can be contained. Both these pre-conditions would be less difficult to meet if there was a common negotiating theme and negotiations, as well as compromises, were allowed to cut across different industries.

Fair Treatment of Participating Countries

In its most general form, fairness can be thought of as extending the GATT's most basic constitutional element, the principle of non-discrimination, to all trade — regardless of sector, industry, commodity or country. In this respect, the GATT system has not fared well, for there are many exceptions to equal treatment, both for industries and for countries. By and large, the exceptions have had the effect, over time, of making the GATT system less and less credible.

Special exemptions for particular industries in a system based on free-trade principles, and moderated only by 'bound' tariffs, indicate that the natural consequences of liberalizing trade — that is, the need for structural adjustment in the face of changes in comparative advantage — are not accepted. Resistance to adjustment, however, is not just a matter of concern to domestic industries. Exemptions affect the distribution of the 'costs' of adjustment among both industries and countries.[1] For example, if agriculture does not adjust to changes in comparative advantage, adjustment costs will be shifted to other parts of the economy[2] as well as to those countries specializing in agricultural exports.[3] This is unlikely to be a fair outcome, either for those industries that do not get special protection or for those industries or countries bearing the economic burden of the lack of adjustment in the agricultural sectors of, in particular, the industrialized countries. In a sense, then, special exemptions for certain industries can be considered a classic 'beggar-thy-neighbour' approach to structural adjustment. They are likely to erode the credibility of the GATT system and make it difficult to argue convincingly for the merits of a partial trade reform, one that improves the trading environment only for those countries that happen to specialize in the 'right' products — that is, those outside the industries which are subject to special exemptions.

Like exemptions for industries, country-specific

exemptions can be considered to be detrimental to the concept of fairness and to breakthrough agreements in the Uruguay Round negotiations. The GATT waiver granted to the United States for quantitative restrictions under Section 22 of the Agricultural Adjustment Act of 1933 is a classic example of a country-specific exemption.[4] Quite apart from its significance for agricultural exporters which might otherwise find a larger market for their produce in the United States, it has created an unfavourable psychological climate, for it is so clearly at odds with the idea of non-discrimination and fairness.

The idea of equal treatment in trade for all countries has also been undermined by the special legal status of developing countries in the GATT.[5] Developing countries have obtained exemptions from most obligations under the GATT. Yet they receive preferential access to developed-country markets through the Generalized System of Preferences and a number of other preferential tariff schemes. Fairness seems to be interpreted, in this case, in the same way as vertical equity is interpreted in tax theory: economic agents that are better off can also better afford to pay taxes. Translated to trade, this idea of fairness suggests that poor developing countries should be given more favourable treatment; that is, they should be taxed less by tariffs in export markets than rich industrialized countries.

Trade preferences for countries, however, tend to favour some countries and some products at the expense of others which are not subject to preferences. But apart from this obvious problem of trade diversion, it is not even clear whether the intended beneficiaries of trade preferences do actually benefit. Although there is evidence that at least some countries could increase their exports to protected markets and gain economic rents, it is questionable whether this is in the long-run interests of developing countries.[6] After all, access to high-price markets can establish artificial incentives to produce commodities for which there is no true world market. This might lead to distortions in the structure of production which, in turn, would create a need for difficult restructuring efforts once producers have to face true world prices.[7] Finally, the economic rents associated with trade preferences create a strong incentive for producers to oppose across-the-board trade-liberalizing efforts which are likely to be much more beneficial than selective preferences.

Being exempted from obligations under the GATT is not necessarily advantageous. As convincingly argued by Robert E. Hudec, in a study for the Trade Policy Research Centre,[8] the no-obligations status has deprived governments in developing countries of an important shield against the demands of domestic producers for protectionist action. As a result, the no-obligations status may be partially to blame for the poor growth performance of numerous inward-oriented developing countries.[9]

Apart from equal treatment of industries and countries, fairness in trade also implies that market access is secure and therefore predictable. Clearly not all preference schemes measure up to this standard. Systems of managed trade, however, such as the Multi-fibre Arrangement (MFA),[10] are clearly the worst in this respect. Managed-trade regimes also violate another important dimension of fairness: the reliance on rules of market access that are easy to understand and to implement as well as being difficult to manipulate. This dimension of fairness is in the particular interest of developing countries, which can least afford to waste scarce resources on keeping up with, or trying to influence, a maze of ever-changing rules and regulations in importing countries. In simplifying trade and shifting resources from information gathering and lobbying to production, assured market access is likely to develop, like little else probably can, the basis for sound entrepreneurship and lasting economic growth.

Issue of Domestic Acceptability

Domestic acceptability of reform of the GATT depends on the relative political influence of those groups in a society likely to gain from it and those that stand to lose, in the sense that trade reform will subject them to the costs of adjustment. As the interests of the potential losers are likely to be heavily concentrated and those of the potential gainers widely dispersed, the former have a natural advantage in convincing politicians of the merit of the *status quo*. Under these conditions, the cause for trade reform requires not only good economic arguments but also, and perhaps more importantly, a sufficient amount of countervailing power.

Although consumers are likely to gain the most from trade reforms aimed towards more liberalization, their countervailing power may be insufficient against well-organized, focussed and financially powerful producers expecting to lose from trade reform. There are a number of well-known reasons why it is difficult to translate the potential welfare gains to consumers into support which is politically relevant:[11]

(a) lack of appropriate information results in small perceived personal gains from trade reform;

(b) high transaction costs frustrate attempts at organizing a large body of people with diverse interests; and

(c) the costs of protection per capita decrease with rising incomes if the income elasticity of demand is less than one (as for most farm products).

As a result, strong support in favour of GATT reform has to come from somewhere else.

It is suggested that producers in the industries likely to gain from trade reform could provide such support or countervailing power. Unlike consumers, they are more focussed and, because of their smaller number, they are also more easily rallied behind a particular cause. Support is potentially most forceful among those producers for whom successful multilateral trade negotiations readily translate into improved market access in other countries.[12] This mercantilist idea of better export opportunities, however, works only to draw the support of exporters and importers that face significant trade barriers. The political counterweight against producers losing from trade reform could be strengthened if producers outside the import-export business are made more aware of the potential gains to them from trade liberalization. The task is to make them understand that higher profits result not only from better access to foreign markets but also from cost reductions resulting from cheaper intermediate products, more competitive factor prices, better quality, improved service and more flexibility, all as a consequence of a more competitive domestic environment. Two intuitively obvious examples illustrate this point.

First, eliminating the protection of cotton production in the United States would reduce the input costs of the textile industry. Lower output prices in this industry would, in turn, decrease the perceived need for protection in the clothing industry. Second, reducing protection of food products in Japan or Western Europe would increase real wages and thereby moderate demands for nominal wage increases throughout the economy. This would raise competitiveness *vis-à-vis* low-income countries even at constant relative productivity levels.

Equally as important as gaining support for trade reform from the appropriate groups, however, is framing the issue properly. A simple example may help to illustrate this point. Consider an economy which consists of industries A, B, C and D. Although industry A, which produces largely for export, can be expected to favour liberalization in industry B, its main supplier of intermediate inputs, industry A's main interest is likely to be in getting better market access in other countries. Industry C, which produces non-tradeable goods, also supports liberalization in industry B. Most of the inputs in industry C, however, come from industry D. Imagine now that negotiations proceed on an industry-by-industry basis. Feeling under considerable pressure to adjust, industry B uses all possible ways and means to prevent a change in the *status quo*. Industries A and C, although clearly in favour of reform in B, are unlikely to focus their lobbying efforts on achieving trade liberalization in B. It is rather more plausible that they will concentrate their efforts on where they see most of their gains coming from: trade liberalization in its products for industry A and trade liberalization in D for industry C. After all, even if no trade liberalization is achieved in B, there is still plenty left to gain from the liberalization of trade in the products of A and D. This is the nature of the incentive when negotiations are conducted on an industry-by-industry basis.

The problem with this approach, however, is that it is difficult to bring pressure or influence to bear on diehard protectionists like industry B. On the other hand, trade negotiations could cut across industries and progress in A and D might be predicated on a breakthrough in B. This situation could arise because the balance of cross-country offers and requests is such that no agreement can be reached for industries A or D unless trade reform in industry B is also part of the deal or because the negotiations are conducted in an all-or-nothing fashion so there will be no final accord unless trade reform includes all industries. In either case, industry B can expect to face a tough problem. The amount of countervailing power could be substantial compared with an industry-by-industry approach. To sum up, it appears that the narrower the focus of the negotiations, the smaller the amount of countervailing power that will be available.

Less countervailing power, however, means that the influence on the negotiations of special-interest lobbying groups is larger. Apart from preventing an agreement altogether, this can also negatively affect the economic nature of any potential agreement in multilateral trade negotiations. If trade negotiations are conducted only on an industry basis, industry specialists rather than the top echelon of government officials will have a determining influence on their outcome. Industry specialists, though, are much less likely to consider the interests of the country as a whole. They operate in a direct shooting line of industrial lobbying groups with whom they have developed close ties over time. Hence they may be less willing to compromise the interests of 'their clientele' with a bold move towards trade liberalization. Rather, they tend to favour 'pragmatic' solutions to current problems. Unfortunately, pragmatic solutions can easily compromise important principles of the GATT and thereby make the trading system even less consistent and credible.[13] Given the power of inertia and legal precedent in international trade relations, important GATT principles should not be compromised, not even temporarily. The MFA serves as a warning sign as to what can happen to exemptions from GATT obligations that purport to meet temporary needs.

Finally, without the option of cross-industry agreements the range of possible compromises could be rather small in the Uruguay Round negotiations, leaving little room for a balancing of offers and requests. For example, there can be no reasonable balance of trade offers and requests in beef or even in all of agriculture between Australia and Japan or in clothing between developing countries and industrialized countries. In both cases, one side has a request for better market access, but nothing to offer in return in the same product group. Negotiations along those lines are unlikely to be successful. What is required instead is an approach that embraces more than one industry. To continue the example, liberalization in the Japanese beef industry, or in agriculture in general, could be balanced with liberalization in Australian manufacturing industry. Similarly, liberalization in clothing by industrialized countries could be compensated by developing countries through concessions on intellectual property rights, services or investment-related issues.[14]

Common Negotiating Theme for All Industries

Deals that cut across industries are made difficult, if not practically impossible, if the ideas of what comprises trade liberalization or trade reform diverge sharply among those affected. Comparison of the economic consequences of gradual enlargements of quotas for the products of one industry with the reduction in producer subsidy equivalents (PSEs)[15] for the products of another and the lifting of certain 'domestic-content' requirements in a third may be too demanding an exercise for a large number of products, industries and participating countries. It could also leave much of the industry-specific structure of current systems of protection intact or, worse, lead to a host of arrangements for managed trade. But the chances for a breakthrough trade agreement could very likely be improved if a common denominator of what comprises trade reform could be found. In other words, there is a need for a general theme for the negotiations that is applicable to all industries, similar in spirit to the across-the-board formula for the reduction of tariffs in the Kennedy Round and Tokyo Round negotiations.[16] In the Uruguay Round negotiations the task of finding such a common theme is complicated because of difficult 'special cases.' This does not invalidate the idea, but makes it all the more important. When the same methods and standards are used in all industries this would ultimately be an application of the GATT principle of non-discrimination or fairness, as discussed above.

Even if there is agreement on the need for a common approach to trade reform regardless of industry, this does not resolve the question of what should replace the across-the-board tariff cuts of the last two rounds of multilateral trade negotiations. Numerous suggestions have been made. They range from minimum access guarantees and global quotas to the conversion of all non-tariff measures into temporary tariff increases which will gradually decline. Although there is no space for discussing the pros and cons of these various reform proposals at this point,[17] the conversion of all non-tariff measures to tariffs appears to be ideally suited to replace the across-the-board cuts in tariffs. The main attraction of this proposal, apart from its applicability across all industries and special cases, is its reliance on the time-tested instrument of tariffs. Tariffs are compatible with GATT obligations; they are predictable, easy both to implement and to monitor; and they do not eliminate the operation of the price mechanism.

INCENTIVES AT THE IMPLEMENTATION STAGE

Every system of rules that tries to discipline the behavior of economic actors by limiting the set of allowable actions faces one central problem: it has to be credible. Credibility depends, *inter alia*, on the system's internal consistency, its perceived fairness and its enforceability at the implementation stage. To make trade reforms as effective as possible, they have to be carefully checked and the political incentives for governments to take decisions in trade matters have to be taken into account. In what follows this idea will be applied to three central issues of the Uruguay Round negotiations.

Article XIX of the GATT

Article XIX contains the main safeguard provision of the GATT. In certain loosely defined circumstances, the article allows a country to impose a tariff or a quota in order to counter import surges of a particular product that inflict or threaten serious injury to the corresponding domestic industry. Any such action is supposed to be temporary, non-discriminatory and subject to compensation. In practice, Article XIX is seldom applied, for the conditions of non-discrimination and compensation have raised the political price of import sanctions. Governments prefer to use politically less dangerous responses, mainly 'grey area' measures such as voluntary export restraints.

The question at the heart of revising Article XIX is whether to make it less demanding in its requirements, thereby reducing the attractiveness of avoidance strategies, such as export restraints, or whether to plug the possible escape routes instead.[18] If it is true that most governments favour binding international restrictions in trade-policy matters as a protective shield against the protectionist demands of special interest groups, then there is a case for the latter approach. Plugging escape routes is preferable also if it is thought that Article XIX can be made more attractive to governments only by revoking the GATT principle of non-discrimination. The credibility of the GATT is clearly not served by an article that is inconsistent with its most basic constitutional principle.[19] But on the other hand, the idea of making Article XIX more attractive also has some appeal. It is as well to remember in this context that it is uncertain whether all possible loopholes can actually be plugged. Even if export restraints could be eliminated, this does not guarantee that other mechanisms will not take their place. Historical experience shows that there is certainly no lack of ingenious ways of restricting trade.[20] Hence the challenge of revising Article XIX would be to find a way to make it more attractive to governments while, at the same time, avoiding a conflict with the GATT principle of non-discrimination and the working of the price mechanism.

To ensure the continuing operation of the price mechanism, safeguard actions under Article XIX could be limited to temporary tariff increases. These tariff increases could be combined with a provision for their automatic decline which would increase the incentive for domestic producers to adjust.[21] Provisions could be added which would give countries further incentives to speed up rather than to retard the domestic adjustment process. An example would be the mandatory payment to affected exporters of all tariff revenue, possibly at an increasing rate over time. Such a provision could also go some way to compensate exporters that are now subject to voluntary export restraints for the loss in quota rents. The combination of these measures, however, would certainly not make Article XIX more attractive to governments; quite possibly, it would be less so. One way to remedy this could be to relax substantially the conditionality of Article XIX revised in this way. This needs some explanation.

The conditions that justify imposing safeguard measures are vague at best, making the safeguard clause less than operational in practice. Rather than trying the standard approach and defining 'serious injury' more succinctly, employing for example a measure that uses data on the historical development of imports, a radically different approach could be tried — that is, to remove the conditionality altogether. In other words, it would be left to each country to decide when to apply Article XIX, but the allowable instruments would be restricted. As mentioned above, only temporary tariff increases should be used, with a maximum duration of x years. In addition, it could be stipulated that a safeguard measure could be invoked only once for a particular product or product group. This assumes that once an industry has been given time to adjust properly, there is no reason for further help through border measures.[22]

There is one danger with this approach. Given the current focus on 'strategic trade policy,' governments may have a tendency to give new products that are considered of strategic importance, such as high-definition television sets, almost automatic protection through tariff increases under the safeguard clause at the beginning of their product cycle. To guard against such misuse, the idea of countervailing power could be applied again: safeguard actions should not be allowed for individual products but only for whole sub-classes of products, for example those identified by the three-digit level of the Standard International Trade Classification. The idea of this is that if a sufficient number of importers are affected by excess tariffs, the chances of passing a safeguard measure are likely to be less. This is especially true if producers in the affected industry can expect to face similar

excess tariffs in their major export markets. With incentives
of this kind, it is possible that momentum would be given to
the idea of determining the economic sense of import
restrictions in an economy-wide perspective, as suggested
inter alia by Samuel Laird and Gary Sampson.[23]
      In short, if properly revised and supplemented with
measures to plug obvious escape routes, Article XIX could
make the GATT system more consistent and credible. The
potential of Article XIX, however, appears to extend beyond
this.   Indeed, the temporary tariff increases under the
safeguard mechanism could be thought of as the central and
possibly the only vehicle for the elimination of non-tariff
measures.   In other words, the conversion of non-tariff
measures into tariffs could be implemented through the
safeguard clause without, in principle, releasing countries
from their bound tariffs.   As it would largely avoid the
problems of precedent, difficult phase-in and irreversibility,
such a move appears to be attractive.

Voluntary Export Restraints

      Voluntary export restraints are currently the preferred
way of circumventing the disciplines of Article XIX. They are
particularly popular among large countries facing import
competition from smaller countries that are politically and
economically less powerful.[24] The established exporters in
the restricted country have no strong incentive to oppose
export restraints because they can usually reap a quota or
scarcity rent on the protected export market.[25] Furthermore,
they are shielded to some extent from potential competitors,
both from within the country, if quota rights are not
tradeable, and from outside the country.
      The influence of export restraints plays an important
role in designing reform proposals intended to reduce their
number. For example, the effect of a simple ban on export
restraints with no auxiliary provisions would be quite unlike
a ban on export subsidies. An importing country is certain to
respond to foreign export subsidies because they hurt its
domestic producers. This ensures that the issue will come out
into the open.   There is no such incentive for export
restraints. Restricted exporters are unlikely to oppose export

restraints, despite a ban by the GATT, if they are economically or politically dependent on the goodwill of the importer. A possible way out of this dilemma is to give the GATT more power to investigate violations of the General Agreement. To minimize the need for independent monitoring, trade associations of affected industries could be given the right to appeal directly to the GATT Secretariat, thereby circumventing their governments.

Yet even these changes would not fully eliminate the problem of export restraints. Those sponsored by governments would diminish, but the suggested reform proposal is likely to increase the incentive for export-restraint agreements that are negotiated at company or industry level, without the tacit agreement, or possibly even without the knowledge of, the respective governments. This problem is most probable in cases where the number of domestic producers and foreign exporters is small and hence the transaction costs of a negotiated solution are low. It is difficult to imagine how private 'cooperation' agreements of this sort can be restrained through the GATT. Progress in this area probably requires tougher cartel legislation at the individual country level, particularly in importing countries. This has already been accomplished to a large extent in the United States, but in much of Western Europe, cartel legislation is far behind in this respect. How changes could come about is an unresolved question. Sufficient political pressure from the United States may help speed up the process.

Domestic Subsidies

A basic principle of the GATT has been its emphasis on containing the use of trade instruments with direct trade effects or what may be called frontier barriers to trade. Hence domestic subsidies have received little attention in the treaty. Some change in this position occurred during the Tokyo Round negotiations when the Subsidies Code was devised.[26] Yet experience with its operation has not been favourable. The Subsidies Code is generally considered to be one of the least effective of the codes negotiated during the Tokyo Round deliberations.

The primary concern of the GATT with frontier barriers rather than domestic subsidies is based on solid economic reasons. Frontier barriers to trade tend to be rather visible and hence more tractable and easier to negotiate than domestic subsidies. Domestic subsidies also have a number of economic advantages when compared with frontier barriers. They can be better targeted to correct market failures, they do not distort consumer prices, they are subject to annual budgetary review and they are more equitable (on the assumption that the tax system itself is judged to be equitable). Another important consideration is that subsidies are expensive to maintain in the absence of frontier barriers.[27] But as the final, if implicit, objective of the GATT is the removal of frontier barriers to trade, this means that the problem of domestic subsidies would, in any case, decline in importance in the long run.

At present, however, the removal of frontier barriers to trade is still a long distance away for many industries. Not surprisingly, then, subsidies have been a cause of considerable friction in trade relations.[28] This is most obvious in high-technology areas and in declining industries, such as agriculture, coal mining, iron and steel and shipbuilding. For certain product groups, implicit subsidies through defence contracts and space research also play a significant role.

One way to reduce the trade problems caused by domestic subsidies would be to impose explicit quantitative limits by amending the existing Subsidies Code. Although such an approach would only bind the Code's signatories, it could be sufficient to diffuse the subsidies issue. After all, most of the problems with subsidies occur among the signatories to the Code.

The suggestion of a quantitative limit on domestic subsidies raises at least two questions. First, is such a limit consistent with the GATT framework and the incentives facing governments? Second, can it be implemented in a way that makes economic sense? On the first question, quantitative rules for domestic subsidies clearly depart from the GATT's focus on frontier barriers and hence policy instruments that affect trade directly. But they do not contradict the long-run goal of open markets. On the contrary, quantitative limits would allow the trading system to respond to the challenges currently facing the General Agreement. By lowering the chances of subsidy wars, quantitative limits on domestic subsidies could actually help the trading system to get closer to its final goal.[29]

From the perspective of domestic political economy, a limit on subsidies is likely to be a welcome idea, even if it may not be admitted publicly by politicians. It is appealing because it gives politicians an argument to withstand demands for handouts by special interest groups. Witness, in this context, the difficulties that governments in industrialized countries have in reducing existing subsidies or in resisting demands for new ones. External pressure resulting from firm rules on domestic subsidies could help to establish a much-needed counterweight. The argument that quantitative limits on subsidies would effectively deprive governments of a flexible and useful instrument of economic policy is overstated. First, it is not suggested that subsidies should be eliminated altogether, just that they should be limited. Second, many subsidies currently in use in industrialized countries are not correcting for market failures, but serve instead as an inefficient form of income redistribution for industries resisting structural adjustment. In these circumstances, a quantitative limit on subsidies is likely to promote rather than impede economic efficiency.

A quantitative limit on domestic subsidies could be implemented by using a modified version of the concept of 'producer subsidy equivalent.' In their original form, PSEs are an enhanced variant of the nominal rate of protection (NRP). They extend the NRP by adding per-unit subsidy payments to the tariff equivalents that result from a simple comparison of domestic and world prices. PSEs could be simplified for the present purpose by dropping the NRP part. Simplified in this form, they could then be calculated for individual products or entire industries by dividing the value of the subsidies going to the product or to the industry by the respective value added.[30] Once subsidy equivalents were estimated,[31] their levels could be negotiated and then written into the Subsidies Code as part of a country's trade concessions. Alternatively, subsidy equivalents could be treated as analogous to tariff increases under a safeguard

code elaborating Article XIX. This would make them subject
to limited duration and automatic decline.

Although there do not seem to be any fundamental
problems in applying this idea, the data collection and
preparation process may turn out to be demanding, at least in
the first instance, because neither governments nor special
interest groups will want to be put in an embarrassing
position. For this reason, the data work would have to be
checked by independent institutions within the country,
under contract to the GATT. To settle trade disputes at the
application stage, consultants from third countries could be
called on to check the figures independently.

CONCLUSIONS

The behavior of governments is conditioned by political (and
economic) considerations. Proposals for GATT reform that
ignore their effects on the motivating influences of
governments are unlikely to get very far. Such proposals may
block agreement altogether; alternatively, they may cause
unintended reactions and consequent trade conflicts at the
implementation stage. As a result, the credibility of
multilateral trade negotiations and the GATT will be
undermined. In this article a number of proposals for the
reform of the GATT that aim at avoiding these problems have
been developed. They can be summarized as follows.

Negotiations and compromises across industries appear
to be mandatory if the objective is to eliminate the particular
treatment of such 'special cases' as agriculture and textiles
and clothing. Without cross-industry agreements, it appears
unlikely that a sufficient amount of countervailing power
could be generated to oppose the industrial lobbying efforts
for the *status quo*. A common negotiating theme for all
industries could further improve the chances of a successful
cross-industry agreement.

The conversion of non-tariff measures into tariffs seems
to be the most useful theme to replace the across-the-board
formula for tariff cuts of the Kennedy Round and Tokyo
Round negotiations. This idea could be integrated into the
GATT framework through a revised Article XIX without
prompting new inconsistencies.

Voluntary export restraints and domestic subsidies, two troubling loopholes in the present structure of the GATT, need separate treatment. A successful fight against export restraints requires more than a simple ban. The GATT Secretariat would need more authority to enforce such a ban. The detrimental trade effects of subsidies could be lessened by adding a quantitative subsidy limit to the Subsidies Code.

FOOTNOTES

1. For a discussion of the 'cost' of adjustment, see Gary Banks and Jan Tumlir, *Economic Policy and the Adjustment Problem*, Thames Essay No. 45 (Aldershot, Brookfield and Sydney: Gower, for the Trade Policy Research Centre, 1986).

2. Compare the studies summarized in *Macro-economic Consequences of Farm-support Policies: Overview of an International Programme of Studies* (Canberra: Centre for International Economics, 1988) or Kenneth W. Clements and Larry A. Sjaastad, *How Protection Taxes Exporters*, Thames Essay No. 39 (London: Trade Policy Research Centre, 1984). The studies in the first title are being published in full in A.B. Stoeckel, D.P. Vincent and A.G. Cuthbertson, *Macroeconomic Consequences of Farm Support Policies* (Durham, North Carolina: Duke University Press, forthcoming).

3. See, for example, Alberto Valdés and Joachim Zietz, *Agricultural Protection in OECD Countries: Its Costs to Less Developed Countries*, Research Report No. 21 (Washington: International Food Policy Research Institute, 1980).

4. The waiver is discussed in, for example, Zietz and Valdés, *Agriculture in the GATT: an Analysis of Alternative Approaches to Reform*, Research Report No. 70 (Washington: International Food Policy Research Institute, 1988).

5. Robert E. Hudec, *Developing Countries in the GATT Legal System*, Thames Essay No. 50 (Aldershot, Brookfield and Sydney: Gower, for the Trade Policy Research Centre, 1987).

6. Compare, on this point, *Trade Policies for a Better Future: Proposals for Actions*, Leutwiler Report (Geneva: GATT Secretariat, 1985) and Rolf J. Langhammer and André Sapir, *Economic Impact of Generalized Tariff Preferences*, Thames Essay No. 49 (Aldershot, Brookfield and Sydney:

Gower, for the Trade Policy Research Centre, 1987).

7. Some evidence for that is presented in Hermann Dick, Egbert Gerken and Vincent, 'The Benefits of the CAP for Developing Countries: a Case Study of the Ivory Coast,' *European Review of Agricultural Economics* 9, no. 2, (Amsterdam: 1982), 157-81.

8. Hudec, *op. cit.*

9. The role of protectionist policies in retarding growth is discussed in some detail in *World Development Report 1987* (New York: Oxford University Press, for the World Bank, 1987).

10. Donald B. Keesing and Martin Wolf, *Textile Quotas against Developing Countries*, Thames Essay No. 23 (London: Trade Policy Research Centre, 1980).

11. Yujiro Hayami, 'The Roots of Agricultural Protectionism,' in Kym Anderson and Hayami (eds), *The Political Economy of Agricultural Protection* (Winchester, Massachusetts, and London: Allen & Unwin, 1986) provides a good account of the case of agriculture.

12. Robert E. Baldwin, 'Multicultural Liberalization,' in J. Michael Finger and Andrzej Olechowski (eds), *The Uruguay Round: a Handbook on the Multilateral Trade Negotiations* (Washington: World Bank, 1987).

13. Agriculture and textiles provide ample evidence for this.

14. On this point, see the article by Bernard M. Hoekman, 'Services as the *Quid Pro Quo* for a Safeguards Code,' *The World Economy* (London: June 1988), 203-15.

15. Producer subsidy equivalents were introduced by T.E. Josling as a way to make support levels in agriculture more comparable across countries. See *Agricultural Protection and Stabilization Policies: a Framework of Measurement in the Context of Agricultural Adjustment*, C75/Lim/2 (Rome: Food and Agriculture Organization, 1975) and Stefan Tangermann, T.E. Josling and Scott Pearson, 'Multilateral Negotiations on Farm-support Levels,' *The World Economy* (September 1987), 265-81.

16. A similar idea is expressed in Henry R. Nau, 'Bargaining in the Uruguay Round,' in Finger and Olechowski (eds), *op. cit.*

17. See Zietz and Valdés, *Agriculture in the GATT, op.*

cit., for a thorough discussion of alternative reform ideas for the case of agriculture.

18. The next section contains a brief discussion of how to keep countries from resorting to voluntary export restraints, the main avoidance strategy in this context.

19. See Brian Hindley, 'Voluntary Export Restraints and the GATT's Main Escape Clause,' *The World Economy* (November 1980), 313-41.

20. *Ibid.*

21. Compare, for example, the similar points raised in the *World Development Report 1987, op. cit.*

22. This does not exclude the possibility of assisting an industry with payments that are 'decoupled' from production.

23. Samuel Laird and Gary P. Sampson, 'Case for Evaluating Protection in an Economy-wide Perspective,' *The World Economy* (June 1987), 177-92.

24. Julio J. Nogués, Olechowski and L. Alan Winters, 'The Extent of Non-tariff Barriers to Industrial Countries' Imports,' *The World Bank Economic Review* (Washington: September 1986), 181-99, provide a detailed analysis of the frequency of export restraints and other non-tariff measures.

25. The quota rents can be large. Carl Hamilton, 'An Assessment of Voluntary Restraints on Hong Kong Exports to Europe and the USA,' *Economica* (London: August 1986), 339-50, reports that Hong Kong's rent on clothing exports amounts to about 2 per cent of her gross national product.

26. The Subsidies Code is discussed in some detail by Gary C. Hufbauer and Joanna S. Erb, *Subsidies in International Trade* (Washington: Institute for International Economics, 1984).

27. Richard H. Snape, 'The Importance of Frontier Barriers,' in Henryk Kierzkowski (ed.), *Protection and Competition in International Trade: Essays in Honour of W. Max Corden* (Oxford: Basil Blackwell, 1987) provides a detailed account of this argument.

28. See Richard Blackhurst, 'The Twilight of Domestic Economic Policies,' *The World Economy* (December 1981), 357-73, and the references cited therein for a discussion of this point.

29. Putting the subsidy policy into the existing GATT Subsidies Code makes it clear that it does not mark a reversal

in long-run focus, but merely a response to temporary needs.

30. Subsidy equivalents would have to be fixed for product groups at a fairly low level of aggregation in order to avoid cases where the subsidy available to a country is concentrated all on one product, thereby forcing producers in other countries out of the market.

31. Compare, for example, the estimates for agricultural products produced by the Organization for Economic Cooperation and Development, as discussed in *National Policies and Agricultural Trade* (Paris: OECD Secretariat, 1987).

Chapter V

The International Atomic Energy Agency (IAEA)

The International Atomic Energy Agency (IAEA) was established in July 1957. It is not a specialized agency, but an independent inter-governmental organization under the aegis of the United Nations. Thus, it is autonomous but administratively a member of the UN Common System. The 113 member countries meet as a Conference once a year, and the Secretariat consists of two thousand employees at the Vienna headquarters. The IAEA budget is financed by regular and voluntary contributions from member states, and for 1989 it amounted to US$150 million. The agency's goal is to "enlarge the contribution of atomic energy to peace, health and prosperity throughout the world and to ensure, so far as it is able, that assistance provided by it or at its request or under its supervision or control is not used in such a way as to further any military purpose." Programmatically, this corresponds to a number of general activities. First, the IAEA provides technical aid and encourages technical co-operation in the research and practical application of atomic energy for peaceful use. Second, the IAEA provides safeguards, ensuring that special fissionable and other materials, services, equipment and information provided by or at the request of the agency not be used for any military purpose. This includes the agency's role in enforcing the nuclear Non-Proliferation Treaty. Third, the IAEA provides emergency response and preparedness in case of a nuclear accident. Much of the international response to the Chernobyl accident was coordinated by the IAEA. These actions and others by the agency serve to increase the safety of nuclear power production throughout the world.

Nuclear Power Safety and the Role of International Organization

Jack Barkenbus

The very first fissioning of the uranium atom showed clearly that the potential impacts of nuclear energy are global, and that one could not simply assume that nations would accommodate international interests in their national decision-making or regulation. One of the very early proposals for incorporating international interests was the

87

Acheson-Lilienthal Report, which called for the creation of the supranational Atomic Development Authority to construct and operate nuclear reactors around the globe, with international civil servants to license, regulate, and inspect the reactors.[1] The proposal for the creation of a supranational authority, embodied subsequently in the Baruch Plan put forward by the United States in the United Nations, died in the late 1940s, caught in the web of superpower politics.

No remotely comparable vision has been considered since that time. Still, the dilemma of how to spread the energy benefits of civilian nuclear power without also spreading the materials and capabilities required for building nuclear bombs (the uranium and plutonium used in, and produced by, nuclear power reactors can be used as source material for nuclear weapons with additional treatment), has resulted in an elaborate set of international norms, practices, laws, and institutions that we frequently term the "nonproliferation regime."[2] The centerpiece of this regime is, of course, the international safeguarding of fissionable material, partly ensured by inspections of nuclear reactors.

Proliferation, however, is not the only possible transboundary impact of nuclear power reactors. Serious nuclear power accidents can disperse radioactive materials well beyond national boundaries. Yet the health risks associated with nuclear power have not led to a "safety regime" comparable in scope and activity to the "nonproliferation regime." Though some states have willingly ceded some control of nuclear power operations to private entities,[3] virtually all have been unwilling to compromise their autonomous decision-making powers in the health-safety arena to supranational authorities.

The Chernobyl nuclear reactor accident of April 1986, which claimed thirty-two prompt fatalities and could, over time, claim many more, may occasion fundamental rethinking. Prior to the Chernobyl accident, transboundary health threats were largely ignored by states and treated hypothetically. The change in perspective revealed itself in the words of U.S. Department of Energy Secretary John Herrington: "Chernobyl has made it abundantly clear that nuclear safety is not, and cannot be, a solely national concern."[4] Hence, alternative technical and institutional paths for the future of nuclear power, which would have been dismissed out-of-hand prior to the accident, now receive serious consideration.

This article examines the tension between the transnational concern for safety and the state's decision-making autonomy on nuclear power. I shall attempt to foresee where the concern over safety interdependencies may lead, at least throughout the rest of this century. A brief section describing the extent and growth of nuclear power follows. I shall also cite the kinds of transboundary disputes that have developed both before and after Chernobyl. I then describe the safety responsibilities of the primary international organization in this field, the International Atomic Energy Agency (IAEA), and discuss the extent to which this agency exercises supranational responsibilities. I also review the kinds of tasks now being proposed for the agency in the post-Chernobyl environment. While a frontal assault upon state-based health regulatory authority is unlikely, I shall show that we can expect modest and incremental inroads into autonomous state decision-making.

Nuclear Power Today

Nuclear power is a major energy source today, generating approximately 15 percent of the world's electricity.[5] As seen in Table 1, this power involves 388 operating nuclear reactors, which produce over 260,000 megawatts (MWe) of generating capacity. Another 142 reactor units, potential producers of 126,000 MWe of generating capacity, were under construction in late 1986.

The use of nuclear power, however, is not evenly distributed across the globe. Over 80 percent of all operating generating capacity (and three-quarters of the reactors) is found in Organization for Economic Cooperation and Development (OECD) countries. Very few developing countries are either operating or constructing nuclear power plants. Only India, South Korea, and Taiwan have major nuclear power programs. The absence of nuclear power in most developing countries can be primarily attributed to high capital costs, the lack of sufficient technical expertise, and a

TABLE 1. *Nuclear power capacity: Operational and under construction (as of 31 October 1986)*

Country	Operational Units	Operational MWe	Under construction Units	Under construction MWe
Belgium	8	5,486	0	0
Finland	4	2,310	0	0
France	48	43,428	15	19,067
West Germany	20	17,720	5	5,278
Italy	3	1,273	5	3,899
Netherlands	2	508	0	0
Spain	8	5,528	2	1,920
Sweden	12	9,455	0	0
Switzerland	5	2,884	0	0
United Kingdom	38	10,170	4	2,530
OECD Europe	148	98,762	31	32,694
Canada	18	11,107	4	3,458
United States	95	80,117	24	26,795
OECD N. America	113	91,224	28	30,253
Japan	34	24,754	10	8,658
OECD total	295	214,740	69	71,605
Bulgaria	4	1,632	2	1,906
Cuba	0	0	2	816
Czechoslovakia	6	2,411	10	5,896
East Germany	5	1,694	6	3,432
Hungary	3	1,235	1	410
Poland	0	0	2	880
Romania	0	0	3	1,980
U.S.S.R.	50	26,806	34	31,816
COMECON total	68	33,778	60	47,136
Argentina	2	935	1	692
Brazil	1	626	1	1,245
India	6	1,164	4	880
Mexico	0	0	2	1,308
Pakistan	1	125	0	0
Philippines	0	0	1	620
PRC (China)	0	0	1	300
South Africa	2	1,840	0	0
South Korea	6	4,475	3	2,685
Taiwan	6	4,918	0	0
Yugoslavia	1	632	0	0
OTHER total	25	14,715	13	7,730
World total	388	263,233	142	126,471

Note. Austria's completed reactor and Iran's two partially completed reactors are not included, since they have been abandoned by both governments.

Source, International Atomic Energy Agency Power Reactor Information System, reproduced in *IAEA Bulletin,* Winter 1986, p. 61.

mismatch between the large size of generating capacity of nuclear power plants and the relatively small electric grid systems in these countries. The communist world, with the exception of the Soviet Union, has only a modest operating nuclear power effort. That situation is destined to change in the near future, however, because Council for Mutual Economic Assistance (COMECON) countries are now constructing a number of nuclear power plants. In fact, if one compares the number of operating nuclear power plants with those under construction, the ratio in OECD countries is 4:1, while the ratio in Eastern Europe is close to 1:1. Clearly, the most vigorous expansion of nuclear power is occurring in communist states, and the Soviet Union is constructing more nuclear power plants than any other state. Some speculate that nuclear power technology can only thrive in centralized, autocratic societies,[6] but I shall not explore that intriguing political issue in this article.

Table 1 does not reveal the importance of nuclear power in the electrical systems of individual states. Figure 1 provides this perspective and illustrates that while the United States and the Soviet Union have more operating nuclear power reactors than any other states, they are less dependent upon nuclear power for the generation of electricity than many others. France and Belgium, two states vigorously seeking to displace their oil import dependency, lead all others by generating approximately 60 percent of their electricity through nuclear power.

Transboundary Fears

The Chernobyl accident reveals the inadequacy of placing nuclear power development solely within a state context. Though the damaged reactor is approximately 250 miles away from the closest international border, its enormous levels of radioactivity spewed far into Europe and Scandinavia. Most, but not all, experts discount the probability of widespread health effects in Europe resulting from the radioactive fallout.

The "political fallout" may be more long-lasting and tangible. Chernobyl energized the large, but quiescent, anti-nuclear force in Western Europe. This activity is particularly

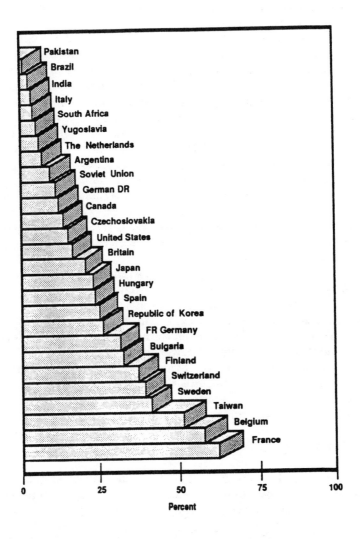

FIGURE 1. *Nuclear power generation (1985), by country as a percentage of all national electricity generation.*
Source.   Richard Masters, "Still Working Through the Backlog," *Nuclear Engineering International,* June 1986, p. 46.

apparent in West Germany where, despite a considerable investment in, and dependence upon, nuclear power (twenty operating reactors and five under construction), there is serious discussion about phasing out nuclear power.[7] In the Netherlands, the government abruptly canceled plans to announce the construction of two new nuclear reactors. In Austria, the government announced that it would dismantle the completed, but never operated, reactor at Zwentendorf. It is indeed ironic that the political fallout occurred in the West. The accident involved a reactor type that would never have been licensed in the West because of its inherent safety deficiencies. The Soviets, and other Eastern bloc states, have announced their intention to move full-speed ahead with nuclear power development, making only modest safety backfits to their Chernobyl-type reactors.[8]

Nuclear safety concerns have transcended boundaries. The vast majority of European nuclear reactors are closer to international borders than Chernobyl. Though transboundary safety fears predate the Chernobyl accident, they, too, have been invigorated by it. Illustrative of the fears are the following:

1. Environmentalists in West Germany and Luxembourg have vigorously protested French nuclear energy expansion at Cattenom, just thirteen kilometers from the West German border and nine from Luxembourg. One large nuclear power plant (1300 MWe) is already operating there and three more are in various stages of construction. Relatively minor accidents have occurred at the site with no releases of radiation, but the incidents have raised considerable concern nonetheless. Neighboring states tried to get the French to reduce the scale of their plans at the site—and were rebuffed.[9] The Belgians also expressed concern over French reactor construction at Chooz, just two miles inside the French-Belgian border.[10]

2. Some European states, explicitly rejecting the nuclear power option because of safety concerns, now find themselves uncomfortably close to reactors in neighboring states. Austria — which rejected nuclear power in a 1977 referendum — has expressed its concern to Czechoslovakia over the four operating

reactors just forty miles away from the Austrian border.[11] Austrian environmentalists have also protested the construction of a nuclear reprocessing plant in neighboring Bavaria.[12] Denmark, another state that has rejected nuclear power, has sought safety assurances from Sweden regarding their Barsebaeck reactors located just twenty kilometers from Copenhagen.[13]

3. Over a million people in Hong Kong, one-fifth of the population, signed a petition opposing China's plan to construct and operate a nuclear power plant at Daya Bay, just thirty miles northeast of Hong Kong.[14]

Despite the safety concerns of their neighbors, states have resolutely maintained the sole right to determine the scope and placement of nuclear power developments within their borders. As we have seen, these determinations have varied widely among states, even neighbors. Moreover, the state, through regulatory guidelines, determines the level or degree of safety embodied in its nuclear power technologies and operations (in other words, it alone determines "how safe is safe enough"). While there is much overlap in the kinds of requirements states impose upon reactor designers, constructors, and operators, the requirements generally achieve varying levels of safety.[15] As noted previously, the Chernobyl reactor was of a type that would never have passed licensing requirements in a Western state; nor would a Western state have approved a design without a sturdy reactor containment. Even within the West, however, more subtle differences distinguish the degree of safety system redundancy nations require to mitigate the consequences of a major accident. United States and European regulatory approaches to nuclear power differ significantly, though it would be hard to prove that one regulatory approach ensures a higher degree of safety than the other.[16] The fact that nuclear reactors differ in the way they are built, the way they are operated, and the way they are regulated provides sufficient grounds for both interest and anxiety of neighboring states.

Though states jealously guard their sovereignty over

nuclear power decision-making, some bilateral accommodations have assuaged the fears of "outsiders." Most states have accepted a general obligation to provide neighboring states with information about border plants. No universal rules, however, determine what information to share, the frequency with which it is to be shared, or its level of detail. Perhaps the most notable example to date is the Swedish-Danish commission that meets regularly to confer on the status of Barsebaeck.[17] France and West Germany have also established a joint commission on nuclear safety, a major purpose of which is to jointly evaluate safety levels at the Cattonem site. France has also invited politicians from both West Germany and Luxembourg to tour the reactor site.[18]

Safety critics asked states to go much further than information-sharing, but so far the states have resisted. Attempts by foreign governments or environmentalists to gain legal standing in licensing proceedings have been rebuffed. Nor have inspection rights been granted. Denmark sought such rights in East Germany recently, as did West Germany in France.[19] Both requests were dismissed. The director of France's nuclear inspectorate stated the French position succinctly: "We are old enough to do our own inspections. Inspections are a matter of national sovereignty."[20]

Hence, while states have shown some sensitivity to the anxiety of neighboring states, this sensitivity has been limited and indeterminate. The continuing growth of nuclear power and the Chernobyl accident are likely to lead to demands that go beyond the basic, amorphous obligation for information sharing. When nations are not allowed to participate in the nuclear power decision-making that potentially impacts the health and safety of their citizens, they will reasonably seek recourse in the international arena.

International Norms

Strong arguments can be marshaled against common or international health and safety standards. Various populations perceive the risks and benefits associated with any activity according to the risks and standards of living in their societies. Generally, the balancing of risks and benefits should be the responsibility of governments close to the people at risk. For the most part, this means that national governments establish environmental, health, and safety standards for activities within their borders. This principle was reiterated clearly by a panel of environmental experts and business leaders: "We do not believe internationally uniform environmental ambient or emission standards are desirable. Each country should consider its own social, economic, and physical characteristics and values to determine *for itself* appropriate environmental protection levels."[21]

Though public and private leaders hold this principle with considerable conviction, they sometimes append a notable qualification to it; namely, when the technologies' injurious side-effects cannot be confined within national borders, then strictly national decision-making is no longer appropriate.[22] Nuclear power presents an interesting case. Unlike coal, its major competitor, nuclear power has few, if any, transboundary effects during normal operation. Coal-fired plants are major emitters of the pollutants which contribute substantially to acid rain and possible climate change. Yet nuclear power potentially contains the most sudden and catastrophic kind of transboundary impact. Until very recently, the argument that a severe nuclear power accident was extremely improbable led to the nearly unchallenged assumption that state authorities were the obvious and proper locus for safety and regulatory decision-making. The Chernobyl accident has shaken, if not destroyed, that presumption.

The transboundary political effects of a nuclear accident provide still another reason to question the appropriateness of solely state decision-making. Even before the accident in the Soviet Union, it was sometimes said, "A nuclear accident anywhere in the world is a nuclear accident everywhere in the world." This statement was, in large part, borne out by the intense public reaction everywhere to the Chernobyl accident.

If national decision-making is not enough, and bilateral agreement difficult to achieve, where do we turn? The answer so far has been primarily the International Atomic Energy Agency (IAEA), an independent, inter-governmental organization within the United Nations system, headquartered in Vienna.[23]

IAEA

IAEA was founded in 1957 and now has 113 member states. Its current functions reflect the fundamental bargain behind its creation. The United States and other major powers agreed to spread nuclear power technology abroad provided nations would agree not to use nuclear technologies for military programs. IAEA was created to provide these assurances by applying international or nonproliferation safeguards. Safeguards track the use and location of fissionable material with physical inspections, seals and surveillance systems, and review of accounting records. Safeguards are designed to detect diversion and, through the threat of disclosure to the United Nations and the international community, to deter it. The agency claims that it has never detected a diversion of fissionable material from civilian nuclear power plants — a claim supporters use to praise the safeguarding system and detractors use to condemn it.[24]

The establishment of international safeguards over fissionable material and the monitoring of compliance within states provides IAEA with more supranational authority than any other international organization. The Soviet Union initially opposed IAEA for this reason but eventually it became a fervent convert due to its special interest in nonproliferation. A few years ago a former IAEA official asked the agency's Soviet representative to describe a future mandate for IAEA. The Soviet representative replied, "The IAEA should have three tasks: safeguards, safeguards, and further safeguards."[25]

Other member states do not share the Soviet viewpoint. Indeed, many feel that IAEA's focus on safeguards already neglects its other primary task, namely, the provision of technical assistance for the peaceful uses of the atom. Many developing countries would prefer to see a more vigorous promotion of nuclear power and other nuclear science applications in agriculture, medicine, and health.

In recent years safeguards have claimed approximately half of the agency's $100 million annual budget, with all other activities involving peaceful uses of the atom taking the other half. Within the latter half, the Nuclear Safety Program has been accorded approximately $5 million, with a supporting staff of thirty professionals. Budgetary allocations clearly show that IAEA's safety program is not high on the agency's priority agenda (and it is minuscule in comparison to national safety programs; the United States Nuclear Regulatory Commission, for example, has a budget exceeding $400 million and employs approximately 3,400).

IAEA carries out several distinct nuclear power programs. If we were to categorize the programs according to the supranational hierarchy described by Eugene Skolnikoff (service-facilitating, norm creation, rule observance, and operation),[26] nearly all would be service-facilitating — the least supranational of activities. One observer stated the agency's focus: "The principal contribution of IAEA is to provide different forms of technical assistance to countries beginning nuclear power programs, especially those with a limited technological base."[27] This assistance is carried out through such means as conferences, staff publications, and exchanges of experts.

Largely in response to the Three Mile Island (TMI) accident in 1979, IAEA embarked upon activities focused exclusively on nuclear safety — for example, the establishment of a data collection system which draws upon national reports of incidents and malfunctions at operating nuclear power plants all over the globe; and the Operational Safety Review Teams (OSART) which audit the safety practices at nuclear power plants on request.

Post-Chernobyl Developments

The Chernobyl accident will probably impact IAEA's safety mandate even more than the TMI accident. IAEA has been the focus of international response to the accident. The legitimacy of IAEA's safety program was surely enhanced when the IAEA director-general and the safety director were the first foreign experts invited by the Soviets to assess the damage at Chernobyl. Moreover, the Soviets chose IAEA as the proper forum for a detailed account of the Chernobyl accident (August 1986). Given past Soviet disinterest in

IAEA's nuclear safety program, the sudden attention was a dramatic turn of events.

Member states have already concluded that the IAEA safety program's 1987 budget required a boost from $5 million to $8 million. Additional funding has also been allotted for the almost continuous meeting of IAEA representatives and technical experts since summer 1986. The most immediate results of these meetings have been two legal conventions drawn up by IAEA-convened experts and adopted in September 1986 by the IAEA general conference. The first obligates nations to give early warning when civilian nuclear power accidents have potential transboundary consequences. Signatories to this convention must report such accidents immediately to IAEA and to neighboring states. The impetus for this convention, of course, was the Soviet's late reporting of the Chernobyl accident.

The second convention creates a mechanism for multinational emergency assistance after a nuclear accident. IAEA will house an emergency control center and, on request, organize teams of experts for prompt response.

IAEA could produce these conventions in record time because they had prepared for them in earlier years. IAEA convened experts in the early 1980s to advise the agency in these two areas, and their deliberations produced the foundation for the accords. Only the Chernobyl accident, however, created the political will for their implementation.

Some have hinted that the two legal conventions are only the beginning of what will eventually become a greatly expanded international presence in global nuclear power affairs. The most ambitious visions include IAEA forging a set of universal safety standards and creating an international inspectorate to ensure these standards are followed. Enaction of this vision would raise the IAEA safety program another notch on the supranationality scale, as it would involve binding norm creation and enforced rule observance.

Exactly what would be involved in creating international safety standards is not entirely clear. IAEA, under its Nuclear Safety Standards Program (NUSS), has already provided a very basic and general set of guidelines for states embarking upon a nuclear power program. These guidelines, consisting of over sixty separate documents, are only a framework for regulation and organization. They do not contain specific or detailed standards and cannot be enforced. Would the standard-setting process simply update these guidelines and require their observance? Or would IAEA effort go well beyond NUSS generalities and become increasingly detailed and prescriptive?

Though there now is considerable talk about vigorous, internationally approved standards or regulations, it is quite unlikely that anything other than a "lowest common denominator" set of standards will result. Despite the specter of Chernobyl, states are unlikely to accept the consensus of experts convened in Vienna as to "how safe is safe enough." The socioeconomic factors which vary the assessments of risks have not disappeared. We cannot assume that the United States government's desire to see hundreds of millions of dollars spent at each nuclear reactor to protect against low-probability events (for example, earthquakes) will be realized elsewhere. Other practical difficulties to standardization include differing national atomic energy laws, the differing nature of nuclear reactors, and differing industry practices and organization.

The president of the American Nuclear Society, Manning Muntzing, attempted to interest the international community in developing a common safety philosophy in 1982. He proposed the creation of an International Institute on Nuclear Safety which would promote common, fundamental reactor safety principles that all nations could follow and build upon.[28] The private American initiative received considerable review, but in the end was rejected. Some claimed it would blatantly violate state sovereignty; others felt that the impetus for the initiative came from the American nuclear industry, which hoped for relief from its own regulator (the United States Nuclear Regulatory Commission) by agreeing to less rigorous, but universally adopted, international regulations.[29] The initiative did not die, but rather was transformed. IAEA Director-General Hans Blix agreed to establish the International Nuclear Safety Advisory Group. But this new group's mandate did not mention the idea of forging a common nuclear safety philosophy.

It is even less likely that IAEA will become an unrelenting international inspectorate, or "watchdog." IAEA/OSART audit teams conducted only six inspections in 1986. IAEA would need an enormous influx of new personnel and money to inspect the approximately 400 operating reactors every year or two. Post-Chernobyl plans now call for approximately twenty reactor inspections in each of the next two years, based upon requests IAEA is receiving from states.

The agency must also carefully evaluate the motive behind the increasing calls for its OSART services. States may be less interested in the OSART team's advice and recommendations than in receiving a clean bill of health that it can wave in front of a questioning domestic public. This motive certainly underlies the Federal Republic of Germany's requested OSART audits for all its operating reactors, especially the Biblis A plant, that country's oldest large-scale nuclear reactor.[30] The chances of IAEA being used by national governments as a "puppydog" are at least as great as the agency turning into a "watchdog."

What We Can Expect

If we cannot or should not expect in-depth international safety standards, monitored and enforced by a tenacious IAEA, what can we expect in the way of international action or [programs over the next decade? First, we should not expect the tensions between state decision-making autonomy and transboundary safety concerns to wither away. Despite the Chernobyl accident, and the widespread radioactive and political fallout which resulted from it, states will jealously protect their nearly exclusive right to decision-making and operation. But those citizens most fearful of continued nuclear power operation will continue to seek international remedies when national governments ignore their voices. Obviously, the more errors, incidents, and accidents there are at nuclear power plants, the stronger the pressures will be for more international action. It is impossible to predict how turbulent a future is in store for nuclear power. The following assessment of probable international action over the next decade is based upon the assumption that no accident of Chernobyl's magnitude will occur, but that relatively minor incidents will continue to plague the industry and fan public fears.

1. A significantly expanded IAEA/OSART program

Though the OSART program will not be transformed into an international inspectorate, it will probably be expanded significantly. As noted previously, states may seek to use OSART for their own purposes. IAEA must guard against this possibility, and it can easily do so. The OSART program is in some ways analogous to the inspection of U.S. nuclear facilities carried out by the industry-formed Institute of Nuclear Power Operations (INPO) in the United States. OSART can learn lessons from the experience and evolution of INPO.

INPO was established in the wake of the TMI accident. One of its primary tasks was to form small teams of experts for the auditing of nuclear power operations.[31] INPO audits were not intended to duplicate the inspections of the Nuclear Regulatory Commission, but rather to understand the practices being carried out at the audited facility and recommend improvements based upon the accepted "best practices" of nuclear utilities. The recommendations typically follow a three-tier hierarchy. The highest, "red tab" items signify areas deserving "immediate attention." Follow-up audits note how many of the previous year's recommendations have been implemented, particularly "red tab" items.

Although INPO never sought the regulator's mantle, a few U.S. nuclear utilities, by ignoring INPO's recommendations, pushed the organization further into a regulatory mode. A recent report by influential nuclear power leaders called for INPO to publicly rank high and low industry performers.[32] This is a far cry from what industry leaders envisioned when INPO was first formed, but such actions are now viewed as necessary to ensure a uniform standard of operating excellence.

OSART could evolve in a similar fashion. While the primary explicit goal of OSART audits should be the transfer of "best operating practices" to reactor operations worldwide, OSART should not begin an audit without getting a commitment from the state that it will allow follow-up rights; that is, OSART's right to come back in a year or two and examine how many of its recommendations have been implemented. While one cannot really envision IAEA being given the power to shut recalcitrant reactor operators down, one can envision IAEA publicizing the actions (or inaction) of a low performer, and thereby significantly affecting public opinion in that state and its neighboring countries.

Will OSART teams be invited under these terms? Undoubtedly, some nations will express reluctance. With the backing of a few influential states, however, OSART audits can become an international norm. In the long run, even the states most adamant about sovereignty will recognize the benefits from an IAEA list of low performers. Currently, low safety performers are not distinguished from high performers. When accidents or incidents occur at low performing facilities, therefore, the entire industry is subject to opprobrium. OSART's discrimination, consequently, can lead to more discrimination in the public mind, something those operating nuclear power plants properly and conscientiously can only applaud. Those rejecting OSART audits can bear the onus when they are publicly questioned, "What do you have to hide?" There is considerable potential for an evolving, significant, international role in nuclear safety through this means.

2. Operator accreditation

The Soviets insist that human error caused the Chernobyl accident, and there is no question that the man-technology interface in the operation of nuclear power plants has been a source of concern. One way to deal with this concern is to promote a higher and more uniform level of operating capabilities through the creation of international or regional operator training centers, and the accreditation of these centers. The type of training prospective operators receive just in the United States varies significantly. This situation has led to proposals for the establishment of a federally run national academy for plant operators, and the actual establishment of a training academy for plant operators under the auspices of INPO.[33] Two post-Chernobyl

IAEA meetings have proposed that IAEA become more deeply involved in international accreditation of operator training programs.[34] This kind of proposal that would cost member states relatively little to implement, would not constitute a major assault on state decision-making, and could produce benefits obvious to all. For these reasons, an accreditation program could be set up in the near future and perform a valuable service.

3. Defining transboundary obligations

The accord drawn up by IAEA members in September obligates states to notify neighbors immediately of accidents with potential transboundary consequences. Yet the obligations states have to inform or involve neighbors during construction or normal operation remain undefined. No standards are generally recognized for what information is to be transferred, and in what detail. Moreover, neighboring states have no legal standing in the licensing or regulation of border plants. It is likely that member nations will ask IAEA to convene a body of experts for the purpose of better defining transboundary obligations and responsibilities. This purpose will include examining whether a firm liability and compensation scheme should be established to cover accidents causing transboundary injuries.

IAEA will have to grapple with several key questions in preparing these guidelines: At precisely what distance from international borders do states incur transboundary reporting obligations? Within the distance chosen, are states obligated to share all documentation that goes into licensing? Are joint-state commissions to be formed to handle possible disputes? Should the neighboring country have inspection rights? Should emergency planning be coordinated? How are legitimate injury claims to be validated? IAEA certainly has a number of difficult issues to wade through before achieving consensus. Yet we have gone beyond the stage where we can simply rely upon the goodwill of states with border facilities to satisfactorily address transboundary concerns.

4. A central clearinghouse for radiation data and information

Much of the near panic that gripped Europe during and after the Chernobyl accident resulted from conflicting and confusing radiation readings and pronouncements. Citizens could hardly be blamed for what now appears to have been excessive concern, given the bewildering news accounts they heard. Even the units in which radiation levels were reported frequently differed. Until we know more about the health effects of radiation, worst fears will always be present. Yet these worst fears should not be compounded by confusion over the radiation readings themselves.

Since the accident, there have been calls for either IAEA or the World Health Organization (WHO) to serve as a central clearinghouse for radiation information, coordinating the collection, dissemination, and interpretation of radiation data.[35] This clearinghouse would presumably still rely on state monitoring services, but it would speak with a single, authoritative voice across state boundaries. Such a clearinghouse would more likely be set up at WHO than IAEA, but the establishment of a radiation data bank would involve efforts on the part of both organizations.

Conclusion

Many scholars have noted that the use of modern technologies inevitably produces transboundary impacts which impinge upon autonomous state decision-making and produce what one observer has termed "perforated sovereignties."[36] Despite recognition of potential, widespread health risks associated with nuclear power, states had resisted even modest encroachments upon their regulatory authority prior to the Chernobyl accident. IAEA had been accorded very little responsibility for ensuring safe nuclear power operations globally. This situation will probably change in the future, but only in an evolutionary, not a revolutionary, manner. Prior to 1980, IAEA served almost exclusively in a technical assistance capacity with civilian nuclear power. The TMI accident brought new nuclear safety responsibilities to IAEA, but it was still squarely within the category of service-facilitating functions.

Chernobyl will likely provide the impetus to involve IAEA in more norm-creation functions in such areas as nuclear power operations, operator qualifications, and transboundary obligations. IAEA could also move subtly into a rule observance role with its OSART program. States are not prepared to countenance an international regulatory body setting forth and monitoring universal rules and standards. However, as the experience of INPO in this country has shown, even organizations with no formal enforcement powers use the threat of public disclosure to enforce compliance with acceptable operating practices. In any event, Chernobyl has shown that nuclear power safety choices cannot rest solely with states.

FOOTNOTES

1. Congressional Research Service, *Nuclear Safeguards: A Reader* (a report prepared for the House Subcommittee on Energy Research and Production, 98th Congress, 1st sess., December 1983), 46-56.
2. Lawrence Scheinman, "Nonproliferation Regime: Safeguards, Controls, and Sanctions," in Alvin M. Weinberg, Marcelo Alonso and Jack N. Barkenbus, eds., *The Nuclear Connection* (New York: Paragon House Publishers, 1985), 177-210; David Fischer and Paul Szasz, *Safeguarding the Atom: A Critical Appraisal* (London: Taylor & Francis, 1985); Lawrence Scheinman, *The Nonproliferation Role of the International Atomic Energy Agency: A Critical Assessment* (Washington, D.C.: Resources for the Future, 1985).
3. Lawrence Scheinman, "Security and a Transnational System: The Case of Nuclear Energy," *International Organization* 25 (Summer 1971), 626-49.
4. John Herrington in *The Energy Report* (newsletter), (9 September 1986), 722.
5. Atomic Industrial Forum, *INFO* (newsletter), (June 1986), 4.
6. John Graham, "The Graham Thesis," *Nuclear News* (29 September 1986), 37.
7. *European Energy Report* (newsletter), (3 October 1986), 3-4.
8. David A. V. Fischer, "The International Response,"

Bulletin of the Atomic Scientists 43 (August/September 1986), 47.

9. *The Economist* (6 September 1986), 45.

10. *World Environment Report* (newsletter), (5 May 1980), 4; *Nucleonics Week* (newsletter) (12 June 1980), 1.

11. *The New York Times* (1 September 1980), 35.

12. "Austrians Fume over Wackersdorf," *Nuclear Engineering International* (31 September 1986), 12.

13. *Nucleonics Week* (newsletter), (22 May 1986), 10-11.

14. *The New York Times* (4 January 1987), 6.

15. Morris Rosen, "The Critical Issue of Nuclear Power Plant Safety in Developing Countries," *IAEA Bulletin* (19 April 1977), 12-21; "Do We Need a New International Safety Body?," *Nuclear Engineering International* (30 March 1985), 19-21.

16. Jack N. Barkenbus, *Prospects and Opportunities for Nuclear Power Regulatory Reform*, Institute for Energy Analysis Research Memorandum (Oak Ridge, Tenn.: Oak Ridge Associated Universities, April 1983), 23-30.

17. *Nucleonics Week* (newsletter), (22 May 1986), 11.

18. *Nuclear News* (29 September 1986), 75.

19. *Nucleonics Week* (newsletter), (11 May 1986), 11.

20. *Nucleonics Week* (newsletter), (4 September 1986).

21. World Resources Institute, *Improving Environmental Cooperation* (a report of a Panel of Business Leaders and Other Experts Convened by the World Resources Institute, Washington, D.C., 1984), 42.

22. Harold K. Jacobson, "Technological Developments, Organizational Capabilities, and Values," *International Organization* 25 (Autumn 1971), 778.

23. There are regional organizations active in nuclear safety issues, notably: the Nuclear Energy Agency of OECD; EURATOM, which comes under the European Economic Community; and the Council for Mutual Economic Assistance which serves Eastern European nations and the Soviet Union. These organizations will not be discussed in this article.

24. Lawrence Scheinman, *The Nonproliferation Role*; Ashok Kapur, "Nuclear Energy, Nuclear Proliferation, and National Security: Views from the South," in Robert Boardman and James F. Kelley, eds., *Nuclear Exports and*

World Politics (New York: St. Martin's Press, 1983), 163-93.
  25. Personal communication from David Fischer (5 December 1983).
  26. Eugene B. Skolnikoff, *The International Imperatives of Technology* (Berkeley: Berkeley Institute of International Studies, University of California, 1972).
  27. K. B. Stadie, "Sharing Safety Experience in IAEA," *Current Nuclear Power Plant Safety Issues* 1 (Vienna: International Atomic Energy Agency, 1981), 435.
  28. *Nuclear News* (newsletter), (January 1983), 14.
  29. *Nuclear Engineering International* (30 March 1985), 19-21.
  30. *The Energy Daily* (newsletter), (12 September 1986), 3.
  31. Edwin Zebroski, "The Dynamics of Institutional Changes Following the TMI Accident," in M. R. Williams and N. J. McCormick, eds., *Progress in Nuclear Energy* 10 (Oxford: Perganon Press, 1982), 249-58.
  32. Lelan, Sillin et al., *Leadership in Achieving Operational Excellence: The Challenge for All Nuclear Utilities* (report to the U.S. Nuclear Utility Industry, August 1986).
  33. *Inside N.R.C.* (newsletter), (3 February 1986), 8-9.
  34. *Inside N.R.C.* (newsletter), (29 September 1986), 2-3.
  35. *Washington Post* (7 May 1986), A34.
  36. Ivo D. Duchacek, *The Territorial Dimensions of Politics: Within, Among and Across Nations* (Boulder: Westview Press, 1986).

Chapter VI

International Bank of Reconstruction and Development, World Bank (IBRD)

The International Bank of Reconstruction and Development (IBRD), also known as the World Bank, was established in 1944. Its original task was to deal with post-war reconstruction of Europe. Since that time, however, its focus has shifted to the assistance of the developing world in attaining economic development. The IBRD has three affiliates: the International Development Association (IDA), the International Finance Corporation (IFC), and the Multilateral Investment Guarantee Agency (MIGA). The "World Bank Group" comprises IBRD and IDA, and it has 151 member nations. The Bank's capital is derived from member countries' subscription to capital shares, the calculation of which is based upon their quotas in the IMF. In 1988 World Bank capital totaled US$171.4 billion. The World Bank assists the economic development of member nations by making loans where private capital is not available on reasonable terms to finance major investments. Loans are made either directly to governments or to private business with government guarantee. IBRD loans usually have a five year grace period and are repayable over fifteen years or fewer. The World Bank has supported the world-wide agricultural green revolution, which attempts to alleviate hunger and scarcity by introducing modern agricultural technology. The Bank has also been instrumental in the "basic human needs" program.

The World Bank and Poverty:
The Plight of the World's Impoverished is Still a Major Concern of the International Agency

Jonathan E. Sanford

Abstract. Since the early 1980s, the *World Bank* has taken on new tasks in addition to its regular *development finance* function: preventing economic collapse in borrower countries, helping heavily indebted countries cope with their *international payments* difficulties, and encouraging basic *economic policy reform* and *structural adjustment* in *developing countries*. Many critics worry that, as the World Bank has taken on these new responsibilities, it has lessened its concern about *poverty*. The Bank and its friends argue that poverty alleviation remains a central element of the Bank's agenda, but the *world situation* is different than it was during the 1970s and new kinds of action are needed today. The Bank believes that economic reform and structural adjustments are crucial elements of a modern *anti-poverty program*. Many critics believe that structural adjustment programs may seriously hurt the *poor*. Exploring the arguments and reporting the ways the World Bank has sought to respond to this controversy, the author concludes that the issue is a fundamental disagreement about whether the new modes of Bank lending and the Bank's new policy emphasis will have a positive or negative effect on the poor.

The Controversy Over World Bank Policy

When Robert McNamara retired from the presidency of the World Bank in 1981, the international development lending agency lost its most prominent advocate for the poor. There has been concern, in some quarters, that since his departure the World Bank has reduced its emphasis on poverty alleviation. The World Bank and its friends insist that there is no real basis for this concern. Poverty alleviation remains a major element of the bank's program, they argue. The Bank has changed some of its methods and has taken on additional challenges in the area of Third World debt and economic reform, but they insist these are fundamental expressions of — not digressions from — its poverty agenda.

The observer has difficulty resolving this argument. There is no consensus about what the appropriate elements of a poverty alleviation program might be.   Are lending for poverty-alleviation and economic growth or stabilization different things? Is poverty-alleviation mainly programs that meet basic needs, target assistance to the needy, and improve income distribution? Is the Bank fighting poverty when it promotes economic policy reform and fundamental macro-economic change?   Different analysts have very different answers to these questions.   What one analyst sees as progress in the struggle against poverty another may see as an abandonment of that basic concern. [1]

This article sorts through some of the ambiguities and conflicting arguments. A sequel examines the World Bank's lending program, to see if there is any demonstrable change in the emphasis it gives to poverty alleviation loans.   The Bank lends more now for programs to help restructure national economies and less for regular development projects, including anti-poverty projects. The Bank also changed the way it talks about development issues. "At the end of the 1970s almost no World Bank country economic report was regarded as complete without a section on meeting basic needs," one Bank staffer wrote. "Indeed whole reports are devoted to this topic. Nowadays references to basic needs would be the exception rather than the rule."[2] The Bank also seems to be putting more emphasis on economic policy and management issues in its policy dialogue with borrower countries, and perhaps less direct emphasis on poverty concerns.

The author believes that poverty alleviation remains, nevertheless, a major World Bank priority. The shifts in the composition of the Bank's loan program and in its rhetorical style have complicated the analytical problem and obscured the continuity of Bank concern about poverty issues. The bank believes that economic policy reform and structural adjustment are basic and key elements of a modern anti-poverty program. The critics believe, on the other hand, that adjustment programs may hurt the poor and that the Bank's support for adjustment demonstrates a basic insensitivity to poverty concerns. In many ways, it seems the debate regarding the World Bank's concern about poverty is really a debate about the poverty-impact of adjustment lending. Ultimately, to resolve the one controversy analysts will have to resolve the other.

Is Poverty Still a Priority Concern?

Under Robert McNamara, the World Bank took the lead in seeking to make poverty a priority item on the world agenda. Like Theodore Roosevelt, who used the U.S. presidency as a "bully pulpit" to help build public support for his proposals, McNamara used his World Bank presidency as a vehicle for raising public consciousness about the poverty issue. In his address to the Bank's 1973 annual meeting at Nairobi, McNamara first used the term "absolute poverty" in describing conditions of life in the Third World so degraded by disease, malnutrition, illiteracy, and squalor "as to insult human dignity."[3] In 1980, in his final address to a Bank annual meeting, McNamara warned against the temptation to shelve the anti-poverty effort in order to focus on the immediate economic crisis. He agreed that the developing countries' growing international payments deficits cannot be sustained forever. He also insisted, though, that absolute poverty could not be sustained forever either.[4]

His successors — A. W. Clausen (1981-86) and Barber Conable (1986-present) — spent more of their time struggling with the effects of the international debt problem, recession, and inadequate World Bank resources. Clausen said little about poverty in the first year of his presidency, a silence which may have stimulated many of the critics' concerns.[5] Subsequently, however, he and Conable spoke eloquently on several occasions, about the need for continued emphasis on poverty alleviation and the needs of the poor. Unlike McNamara, though, they did not make poverty their principal public theme. They also took a different approach to the issue. McNamara emphasized income distribution and the need for projects targeting direct benefits to the poor. Clausen and Conable emphasized, on the other hand, the parallel need for basic economic growth.

Clausen stressed that "efficient growth and the alleviation of poverty are complementary objectives."[6] Conable said that "There is no simple remedy" for the problem of poverty, but "without continuing growth in the economies of the developed and developing nations and in the commerce among them, there is no cure at all."[7] Conable pledged that the Bank would "increase lending aimed directly at improving the access of the poor to better food, shelter, health care, and schooling," as well as to public services.[8] He also promised that "...we will target an increased proportion of our IDA lending to help tackle the poverty which has remained largely impervious to the benefits of growth."[9] Even so, the two presidents argued, special programs to help the poor are not enough. Growth is vital and serious policy change is imperative, they argued, if developing countries are going to improve their situation and the poor are to have meaningful opportunities in the future.[10]

Critics worry that the Bank no longer seems to be playing a leading role by stressing the need for international action on poverty. They fear that other issues, such as debt and structural adjustment, have been put first and poverty has been put second in the list of priorities — exactly what McNamara warned against in 1980.[11] Sheldon Annis says there has been less emphasis on poverty lending and less interest in the issue because the Bank's system of management controls and staff incentives has changed.[12] Paul Mosley says that the balance between equity and efficiency concerns has shifted and the Bank's new emphasis on policy reform and adjustment reflects a sharp shift towards the efficiency end of the spectrum and less interest in economic fairness.[13] Lane Vanderslice says that the Bank's level of concern about poverty — which he believes was never very high — has declined in recent years and hunger activists should withhold their support unless the Bank makes substantial improvements.[14]

Many believe the fate of the World Bank's Poverty Task Force demonstrates the agency's problems balancing its various priorities. Established by Conable in December 1986, the Task Force began work diligently in 1987 studying poverty concerns.[15] After giving the president a preliminary report in April, however, the Task Force fell victim to the World Bank's 1987 reorganization process. Its staff members were reassigned, the Task Force broke up, and the job of preparing its final report was reassigned to another office, where it has languished. The Task Force's official report was never issued. Instead of highlighting the Bank's continued interest in poverty concerns, the critics suggest, the fate of the Task Force underscores the Bank's difficulties translating good intentions into concrete action.

The key question, the critics argue, is how much weight the anti-poverty goal is getting within the Bank's policy process. "It's an exaggeration to say they have abandoned poverty and their concern about poor people," one critic told the author. "But those considerations are definitely taking a back seat." The critics fear that other priorities — growth, structural adjustment, incentives, and export promotion — are now claiming higher priority, if only because top Bank management has not given the poverty issue sufficient care and attention. Too much emphasis has been given to structural adjustment, policy reform, and debt problems. Top management mentions poverty alleviation as a goal, they say, but it is generally presented as one of several major

concerns.[16]   Because the other issues usually get more
prominent emphasis, the critics argue, Bank personnel
usually put poverty in second place when they have to choose
between it and other Bank priority concerns in the
formulation of their programs.

The Bank's supporters respond that these criticisms
are unfair. The Bank did not focus as strongly on poverty
during the McNamara period as the rhetoric then might
suggest, they argue.   It took time to overcome the
institutional momentum and to build a sensitivity to poverty
into the Bank's operations.[17] There is now more substantial
emphasis on poverty in Bank operations than the public
rhetoric might otherwise suggest.[18] The Poverty Task Force
may not have issued its report, they say, but most of its
suggestions were publicized by the Development Committee
or put into effect in other ways.   The Task Force was
reconstituted later in 1987 and, under a new chair, it
continues to focus staff attention on relevant issues. The staff
may talk less now about the need for action to reach the
poorest of the poor, they add, but the Bank's projects are often
more effective than before.   Attention to the borrower's
broader economic situation can enhance the Bank's
effectiveness in this regard.[19] The Bank's new system for
monitoring the poverty impact of its operations, created in
1983, has helped the Bank assess its loan program and give
poverty alleviation a more direct role in the formulation of
Bank country policy.

In any case, the Bank's supporters argue, the world
economy is suffering from new and different problems from
those experienced in McNamara's time. The world recession
has increased the number of people living in marginal
situations.   The Third World debt crisis has further
suppressed economic activity in many countries. The Bank
would be wrong, they insist, to limit itself to traditional
poverty or development projects in this situation. Furthermore, in many middle-income countries, the needs of the poor
are rather different from what they were before.[20] The Bank
needs to use new techniques if it is to help them adequately.
The Bank's performance in the anti-poverty sphere should be
judged in terms of these new conditions, they say, rather than
those which prevailed during an earlier period.[21]

New Roles for the Bank

Maintaining Growth

During the recession of the early 1980s, the World Bank had to shift its aid strategies quickly. In many countries, instead of financing new development projects, it had to work at preventing economic collapse and keeping its existing projects afloat. Through its Special Action program in 1984-5, for example, the Bank pumped $4.5 billion in fast disbursing aid into 44 countries, thus assuring that some 260 priority projects would be completed in spite of the borrowers' inability to cover their originally agreed share of the cost.[22] In fiscal 1984, over 40 percent of the Bank's lending program was altered during the course of the year to reflect the acute changes in the borrowers' needs. "Our projects were just grinding to a halt," said one loan officer for an African country. "The poor are not being helped if you let projects fall apart because governments can't afford to put money in from their side." In many heavily indebted Third World countries, the debt crisis has had a continuing negative effect on domestic growth and employment.

Third World Debt

Since the debt crisis flared in 1982, the World Bank has been under considerable pressure to expand its emphasis on international finance and debt issues.[23] "Where have you been?" Federal Reserve Board Chairman Paul Volcker reportedly asked the World Bank's top managers in July 1984, when they met with other financial leaders to discuss the debt issue.[24] He reportedly complained that the Bank had failed to do its share, leaving the Fed and the IMF with the main burden of responding to the financing crisis in the Third World. In October 1985, Treasury Secretary James Baker proposed that the multilateral development banks should make $20 billion in new loans to the top debtor countries during the 1986-9 period, in conjunction with a corresponding increase in commercial bank loans and new commitments by borrower countries to implement additional market-oriented policy reforms.

In early 1986, the joint World Bank-IMF Development Committee agreed on a strategy for responding to the growth problems of the highly indebted countries. The plan called for greater flows of World Bank Lending, leadership in developing comprehensive medium-term adjustment programs, and encouragement of new private capital flows.[25] In the two years since the initiation of this strategy (1986-87), the World Bank made $12.6 billion in new loan commitments to the 15 highly indebted Baker Plan countries, a substantial increase in its level of activity.[26] The World Bank appears to be the only one of the actors to fulfill its role in the Baker Plan scenario. Conable told the 1987 annual meeting that "The Bank has a central responsibility in assisting heavily indebted countries to grow out of debt and recession." In many cases, these countries have few other sources of growth capital. "The resolution of debt problems is crucial," Conable said, "if our common development objectives are to be achieved."[27]

Structural Adjustment

Economic reform and policy change have been another growing element of World Bank operations in recent years. Ten years ago, the Bank was mainly a project lender. Now, as Table 1 indicates, a major share of its aid goes for non-project assistance, mainly structural adjustment loans (SAL) and sector adjustment loans. The Bank also makes a small number of program loans (non-adjustment) each year, to finance purchases of scarce imports for the poorest countries or to provide post-disaster reconstruction aid. Sector adjustment loans seek to finance the restructuring. Initially, most adjustment lending was financed with market-rate loans. More recently, an increasing share of the Bank's concessional aid had gone for this purpose. The Bank's members agreed in 1986, for example, that, during the 1987-89 IDA 8 replenishment, special emphasis would be put on Africa and on the promotion of structural adjustment and economic policy change.[28]

Economists say that, without basic reforms in their economic policies, many developing countries are trapped.

Table 1. World Bank Lending by Type, 1978-1986
(percent of total lending; millions of U.S. dollars)

	1978	1979	1980	1981	1982
Structural Adjustment*	--	--	2.5%	5.8%	8.2%
Sector Adjustment	--	0.3%	0.6%	1.1%	--
Program Loans	1.8%	3.5%	0.5%	0.6%	1.3%
Project Loans	98.2%	96.2%	96.3%	92.5%	90.5%
Total lending for year	$8,411	$10,011	$11,482	$12,291	$13,016

	1983	1984	1985	1986	1987
Structural Adjustment*	8.9%	7.0%	1.1%	4.6%	4.5%
Sector Adjustment	4.4%	8.5%	10.3%	15.3%	19.5%
Program Loans	0.8%	1.4%	--	1.2%	1.1%
Project Loans**	85.9%	83.1%	88.6%	78.9%	74.9%
Total lending for year	$14,477	$15,522	$14,384	$16,319	$17,674

*includes Technical Assistance, most of which is aimed at improving the capacity of the borrower to manage aspects of the adjustment effort.
**includes specific investment loans, sector investment loans, and loans through financial intermediaries.

Source: World Bank, letter to author, 1987 calculated by author. The data differ somewhat from those in World Bank 1987 annual report (p. 26) because technical assistance is grouped here with adjustment lending while program and emergency reconstruction aid is distinguished here from adjustment aid.

They cannot stimulate domestic growth without making their balance of payments (BOP) problems worse, but fixing the BOP problem requires them to suppress domestic economic activity. Since 1979, the Bank has lent over $16.1 billion for adjustment purposes. Sector adjustment loans seek to promote economic reform in one sector of the economy. Structural adjustment loans aim at promoting economic reform and adjustment in several sectors simultaneously. The loan agreements for structural and sector adjustment loans usually contain lists of anticipated macroeconomic and sector policy changes, as well as timetables for the reforms. Unlike project loans, which can take from 4 to 9 years to fully disburse their funds, SAL and sector adjustment loans can move money very quickly. In most cases, the proceeds are fully disbursed within 1 to 4 years, depending on the situation.[29]

In a series of reviews issued since 1981, assessing Africa's development needs, the Bank stressed the need for new policies and approaches if the countries of the region are to deal successfully with their economic problems.[30] According to the Bank, major adjustments in their exchange rates would make the Africans' exports more competitive and would eliminate distortion which favored imports over domestic products in their marketplaces. Better domestic pricing policies and more incentives for agricultural production would encourage local producers to expand their output and take fuller (and more economic) advantage of their opportunities.[31] More freedom for the private sector, and less reliance on public enterprise (especially State-owned firms running chronic losses) would stimulate the economy, lessen the pressure on government budgets, and encourage better use of national resources. In this way, the Bank believes, the development prospects of the Africans could increase significantly.[32]

Structural Adjustment and Poverty

The World Bank's concern with adjustment and policy reform is not new. To a degree, country policy issues have long been a factor influencing World Bank loan considerations. The SAL program broadened and formalized this concern in 1980. In the early years of the SAL program, the Bank's comments about adjustment were usually intermixed with statements about the need for continued attention to basic needs. Later statements sometimes failed to make this parallel emphasis. On several occasions, senior Bank executives have been quoted as saying that the Bank's current efforts to revive growth in stagnant economies must necessarily take precedence over the distribution of benefits within those countries. This latter word circulates quickly and is often given more credence than are the Bank's more "balanced" public pronouncements.

The critics worry that this stress on economic reform may diminish the amounts of money available for social programs and other poverty-oriented lending. If the Bank lends more to the top debtor countries, to help them keep their economies afloat, then it has less to lend to others. Furthermore, for many poor countries, they say, the problem is not one of excessive commercial debt or even debt management, but rather the government's basic incapacity to meet the people's needs. They complain that the increase in non-project lending does not expand the productive capacity of the borrower country. Too often, the funds are used to repay creditors and to persuade borrowers to make policy changes rather than to help finance productive new activities.[33]

Many critics worry that more policy conditionality on World Bank lending will have negative effects on the poor. If the Bank staff is paying more attention to policy and macroeconomic issues, for example, they will presumably have less time for poverty concerns. Furthermore, critics argue, if projects are more rigorous and less concessional there will be fewer benefits to distribute to the poor. Subsidies will be cut, resources will be shifted from sectors producing for domestic consumption to those producing for export, and the levels of spending for domestic employment and social amelioration will decline. Critics also contend that the Bank seems more interested in strengthening the private sector and promoting pro-market reforms than in helping needy people. If this trend continues, they worry, the World Bank's future loan levels will be determined more by macroeconomic or balance of payments considerations than by any concern about poverty or countries' development needs. The World Bank will have become merely an adjunct of the IMF, another conservative tool for promoting financial stability and "sound" economic policy. They fear that the Bank will be less interested in practicing "economics as though people matter."

The Bank's supporters contend that the critics have grossly misread the purpose and effect of the Bank's new emphasis on adjustment and policy reform. The effort to improve market conditions and economic policy is an integral part of the Bank's poverty-alleviation effort, they argue. "Adjustment is not the opposite of poverty lending," one Bank spokesman told the author. "If growth doesn't start up in these countries, then poor people will take the rap." From this point of view, the most effective way to deal with poverty is through growth, and the best method for stimulating growth is through structural reforms that allocate resources more effectively and stimulate the small farmer and the private sector's productive energies.[34]

It is not a question of whether there should be adjustment, the Bank's friends insist, but how the inevitable adjustments should proceed. Given the chronic deficits in the developing countries' international payments and the current strains in the world financial system, these countries eventually will have to make major changes in their domestic economic policies in any case. Delay will only make the inevitable adjustment process more painful. The poor will probably be hurt more if it comes as a result of economic collapse rather than through a managed process.

The critics' comparison of the World Bank and IMF is also inappropriate, the Bank's supporters argue. Both agencies are interested in macroeconomic issues, they say, but there are major differences between them in terms of their time horizons and their instruments. The IMF focuses on short-term balance of payments stability — the demand side of the equation. Its instruments are mainly those bitter medicines — currency devaluation, rapid reductions in budget deficits, and cuts in subsidies — which depress the country's aggregate income in order to reduce inflation, cut imports, increase exports, and lessen its balance of payments deficit.[35] The Bank works on the supply side of the equation, its spokesmen argue; its programs have a much longer time period in which to accomplish their ends. Rather than suppressing income levels, the Bank aims at laying the foundation for increased production through the development of new skills and capacity and through changes in relative price levels (which can lead to changes in comparative advantage) in borrower countries.

The critics are also wrong, Bank experts insist, when they say the poor must inevitably bear the burden of adjustment. The elimination of subsidies has never been a major goal of the Bank's adjustment programs, they argue.[36] The Bank has sought some reductions in subsidies (particularly those that benefit urban residents) but there have usually been good economic reasons for these cuts. Sometimes, the cost of the subsidy had grown beyond the point where it could be maintained, given the borrower's available resources. Often, the experts maintain, the greatest burden of the adjustment process has been borne by middle-income groups (particularly government employees) rather than the poor. Frequently, during periods of retrenchment, they say, developing countries cut their social expenditures less than they cut their outlays for defense or their investments in infrastructure and productive facilities.[37] The Bank tries to offset some of the effects of these cuts in government spending by financing some of the investments in productive facilities and infrastructure which are needed if there is to be continued growth and development in hard-hit countries.

One point of dispute is whether economic adjustment and policy reform should now become the principal focus of the World Bank's lending program, at least in the countries with the heaviest debt burdens. Another controversy has to do with how these adjustment programs should be designed. Many experts agree that, at least in theory, economists should be able to devise adjustment programs that have no negative effects on the poor. Stanley Please — a former Bank official who was responsible for developing the Bank's structural adjustment loan program — contends, in fact, that adjustment can be achieved rapidly and "at a higher level of real income and with greater attention to the needs of developmental policy" if close attention is paid to the appropriate issues and concerns.[38] UNICEF also made a similar examination of adjustment issues and published guidelines for "adjustment with a human face."[39] Many analysts believe that adjustment will help save the poor from the consequences of the economic collapse — where they will be the first and the most vulnerable victims — that must inevitably occur if their governments continue pursuing unsound economic policies.

The Bank has given considerable attention, in the past few years, to the question whether structural adjustment and poverty alleviation goals are compatible.[40] Before it was temporarily overwhelmed by the effects of the 1987 reorganization, the Poverty Task Force recommended that the Bank adopt an expanded lending program aimed at addressing social problems and that improved mechanisms should be developed — in consultation with non-governmental organizations — for addressing the problems of the most vulnerable groups. Conable told the Development

Committee that these ideas merited future action.[41]   The
Bank commissioned several studies of the adjustment process
and its effects on poverty.   These found that adjustment can
have negative effects on the poor.   World Bank structural
adjustment programs can have an ameliorating effect,
however, and "given the right policies, the conflict between
adjustment and poverty alleviation need not be as severe as
some suppose."[42] The Bank published a series of studies of
the adjustment experiences of different countries[43] and
related issues.[44]   Together with the IMF, it sponsored a
major symposium on the relationship between growth and
adjustment.[45] The Development Committee issued a report
detailing ways the Bank could protect the poor from injury in
its adjustment programs.[46]   High level Bank officials also
held several discussions on this issue with private voluntary
organizations, international agencies, and other parties.[47]

    Despite statements from the World Bank evidencing
belief that structural adjustment need not necessarily hurt
the poor, the critics remain unconvinced.   In 1987, the U.S.
Congress adopted legislation which sought to give poverty
alleviation higher priority in World Bank operations.   The
House Appropriations, Senate Foreign Relations, and House
Banking Committees all expressed concern about the issue.[48]
The final authorization law directed that the U.S. executive
directors (EDs) at the multilateral development banks should
encourage the multilateral agencies to undertake programs
that help the poor, particularly the rural poor.   The law
required the U.S. EDs to urge the multilateral banks to create
institutionalized procedures within their bureaucracies for
regular consultation with private voluntary organizations and
other grassroots organizations about poverty issues.   The law
directed the U.S. EDs to urge the multilateral banks to do
studies assessing whether their loan operations help or hurt
the poor. The EDs were also required to recommend that the
multilateral banks adopt formal guidelines which would be
designed to identify and minimize any such negative impact
on the poor.[49]

Conclusion

The World Bank cannot control the implementation of the

adjustment programs it finances. Even if the Bank's adjustment plans are perfectly designed, there may still be problems. The Bank can offer its policy advice, but it is still up to the borrower to take it and up to the borrower to see that it is carried out effectively. The political process in the borrower country can generate effects that the program managers at the World Bank may not prefer. Bank officials may not want their adjustment programs to have negative effects on the poor. The leaders of the borrower country may have other concerns. It is not always clear beforehand what the effects of the adjustment program will be, and there may be disputes even if the results could be known. How to keep from having a negative impact on the poor still seems to be a source of concern, even among those at the Bank who are most convinced that the long-run benefits from adjustment are clear.

Critics have noted that the World Bank seems to put less emphasis on direct poverty alleviation than do other organizations, such as the International Fund for Agricultural Development (IFAD) and the Inter-American Foundation, a U.S. government agency.[50] Suggestions have been made that congress might shift funds from the World Bank to these other agencies, in recognition of their supposed superiority in this area.

It is unreasonable to argue that the World Bank should be mainly an anti-poverty agency and that someone else — perhaps the IMF or bilateral lenders — should lend for economic stabilization and basic growth. The World Bank is a large institution, and it plays many more roles in the international system than do the smaller and more specialized agencies. Whoever got its funds would probably also get its enlarged responsibilities.[51] Even with poverty as a principal concern, the World Bank cannot neglect the economic context within which the poor exist nor the economic track record of their home countries.

The relationship between economic adjustment and poverty is a great area of uncertainty. Many analysts have strong views on the issue, but (save for case studies) there are few really good general studies on the subject. It may be, in fact, that nobody really knows what the overall impact of these adjustment programs on the poor may actually be.[52]

Analysts who say they know may be telling us more about
their own economic assumptions and their own concepts of
poverty (and poverty alleviation) than they are about
empirical reality.

Whatever impact its loans might have, the World Bank
clearly does not believe it is making poverty worse through
sponsorship of structural adjustment programs. In that
respect, it has not pulled back from its concern about poverty,
for it believes that in addressing the problems of
macroeconomic policy mistakes and needs for adjustment it is
helping countries address the underlying problem of poverty.

The author believes that the poorest people in the
developing countries probably are being injured initially by
many of the changes mandated by Bank adjustment
programs and World Bank-sponsored economic policy
reforms. He also believes, however, that the poor will
probably be hurt even more, in the long run, by the
stagnation and misallocation of resources that can result if
unsound economic policies persist. So long as there is a
strong perception in the developed and the developing nations
that structural adjustment means austerity and broad-scale
dislocation and suffering, however, the World Bank's
increased activities in the adjustment area will be a serious
source of concern to those who are interested in the poverty-
alleviation impact of the program. Greater attention needs to
be paid to this issue and to the development of ways for
softening the impact of necessary adjustment steps.

NOTES

1. Several schools of thought can be identified: (1)
Critics of the World Bank who believe it could do more about
poverty, (2) *Defenders* of the Bank's overall record, (3)
Conservative Skeptics who doubt the validity of any
multilateral development bank program, and (4) *Liberal or
Leftist Skeptics* who fear the *Multilateral Development Banks*
(MDBs) are fundamentally biased against social reform and
equity.

For the first group, see, for example: Sheldon Annis,
"The Shifting Grounds of Poverty Lending at the World
Bank," in *Between Two Worlds: the World Bank's Next*

Decade, Richard E. Feinberg, ed. (Sponsored by the Overseas Development Council. New Brunswick, NJ: Transaction Books, 1986), 87-110. See also Feinberg's comments in "An Open Letter to the World Bank's New President," 18-20 in the same publication.

For the second group, see, for example: David Beckmann, "The World Bank and Poverty in the 1980s," in *Finance and Development* 23, no. 3 (September 1986), 26-29. See also Beckmann's reply to critics in "A Letter to Christian Hunger Activists," in *Seeds* (February 1987), 20-23. For broader discussion, see: Robert Ayres, *Banking on the Poor* (Cambridge, MA: MIT Press, 1983).

For the third group, several biting commentaries are available questioning the results of the MDBs and the humanitarian justification of its program. See, for example: E. Dwight Phaup, *The World Bank: How Can it Serve U.S. Interests* (Washington, D.C.: The Heritage Foundation, 1984), especially pp. 13-16, 22-25. For a broader discussion, see: Morris B. Goldman, "Multilateral Institutions and Economic Development," in *U.S. Aid to the Developing World: a Free Market Agenda*, Doug Bandow, ed. (Washington, D.C.: The Heritage Foundation 1985), 93-115.

The fourth group harbors a more diverse collection of views. Some liberals question whether the Bank put sufficient emphasis on the poor even during the McNamara period. See: Aart van de Laar, *The World Bank and the Poor* (Boston: Martinus Nijhoff Publishing, 1980), especially pp. 109-140. Many leftists doubt whether the World Bank has ever really been serious about poverty, whatever McNamara may have said. See: Cheryl Payer, *The World Bank* (New York: Monthly Review Press, 1982), especially pp. 55-71.

2. Pierre Landell-Mills, Reviewing Frances Stewart's book, *Basic Needs in Developing Countries, in Finance and Development* 22, no. 4 (December 1985), 58.

3. Robert S. McNamara, "Address to the Board of Governors, Nairobi, Kenya," September 24, 1973. (Washington, D.C.: World Bank, 1973), 6-7.

4. "To ignore it, to temporize with it, to downgrade its urgency under the convenient excuse that its solution is 'longterm' — and that there are other immediate problems that preempt its priority — is dangerous self-deception," he

said. Poverty must still be the fundamental issue. "To reduce
and eliminate massive absolute poverty lies at the very core
of development itself. It is critical to the survival of any
decent society." Robert S. McNamara, "Address to the Board
of Governors, Washington, D.C.," September 30, 1980.
(Washington, D.C.: World Bank, 1980), 18-19.

5. Critics note, in addition, that as late as 1984,
Clausen still did not include poverty alleviation or aid to the
poor as key goals for the Bank in his 1984 message to the
staff outlining "Priority Issues for 1984.," *Bank's World* 3
(January 1984), 11-13.

6. The World Bank, *Focus on Poverty: Report of a Task
Force of the World Bank* (Washington, D.C.: World Bank,
December 1982.)

7. World Bank, "Address to the Board of Governors by
Barber B. Conable, President, the World Bank and
International Finance Corporation." (Washington, D.C.:
World Bank, September 30, 1986), 7.

8. "The Bank will increase lending aimed directly at
improving the access of the poor to better food, shelter, health
care and schooling. We shall strive to protect the poor during
periods of adjustment. We will support policy and
institutional changes to ensure that public programs more
efficiently direct their benefits to poor people. In these vital
social investments we shall work more closely with the
private sector and non-governmental organizations in order to
multiply their effectiveness at the grassroot level." World
Bank. Address by Barber B. Conable to the Board of
Governors of the World Bank and the International Finance
Corporation. (Washington D.C., September 29, 1987.) Text of
speech, as prepared for delivery, distributed by World Bank.
9. *Ibid.*, p. 16.

9. *Ibid.*, p. 16.

10. For a broader representation of Clausen and
Conable's statements, see: A. W. Clausen, "Address to the
Board of Governors, Toronto, Canada," September 6, 1982.
(Washington, D.C.: World Bank, 1982); A. W. Clausen.
"Accelerating Growth and Reducing Poverty: a Multilateral
Strategy for Development." (Remarks prepared for delivery
to the Atlantik-Brucke and the Deutsch Gesellschaft für
Auswartige Politik, Bonn, Federal Republic of Germany, April

18, 1983). Photocopy provided by the World Bank; A. W. Clausen. "Poverty in Developing Countries — 1985." (Address prepared for delivery at the Martin Luther King Jr. Center, Atlanta, Georgia, January 11, 1985). Photocopy provided by the World Bank; A. W. Clausen, "World Bank Focuses on Reducing Poverty," *Journal of Commerce* (January 18, 1985), 4A; Barber B. Conable, "Address to the World Resources Institute, Washington, D.C.," May 5, 1987. (Washington, D.C.: World Bank, 1987); Barber B. Conable. "The Safe Motherhood Initiative: Address and Proposals for Action," Nairobi, Kenya, February 10, 1987. (Washington, D.C.: World Bank, 1987).

11. Robert F. Wasserstrom, "The World Bank and World Poverty," in the *Christian Science Monitor* (June 25, 1984), 12.

12. Annis. *op. cit.*

13. Paul Mosley, *Foreign Aid: Its Defense and Reform* (Lexington, KY: Univ. Press of Kentucky, 1987), 29.

14. Lane Vanderslice, "IDA, the World Bank, and the World's Poor" (Washington, D.C.: Bread for the World, March 1987), 2-4, Background paper Number 95.

15. World Bank. "For Your information: Poverty Task Force," FYI/86/133 (December 27, 1986). Message by Barber B. Conable establishing the task force and setting its terms of reference.

16. Mention was made, for example, of the limited emphasis which poverty alleviation received in Conable's 1986 interview with *Finance and Development*. Barber B. Conable, "The Bank's Mission in a Changing World," *Finance and Development* 23, no. 4, (December 1986), 2-5.

17. Michael Lipton and Alexander Shakow, "The World Bank and Poverty," *Finance and Development* 19 (June 1982), 16-19.

18. For a review of proposals to redirect the World Bank's efforts and the staff's reaction to demands for change, see: William Ascher, "New Development Approaches and the Adaptability of International Agencies: the Case of the World Bank," *International Organization* 37 (Summer 1983), 415-39.

19. Montague Yudelman, "Agricultural Lending in the Bank, 1974-84: a Retrospective Analysis," in *Finance and Development* 21 (December 1984), 45-47. Yudelman was

formerly director of the Bank's agriculture and rural development department.

20. See, for example: Guy Pfeffermann, "Economic Crisis and the Poor in Some Latin American Countries," *Finance and Development* 24, no. 2 (June 1987), 32-35.

21. See, for example: Stanley Please, *The Hobbled Giant: Essays on the World Bank* (Boulder, CO: Westview Press, 1984), 4-5, 12-13, 81-85. He believed that reorganizing the Bank would sharpen its effectiveness in achieving its several goals, one of which is poverty alleviation.

22. World Bank, *Annual Report* (1985), 54.

23. Bruce Stokes, "Liberals and Conservatives Struggling Over the World Bank's Proper Role," *National Journal* 18 (February 8, 1986), 334-37; *The Future Role of the World Bank* (Washington: The Brookings Institution, 1982); James Rowe, Jr., "World Bank Role in Debt Crisis Grows," *Washington Post*, (October 15, 1986), F1, F7; Paul Bernstein, "Conable to Seek to Alter Role of World Bank," *Wall Street Journal* (July 3, 1986), 21; Hobart Rowen, "Transition at Top May Alter World Bank's Global Role," *Washington Post* (June 22, 1986), F1, F6-7; "The Baker Initiative: the Perspective of the Banks," *World Financial Markets* (February 1986), 1-9; G. K. Helleiner, "Policy Based Program Lending: a Look at the Bank's New Role," *Between Two Worlds*, 47-66; Geoffrey Bell, "Dealing with the Debt Crisis: Only the World Bank has the Means," *New York Times* (August 25, 1986), Sec. 3, 3; David Francis, "The World Bank and the Third World Debt Crisis," *Christian Science Monitor* (September 20, 1985), 20; Steven K. Becker, "World Bank Mulls New Debt Policy," *Washington Times* (August 8, 1984), 7B, 10B.

24. See: Clyde Farnsworth, "A Troubled Rule at the World Bank," *New York Times* (Sept. 2, 1984), Sec. 3, 20.

25. Joint Ministerial Committee of the Boards of Governors of the World Bank and the International Monetary Fund on the Transfer of Real Resources to Developing Countries (Development Committee), "A Strategy for Restoration of Growth in Middle-Income Countries that Face Debt-Servicing Difficulties" (Washington, D.C.: World Bank, July 1986).   See also: David Block and Constantine Michalopoulos, "The Emerging Role of the Bank in Heavily Indebted Countries," *Finance and Development* 23, no. 3

(September 1986), 22-25.
  26. World Bank, *Annual Report* (1987), 17-21, 25-27.
  27. Conable speech to 1987 World Bank-IMF annual meeting, 5,7.
  28. See the Administration's testimony in support of the proposed IDA 8 replenishment legislation. U.S. Congress, House, Committee on Banking, Finance, and Urban Affairs, Subcommittee on International Development Institutions and Finance, "Multilateral Development Banks," Hearings 100th Cong., 1st sess., April 2, 1987 (Washington, D.C. U.S.G.P.O., 1987), 2 and following. See also World Bank *Annual Report* (1987), 16, 26-30.
  29. In addition to the material cited in footnote 26, see: World Bank, *Annual Report* (1985), 52-4; World Bank, *Annual Report* 1986, 47-9; Karl Wohlmuth, "IMF and World Bank Structural Adjustment Policies: Cooperation of Conflict," *Intereconomics*, no. 5 (September-October, 1984), 226-34. For additional background on the World Bank, poverty, and structural adjustment, the reader might also consult J. Sanford, *U.S. Foreign Policy and the Multilateral Development Banks* (Boulder, CO: Westview Press, 1982). A survey of current congressional action is presented in J. Sanford, "Multilateral Development Banks: Issues for Congress (Congressional Research Service Issue Brief 87218, March 10, 1988), updated periodically.
  30. See: World Bank. "Accelerated Development in Sub-Saharan Africa: An Agenda for Action," (World Bank, 1981); "Sub-Saharan Africa: Progress Report on Development Prospects and Programs" (World Bank, 1983); "Financing Adjustment with Growth in Sub-Saharan Africa, 1986-1990." (World Bank, 1986). For an example of the reaction which the World Bank approach has engendered, see the published papers for a symposium on the Accelerated Development report, published in the *African Studies Review*, 27 (December 1984), entire issue. See also Anthony G. Hopkins, "The World Bank in Africa: Historical Reflections on the African Present," *World Development* 14, no. 12 (December 1986), 1473-87.
  31. For a discussion of changes in World Bank agriculture policy, see: Yudelman, 19. For a further analysis, see my "Foreign Assistance for Agricultural Development:

Trends in Policy and Operations Since the Early 1970s," in
U.S. Congress, House, Foreign Affairs Committee." Feeding
the World's Population Developments in the Decade
Following the World Food Conference of 1974," (prepared by
the Congressional Research Service, Library of Congress; 98
Cong., 2d sess. October 1984), 244-312.

32. The World Bank's approach differed significantly
from the one preferred by many of the African countries. See,
for example, Robert S. Browne and Robert J. Cummings, *The
Lagos Plan of Action vs. the Berg Report* (Lawrenceville, VA:
Brunswick Publishing Company, 1984). One in a series of
Monographs in African Studies, by the African Studies and
Research Program, Howard University, Washington, D.C.

33. Critics cite, for example, a 1986 agriculture sector
loan in which the Bank lent Argentina $350 million on
condition that it cut its export taxes on agricultural goods.
No new facilities were created as a result of the loan, the
country was urged to take policy steps which were in its
demonstrable interest anyway, and the money went to the
country's central bank in order to help it repay its debts. This
was called an agriculture loan, the critics say, but it was
really a form of balance of payments assistance.

34. John Williamson. *The Lending Policies of the
International Monetary Fund* (Policy Analyses in
International Economics 1), (Washington, D.C.: Institute for
International Economics, August 1982), especially pp. 21-4;
Manuel Guiteran, "Economic Management and International
Monetary Fund Conditionality," *Adjustment and Financing in
the Developing World*, Tony Killick, ed. (Washington, D.C.:
The International Monetary Fund, 1982), esp. p. 88; Richard
Erb, "Collaboration Between Aid Agencies and the IMF," in
Finance and Development, 23 (March 1986), 15-16; Hiroyukin
Hino, "IMF-World Bank Collaboration," *Finance and
Development* 23 (September 1986), 10-14.

35. See, for example: Manuel Pastor, Jr. "The effects of
IMF Programs in the Third World. Debate and Evidence
from Latin America," *World Development* 15, no. 2 (February
1987), 249-62. The IMF argues that its loan programs do not
necessarily have the negative impact on growth and
development that the criticism suggests. Its experts argue
that there are also many cases where successful IMF

adjustment loan programs did not seriously injure growth or where the loss of growth was no more than would have occurred anyway if the country had not undertaken the IMF-supported adjustment program. See, for example, Moshin S. Khan and Malcolm D. Knight, "Fund-Supported Adjustment Programs and Economic Growth," Occassional Paper 41 (Washington, D.C.: International Monetary Fund, November 1985); Fiscal Affairs Department of the International Monetary Fund (author), "Fund Supported Programs, Fiscal Policy, and Income Distribution," Occasional Paper 46 (Washington, D.C.: International Monetary Fund, September 1986).

36. See Mosley, *op cit.* fn. 13, 38-42, for a discussion and table summarizing the essential components of the World Bank's structural adjustment operations between 1980 and 1985.

37. See: Norman Hicks and Anne Kubisch, "Cutting Government Expenditures in LDCs," *Finance and Development* (Sept. 1984), 37-39.

38. See: Stanley Please, "The World Bank: Lending for Structural Adjustment," Richard E. Feinberg and Valeriana Kallab, eds. *Adjustment Crisis in the Third World* (New Brunswick, N.J., published by Transaction Books for the Overseas Development Council, 1984.) Among these criteria were: the relative roles of the public and private sectors in economic activity, the way markets are allowed to develop or are organized by governments, the process and criteria for agricultural pricing, the industrial policy framework, the effects of the pricing and taxation on domestic and imported energy costs and energy conservation, and the public expenditure program. Besides focusing on policy issues, Please says, adjustment loans should push for more — not less — spending on development programs. Many subsidy programs should be cut, though, as he says they often become "counter-developmental" in their impact on economic efficiency and in their poverty-alleviation effects. The Bank must try to assure, he says, that aggregate social and economic expenditures are not cut as the developing countries struggle to meet the guidelines in IMF stabilization programs. The Bank also needs to strive to design good programs for financing development within the constraints of

a tight budget.

39. G. Cornia, R. Jolly, and F. Stewart, eds., "Protecting the Vulnerable and Promoting Growth" (Oxford: Clarendon Press, 1987), especially Chapter 6. *Adjustment with a Human Face* 1. The compilation of studies was prepared with the cooperation and support of UNICEF, the United Nations Children's Fund. The authors maintain that six elements are necessary for the implementation of a humane adjustment program: (1) macroeconomic policies which are more expansionary, (2) meso (middle range) policies designed to help fulfill priorities in meeting the needs of vulnerable groups and promoting economic growth, (3) sectoral policies to achieve restructuring in the productive sector, (4) policies designed to increase the equity and efficiency of the social sector, (5) compensatory programs to protect basic living standards, health, and nutrition of the low-income groups during adjustment, and (6) monitoring of the living standards, health, and nutrition of the vulnerable during adjustment.

40. See the Bank's concise statement of its views in its 1987 *Annual Report*, 15-16.

41. Address by Barber B. Conable, President of the World Bank, to the Joint World Bank-IMF Development Committee (April 10, 1987). Photocopy supplied by the World Bank.

42. Tony Addison and Lionel Demery, "Alleviating Poverty under Structural Adjustment," *Finance and Development* 24, no. 4 (December 1987), 41-43 and their larger study of the same title (Washington, D.C.: World Bank, November 1987); Overseas Development Institute, "Adjusting to Recession: Will the Poor Recover?" ODI Briefing Paper (London: Overseas Development Institute, November 1986).

43. For example, Miguel Schloss and Vinod Thomas, "Adjustment with Growth: Colombia's Experience," *Finance and Development* 23, no. 4 (December 1986), 10-14; George Kopits, "Turkey's Adjustment Experience, 1980-85," *Finance and Development* 24, no. 3 (September 1987), 8-11; Bijan Aghevli *et al.*, "Growth and Adjustment in South Asia," *ibid.*, 12-15; and Nils Borje Tallroth, "Structural Adjustment in Nigeria," *ibid.*, 20-22.

44. Constantine Michalopoulos, "World Bank Lending for Structural Adjustment," *Finance and Development* 24, no. 2 (June 1987), 7-10; Marcelo Selowskyu, "Adjustment in the 1980s: an Overview of Issues," *ibid.*, 11-14; Yukon Huang and Peter Nicholas, "The Social Costs of Adjustment," *ibid.*, 22-24. In addition, an integrated IMF-World Bank approach to structural adjustment was reviewed in Michael Bell and Robert Sheehy, "Helping Structural Adjustment in Low-Income Countries," *Finance and Development* 24, no. 4 (December 1987), 6-9.

45. Vittorio Corbo, Morris Goldstein, and Mohsin Kahn, eds. *Growth-Oriented Adjustment Programs*, Proceedings of a Symposium Held in Washington, D.C., February 25-27, 1987 (Washington, D.C.: International Monetary Fund and World Bank, 1987).

46. Joint Ministerial Committee of the Boards of Governors of the World Bank and the International Monetary Fund on the Transfer of Real Resources to Developing Countries (Development Committee) *Protecting the Poor During Periods of Adjustment* (Washington, D.C.: World Bank, August 1987).

47. World Bank, International Relations Department, "Cooperation Between Nongovernmental Organizations and the World Bank: Fourth Progress Report," (October 20, 1986); International Relations Department. "World Bank/UNICEF Collaboration on Adjustment Issues," (memorandum of meeting on May 28, 1987 between Bank and UNICEF staff following up on meeting of the heads of the two organizations in March); Nancy Alexander, Friends Committee on National Legislation. "Collaborative Problem-Solving in Development," (a World Bank — US NGO Consultation Background Paper for June 3, 1987 Meeting). Photocopies obtained from the World Bank or other sources.

48. U.S. Congress, House, Committee on Appropriations, *Foreign Operations and Export Financing, and Related Programs Appropriation Bill*, 1988,H. Rept. 100-283, accompanying H.R. 3186 (August 6, 1987), 47, 49; Senate. Committee on Foreign Relations. *International Security and Development Cooperation Act of 1987*, S. Rept. 100-60, accompanying S. 1274 (May 22, 1987), Title VIII, summarizing the MDB portion of the legislation, particularly

sec. 802. The House Banking Committee addressed the structural adjustment issue in its amendments to H.R. 3, the omnibus international trade bill, House, Committee on Banking, Finance, and Urban Affairs, Title 4 of the *Trade and International Economic Policy Reform Act of 1987*, H. Rept. 100-40, part 4 (April 6, 1987), specifically Title IV, sec. 427. The Banking committee also considered, but did not report, MDB authorization legislation in 1987. On June 2, the Subcommittee on International Development Institutions and Finance included several sections on structural adjustment and poverty among the amendments it adopted during its markup of H.R. 2403.

49. See H.R. 3750, introduced December 11, 1987, by Representative Mat McHugh, sec. 1402 (1), sec. 1501 (a)(1) and (b)(1), sec. 1601, sec. 1602, and sec. 1603. H.R. 3750 was enacted into law by reference through a clause in H.J. Res. 395 (P.L. 100-202), the omnibus continuing resolution for fiscal year 1988. The text of H.R. 3750 was not included in the continuing resolution. See U.S. House, Conference Report to accompany H.J. Res. 395, "Making Further Continuing Appropriations for the fiscal Year Ending September 30, 1988," H. Rept. 100-498 (December 22, 1987), especially p. 141.

50. See, for example: Larry Hollar. "The Enterprising Poor," Background Paper No. 96. (Washington, D.C.: Bread for the World, April 1987), especially the last page; "IFAD fosters self-help," *Development Forum* (July-August 1987), 7; testimony by Sheldon Annis, Peter Kilby, and Judith Tendler before the House Banking Committee in hearings, *op. cit.*, fn. 28, 308-330.

51. See the comment by Annis, in the hearings, *ibid.*, 280, suggesting that the transfer of funds from the World Bank to these smaller agencies would not necessarily be a good idea.

52. In addition to the other publications referred to above, see: Mohsin S. Khan, "Macroeconomic Adjustment in Developing Countries a Policy Perspective," *The World Bank Research Observer* 2, no. 1 (January 1987), 23-42, especially 37, 39; Stanley Fischer, "Issues in Medium-Term Macroeconomic Adjustment," *The World Bank Research Observer* 1, no. 2 (July 1986), 163-82, especially 179; Deepak

Lal, "The Political Economy Liberalization," *The World Bank Economic Review* 1, no. 2 (January 1987), 273-300, especially 285-288; Gerald K. Helleiner, "Update" and "Balance-of-Payments Experience and Growth Prospects of Developing Countries: a Synthesis," *World Development* 14, no. 8 (August 1986), 875-76 and 877-908; and Edmar L. Bacha and Richard Feinberg, "The World Bank and Structural Adjustment in Latin America," and J. Kydd and A. Hewitt, "The Effectiveness of Structural Adjustment Lending: Initial Evidence from Malawi," both in *World Development*, 14, no. 3 (March 1986), 333-46 and 347-65. Two aspects of these studies merit comment. First, there are many variables in the complex models for adjustment and many of the relationships among them are uncertain or variable. Second, only in the Malawi case study — a small country and a limited set of data — did the authors explore directly the relationship between structural adjustment and poverty. Generally, analyses of changes in the welfare function or wage rates must serve as a partial and not an adequate representation of poverty.

The views expressed in this article are solely those of the author and should not be attributed to IBRD.

Chapter VII

International Civil Aviation Organization (ICAO)

The International Civil Aviation Organization (ICAO) was established as a United Nations specialized agency in 1947. Currently it is comprised of 161 member nations, and its headquarters is in Montreal, Canada. Budget appropriations for 1989 totaled US$3.7 million. ICAO's primary role is "to develop the principles of international air navigation and to help in the planning and improvement of international air transport." In order to perform this function, the organization strives to maintain a number of activities and programs. First, the ICAO attempts to ensure the "safe and orderly growth of civil aviation." Second, the organization encourages aircraft design and operational skills. Third, it attempts to improve airports, air navigation, airways and air facilities in general. The ICAO also strives to prevent unreasonable competition which threatens to waste resources, to guarantee the right of contracting parties to operate international air transport, to prevent discrimination against or between contracting parties, and to provide technical assistance to developing countries. Top priority is given to the security of international civil aviation. This takes on particular significance when considering the periodic "sky-jacking" and aerial bombing episodes which have terrorized air line passengers from a number of countries. The ICAO convened a conference on Air Law in 1988 that ended in the signing by 47 countries, including the United States, of a protocol on unlawful acts of violence in civil aviation. This protocol serves to supplement the 1971 Montreal Convention for the Suppression of Unlawful Acts Against the Safety of Civil Aviation.

Conflicts in International Civil Aviation: Safeguarding the Air Routes

Eugene Sochor

Abstract: The International Civil Aviation Organization (ICAO) has been spared the bitter confrontations and acrimonies that have reverberated in the United Nations and other agencies over the years. Since all nations, big or small, have a vested interest in the safe and orderly development of air transport which are ICAO's major objectives, it would be against the interest of any nation to jeopardize its own access to international airways. The solid confidence all states have placed in the Organization from its earliest days has helped create an environment conducive to compromise. Nonetheless, this conciliatory inclination has been tested to the limit as international and regional conflicts have drawn the Organization into political issues outside its traditional competence. This challenge has been to reconcile the sovereignty principle over the airspace with the obligation of states to assure the security of commercial air travel and the safety of air routes.

The politics of international civil aviation, like all politics in a world of nation-states, is primarily concerned with sovereign rights and national interests — in this case with airspace. For all its expanse, the sky has definite limits for civil aviation, since airlines require the safest and shortest routes to their destinations.

The basic rule of law which gives a state full and absolute sovereignty over its airspace also gives it the right to exclude foreign carriers from its territory.[1] In the absence of a multilateral system governing air services, most states have agreed to allow overflights and technical stopovers on a nondiscriminatory basis and to reserve commercial rights for bilateral agreements. Conflicts of interests are inevitable when political claims take precedence over the principle of freedom of navigation and a state closes its airspace for reasons other than hostilities or national emergency, thereby denying rights previously enjoyed by other states.[2]

Conflicts also arise when states defy international agreements and claim control over airspace which is not within their jurisdiction. The airspace around the world is divided into a series of contiguous Flight Information Regions (FIRs) within which air traffic control and flight information services are provided. Unless states decide to delegate responsibilities, they are expected to provide these services not only within their national airspace, but over oceanic areas as determined by the ICAO Council in accordance with regional air navigation plans and the capability of each country.

These conflicts are aggravated when the state responsible for providing air traffic control fails in the event of disruption of these services to institute contingency measures to ensure the safety of international flights. ICAO will step in and work out alternate routings with adjoining states only when the national authorities cannot adequately discharge their responsibilities or when specifically requested to do so by the state concerned.

Flight Information Regions which encompass the high seas may give the illusion of sovereign power beyond national territory, causing states at times to act as if they own the airspace in which they provide services. While a state has complete freedom to organize its national airspace as it sees fit, so long as it conforms with established procedures, it is not a free agent in respect of the high seas and airspace of undetermined sovereignty. The Council is specifically empowered under Article 11 (Article 2) of the Chicago Convention to apportion these areas on the basis of regional agreements and technical and operational requirements. FIR boundaries are not demarcation lines which shift according to the changing political winds. A pilot must be able to rely on clearly defined charts so that before he takes off he knows exactly what to expect in the way of navigation and communications facilities. Since undefined or contested boundaries can create safety hazards, the aviation community cannot tolerate confusing situations brought about by states extending their rivalries over the airspace outside their jurisdiction.

Since a state is the only judge of its actions when it contests ICAO-approved boundaries or when it closes its airspace to press a political claim, it is up to the other states concerned to protect their interests and ensure the safety of air travel. Those who doubt the ability of states to settle their conflicts through bilateral negotiations or mediation look to the regulatory capacity of the system to bring about a solution.

In this regard, the International Civil Aviation Organization (ICAO) is an interesting subject of study. As a regulatory regime within the United Nations system, it possesses distinctive attributes such as a double-headed executive consisting of a council president concerned with political matters and a secretary general who is the top administrator. Both are international public servants who cannot seek nor accept instructions from any authority external to the Organization.[3] The most noteworthy feature of the Organization is a permanent governing body (presently consisting of thirty-three states elected by the assembly) which provides immediate channels of communications in times of crisis. The ICAO Council, which has final authority in setting the Standards and Recommended Practices governing all aspects of civil aviation worldwide, is also unique among United Nations bodies in that it is empowered to act as a tribunal to settle disputes which affect the safety, efficiency, and regularity of air transport. This article focuses on current conflicts which affect the continued operations of international routes and assesses the effectiveness of the conflict management mechanisms within ICAO. Effectiveness, according to Haas, consists in the ability of the international community to use "the routines enshrined in the principles, norms, rules and procedures to moderate successfully the conflicts" referred to an organization.[4] A corollary is the capacity of an organization to modify its constitutional charter or find pragmatic solutions outside the prescribed mechanisms. An example in the case of ICAO is the way the Organization has used the adjudicative process in conflict management.

The Council as Tribunal

Under the provisions of Chapter XVIII of the Chicago Convention, the ICAO Council is specifically charged with adjudicating disputes between states concerning the interpretation or applicability of the terms of the Convention and its annexes. This was thought to be the first postwar mechanism for the pacific settlement of disputes incorporated in an international instrument and, as such, it was hailed as a significant innovation in international law.[5]
    Specifically under Articles 84-88, the Council is empowered to adjudicate any disagreement between two or more contracting states relating to disputes which cannot be settled by negotiation. The Council must decide such a dispute "on the application of any state concerned in the disagreement." The council's decision may be appealed either to the International Court of Justice or to an ad hoc international tribunal whose judgment shall be final and binding. The Council under Article 66 also assumed judicial functions (including the settlement of differences and the hearing of complaints) with respect to the International Air Services Transit and Air Transport Agreements. Several other multilateral conventions signed under the auspices of ICAO refer to the council's jurisdiction for the settlement of

disputes. The judicial cases before the Council had in common the arbitrary suspension of overflights. Under Article 9 of the Chicago Convention each state is free to restrict or prohibit the aircraft of other states from flying over certain areas of its territory provided that the same applies for the aircraft of the state concerned. The qualifying criterion is that such prohibited areas should be of reasonable extent and location so as not to interfere unnecessarily with air navigation.

In the first case, presented in 1952, India alleged discrimination under Articles 5 and 9 of the Chicago Convention when it claimed that it was not allowed overflights over a prohibited zone along the Pakistani border with Afghanistan when aircraft of other countries were permitted to do so. The second case, in 1967, involved the United Kingdom against Spain over a prohibited zone in the Bay of Algeciras opposite the airport of Gibraltar. In 1971, it was Pakistan's turn to file charges against India after that country suspended all overflights by Pakistani aircraft over its territory.

The Council did not make any decision in the first case, although it helped the parties reach an amicable settlement. The second case was adjourned *sine die* when the parties decided to negotiate their differences in the United Nations and on a bilateral basis. Milde has noted that technically the Gibraltar case is still pending before the Council and could be revived at any time.[6] Action on the underlying political problem has long since shifted to the U.N. Fourth Committee and more recently to the European Economic Community (EEC), where the status of Gibraltar Airport almost brought to a standstill the plans for the liberalization of Europe's air transport system. As Fox puts it: "Here is an example of a dispute which could be settled only by the two parties agreeing to continue to disagree until time and changed circumstances caused both to forget about it, or by changed circumstances which would incline Britain to negotiate the Spanish claim seriously."[7]

The third case was the most contentious as it arose against the background of armed hostilities between the two countries and the alleged complicity of Pakistan in the hijacking and subsequent destruction of an Indian aircraft in

Lahore in full view of TV cameras. The underlying problem was the confrontation over Kashmir which led India to suspend the overflights by Pakistani aircraft, thereby cutting off air communications between West and East Pakistan. India questioned the jurisdiction of the ICAO Council, arguing that the suspension was the result of hostilities. Eventually the case went to the International Court of Justice, which ruled that the Council did have jurisdiction to entertain Pakistan's application. With the creation of an independent Bangladesh in East Pakistan, the matter was not pursued and the proceedings were discontinued by mutual agreement.[8]

Early misgivings as to whether the Council could be expected to fulfill its judicial mandate in a political confrontation proved to be well founded in the last case.[9] At one point in the proceedings, several council members requested a postponement on a vote to seek instructions from their respective governments. When Article XVIII was drafted in 1944, the participants in the Chicago Conference had visualized that the council would become a tribunal composed of impartial judges to settle disputes between states. It was an unrealistic expectation, since council members do not act in their individual capacity but only as spokesmen of their respective governments. Consequently, as Milde has pointed out, "The Council cannot be considered to be a true judicial body composed of judges who would be deciding strictly and exclusively on the basis of respect for law."[10]

It is significant that in none of the three cases in which the judicial machinery of Chapter XVIII has been invoked did the Council take any decision on the merits of the case. Equally significant is the fact that all cases were aviation disputes arising against the background of a larger political dispute. Morgenthau has underscored the problem of reconciling legal claims with conflicts of power and concluded that political disputes which affect the overall distribution of power between two nations cannot be settled by judicial methods.[11]

The disuse of the Council's judicial process is shown in the way India has handled further grievances against Pakistan. In a complaint to the Council president, India in

1985 accused Pakistan of arming the hijackers of an Indian Boeing 737 during a stopover in Lahore. The Boeing, with a full complement of passengers, was taken over by Sikh extremists after it took off from Lahore. It was subsequently flown to Karachi for refueling and on to Dubai where the incident ended with the release of the passengers and the arrest of the offenders. The Indian complaint citing Pakistan's "encouragement and cooperation with the hijackers" requested ICAO to take "appropriate measures."[12] India did not, however, call for a Council meeting, so that there was in fact no follow-up on its complaint.

The Nonjudicial Means for Settling Disputes

Short of invoking the judicial machinery of Chapter XVIII, states can rely on other provisions of the Chicago Convention to air their grievances before the Council. Under Article 54, it is incumbent on the Council "to report to contracting states any infraction of the convention" and to report to the assembly "any infraction where a state has failed to take appropriate action within a reasonable time after notice of the infraction." Under the same Article (n), the Council must consider "any matter relating to the convention which any contracting state refers to it." The latter provision is so broadly worded as to invite any type of grievances, ranging from the strictly technical or legal to those with obvious political implications.

Milde has rightly observed that the nonjudicial proceedings under Article 54 (n) have been used when adjudication would have been fully justifiable. A typical example is the protest of Nigeria in 1967 against Portugal concerning flights from the then Portuguese territory of Sao Tome to Port Hartcourt to supply rebels in Biafra with arms and other supplies. Milde has stated that if the allegations were proved true, Portugal would have violated provisions of the Chicago Convention with respect to the sovereignty of Nigeria (Article 1 and 2), misuse of civil aviation (Article 4) and violation of a prohibited zone (Article 9). The Council procrastinated with the matter for some eighteen months, during which time fact-finding questions were addressed to both parties. Finally, in June 1969, Nigeria requested that the matter be postponed *sine die*, by which time the situation in Biafra was settled.   Nigeria's action, however, did have a positive outcome in that the controversial flights stopped shortly after the filing of the complaint.[13]

It is clear that when alleged infractions are part of an underlying political dispute, states are more inclined to seek redress through the political process under Article 54 than through the judicial process, the more so if they can be assured a majority vote on the Council.

Under the circumstances, the Organization has been understandably careful not to take sides even when states have designated restricted zones in apparent violation of international procedures.   In one such case, Chile in 1978 abruptly deleted a segment of an international route which provided the most direct routing for the ten weekly flights between La Paz and Santiago.   Chile's action, which caused heavy penalties to landlocked Bolivia, was allegedly taken to relocate radio navigational aids.   The move was clearly political, coming after Bolivia had broken off diplomatic relations over protracted negotiations on the question of its access to the sea.   In the meantime Bolivia had imposed restrictions of its own but was quietly dissuaded from bringing a complaint before the council.   The issue was therefore never raised officially and does not appear in official records.

The Evolving Role of the Council President

As ICAO became involved in a growing number of conflicts, the council president gradually assumed a more prominent role as an arbiter and conciliator.   This is unusual since he is not specifically assigned such a role under Article 51 of the Chicago Convention, which spells out his responsibilities. Not only is the Chicago Convention silent on the president's good offices, but the Council, in defining the circumstances in which these would be made available with respect to unlawful interference with civil aviation, specifically limited the scope of ICAO's action.   It decided *inter alia* that "good offices shall be made available to contracting states only if the Council satisfies itself that in the specific case ICAO is not likely to be involved in questions of a political nature or in disputes between two or more states...."[14]

Notwithstanding the limitations imposed on his authority as an agent of the Council, the current president (Assad Kotaite) has increasingly used his influence to bring the parties involved in a dispute to refrain from interfering with international air operations. Most of the President's missions have revolved around questions of the safety of air routes in various trouble spots of the world. He has on numerous occasions been able to moderate conflicts before they developed into confrontations.

In fact, as soon as he took office, he was asked by the Council to use his good offices in a dispute between Senegal and Cape Verde over flight information services to be provided over a portion of the ocean intersecting the heavy north-west/south-east traffic flow between Dakar and North America. The case was particularly sensitive because it affected major air routes and brought into conflict the aspirations of a small outsider which wanted to reap some of the economic benefits of this traffic and was challenging the dominant joint air traffic control system created by the Francophone African States with French help. The President's mediation efforts resulted in a compromise to split the disputed flight area between the two countries.

Such good offices have also resulted in opening an air corridor in the South China Seas after China closed its airspace in the vicinity of Hainan Island, affecting traffic on the main air route to Hong Kong. Efforts are still under way for opening a shorter route between China and Japan over the divided sky of Korea — the President acting in this case as the middleman between states which do not have diplomatic relations. His effectiveness has been dependent on the willingness of the parties concerned to extricate the purely technical problems from their political context.

Diplomatic Moves in the Far East

These diplomatic efforts have resulted in the improvement of the route structure over the Indochina peninsula and the South China Sea, particularly with respect to the use of the Amber-1 route. This airway, which carries the heavy traffic between Europe and the Far East, has been discontinued following the closure of the airspace over Indochina in 1975. As a result, ICAO found it necessary to establish a network of contingency routings over the South China Sea to avoid the peninsula. The unification of Vietnam allowed Hanoi to reactivate the direct route Bangkok-Danang — Hong Kong on Amber-1, following talks in Vientiane in February 1978 initiated by the Council President and attended by Thailand, Laos, Vietnam, and the United Kingdom (representing Hong Kong). The successful outcome of the meeting also opened the way for Vietnam to join ICAO in 1980.[15]

The reactivation of the Far-Eastern segment of Amber-1 was followed by the opening later that year of the more direct routing Manila-Lubang-Danang-Bangkok, which resulted in a considerable saving in time and fuel for the airlines. The military skirmishes between Thailand and Kampuchea on the one hand and between Kampuchea and Vietnam on the other have prevented further improvements.

International air traffic in the Far East faced a more serious problem in 1980 as the result of renewed tension between China and Vietnam, when China designated four danger areas over the high sea along Amber-1 in the vicinity of Hainan Island.[16] The restrictions forced international flights to use a costly detour on the Bangkok — Hong Kong segment of the route. The Chinese relented, following consultations with the Council President. While maintaining that their action was motivated by safety considerations to prevent aircraft from straying into Chinese airspace, they nevertheless agreed to allow flights at certain hours, as well as to other temporary measures to improve operating conditions.[17]

More complicated are the consultations with China, Japan, and the two Koreas for the purpose of establishing shorter air routes between points in China and Japan. These talks are linked to the subtle shifts of relationships that have kept tensions high on the Korean peninsula for more than thirty years. They concern a northern route Beijing-Tokyo through Pyongyang, a middle route Beijing-Tokyo through Pyongyang, a middle route Beijing-Tokyo through Taegu (Republic of Korea), and a southern route Shanghai-Tokyo over the high seas. After prolonged consultations, the President was able to report that all the parties had accepted the southern route, thereby considerably reducing the flying time between China and Japan.[18] The corridor allows nearly 100 flights per week, one third of them operating nonstop to Beijing pending the opening of the shorter northern route. As for North Korea, it agreed to opening its airspace for a northern route to all civil aircraft (including U.S. carriers) without discrimination; but permission to operate on the route would have to be obtained on the basis of bilateral negotiations with the states concerned.[19] The route has yet to be inaugurated. The settlement hinges on agreement of North Korea to the middle route via Seoul (which would mean its tacit recognition of two Koreas) and that of South Korea to the northern route, which is conditional on Korean Air Line being given the right to fly over North Korea in order to compete with airlines using the trans-Siberian route between the Far East and Europe.

The real issue seems to be that the northern routing favored by North Korea has the support of China, while the middle route over South Korea is supported by Japan. North Korea would seem to be motivated by ambivalent feelings towards Japan. While seeking closer ties, it has criticized that country for its friendly relations with the United States and South Korea. The biggest stumbling block, however, is the continued animosity between the two Koreas.[20]

The airlines operating to and from Hong Kong, which at present use a circuitous route over Pakistan, have also complained about the route restrictions on the Central Asia segment of Amber-1. After initial talks with representatives of Afghanistan, India, and Pakistan in 1983, the Council President reported that Afghanistan had agreed to a more direct routing between Delhi and Kabul via Islamabad. Also, various technical measures would be taken by the state concerned to provide direct communication between the area control centers.[21] These efforts admittedly have not yielded the expected results due to the continuing tension on Pakistan's northern border with Afghanistan.

Military and Political Maneuvers Over the Aegean Sea

For years, ICAO has been trying to resolve an intractable issue between Greece and Turkey concerning the realignment of an air route linking northern Europe to Greece to improve the flow of traffic and ease congestion on an important vacation destination. While on the surface this realignment is of a purely operational and technical nature, it involves a segment over the Aegean Sea (between Limnos and Mesta) which Turkey finds unacceptable on the grounds that it would affect its freedom to conduct naval and air exercises in the area. Turkey further contends that the geographical configuration of the Aegean Sea does not provide other sites for such exercises.

Even though Greece and Turkey are both members of NATO, the dispute has led to innumerable complaints by Turkey of harassment and interceptions by Greek fighters during military maneuvers in Greek-controlled airspace even though prior clearance had been obtained and flight plans filed according to ICAO procedures. The fact that the realignment had first originated in the European Air Navigation Plan and had been approved in line with a Council resolution did not deter Turkey, which saw in the move "the predominantly political objective of excluding Turkey from freely using the international airspace of the Aegean."[22] The realignment of the air route is part of a broader agenda which has bedeviled Greek-Turkish relations for years: Turkish exploration rights on the Aegean continental shelf claimed by Greece, the limit of Greek territorial waters; the militarization of the Greek islands off the coast of Turkey; and, finally, the unresolved problem of Cyprus, which has brought the two countries to the verge of war a number of times.

The specific issue of airspace control arose as a result of the 1974 crisis on Cyprus. Turkey challenged the arrangements existing since 1952 and contested a presidential decree extending the Greek airspace to ten miles beyond the Greek coast so as to cover the Lemnos terminal area and the NATO operational control areas. On August 4, 1974, Turkey advised all carriers operating in the region to contact Izmir instead of the Athens control center when approaching the Turkish coast. Since this unilateral action by Turkey affected international flights over several Greek islands, Greece closed the Aegean air corridors as unsafe. These air corridors were reopened early in 1980 when, in order to facilitate the reintegration of Greece in NATO, Turkey no longer insisted on its demand.[23]

The issue of airspace control in the Aegean, yet to be resolved, has clearly placed ICAO in a predicament since the organization is committed to speeding the flow of traffic on the congested air routes of Europe. It has been a recurrent headache for the ICAO Regional Office in Paris, which has bravely attempted to coordinate such efforts, and for the Air Navigation Commission — the ICAO Council's technical body — which has tried so far in vain to find a solution acceptable to both parties. The Council itself has been loath to take a firm position on the matter and to exert sufficient pressure on the two NATO partners to settle their differences.

It is a case which on the surface would require arbitration to reconcile opposing interests and conflicting interpretations of the Chicago Convention. Neither party in the conflict has so far shown an inclination to do so in the context of their wider quarrel. Unlike the sea bed issue, which almost resulted in a military confrontation in April 1987 over a Turkish threat to start prospecting for oil in the Aegean sea bed, there are with respect to the airspace no hard-core economic arguments involved. Various technical questions might be resolved by arbitration with respect to the obligations of states under Article 3(d) of the Chicago Convention and problems of coordination between civil and military aircraft under Annex 11 (Air Traffic Services).

There have been intermittent attempts in the past to seek a negotiated settlement on some of the issues at the level of technical experts and in the context of the seasonal NATO meetings. However, Greece's preference for the adjudication of outstanding issues has met with Turkey's persistent demand for a political settlement.[24]

Rivalries in the Cypriot Sky

Cyprus has been a thorn for the United Nations ever since a peacekeeping force was installed on the island in 1964 to separate the embattled Greek and Turkish communities. It became a perennial issue as well for ICAO in 1974, when Turkey launched a largescale military operation and established a de facto Turkish Cypriot government in a northern enclave of the island.

Turkey meanwhile tried to assert control over the airspace and requested pilots to contact the Ankara Area Control center while operating within the Nicosia flight region. This was followed by the promulgation of a NOTAM (Notice to Airmen) in March 1977 announcing the establishment of the "ERCAN" FIR as the only authorized flight information center in the area.[25]

The existence of two Flight Information Centers inevitably created confusion for airlines using the air corridors over the region. Turkey's insistence that all aircraft take guidance from the "ERCAN" FIR, combined with the fact that this service was not recognized by ICAO and was therefore not listed in the European Regional Plan, brought repeated complaints and calls for action from Greek and Cypriot authorities as well as airlines and pilots associations.

The ICAO position was made clear in a circular by the ICAO president (March 18, 1977). This circular states that the creation of the ERCAN advisory airspace was illegal and that the responsibility for providing air traffic services rested with the Nicosia Air Control Center in accordance with established ICAO provisions.[26] The International Air Transport Association (IATA) entered into the picture when Turkish Cypriot authorities refused to discuss the matter and advised its member airlines to remain in strict accord with the ICAO position and not to accept instructions from the "ERCAN" station without informing the Nicosia Center.

IFALPA — the International Federation of Air Line Pilots Associations — has been particularly concerned about the deadlock, which it claims has caused the situation to deteriorate to the point of endangering civil air transport. An IFALPA memorandum notes that "pilots overflying the northern Nicosia FIR maintain two-way radio contact with at least two and often three air traffic control centers simultaneously. The combination of heavy traffic congestion in a small area, the absence of coordination between adjacent ACCs and the assignment of conflicting flight levels to aircraft in the vicinity can only jeopardize the safety of flight operations through the whole area." Furthermore, in 1982 and again in 1984 the IFALPA Conference classified the northern position of Nicosia FIR and adjacent air spaces as "critically deficient."[27] Since then radar facilities have been installed or ordered to alleviate these deficiencies.

Cyprus has raised the illegal operation of the "ERCAN" station at various ICAO assemblies, calling it "the most flagrant violation of international procedures and practices."[28] Thus far, the aviation community has learned to live with the political status quo. The periods of crises and lulls seem to follow an established pattern in that they appear to relate to the prevailing political climate and the ups and down of the diplomatic moves with respect to the Aegean Sea.[29]

The Gulf War and the International Routes

The worst trouble spot with respect to civil aviation has been the Gulf area, where the protracted hostilities have long threatened the safety of air routes. The organization has also been enmeshed in a web of conflicting defense interests and boundary disputes of the flight information sectors assigned to the Gulf states.

The protracted conflict between Iran and Iraq inevitably became a concern for ICAO when the two warring countries threatened to interfere with international traffic over their airspace. This threat was particularly ominous for the world's airlines flying dangerously close to the Iranian airspace in the Gulf of Oman along the Amber-1 route to the Far East.

Air safety had already become a concern in Iran in the turmoil that preceded the takeover by Ayatollah Khomeini in February 1979. With erratic Air Traffic Control and Communications being provided by the military or being improvised by the airlines, air operations were deemed so risky that IFALPA urged the cessation of all flights except for evacuation purposes. Overflights over Iran had already been suspended. On behalf of the airlines concerned, IATA sent a mission to Teheran, which found the situation worse than expected. Under these circumstances, the Council President sent an urgent cable to the Iranian Foreign Affairs Minister on January 12, 1979, offering "all possible assistance by ICAO in the interest of safety of operation of international civil aviation."[30] No acknowledgment was ever received.

With a number of airlines suspending operations into

Iran and avoiding Iranian airspace, the council president was able to secure the cooperation of Bahrain to provide air traffic services to international flights over the water portion of the Teheran FIR, thus assuring direct routings between Europe and Southeast Asian destinations.

Fast-moving developments required the council president to take immediate action on his own. This was the case when Iran on November 26, 1979, at the height of the U.S. Embassy hostage crisis, warned international air carriers flying to Teheran and overflying Iranian territory to maintain altitudes of more than 15,000 feet and not to stray from established airways, or they would face the risk of being shot down by Iranian air force fighters. Iran's decision requiring airlines to establish contact with Iranian Air Defense or submit a flight plan caused consternation among airlines, considering the history of poor communications control in the area. The day after the order was issued, the Council President cabled Iran to warn of the danger to international flights on account of the difficulties of complying with the requirements. He also called attention to the provisions of Annex 2 (Rules of the Air) to the effect that intercepting aircraft should refrain from the use of weapons. The admonition proved to be effective, since Iran rescinded its threat to use force against straying aircraft.[31]

The modified stand did not for that matter allay the fears of the airlines, since Iran was still using old interception procedures which predated those in the current ICAO Annex, the notable difference being air-to-air signaling which was not familiar to most airline pilots. The situation was somewhat eased when Iran sent an advisory to airlines operating into its airspace that their fears were groundless and that interception would only be used as a last resort and according to ICAO-approved procedures. To overcome the air communications deficiencies, the council president formally requested Bahrain to provide Air Traffic Control services along Route R-21 within the Teheran flight region. He received the accord of Bahrain in spite of that country's continuing suspicions of Iran's intentions.[32]

The semblance of normalcy in air operations was shattered when the border dispute between Iran and Iraq erupted into open warfare on September 27, 1980.

Immediately after the start of hostilities, both Iraq and Iran
closed their airspace to commercial flights, causing delays on
the trunk route A-1 at a time of heavy traffic during the Haj
pilgrimage season. Problems were also encountered at other
route crossings affecting traffic over the Gulf.

Following urgent consultations with Iran, Iraq, and the
Gulf States, Bahrain was once again called upon to assume
temporary responsibility for services on the high sea portion
of international routes (B-56 and R-21) in the Teheran FIR.
Similar consultations resulted in relieving congestion on
traffic originating from European, Far East, and Gulf airports
through alternate routings at a safe distance from the Iranian
coast.[33] The contingency routes through Saudi Arabia and
the Southern part of the Gulf, which required Saudi Arabia,
Bahrain, Kuwait, Jordan, and Syria to provide emergency
services with little notice, represent a remarkable (albeit little
publicized) example of international cooperation in civil
aviation.

Despite occasional delays and problems of coordination,
the contingency plans have worked out well. There was some
concern when the Iranian military authorities in November
1983 threatened to fire upon any aircraft overflying Iranian
offshore installations.   The identified area presumably
included the important routings outside Iranian airspace and
within the Bahrain Flight Information Region. As a result,
the airlines felt the threat covered all the civil operations in
the international waters of the Gulf.   Because of safety
considerations, Bahrain closed its sector of the Route A-1.
The situation was finally resolved when the Iran Civil
Aviation authorities gave assurances that the order in
question was invalid and had not been authorized by the
highest military authorities.[34]

As for Iraq, notwithstanding the fact that there had
never been a formal declaration of war, it officially notified
ICAO in October 1980 that a state of emergency existed
under Article 89 of the Chicago Convention and that it would
therefore not be able to comply with any or all the provisions
of the convention. The state of emergency became an
immediate danger at the height of a fierce battle for the
control of a strategic road to Basra, when Iraq warned all
airlines to stay out of Iranian airspace or face the

consequences. The Notice to Airmen NOTAM (No. 9016) issued on March 17, 1985 was immediately circulated to the ICAO Council, along with a strong protest by Iran, while the council president cabled Iraq to make sure that there would be "neither interruption nor cessation of civil flight operations on international routes."[35]

The seriousness of the situation was underscored when an Iraqi military spokesman warned international carriers that Iranian airspace would be "a prohibited war zone" and that Iraq intended to continue air attacks on Iranian cities and would not be responsible for the safety of commercial aircraft. The Iraqi NOTAM had a chilling effect on the airlines still operating in Iran, leading them to cancel their operations and leaving Iran Air as a possible target. The NOTAM also caused uncertainty for international carriers using Route A-1.

While developments in the Iran-Iraq conflict were left to the discretion of the president, Iran felt that the Iraqi threat, because of its "extra-territorial extensions of authority and unlawful interference with civil aviation," required council action. It therefore requested an urgent meeting of that body under Article 54(n) of the Chicago Convention.

The ICAO Council took an even-handed attitude when it debated the Iran-Iraq issue. After a two-day Extraordinary Session (April 22-23, 1985), it unanimously urged both countries to take immediate steps to assure the safety of civil aviation along international routes. It was left for the Council President to seek the withdrawal or cancellation of the controversial Iraqi NOTAM.[36] There followed numerous cables and repeated complaints from Iran about Iraq's noncompliance with the Council's decision. Without formally withdrawing its NOTAM, Iraq, however, gave formal assurances that international traffic would not be affected.[37]

Unrelated to the Iran-Iraq conflict, but very much central to the safety of the air routes over the Gulf, is the mini-dispute involving Qatar and Bahrain over the ownership of the minuscule Fasht al Dibal island, which caused Qatar to launch a military attack and dismantle the sandbar in April 1986. The otherwise minor incident had immediate effect on civil aviation, given the strategic importance of the various Gulf states in assuring the flow of air traffic in the area. The closure by Qatar of its airspace to overflights in April 1986 because of defense considerations caused serious congestions and disruptions affecting all airports in the Gulf area. The situation was made even worse when Bahrain, citing unauthorized military activity near its airport, established a restricted area which encroached upon the territory of Qatar and Saudi Arabia. Qatar, as expected, objected to this violation of its sovereignty. Bahrain rejected the objection and vowed to continue "to use the area for its aviation in an unrestricted manner." It said the restrictions were justified to protect civil aircraft from encroaching in a military danger zone that affected only a small segment of route B-39 (Dhahran-Doha).[38]

The Council President expressed the concern of the airlines in personal visits to the four Gulf states in March 1987 and asked them to return to the "status quo" existing before the restrictions or seek adjustments in the approved Air Navigation Plan through the normal process of securing the agreement of all the parties concerned. Even after this goodwill mission, the United Arab Emirate issued a NOTAM on June 22, 1987 banning overflights of its oil installations, thereby forcing all traffic into a single airway. Qatar and the UAE eventually agreed to the modus operandi proposed by the council president and issued a joint NOTAM after a meeting in Abu Dhabi to smooth the transfer of traffic to other routes. Bahrain also temporarily lifted some of the restrictions which would have stopped all traffic on the Dhahran-Doha segment of Route B-59.[39] The lifting of the remaining restrictions would require a political solution which is still eluding Saudi mediation efforts after the failure on an agreement at the Islamic Summit Conference in Kuwait (January 1987).[40]

There have been also several other disputes involving FIR boundaries which, however, have had little impact on international traffic. One such case has involved Saudi Arabia and the People's Democratic Republic of Yemen. The controversy regarding the boundary between the Aden and Jeddah FIRs has had its roots in the fact that national borders in the area are largely undetermined. In another such dispute, Iraq has long claimed jurisdiction of disputed airspace over the high seas which had been assigned to the

Teheran FIR. In this case, the continued promulgation by Iraq of conflicting aeronautical information tended to confuse pilots and forced the Council President to send a stern reminder to Iraq that it was acting against the provisions of Annex 11 covering air traffic services and relevant council decisions.[41]

Conclusion

"Even though the principles of sovereignty and the absence of a superior authority limit the degree of confidence placed in international agreements, states engaged in open conflict can still find it possible to cooperate."[42] This observation by Keohane is borne out in conflicts affecting civil aviation in which the states concerned have cooperated with ICAO to avoid a serious disruption of international traffic in their particular region.

Conflict management mechanisms may exist and yet not be used, as in the case of ICAO. If so, an organization must find pragmatic solutions which are not challenged by the prevailing consensus. As noted by Buergenthal, ICAO has demonstrated an unusual capacity for reshaping the Chicago Convention without going through a cumbersome amendment process which would have challenged such consensus.[43] A noteworthy development brought about by the reluctance of states to resort to the judicial process in ICAO, as envisaged in the Chicago Convention, and the inability of the Council to resolve conflicts which are essentially political in nature, has been the gradual evolution of the office of the Council President. The President, whose authority flows from the council, has tried to exert a restraining influence in critical situations, but he cannot be expected to resolve political differences unless the parties concerned are predisposed to do so or can agree on their technical aspects.

Regardless of personal qualities and the perception he has of his role, the council president is too much an agent of that body to perform as an autonomous actor in the international system. Nevertheless, when the need has arisen, he has acted with skill and he has effectively used his good offices to uphold the principles and norms which guarantee the safe and unrestricted movement of people and goods across international routes. These attributes, however, cannot make up for the failure of the council to act decisively against states which do not comply with their international obligations. At best, as has been said of the U.N. Secretary General, "He can only speak with the voice of a universal conscience, even if his voice is muted, his admonitions faintly heard and his advice often unheeded."[44]

NOTES

1. The basic instrument which governs all aspects of international air transport is the Convention on International Civil Aviation signed in Chicago in 1944, now ratified by 160 states which together compose the International Civil Aviation Organization (ICAO). The ninety-six articles of the Chicago Convention establish the privileges and obligations of all contracting states and provide for the adoption by the ICAO Council of international standards and recommended practices covering all aspects of civil aviation. The convention accepts the principle that every state has complete and exclusive sovereignty over the airspace above its territory (Article 1) and provides that no scheduled international air service may operate over or into the territory of contracting state without its previous consent (Article 6). The Chicago Conference was unable to reach agreement on the exchange of commercial rights in international civil aviation. It therefore also set up two supplementary agreements: the International Air Services Transit Agreement and the International Air Transport Agreement. The first, ratified by 100 countries, made provisions for aircraft of any signatory power to fly over or to land for technical reasons in the territory of any other signatory. The second agreement, which has never come into force, provided among other things for the carriage of traffic between the state of registration of the aircraft and any other signatory state.

2. Article 89 of the Chicago Convention, which gives states the right to suspend provisions of the convention in case of war or emergency conditions upon due notification to the council, raises several problems of interpretation since it applies equally to both circumstances. If, however, a state of

war can be readily determined, this is not the case with a state of emergency. Fitzgerald has pointed out that such a declaration to the council presumably would be based on military necessity or public safety. On that basis, he doubts that an international tribunal faced with this problem would accept a subjective determination and would need to review the conditions which led to the declaration. Gerald Fitzgerald, Lecture, Institute of Air and Space Law, McGill University, Montreal.

3.   The council has had only three presidents during its whole history: Dr. Edward Warner (USA) 1947-58; Walter Binaghi (Argentina) 1958-76; and Dr. Assad Kotaite (Lebanon) since 1976.

4.   Ernest B. Haas, "Regime Decay: Conflict Management and International Organizations, 1945-1981," *International Organization* 37, no. 2, (1983), 193.

5.   J. Schenkman, *International Civil Aviation Organization* (Geneva: H. Studer, 1955), 376.

6.   M. Milde, "Dispute Settlement in the Framework of the International Civil Aviation Organization (ICAO)," *Studies in Air and Space Law* (Koln: Carl Heymanns Verlag, 1979), 91.

7.   William T. R. Fox, "World Politics as Conflict Resolution," in Matthews, Ruhnoff, and Stein, eds., *International Conflict and Conflict Management* (Scarborough: Prentice-Hall of Canada, 1984), 10. See also Paul Delaney, "283 Years Later, Dispute Over Gibraltar Persists," *New York Times* (30 July 1987), A15. *Interavia Air Letter*, No. 11.277 (30 June 1987).

8.   Milde, op. cit., 93. The Indian position is outlined in S.K. Agrawala, *Aircraft, Hijacking and International Law* (Dobbs Ferry, N.Y.: Oceana Publications, 1973), Chapter 10.

9.   Dr. Edward Warner, the first Council President, wrote in 1945:   "No international agency composed of representatives of states could be expected to bring judicial detachment to the consideration of particular cases in which large national interests were involved...."   "The Chicago Air Conference," *Foreign Affairs* (April 1954). His two successors have expressed similar reservations.

10.   Milde, op. cit., 90.

11.   Hans J. Morgenthau, *Politics Among Nations* (New

York: Alfred A. Knopf, 1973), 425. Morgenthau specifically refers to the Kashmir issue and Nehru's rejection of a resolution of the United Nations Security Council calling for arbitration of the India-Pakistan dispute. As Nehru put it: "Great political questions — and this is a great political question — are not handed over in this way to arbitrators from foreign countries or any country."

12. *The Times of India*, New Delhi (19 December 1984); and *Patriot*, New Delhi (19 December 1984).

13. Milde, op. cit., 92.

14. "Good Offices of ICAO," ICAO Document, C-WP/5211, 71st Session of the Council (1970).

15. Air Traffic Services, Southeast Asia Region, AN 13/4.5, Vol. 3, ICAO Archives.

16. The area in question had been a matter of dispute since China in 1974 defeated a Vietnam naval force and reiterated its long-standing claim over Hainan. (See Marwyn S. Samuels, *Contest for the South China Sea* [New York: Methuen, 1982].)

17. President's memoranda to the council, 15 October 1979, 17 January 1980, and 15 July 1981.

18. President's memorandum to the council, 10 February 1983, and ICAO Press Release, PIO 9/83. To avoid signing a formal agreement, a memorandum of understanding was signed by ICAO with each of the states concerned.

19. President's memorandum to the council, 10 February 1983. Report of the president to the council, C-WP/7365, 11 November 1981.

20. As dramatically illustrated recently by South Korea's suspicion that North Korea's agents had planted a bomb on a KAL Boeing 707 which went down in the Thai-Burmese jungle on November 1987 killing all 115 persons on board (Clyde Haberman, "Seoul Suggests It Suspects North in Plane Disaster," *New York Times*, 3 December 1987.) For North Korea's ambivalence see: Young Whan Kibi, "North Korea in 1984 — The Hermit Kingdom Turns Outward," *Asia Survey* XXV (1) (January 1985), 73-74.

21. President's memorandum to the council, 10 February 1983.

22. Statement by the Turkish observer to the Air

Navigation Commission, AN Min 115-17, 10 June 1987. See also Council Document C-WP/8435, 12 June 1987, and Air Navigation Commission Document AN-WP/6078, 15 May 1987.

23. Van Coufoudakis, "Greek-Turkish Relations, 1973-1983: The View from Athens," *International Security* 9, no. 4, 199.

24. Andrew Wilson, "The Aegean Dispute," Adelphi Paper No. 155 (London: International Institute for Strategic Studies, Winter 1979-80) 7.

25. ICAO Registry Files AN 13/4.2, Vol. 17. The only international carrier using ERCAN is Turkish Airlines.

26. Ibid.

27. Memorandum from IFALPA to the Secretary General of ICAO, November 1984 (ICAO Registry Files AN 13/4.2, Vol. 8).

28. Statement by the chief delegate of Cyprus to the 24th Assembly, October 1983. In a letter to the council president, he reported more than 120 incidents in 1982 and early 1983 in which aircraft were deliberately prevented from complying with instructions issued by the Nicosia FIR or were intentionally retained on the "ERCAN" frequency and issued instructions not approved or coordinated by Nicosia.

29. That the question is far from settled was made clear by a NOTAM issued by the "Turkish Republic of Northern Cyprus" and promulgated through the Turkish NOTAM Office on March 1987 designating a second international airport for the Northern part of the island.

30. Air Traffic Services, Middle East Region, AN 13/4.3, Vol. 6, ICAO Archives.

31. Idem. See also "Iran Institutes Strict Control Over Its Airspace," *Aviation Week & Space Technology* (3 December 1979).

32. Air Traffic Services, Middle East Region, Vol. 6, ICAO Archives.

33. Idem.

34. Idem.

35. President's memorandum to the council, 19 March 1985.

36. Council Minutes, C-Min, Extraordinary (1985), 194.

37. President's memorandum to the council, 26 March

1985. This assurance was repeated when he visited Baghdad two years later, Council Minutes 120/13.
    38. Air Navigation Services, Middle East Region, AN 13/4.3, Vol. 8, ICAO Archives.
    39. Idem.
    40. *The Economist Intelligence Unit*, No. 1 (1987), 10-11.
    41. Letter to the Chairman of the State Organization for Iraqi Civil Aviation, Air Navigation Services, Middle East Region, AN 13/4.3, Vol. 6, ICAO Archives.
    42. Robert Keohane, *After Hegemony* (Princeton: Princeton University Press, 1984), 62.
    43. Thomas Buergenthal, *Lawmaking in the International Civil Aviation Organization* (Syracuse University, 1969), 226.
    44. Yves Beigbeder, "Le Rôle politique, administraitif et operationnel du Secrétaire Général de l'Organisation des Nations Unies," *International Review of Administrative Sciences*, LI(4).

The views expressed in this article are solely those of the author and should not be attributed to ICAO or its Secretariat.

Chapter VIII

International Fund for Agricultural Development (IFAD)

The International Fund for Agricultural Development (IFAD) was established in 1977 after a proposal from the 1974 World Food Conference. Its membership includes 143 countries, divided into three categories. The first category contains the developed (OECD) countries, and there are twenty-one of these. The second group contains twelve OPEC countries. The third includes 110 developing countries. The governing structure of IFAD is unique in that each of the three categories of members has an equal number of votes. Decisions are, however, generally made by consensus. IFAD employs 189 regular staff members at its Rome headquarters. Its budget is financed by resources pledged by members (primarily from the OECD and OPEC countries) and in 1989 it amounted to US$36.3 million. The organization's primary task is to "fund rural development programs specifically aimed at the poorest of the world's people." IFAD sponsors agricultural development projects in developing countries which will serve to improve the lives of the landless poor and increase food production. To do so, it must mobilize additional resources in order to make grants and loans. In 1986 IFAD began a special program for sub-Saharan Africa, one of the poorest regions in the world. Many of IFAD's loans have been designated for projects designed by the World Bank and other international and regional lending institutions. IFAD contributes input on aspects of such projects related to small farmers and landless laborers.

The International Fund for Agricultural Development: The First Six Years

John Andrews King[1]

At the end of October 1984, the Governing Council of the International Fund for Agricultural Development (IFAD) ended its eighth annual meeting without agreement on the provision of financing for the Fund's investment projects and programmes for its third triennium — 1984-6. The Council, however, adopted a resolution to continue negotiations for replenishment of its funds requesting Member Countries to make advance contributions to enable operations to continue prior to the conclusion of the agreement on the second replenishment. This paper will look at IFAD's origins, structure and mandate, its operational history and its financing and attempt to indicate some of the reasons for this state of affairs.

IFAD's origins are found in the World Food Conference of November 1974, which took a new view of the world food problem by recognizing that the problems of food and nutrition in the developing countries were not the result of occasional crop failures or natural disasters, but were part and parcel of the whole fabric of underdevelopment and poverty. It concluded, therefore, that unless the employment, productivity and incomes of the rural poor could be increased, they would remain hungry and malnourished.

To attack these problems, the Conference proposed the establishment of an International Fund for Agricultural Development to mobilize additional resources for investment in agriculture. At the time, the United States was among the leaders in support of this. Basic to the proposal was the notion that contributions to IFAD would provide additional resources and oil exporters were seen as a major source of additionality. The UN General Assembly endorsed the proposal, and in due course IFAD began operations with the first meetings of its Executive Board and Governing Council in December 1977, its first two loans being approved in April 1978.

The Fund's mandate and structure set forth in the Agreement of June 1976 establishing IFAD is to finance projects and programmes specifically designed to improve food production systems particularly in the poorest food deficit countries, and to raise the incomes, productivity and nutrition of the rural poor.[2] A somewhat unusual provision requires the Fund normally not to finance projects which have a negative impact on income distribution, i.e. projects which do not provide a proportionately greater share of benefits to the poorest among the project beneficiaries. Though the Agreement may appear to permit a fairly broad approach to increasing food production in the developing world, it has been consistently interpreted as having a distinct small-farmer focus. For example, though the Fund has concentrated on increasing food production, it would probably not finance a project to increase, say, maize production by plantation agriculture, while it would consider a project to increase smallholder incomes based largely on the production of coffee or cotton if this appeared to be the best way of improving living conditions.

IFAD is, in principle, another international financial institution like, for example, the World Bank or the Regional Development Banks, charged with lending for development projects. Like them it has a Governing Council composed of representatives from each of its Member Countries; an Executive Board with responsibilities, delegated by the Governing Council, for the general operations of the Fund, including approval of loans; and a President and staff to carry out its work. But it differs from them in several important respects.

First, IFAD has a narrow mandate; it is limited to a single sector, agriculture, and within that sector its attention is directed at increasing food production and improving the productivity, incomes and nutrition of the rural poor, its sole target group. Most of the other international financial institutions have broader responsibilities and lend for a wide variety of projects in many sectors with a broad range of beneficiaries.

Second, for most of the existing international financial institutions, the great bulk of the funds available for lending for development, whether in the form of (i) contributed capital, (ii) funds borrowed in private capital markets or from public sector institutions, or (iii) grants, come from the developed countries. In the case of IFAD, however, though the OECD countries provided slightly more than half of the approximately US$1,000 m. making up its original resources, the OPEC countries, which are still developing, provided a substantial share, slightly less than half.[3] This is a major change.

Third, in the existing international financial institutions, voting power is determined largely by formulas which measure the strength and size of each country's economy or by the size of the country's contribution to the institution. This method tends to place control in the hands of the developed countries. On the other hand, in the UN General Assembly and most of its specialized agencies, the method of voting is one country, one vote, a formula which places the developed countries in a distinct minority. In IFAD the method adopted represents a middle ground. Voting power is divided equally among three categories of members: I, OECD countries; II, OPEC countries; and III, other developing countries. Within Category I, voting power is determined primarily by the size of each member's initial and any additional contributions; 82.5 per cent of the votes in that category are so allocated with the remaining 17.5 per cent being allocated equally. Within Category II, the principle is similar, with 75 per cent being allocated in proportion to size of contribution and 25 per cent equally. The votes of Category III, however, are allocated equally among members in that Category. This system of voting is a major change and gives the donors (Categories I and II) and the developing countries (Categories II and III) each an opportunity to achieve a majority. This structure is intended to permit greater interaction between North and South and to give the developing countries a larger role in influencing the management of development aid.

Fourth, existing international financial institutions normally are directly involved in the entire cycle of the projects for which they make loans, from identification and design of the project through its appraisal and implementation. Though most of the steps in the cycle are primarily the responsibility of the borrower, the lending institutions have sole responsibility (i) for appraising the technical, institutional, financial and economic soundness of the projects for which they make loans, before these are presented for approval to their respective Executive Boards, and (ii) for supervising their execution by the borrowers after they have been approved. This work is carried out by their own staff, supplemented by consultants hired by the institution for this purpose. In contrast, IFAD is directed, as a general rule, to use the services of 'international institutions' for appraisal and supervision of implementation. It is thus directly involved only in the first half of the project cycle — from identification and design through preparation. This too is a major change. It results from a compromise between (i) most of the OECD countries who were opposed to the creation of yet another international institution with the

TABLE 1: Loans and grants provided by IFAD 1978-83 (SDR m.)

	1978		1979		1980		1981		1982		1983		Total	
	No.	Amount	No.	Amount	No.	Amount	No.	Amount	No.	Amount	No.	Amount	No.	Amount
A. Loans														
Africa	2	12.1	6	43.6	8	76.4	12	101.0	7	64.1	11	103.7	46	400.9
Asia	5	63.3	5	136.8	8	99.2	9	137.0	7	98.7	6	91.9	40	626.9
Latin America	1	2.7	5	35.4	5	54.9	7	52.4	5	51.1	4	20.3	27	216.8
Near East & North Africa	—		5	53.9	6	67.7	2	14.2	6	77.5	3	32.1	22	245.4
Total loans	8	78.1	21	269.7	27	298.2	30	304.6	25	291.4	24	248.0	135	1,490.0
B. Grants[a]		—		4.4		12.1		20.3		16.4		18.3		71.6
Total loans and grants		78.1		274.1		310.3		324.9		307.8		266.3		1,561.6

a. These figures have been adjusted for provisions made for the write-off against grants for project preparation to countries receiving loans on intermediate terms which are ultimately converted into loans.

Source: IFAD, *Annual Report 1983.*

proliferation of staff and costs involved and who preferred to give the additional funds intended for this new effort to one or more established international financial institutions (for example, the World Bank) for administration, and (ii) the developing countries who regarded the established international financial institutions as donor-oriented and who wished for a new, fully fledged lending institution which would be borrower-oriented.

Operations

During its first six years ending 31 December 1983, IFAD helped to finance 135 projects through loans totalling US$1,580 m. In addition, it provided technical assistance grants, primarily for agricultural research and training, totalling US$75 m. over the same period. These funds benefited some eighty of its member countries. Table 1 provides a breakdown of these activities.

Table 2 gives an indication of the types of projects financed, but the picture presented is neater than the reality. For example, agricultural projects often contain credit or research and extension elements; rural development projects may well include irrigation or livestock sub-projects; irrigation projects are intended to increase agricultural production but are customarily listed separately because of the heavy investment costs usually required.

Table 2 indicates that IFAD has emphasized four types of projects

	% of projects	% of loans
Rural development	31.1	31.0
Agricultural development	20.0	17.0
Credit	15.6	14.9
Irrigation	14.8	21.0
	81.5	83.9

Special attention has been paid to the poorest developing countries; 67 percent of the total loan commitments, or about SDR991m. were made to countries with per capita incomes of less than US$300 (1976 dollars). The countries categorized by the UN as 'least developed' received about 31 percent of the commitments, and in its loans to countries with somewhat higher per capita incomes

IFAD has consistently sought to assist small farmers located in the poorest regions or who are otherwise at a disadvantage.

TABLE 2: Number of IFAD projects by sub-sector

Sub-sector	1978-80	1981-3	No.	Total Amount (SDR m.)[a]
Rural development	17	25	42	461.2
Agricultural development	13	14	27	252.9
Credit	10	11	21	221.3
Irrigation	8	12	20	312.8
Livestock development	3	4	7	74.0
Fisheries	1	5	6	22.2
Research/extension/training	1	5	6	52.2
Programme loan	1	3	4	62.3
Settlement	2	—	2	31.1
Total	56	79	135	1,490.0

a. Loans approved in 1978 were denominated in US$, but all subsequent loans have been denominated in Special Drawing Rights (SDR), one of IFAD's innovations. Loans in 1978 in Table 2 are based on the US$-/SDR conversion rate as of 31 December 1983. In operational terms the use of SDRs for accounting purposes leads to some distortions because all projects were conceived and appraised in current dollars.

Source: as for Table 1.

In operational terms, Table 1 indicates that IFAD got off to a quick start, presenting more than twenty projects for approval to its Executive Board in its second year. It also shows that operations have suffered since 1981 because of uncertainties relating to the replenishment of its funds after the completion of the first triennium in 1980.

As noted above, when IFAD was created it was endowed with several new features which made it different in some respects from other international financial institutions, such as the World Bank and the Regional Development Banks. These may be summarized as follows:

a) a focus on a limited area, food production, and a single target group, the rural poor;

b) a markedly increased reliance on the developing

(particularly OPEC) countries for funds, coupled with a new voting structure intended to give the developing countries greater influence in the management of development aid; and

c)   a required sharing of management of the project cycle with other international financial institutions, leaving to them the functions of project appraisal and supervision of implementation.

As far as the first of these is concerned, the Fund has had no difficulty in consistently concentrating on projects aimed at increasing food production and improving the income and living conditions of the rural poor. These objectives have been central to all the loans approved by its Executive Board. Furthermore, it has sought to apply its funds to support the 'people elements' rather than the 'bricks and mortar elements' of projects; that is, to finance agricultural extension services and the construction of the tertiary and quarternary watercourses needed to bring irrigation water to the farmers' fields rather than, say, financing big dams or housing in settlement projects.

It can also be said with considerable assurance that the narrowness of the Fund's mandate has compelled staff to work harder on conceiving, identifying and designing projects which specifically and primarily benefit the rural poor. This is not to say, however, that more could not be done in this respect. Because the rural poor are often outside the normal reach of government development activities and institutions (e.g. extension and credit) such projects are difficult to conceive and design and do require a special focus and effort. Other international financial institutions are not subject to this sort of discipline. Even in the agricultural sector, for example, an agriculture projects division in, say, the World Bank's Western Africa region might well be working at any one time on cotton or coffee production projects, pineapple or palm oil plantation projects, and smallholder rice or millet projects. If they cannot complete preparation of a suitable project benefiting the rural poor in a given country in a given year, these institutions can lend for something else, but IFAD cannot and it must work harder if it is to lend at all. The narrow focus also gave IFAD's staff a sense of purpose and dedication which strengthened its efforts. The establishment of a new and separate institution with this narrow mandate can thus be seen as a constructive step. The unique focus which it provides means that more attention is given to the needs of small farmers, the obstacles they face in increasing their production and the measures which can help them to overcome these obstacles.

IFAD's second new feature, the new voting structure, seems also to have worked reasonably well. It has not been the practice in Executive Board meetings to take formal votes; decisions are normally reached by consensus. But the underlying structure has tended to give the developing countries a greater voice in managing IFAD and directing the aid which it provides than they have in most of the other international financial institutions. This influence has been felt in two ways. First, within the Governing Council the developed countries have modified their views on a number of issues such as the level of IFAD's administrative budget or the terms and conditions of its assistance in response to views expressed by the developing countries. Second, and perhaps more important, the staff have, as a result of IFAD's origins and structure, a strong sense of service toward the developing countries and IFAD's target group. This is not to say that many individual staff members of other international financial institutions do not have similar feelings, but it has meant that the institutional climate in which projects are processed at IFAD is perhaps more borrower-oriented than at most other international financial institutions. This climate is enhanced by IFAD's strong policy of hiring a significant number of staff from developing countries; most key management and operational positions are occupied by Third World nationals. This orientation has had an important side effect. It has made borrowers more willing to accept advice and difficult but desirable conditions in loans. For example, IFAD joined the World Bank in co-financing the third of a series of projects aimed at increasing food production in a Near Eastern country with a skewed pattern of landholding. Though the Bank had tried to use these projects to improve the situation of the tenant farmers, it had been unable to secure government agreement to a change in landlord/tenant relationships. But the presence of IFAD as a co-financier helped persuade the government to agree to initiate some changes in favour of the tenants under the third project.

This 'borrower-orientation' is not, however, unbalanced. While IFAD is particularly sympathetic to borrowers' needs and sensitivities, it does set high standards for its projects in terms of economic and technical requirements and its loan agreements establish conditions which must be met. While these may be fewer than those required by other institutions, IFAD is still criticized by developing countries for being too conservative in this regard. It can be concluded, therefore, that the innovation in voting structure has produced a modest change in the management of development aid.

The third innovation, sharing management of the project cycle with other international institutions, must be regarded as less successful. Its explicit purpose was to prevent or limit a proliferation of staff and other costs associated with the creation of another international institution, and it appeared to assume that the existing international financial institutions had 'excess capacity' which would enable them to appraise and supervise the implementation of IFAD projects. It had a number of financial and operational consequences.

The first relates to the selection of projects. IFAD has two choices. One alternative is to identify projects in the pipeline of a sister institution such as the World Bank or one of the Regional Development Banks — projects which appear to fall within IFAD's mandate and to assist its target group to a reasonable degree — and co-finance such projects. Indeed, these other institutions need co-financiers for their projects and frequently invite or even press the Fund to join in. From the Fund's point of view, this approach has advantages and disadvantages. The principal advantage is cost; under the Fund's operating agreements with these sister institutions, such a project is essentially 'free' with no charges for the sister institution's costs incurred in the course of identification, preparation, appraisal or supervision of implementation (though the Fund might incur costs of its own by sending its staff to participate in one or more of the missions fielded by the sister institution). Another advantage can be flexibility; for example, co-financing in this sense may make it possible to assist a member country sooner than might otherwise be possible. The principal disadvantage of this approach is that it limits IFAD's creativity and leadership in the areas of its special responsibility. Though the Fund can and does try to modify the design of a project to make it more responsive to the needs of its target group, the possibilities are limited and the project tends to remain substantially as originally conceived and designed. Inasmuch as IFAD's creation reflects a certain dissatisfaction, at least on the part of some countries, with the existing patterns of project design and project lending as they concern the rural poor, co-financing in this sense cannot be the complete answer.

The Fund's other alternative is to help Member countries to identify, design and prepare projects which fit its mandate more closely. This approach gives it greater opportunities to be innovative. It requires (i) more IFAD staff and consultants, primarily but not exclusively for the phases of the project cycle up to appraisal, and (ii) payments to the international institution appraising the project, supervising its implementation and administering IFAD's loan, as provided in the Agreement establishing IFAD and its operating agreements with these institutions.

All projects approved in IFAD's first year were 'co-financed'; as a practical matter, if IFAD was to lend at all in that year it had to find projects already prepared and appraised and more time was needed to design and prepare 'IFAD-initiated' projects. During the next five years, slightly more than half the projects approved were 'initiated' by IFAD, for a six-year total of sixty-seven 'co-financed' and sixty-eight 'IFAD-initiated.'[4] The important issue here, of course, is not who is financing the project, but which institution took the lead in its design and preparation, and it must be recognized that a number of the projects listed as 'IFAD-initiated' were in fact substantially designed by sister institutions. As might be expected, some of the developed countries appear to prefer to limit the number of 'IFAD-initiated' projects for the reasons that led them during the period of IFAD's foundation to oppose the creation of a new and separate lending institution to carry out IFAD's objectives, while most developing countries appear to favour a larger proportion of 'Fund-initiated' projects.

There can be no question that the arrangements for sharing management of the project cycle were very effective in limiting the growth of IFAD staff. As a crude indication of this success, IFAD's Project Management Department presented an average of twenty-six professional staff; in contrast the World Bank's West Africa Region (a comparable operational unit in terms of general functions) had more than five times that number to present a somewhat higher number of projects, an average of thirty-four annually, to the Bank's Executive Board. This is not to suggest that IFAD was five times as efficient as the Bank; it was not, but a lot of work was being done elsewhere and some of it at a cost to IFAD. IFAD's co-operating institutions were hiring staff and consultants to carry out appraisals and supervision of IFAD projects and being paid by IFAD for these services under its operating agreements with them. The assumed 'excess capacity' was not there; in particular, operations were hampered by a shortage of qualified mission leaders to do the work of both institutions (partly because projects to reach the poor are particularly difficult).

Though the charges paid by IFAD under the operating agreements to its co-operating institutions for these services were reasonable (they were based on either average or actual costs, excluding overheads), the system may be less cost-effective than if IFAD had been given staff to handle appraisals and supervision itself. Apart from those few cases where the work was unsatisfactory and had to be redone, the system tends to duplicate supervision or to review it, or both, to ensure that IFAD's objectives have not been lost or diluted in the process, and to be able to apply the lessons learnt in appraising and supervising ongoing projects to the design of new ones.

More significant than financial cost, however, were the operational consequences. There can be no question that the existing international financial institutions went out of their way to co-operate with IFAD both as it was getting under way and subsequently. Without that co-operation, the Fund could not have achieved its rather remarkable success in committing its funds, particularly in its first triennium. But even with the best will in the world on both sides, there were difficulties. One of these, already alluded to, arose from the mistaken assumption that excess capacity existed in the sister institutions enabling them to process IFAD's projects as well as their own without delays or hiring additional staff. Faced with the impossibility of doing so, these institutions found it necessary in some cases to postpone appraisal of IFAD's projects, sometimes because they believed these projects were not ready for appraisal and required further preparation. With the inflexibilities imposed by its relatively small lending programme and the time required to identify, design and prepare suitable alternative projects, any postponements caused IFAD problems. It responded by seeking additional 'co-operating institutions' outside the original circle of the World Bank and the Regional Development Banks, and was successful in doing so.[5] But these new allies had only a relatively limited capacity and experience, and the Fund continued to depend heavily on the original circle. For more than half of its projects, the World Bank is the co-operating institution, and it and the three Regional Development Banks (inter-American, Asian and African) are co-operating institutions for 86 per cent of these projects.

But more difficult were the philosophical and technical differences between the co-operating institutions and IFAD which flowed from the Fund's narrow and special mandate. These differences arose for both country and project reasons. For example, the Fund might wish to proceed with a project which seemed well designed, say, to increase maize production and improve the incomes of a group of smallholders in a country where the co-operating institution had suspended lending because, say, it was seeking changes in economic and fiscal policies. In such cases, the co-operating institution usually considers it inconsistent and counter-productive to process IFAD's project, even though it may concede that it is a sound project benefiting IFAD's target group.

Differences over projects can arise in a variety of sub-sectors, but can perhaps be most clearly illustrated in agricultural and rural credit. In such projects, IFAD is usually seeking to make credit available to small farmers and the landless, groups which have traditionally not had access to institutional credit and which can only be reached through special efforts. Lending to these groups imposes additional costs and risks on the credit institution. In most countries, the agricultural financial institutions have been clients of the existing international financial institutions for a number of years, and the latter have tried, through a series of loans, to build up their financial and managerial strength and their capacity to provide credit and related services to the agriculture sector as a whole. IFAD's project, therefore, may appear, because of the additional costs and risks involved, as a threat to the credit institutions and to everything the co-operating institution has been trying to achieve. Under these circumstances, the co-operating institution may seek to modify IFAD's project in ways which make it less risky or burdensome, but at the same time less effective in reaching IFAD's target group. Or it may even refuse to proceed with it at all. Similar conflicts in objectives can arise in other subsectors as well.

Experience suggests that a further difficulty can arise because of the shift of operational responsibility from IFAD to the co-operating institution at the time of appraisal, and it is a most serious one. The ultimate objective of every IFAD project is, of course, to benefit its target group, but with this shift, attention can be diverted more easily to intermediate objectives such as the satisfactory design and economic completion of physical works or other technical issues. Of course, if IFAD had operational responsibility for the whole project cycle from identification through supervision, this could still happen because project experts like to grapple with these problems, if only because they are more familiar and more open to solution. But the shift, which removes IFAD staff with their special focus and dedication from operational responsibility for these crucial phases, increases the risk. In other words, the 'partnership' weakens the benefits provided by IFAD's narrow mandate.

Funding

These operational issues were, of course, entwined with IFAD's funding. The fact that IFAD exists as a separate institution with operations of its own is, as has been already noted, one consequence of that relationship. From the

beginning, the concept of 'rough parity' between the
contributions of the OECD and OPEC countries was
fundamental and the basis for the equal voting power of these
two blocs of donors. In the initial funding, which amounted to
US$1,052.7 m. (US$1,034.1 m., or 98 per cent from the OECD
and OPEC countries), 'rough parity' turned out to be 58 per
cent OECD and 42 per cent OPEC.[6] There does not, however,
appear to have been any real agreement on what 'rough
parity' really meant, and almost at once some OECD
countries, notably the United States, began contending that it
meant equality or something closer to equality than 58/42.

It is easy to understand this attitude. In the climate of
the late 1970s and early 1980s with declining popular support
for external aid, it would have been good for IFAD supporters
in the OECD countries to have been able to say that every
dollar they gave to the Fund was matched by a petrodollar
from the OPEC countries. But that is quite different from
contending, as some OECD countries are now doing, that
IFAD was jut another institution created for recycling
petrodollars. The history and timing seem a clear indication
to the contrary, and the amount, less than US$500 m. from
the OPEC countries in the initial funding, seems too small to
be significant in this regard.

To the call for greater equality, spokesmen for the
OPEC countries responded that by no conceivable standard —
population, territory, GNP, level of education or development — could these countries be considered 'equal' to the
OECD countries. The argument continues unresolved.

IFAD's first replenishment (for the triennium 1981-3)
took some time to negotiate and agreement was not reached
until the fifth session of the Governing Council in January
1982. In the first replenishment, 'rough parity' remained at
the same level (58/42) but the two blocs' contribution inched
down to 97 per cent of the total. The first replenishment
amounted to a total of US$1,100 m., which with a carry-over
from the first triennium of US$240 m. and net earnings on
the Fund's liquid assets would permit an operational
programme of about US$1,350 m. during 1981-3.[7] This
replenishment was seen as providing funding in real terms
about equal to the initial funding (if, of course, one ignored
the fact that slightly less than one-fifth of this total came

directly or indirectly from the initial funding). It must be added that, agreement having been reached, a number of countries, notably the United States, have been slow in providing the funds agreed.

The donors were facing a changed situation. In general, popular support for external aid was declining with the OECD countries. Soft oil prices and large internal development programmes limited the capacity of the OPEC countries to provide funds, and for some the situation was worse because of war and revolution. They have also contended publicly that, while they believe that IFAD is an important innovation in North/South relations and is an institution which they wish to support, it is not essential to their relationships with other Third World countries. For example, they have a variety of other channels for providing development aid. Thus, the climate for IFAD's second replenishment has been poor, and this is reflected in the history of negotiations, extending from July 1983 to October 1984.

As suggested above, the meaning of 'rough parity' remains the central issue, with the OPEC countries arguing that there was no historical basis for an inflexible burden-sharing ratio, and that their situation had greatly changed since 1975-8. The two blocs did agree, however, that the period to be covered by the second replenishment would be 1985-7 and that 1984 would be treated as an extension of the first. The levels of replenishment were initially seen in a range of US$0.9 billion to US$1.1 billion, a further erosion in real terms of the level of the initial funding. Negotiations indicated that this initial level was too high, and in October 1984 the OPEC countries proposed US$295 m. as their target contribution to be matched by US$465 m. from the OECD countries, leaving a gap of US$40 m. in a proposed replenishment level of US$800 m., excluding contributions from Category III. This would have left 'rough parity' at 61 per cent OECD and 39 per cent OPEC. The OECD countries responded that to an OPEC contribution of US$295 m. their contribution to replenishment would amount to only US$405 m., thus falling back to the original 'rough parity' of 58/42. Though negotiations continued, no agreement could be reached before or during the Governing Council meeting.

If IFAD has made some innovative contributions to development lending, it would seem that donors should take a more flexible view of financing so as to permit the Fund to continue its work. Current negotiating positions appear to have produced a position of stalemate, and new approaches are needed.

Underlying these negotiations, of course, were questions as to how effective IFAD has been, how different has been its practice from that of other international financial institutions, and how deserving was it of continued support.

These were hard questions to answer. It is still too early to measure the results of IFAD's lending and its effectiveness in carrying out its mandate. As of December 1983, 115 of the 135 approved projects were effective, but only three had been fully disbursed and only thirty-two (less than a quarter) had been under implementation for more than three years in an average implementation cycle of say six to eight years. A meaningful evaluation cannot be made until several years after a project has been completed and the loan fully disbursed.

Nevertheless, a number of OECD countries have undertaken studies to seek answers to these questions, including the United States, Canada and the Federal Republic of Germany. To the extent that the results of these studies are to hand they support the notion of IFAD's validity and utility as a development institution and conclude that it has been reasonably innovative in carrying out its mandate, and has demonstrated leadership in finding ways to help small farmers. The Brandt Commission, several years earlier, also concluded that the Fund was an effective institution and called for an expanded replenishment.

In addition, during 1984 the Fund itself undertook a 'mid-term evaluation' by teams of consultants of a sample group of fourteen projects (two in Africa, five in Asia, two in Latin America and the Caribbean, and five in the Middle East and North Africa). These projects, all 'IFAD-initiated,' had been approved between 1979 and 1982 and were currently under implementation. A synthesis of these 'evaluations' claimed that, while it was generally too early for project effects and impact to be quantified, all projects were expected to have a positive impact on food production and incomes, although the degree of impact on the poorest and on women was varied, some projects being much more effective in reaching them than others. In addition, most projects were expected to increase on-farm employment and, in some, off-farm employment. Target group participation in decision-making was also being achieved in a number of projects. Most of the fourteen projects had innovative features, and three projects considered as too risky by the appraising institution subsequently turned out to be viable and very effective in reaching the target group.

Though these indications are positive, it must be remembered the sample in the 'evaluation' was made up of 'IFAD-initiated' projects. For the portfolio as a whole, the situation is more complex. IFAD's capacity to be truly innovative and to involve the rural poor in the conception and implementation of projects to improve their lot is in fact limited by the institutional framework with which it was endowed: (i) the lack of operational responsibility for the crucial later phases of the project cycle, coupled with the need for producing projects more or less acceptable to established international financial institutions; (ii) a heavy insistence by the OECD countries on co-financing, which means financing projects identified and prepared by other institutions; (iii) the need to commit funds, at least in the first triennium, to demonstrate that IFAD was viable. These factors may have made IFAD less innovative in practice than it might have been if given a freer hand.

Nevertheless, there is wide agreement in all these studies that in at least one sub-sector, agricultural and rural credit, IFAD has helped to introduce new concepts and practices which benefit its target group. This has been done in two ways. First, IFAD has encouraged its co-operating institutions and its borrowers to regard the poor as 'bankable' — e.g. by broadening eligibility rules for borrowing or by creating special facilities for borrowing by the poor. Second, IFAD has supported an innovative type of project which provides credit to the poor for productive activities without collateral. To date, experience with these projects is very encouraging; rates of loan recovery are high, the credit seems to have been put to good use and the morale and initiative of the beneficiaries has been strengthened.

More generally, during its first six years, IFAD has directly influenced development lending and project design in favour of its target group. As noted above, it has persuaded both its co-operating institutions and its borrowing Member Countries to modify project design and objectives so as to give more attention to the needs of the rural poor. For example, in the field of agricultural credit, it has persuaded governments, local institutions and its co-financiers to modify their policies and practices so that a larger share of the credit being provided goes to smallholders or, in a few cases, to the landless. Or, in agricultural research, a project was modified in response to IFAD's request to improve the linkages between research, extension and disadvantaged small farmers so that the research would be responsive to their needs and the results made available to them promptly. Some of the changes introduced seem modest; others have been more significant. But it is fair to say that their cumulative impact has been noticeable.

Conclusion

There is now a fairly general consensus that problems of hunger and poverty in the developing countries can best be tackled by expanding food production by the rural poor and by increasing their productivity and incomes. IFAD, focused exclusively on these issues with a special sensitivity to the needs of the poorest countries and the rural poor, seems to be effective in helping these countries to attack these problems. Experience to date suggests that such an institution would be more effective if it had more control over its operations than the existing Agreement permits, and if it had more funds so as to give it the leverage required to help countries make the difficult policy changes and structural adjustments which are often needed to produce the results desired.

NOTES

1. The author served as the Senior Operations Officer of IFAD's Project Management Department from October 1978 through January 1982, on leave of absence from the World Bank. The views expressed in this article are his own

and do not reflect those of either IFAD or the World Bank.

2.   The mandate is set forth in the Agreement Establishing IFAD and in the Fund's 'Lending Policies and Criteria.'

3.   Financing and the issue of 'rough parity' are discussed below.

4.   IFAD-initiated projects can receive financing from others, and it is IFAD's policy to try to mobilize such financing.   Twenty-nine of the sixty-eight IFAD-initiated projects receive funding from other external donors.

5.   Among the additional 'co-operating institutions' which have appraised IFAD's projects or administered its loans are the Arab Fund for Economic and Social Development, UNDP's Office of Project Execution (OPE), the Caribbean Development Bank, the Central American Bank for Economic Integration and the Andean Development Bank.

6.   IFAD, *Annual Report 1978*.   The percentages are based on the contributions of the countries and do not take into account the contributions of Category III (other developing countries).   Some OECD countries argue that these percentages do not reflect the parity actually agreed upon, because the OECD total includes supplementary contributions.

7.   IFAD, *Annual Report 1981*.

Chapter IX

The International Labor Organization (ILO) and the United Nations Educational, Scientific and Cultural Organization (UNESCO)

The International Labor Organization (ILO) was established in 1919 as a part of the Treaty of Versailles. In 1946 it became a specialized agency of the United Nations, and in 1969 the ILO received the Nobel Peace Prize. There are 150 member nations, with a unique tripartite representation in the conference for governments, workers, and employer organizations. The staff includes over 3000 officials and technical advisors from 110 countries. The ILO budget for 1990-1991 is US$330 million. The organization is charged with the task of "working for social justice as a basis for lasting peace, and promoting decent living standards, satisfactory conditions of work and pay and adequate employment opportunities." The ILO sets international labor standards, provides technical assistance and co-operation service, researches and publishes on social and labor matters, helps to work out development policies, and attempts to protect the rights of workers. The organization also supports attempts by various countries and regions to achieve full employment, raise standards of living, more fairly distribute the benefits of labor, protect the lives and health of workers, and promote cooperation between employers and workers. Such activities are beneficial for developed and developing countries alike because social problems are universal.

The United Nations Educational, Scientific and Cultural Organization (UNESCO) was established in 1945 in order to "advance, through the educational, scientific and cultural relations of the peoples of the world, the objectives of international peace and the common welfare of mankind." There are 158 members, which provide the financing for the biennial budget. The 1988-1989 budget was US$350.3 million. Extra-budgetary funds, provided voluntarily by members and other sources, like UNDP, amounted to US$213 million. The United States withdrew from UNESCO in 1984, followed by the United Kingdom and Singapore in 1985, and remains out due to allegations of mismanagement and sharp anti-Israeli and anti-Western sentiments in the organization. It has been suggested that over seventy percent of the budget is used to pay for the vast organizational bureaucracy in Paris, UNESCO's headquarters. The United States, were it still a member, would be assessed to pay twenty-five percent of the UNESCO budget. UNESCO attempts to foster international intellectual co-operation, meaning the sharing of knowledge and experience. The organization also offers operational assistance, especially in developing countries, in the planning and execution of various educational scientific and cultural projects.

Through research and studies, UNESCO attempts to promote peace.
UNESCO's efforts to combat illiteracy have been extremely successful.

UNESCO AND THE ILO: A TALE OF TWO AGENCIES

Michael J. Allen

Introduction

On December 31, 1984, the United States withdrew from the United Nations
Education, Scientific and Cultural Organization (UNESCO), a specialized
agency of the United Nations,[1] one year after giving notice.[2] In its notice of
withdrawal, the United States government cited four main reasons for its
dissatisfaction with UNESCO: 1) increased politicization of the agency;
2) increased emphasis on state and collective rights versus individual rights;
3) mismanagement with regard to personnel, financial activities and
programs within the organization; and 4) its unrestrained budget. The
United States had hoped to provide the impetus for improvements in the
problem areas which it saw in UNESCO, but finding the improvements in
UNESCO insufficient to warrant continued U.S. participation, the United
States finally withdrew. Because the United States is a dominant power and
because it was the largest contributor to the UNESCO budget,[3] its
withdrawal from the organization will sap the agency's ability to continue its
programs.
        Prior to this, the U.S. had withdrawn only once from a UN agency:
the International Labor Organization (ILO).[4] In November of 1975,
Secretary of State Henry Kissinger gave the ILO notice of the United States'
intention to withdraw from the organization if certain improvements in the
United States were not made within a two year period. As in the notice of
intent to withdraw from UNESCO, the United States cited certain problem
areas in connection with its potential withdrawal from the ILO: 1) the
erosion of tripartism; 2) the ILO's selective concern for human rights; 3) the
disregard of the process in the ILO; and 4) the increased politicization of the
ILO. As in the case with UNESCO, the United States did not see sufficient
improvements in the ILO, and effectively withdrew on November 1, 1977.[5]
        During the 1970's, U.S. participation in the ILO had been criticized
as ineffective and had been categorized as crisis management rather than a
continuous and thorough monitoring of an international organization.[6] In
response to these criticisms the United States intensified its involvement in
and preparation for ILO Conferences.[7] Although certain problems existed in
the ILO itself, inadequate U.S. participation in that organization had
prevented effective U.S. involvement.
        The more recent withdrawal from UNESCO reveals similar problems
as those surrounding the ILO withdrawal. Although the United States'
involvement in UNESCO and the ILO, and the events surrounding

withdrawal from these organizations, are not identical, it is useful to utilize the ILO experience as a framework through which to evaluate the recent U.S. withdrawal from UNESCO and the future of the U.S./UNESCO relationship. Section One of this article explores the extent of the problems in UNESCO which resulted in the U.S. withdrawal. Section Two discusses the problems in the ILO which the United States cited as reasons for withdrawal, and the degree to which U.S. withdrawal caused improvements in those areas. Section Three evaluates how many of the problems found in UNESCO can be expected to be rectified through withdrawal, and compares the effectiveness of U.S. participation in both UNESCO and the ILO, focusing on the degree of preparation necessary to participate effectively in these organizations. Section Four then analyzes the impact of U.S. withdrawal on each sector of UNESCO. Finally, Section Five recommends guidelines regarding further U.S. role in UNESCO, and the means by which the United States may improve its effectiveness in that organization.

I. The United States and Unesco

Secretary of State George Schultz cited four problems with the present status of UNESCO which create U.S. discontent: politicization, the over emphasis on collective rights, mismanagement, and budgetary abuse. Discussing each of these problem areas enables us to evaluate UNESCO's success in achieving the goals for which it was established.

A. Politicization

One of the four reasons the U.S. cited for giving notice of withdrawal from UNESCO was the use of the organization as a political forum.[8] Although politicization will exist to some extent in all international organizations,[9] the State Department maintained that politicization was much greater in UNESCO than in other UN specialized agencies.[10] The State Department has blamed the politicization on the strong power of the Secretariat and its African bent.[11]

According to the State Department, many examples of politicization in UNESCO exist:

> aid to "liberation" organizations; imbalanced disarmament campaigns; selective anti-discrimination campaigns; the abuse of legitimate interest in cultural preservation to attack Israel, with little or no account taken of UNESCO-sponsored reports on the issues; and the use of the General Assembly for the debate of issues

far afield from UNESCO's area of concern.[12]

Some of the examples listed above, however, cannot be so clearly blamed on the UNESCO forum. For example, UNESCO involves itself with extraneous issues of peace and disarmament (often pro-Soviet Union) because the United Nations General Assembly had "urged UNESCO to intensify its efforts in the disarmament area."[13] Although the complaint regarding politicization is somewhat nebulous and perhaps not isolated to UNESCO,[14] it does have some validity. It is unclear, however, how much U.S. withdrawal will eliminate or reduce politicization; the problem may be better attacked by greater participation within the organization itself.

B. Human Rights

Another reason cited for U.S. dissatisfaction with UNESCO is the apparent disregard of individual human rights in furtherance of states rights or collective rights.[15] For example, UNESCO devotes a considerable amount of funds to national liberation movements. Additionally, the United States has criticized UNESCO studies regarding the "rights of peoples."[16] This problem first arose in 1982 when the Extraordinary General Conference approved for 1984-89 programs which would study collective peoples' rights as well as individual human rights.[17]

Some critics of the United States' withdrawal from UNESCO have stated that, depending on the exact scope of "peoples' rights," there may be some justification for U.S. concern that UNESCO is focusing too heavily on peoples' rights.[18] The critics, however, are even quicker to point out that many third world, non-democratic nations feel the need to ensure peoples' rights as well as human rights.[19] The concept of peoples' rights, although supported by the Soviet Union, was not originated by them; it is of great importance to other nations.[20] Moreover, the fact that UNESCO programs discuss peoples' rights does not, in itself, reduce the importance of individual human rights.[21]

Although this focus on peoples' rights provides a possible legitimate criticism of some of UNESCO's programs, it should also provide incentive for the United Sates to rejoin UNESCO rather than stay outside the agency. The United Sates can combat any movement away from concern for individual human rights by using UNESCO as a forum to advocate its views.[22] The United Sates fears that the new concern for peoples' rights is the Soviet Union's ploy to change the focus of human rights discussions in UNESCO. If this fear proves to be true, the United States serves Soviet interest and defeats its own by remaining outside UNESCO.[23]

C. Management/Organization Problems

A third weakness causing U.S. dissatisfaction with UNESCO is the organization's structure and operation. The State Department has strenuously criticized UNESCO for mismanagement of UNESCO's programs. The State Department's criticisms focus on three main problems. First, it believes that the UNESCO General Conference has failed to fulfill its function of determining "the policies and main lines of work."[24] Instead, argues the State Department, the General Conference acquiesces in fulfilling its role and allows the strong Secretariat to perform the responsibilities of the General Conference.[25] Second, the Executive Board fails adequately to oversee the UNESCO program and budget proposed by the Secretariat.[26] This failure results in the Secretariat's having the "last word" with regard to all questions concerning the UNESCO program and budget.[27] Third, the lack of any critical or, at the least, complete information regarding the quality and effectiveness of UNESCO's work greatly inhibits evaluation of and improvements in the agency's work.[28] This "wall of misinformation and illusion: makes it difficult for member states accurately to assess how their contributions are being used and how well the goals of UNESCO are being achieved.[29]

The State Department accurately summarized the United States' dissatisfaction with the management of UNESCO in its report:

UNESCO today functions in a way which it seems

clear, would astound and disappoint its founders and those who wrote its Constitution. Its basic institutions fulfill few of the responsibilities intended for them, and this is particularly true of the parliamentary bodies, the Executive Board and the General Conference. Instead, UNESCO has become almost entirely a creature of the Secretariat; its governing bodies lack the will, the organization, and, above all, the information to perform their functions except in a routine, formalistic fashion. All of their decisions are prepared for them, and the execution of those decisions is entirely within the discretion of an executive, which is not then accountable to the governing councils in any meaningful sense. It is within this environment that the specific concerns of the United States with respect to the politicization of UNESCO, its management, its program and budget, and the suppression of minority views must be seen.[30]

The State Department has also complained about 80% of UNESCO funds being spent and 80% of UNESCO personnel being based in Paris.[31]

D. The UNESCO Budget

The fourth major reason for U.S. dissatisfaction with UNESCO has been its budget. One of the Reagan Administration's policy priorities for multilateral organizations is "[t]o implement, for the first half of the decade, a budgetary policy of zero net program growth and significant absorption of non-discretionary cost increases...."[32] The U.S. government has felt that of the U.N. specialized agencies, UNESCO has done the least in trying to attain zero budget growth.[33] For the 1984-85 program budget, for example, the Director-General originally proposed a budget to the Executive Board that would have resulted in a real budget growth of 5.5 percent.[34] As a conciliatory measure, the Director-General reduced the final budget amount by $10 million, thus making the estimated real budget growth somewhere between 3.6 to 4.3 percent.[35]

In his response to Secretary of State Schultz's notice of

withdrawal, UNESCO Director-General M'Bow addressed the U.S. concern for zero budget growth and UNESCO's efforts to meet this concern. He stated that the budget for 1984-1985 was actually $56 million less than that for 1982-1983, the largest reduction in the history of the United Nations system. Thus, although growth in the UNESCO budget was not totally curtailed, some effort had been made within UNESCO to control spending.[36]

To summarize to this point, there is little question but that the reasons for U.S. dissatisfaction with UNESCO are valid. One question that needs answering, however, is whether the best method by which the United States can make changes is to remain outside UNESCO or whether it should work from within the organization to alleviate the problems. By withdrawing, the United States uses its purse strings (25 percent of the UNESCO budget) to force improvements sufficient to warrant the U.S. return; UNESCO will most likely fall into step. On the other hand, by remaining a member of the agency, the U.S. would retain its voice in shaping UNESCO's programs, as well as continue to reap benefits.[37]

Since the United States withdrew from UNESCO just a few months ago, the full effect of withdrawal cannot yet be assessed. Still it is possible to use the experience of the U.S. withdrawal from the ILO to see what can be expected and achieved from withdrawal, and to understand what the United States and UNESCO need to do to bring about changes sufficient to warrant the rejoining of UNESCO.

II. The U.S. and the ILO

On November 5, 1975, Secretary of State Henry Kissinger sent the Director General of the ILO notice of intent to withdraw from the ILO unless improvements were made in four areas cited as problem areas. The four areas cited in the Kissinger letter were the erosion of tripartism, the ILO's selective concern for human rights, the disregard of due process in the ILO, and the increased politicization of the ILO. By the end of the two year period, improvements were not great enough to warrant the United States to remain a member of the ILO.

The United States' concern with ILO activities, however, did not begin in the 1970's. Some problems existed prior to United States' membership in the ILO, and many existed since the Soviet Union rejoined the ILO in 1954, during the Cold War. The level of intensity of U.S. problems with the ILO increased in the early seventies. In 1970, for example, Wilfred Jenks, the Director-General of the ILO, appointed a Russian assistant Director-General, Pavel Astopenko, even though he knew such an appointment would have serious repercussions, especially concerning the United States.[38] After the appointment, the House Committee on Appropriations held a hearing at which George Meany, then president of the AFL-CIO, testified against U.S. financial support of the ILO.

The hearings resulted in the decision to withhold U.S. funds from the ILO ($3.7 million, or one half our contributions in 1970 and $7.8 million, our whole contribution in 1971). Meany and the AFL-CIO approved of such an approach, although the Executive Branch believed that the U.S. was obligated as a member of the ILO to contribute funds.

The withholding of funds did affect the work of the ILO, and thereafter various improvements in the ILO were made. For example, a Mexican supported by the U.S., was elected Chairman of the Governing Body, defeating a Soviet candidate who had received support from some of the Western European members of the Governing Body. Also, there was a reduction in the use of the ILO as a forum for non-labor political discussion. The United States paid the impounded funds in arrears in 1976.

From 1973 to 1975 certain events occurred which greatly troubled the US. First, at the 1973 Conference the Arab states, along with the Communist countries and some African countries, sought to pass a resolution condemning Israel for racism and for violating Conventions (freedom of association, collective bargaining, and discrimination in employment). This resolution, which failed for lack of a quorum, was submitted without any formal investigation or proven violations.

Another resolution condemning Israel for convention violations was submitted at the 1974 Conference. This time the effort was successful. Also, the Conference refused to adopt the report of the Committee on the Application of Conventions and Recommendations in condemning the USSR for violation of the Convention on forced labor, which it has ratified. In the 1975 Conference, more occurrences caused US disenchantment with the ILO. The most noteworthy of these was the fact that the ILO granted the PLO observer status in both of the Conference committees. The specific sources of United States disenchantment with the ILO are explored briefly as a means of placing the UNESCO withdrawal in context.

A. Erosion of Tripartism

The structure of the ILO as a specialized agency is unique in that not only are the governments represented, but the workers and employers of the member countries are also represented. This structure, conceived when the ILO was first established, is a basic tenet upon which the ILO is to operate. The idea of tripartism becomes jeopardized when the worker groups or employers are not clearly distinct from the government. A tension naturally arises between tripartism and another foundational belief of the ILO (as well as all UN agencies): universality. As an international organization, the ILO desires the participation of all countries, irrespective of their economic systems.

The lack of true tripartite representation from a member country is neither a new development nor one that has been unique to Soviet bloc countries. The ILO Constitution states that the workers and employers of a member country should be represented by organizations "which are most representative of employers or workpeople," if such organizations exist.[39] In 1927, the problem arose for the first time with seating a worker or employer delegate who appeared to be merely a puppet of the government. In that year the worker delegate from Italy was from a fascist-controlled union. Although some members opposed seating the delegate on the ground that the union was a mere agency of the government, the workers' delegate was seated.

The greatest concern over the erosion of tripartism has arisen with regard to eastern-bloc countries, usually with specific regard to the Soviet Union. The first instance occurred in 1937, when the Soviets sat the All Union Central Council of Trade Unions as the workers' delegate for the first time. The concern was even greater when the Soviet Union rejoined the ILO in 1954. There was great dispute as to whether worker and employer delegates should be seated where they appear to be mere puppets of the government rather than entities distinct from the government and truly representative of the workers and employers of that country. The debate concerned the workers and employers committees to the ILO Conference. The heated debate, however, resulted in the seating of the Soviet-bloc delegates in these commit-tees. As long as totalitarian countries are represented — that is, the workers and employers of totalitarian countries — the issue of less than true tripartism will exist.

One commentator stated that the United States' attack on the tripartism problem came twenty years too late. Certain improvements regarding the erosion of tripartism, nonetheless, have been made. For example, in 1979, the ILO enacted a provision which allowed for voting by secret ballot under certain circumstances. Proponents of the secret ballot believed this would relieve pressures on worker and employer delegates to vote in accordance with the government, thus allowing them to further the objectives of their constituents.[40] In the same vein, some believed the secret ballot would increase the autonomy of workers and employers delegates vis-a-vis the government delegates. In 1983, the secret ballot was used in a few instances, the two most important being on a plenary vote by the Conference on the adoption of the report of the Committee on the Application of Conventions and Recommendations, and in the defeat of the Arab resolution condemning Israeli government cities. Although in 1977 a country merely had to label a delegate "worker," "employer" or "government" to satisfy the ILO constitutional requirement, other steps have been taken to strengthen this requirement.[41]

B. Selective Concern for Human Rights

The second grievance was the ILO's apparent selective concern for human rights. This concern has also been termed the double standard, for the U.S. criticized the ILO's excessive concern over unfair application of conventions to non-eastern European countries. This criticism was aimed primarily at the Soviet Union and Soviet-bloc nations. The United States believed that the ILO failed fully to explore and criticize the Soviet-bloc nations for failing to apply conventions which they had ratified. Instead, it appeared to the U.S. and some other countries that the focus was placed on countries which, although they had not fully applied all ratified conventions, had attempted to satisfy ratified conventions and were willing to work with the ILO to alleviate the remaining shortcomings.

Before discussing further the issue of selective concern for human rights, it is helpful to delineate the process by which the ILO decides which countries should be criticized for their failure to ratify its conventions. Like any other agency, the ILO has limited resources; it should, therefore, focus on those violations which are most egregious and need prompt resolution. The two conventions which the committee on the Application of Conventions and Recommendations most closely watches are the Convention on Freedom of Association (No. 87) and the Convention on Forced Labor (No. 29).[42]

Under Article 22 of the ILO Constitution, each member country must report regularly to the ILO as to efforts taken to ensure that the ratified conventions are being applied. The Committee of Experts on the Application of Conventions and Recommendations (Committee of Experts) studies the reports and data, and then reaches conclusions regarding how the countries are actually applying the Conventions which they have ratified. The conclusions of the Committee of Experts can be classified into two types: first, in its report, the Committee publishes "observations" which concern longstanding or severe violations of conventions; second, the Committee makes other findings in unpublished "direct requests," to which governments are to reply. The most egregious of the observations are placed on a special list. This list indicates those countries which have shown a "continued failure to implement" the conventions and recommendations they have ratified.

The Conference Committee on the Application of Conventions and Recommendations, tripartite in structure, studies the report of the Committee of Experts, and votes on whether or not to accept the Committee of Experts' report. If the Conference Committee accepts the report, the countries named in the report are formally placed on the "continued failure to implement" list, the most serious form of censure (short of suspension or expulsion from the ILO). The ILO Conference must then ratify the decision or else the countries listed are not censured.

The facts illustrate certain trends with regard to the countries placed on the "continued failure to implement" list. Most of the countries which have been placed on the list are small developing countries. Also, the list from each conference is usually not repetitive, and the countries on the list are fairly well spread out among the continents. Problems arise in this area because most countries believe in the uniform application of standards (i.e. conventions and recommendations), whereas the Soviet-bloc countries believe otherwise. The latter believes that in judging the application of conventions and recommendations, the various legal, social and economic aspects of each country must be taken into account — a simple uniform application disregards the various essential characteristics of a nation.

C. Concern for Due Process

As a third reason for potential withdrawal, the Kissinger letter cited a concern for disregard of the constitutional guarantees of due process. The main concern regarding due process was that the ILO Conference and certain of the Committees were promulgating (and furthering the promulgation of) resolutions against countries without following the procedure mandated by the ILO Constitution.

Two occurrences at the 59th International Labor Conference in 1974 best exemplify U.S. fears regarding the ILO's move away from due process. First, the Resolutions Committee put before the Conference plenary a "Resolution Concerning Human and Trade Union Rights in Chile." The proposal was published prior to the completion of the investigation of Chile's record regarding freedom of association. The United States fought the resolution in the Resolutions Committee meeting; the Resolutions Committee, however, passed the proposal.[43] The Conference plenary adopted the resolution, though the United States government delegation abstained.[44]

Second, the Conference adopted an Anti-Israel resolution regarding that country's policy concerning racism and free trade unions in Palestine and the occupied territories on the West Bank of the Jordan River. The United States voiced two main objections to the resolution: first, "previous experience in the ILO dealing with serious allegations indicated the wisdom of using in the first instance the available procedures..."[45]; second, the resolution dealt with a problem which was an outgrowth of a political reality, i.e., the absence of peace in the Middle East; the subject was delicate and the adoption of such a condemnatory resolution might disrupt the negotiating process.

The problem of due process in ILO procedures still concerns the United States. Some measures have been taken by various groups, however, to amend the ILO Conference standing orders to strengthen due process procedures regarding adoption of resolutions by the Conference plenary.

D. Politicization

The fourth ILO problem area was the increased politicization of the organization. To be sure, international labor standards and workers' rights are to a certain extent inherently political. The distinction must be drawn, nonetheless, between labor issues necessarily political and the use of the ILO as a forum for purely political, non-labor issues. Clearly, the problem of politicization is not unique to the ILO. In fact, the presence of politicization has been a subject of criticism in other U.N. specialized agencies, particularly UNESCO.[46]

The removal of all politicization from any international organization such as the ILO would be impossible. In its notice of withdrawal letter, however, the United States expressed concern that the ILO had experienced increased politicization. The illustration most cited to support this statement was the anti-Israel movement within the ILO during the 1970's. In 1975, the ILO granted observer status to the Palestine Liberation Organization (PLO), a fact which appears to have exacerbated the "anti-Israel" movement in the ILO.[47]

Prior to the 1970's the ILO had been used as a forum to criticize other countries for non-labor policies.[48] More recently, in 1981, Communist labor delegates introduced a resolution regarding disarmament and social policy. Although this resolution was criticized as being wholly extraneous to the ILO's scope and purpose, the resolution was adopted, with the support of the U.S. government delegation.[49]

III. Effect of Withdrawal on UNESCO's Problems

A. The ILO Experience

Many professionals in the international labor field thought that the U.S. withdrawal from the ILO was successful: the secret ballot stopped, or at the least slowed down the problem of eroding tripartism.[50] The amount of politicization in ILO debates and discussions decreased somewhat[51]; an anti-Israel resolution in 1978 was defeated and no such resolution reappeared in 1979; and progress made regarding amending Article 17 to screen out resolutions which violated ILO due process provisions.

Moreover, U.S. withdrawal from the ILO precipitated a cohesive effort among Western European countries to see that the ILO changed sufficiently to warrant the U.S. return. In 1980, the U.S. government was satisfied enough with changes in the ILO to rejoin.

While changes were occurring in the ILO, the United States was reassessing its own role. The government departments responsible for ILO activities — the Departments of Labor, State and Commerce — recognized the shortcomings in their methods of preparing the U.S. delegations for ILO Conferences. The government realized that it could not increase its effectiveness in shaping ILO programs and policies unless it brought about two internal changes. First, the United States government had to establish clear objectives it sought to achieve in the ILO. Second, in order to achieve these goals, the government (the Labor, State and Commerce Departments) had to increase its expertise and manpower regarding ILO activities. The U.S. could not succeed under the then-existing practice of ad hoc preparation of U.S. delegates to the ILO.

To alleviate these internal problems, the United States government, mainly the Department of Labor, acted to establish concrete objectives of the U.S. with regard to the ILO. The Cabinet Level Committee on the ILO established eleven goals of the U.S. in UNESCO. The President's Committee on the ILO, the successor of the Cabinet Level Committee, approved the objectives in 1983. The objectives concern three major areas: improving the four problem areas, improving the effectiveness of U.S. participation in the ILO and improving U.S. input as to the efficiency of the ILO's programs. Also, greater effort was expended to ensure that the specific duties of the Departments of State, Labor and Commerce were capitalized. The Department of Labor, as a result, has the greatest role in U.S. policy formulation for ILO activities, such as its technical programs and the ILO program budget. The Department of Labor increased the rigor of its study of these areas. Perhaps the best example of a greater U.S. study is the Department of Labor's in depth analysis of the ILO program and budget for 1982-83, with a view to proposing an alternative program and budget for 1984-85. At the least, the Department of Labor's efforts reflect a different, more aggressive attitude by the U.S. Although it expects the ILO and the other members to bring improvements in the ILO, the U.S. also is working to ensure that the ILO adequately performs its programs and functions. Obviously the rationale for actively monitoring the ILO is not solely for the benefit of that organization; the U.S. also wants to ensure that it is putting forth its strongest voice to affect the ILO in ways favorable to the U.S. The best means by which to do this is to be prepared regarding ILO activities.

Because the United States did improve its own participation in the ILO after rejoining, it is difficult to gauge how much of the improvement in the four problem areas resulted from U.S. withdrawal, and consequently, twenty-five percent of the funds for the ILO, and how much was from a more cohesive, assertive U.S. delegation at ILO Conference since returning. At the least, withdrawal substantively improved the areas of U.S. discontent. When a nation, especially a leading nation like the U.S., gets so disenchanted with an agency like the ILO that it withdraws, such an action has great impact.

The impact of withdrawal may be even greater, or at least the reasons given may be considered more sincere by other nations, where the country illustrates its continued support of the basic goals sought by the international organization. During the withdrawal period, the United States provided some funding, approximately $250,000 for a technical program established by the ILO. The United States also exhibited good faith to the ILO by its internal improvements.

In a sense, withdrawal also indicates the serious level of U.S. disenchantment with the organization. By actually withdrawing after giving notice, the U.S. illustrated to the ILO that it meant business with regard to the problems it perceived as clouding the ILO's work. In the ILO situation, the withdrawal had greater impact because the U.S. had never withdrawn from a U.N. agency before. This fact added to the gravity with which the U.S. viewed the ILO's problems.

In summary, U.S. withdrawal provided the catalyst for improvements in the ILO. Also, withdrawal caused the United States to reassess the role it had played in the ILO, and the role it should play in that organization. Thus, the improvements which were started while the U.S. was outside the organization continued as the U.S. worked to have a stronger voice in ensuring that the goals of the ILO were sought, and that the democratic beliefs supported by the U.S. were heard.

B. Implications of Withdrawal from UNESCO

As is illustrated by the ILO experience, U.S. with-drawal from UNESCO will help bring about improvements in the areas of U.S. dissatisfaction. As also was true with the ILO, the United States has illustrated its continued interest in UNESCO. Early in 1985, the U.S. joined UNESCO as an observer. Some UNESCO officials had hoped a rather sudden change of heart in the U.S.'s position regarding UNESCO, but no such drastic change occurred. The participation of the U.S. as an observer does evidence U.S. good faith to see that improvements in UNESCO are made.

Before the U.S. withdrew from UNESCO, the State Department assessed continued U.S. participation in that organization, and came up with possible alternative sources for some of the benefits the U.S. received from its membership. If the U.S. participates in alternative but still UNESCO-related organizations, such participation may also be seen as a strong continued interest in UNESCO activities. Other member countries' perception of such an interest may have effect of creating greater incentive to improve the areas of U.S. discontent in UNESCO.

The chance for improvements in UNESCO is enhanced by the fact that many of the Industrial Market Economy Countries (IMEC) feel much of the same dissatisfaction with UNESCO as the United States. Since none of these countries has given UNESCO notice of withdrawal, these countries will be able to work within UNESCO to eliminate the problems. This fact creates a tension in two ways. First, the presence of the United States in UNESCO would enhance the ability of the IMEC countries to bring about improvements. Second, the fact that these countries remained members of UNESCO even though their governments were unhappy with UNESCO's performance may cause the U.S. to be perceived as unwilling to work to improve UNESCO. In any regard, the fact that other countries realize the problems of UNESCO and are dissatisfied with them helps put greater impact on the U.S. withdrawal. Because of this, the organization must be sensitive to these complaints and try to rectify the existing shortcomings in order that more nations do not follow the U.S. out the UNESCO door.

The United States' withdrawal will probably cause the most rapid improvements in the area of the budget — UNESCO must adjust to the loss of twenty-five percent of its funds. Because of the decrease, the agency will most likely be forced to follow a more restrained budget even if the U.S. returns to the organization. Even before the U.S. officially withdrew from UNESCO, M'Bow had worked to decrease the budget for 1984-85.

The amount of politicization in UNESCO can be reduced in the short run as well as the long run. U.S. withdrawal did appear to reduce the amount of politicization in the ILO.   The combination of U.S. withdrawal from UNESCO and other countries' discontent with politicization may be as effective as was withdrawal from the ILO.   It is questionable, however, whether the United States could better reduce the politicization in the UNESCO forum by returning to the organization and voicing its opinion against such debate.   The concerns existing in the states' rights versus individual rights complaint parallel those regarding the politicization problem.

The one problem in UNESCO which withdrawal may improve but not quickly eradicate is the management and operation problem. Because of bureaucratic inertia, a change in the operation of UNESCO's programs would require much time. Elimination of this problem, if it ever occurred, would require more time than the U.S. could afford to be outside the organization and still have other countries expect a U.S. return.

IV. Impact of Withdrawal from UNESCO

Entirely separate from the question of whether and to what extent U.S. withdrawal from UNESCO will bring about adequate change in the four areas of U.S. concern in that organization, is an equally important question: to what extent will the United States and UNESCO lose the benefits which arise from their mutual association? In addition to the impact which withdrawal has on the UNESCO budget (loss of approximately 25 percent of the budget), U.S. withdrawal also affects UNESCO's programs to the extent that American scientists, scholars, and educators no longer contribute to the agency's programs.   Likewise, withdrawal from UNESCO affects the United States' ability to receive the benefits of these programs, although some have argued that many of the benefits may be derived from other sources.

Because of the recent nature of withdrawal, and the importance of certain intangible foreign policy benefits gained by remaining in UNESCO, it is difficult to determine the actual extent to which the U.S. and UNESCO would be deprived of actual benefits due to the U.S. withdrawal. By exploring the benefits formerly enjoyed in each UNESCO sector as a result of U.S. participation in that organization, the effect of withdrawal on UNESCO and the U.S. may be demonstrated.

A. The Education Sector

The United States has received benefits from UNESCO's Education Sector, it largest sector. The U.S. benefits from this sector in its work as a clearinghouse for information regarding educational materials.[52]   Of UNESCO's role as the disseminator of ideas and educational materials, the State Department in 1984 stated that, "it is unlikely to be duplicated by any other source.... It is the principal and most authoritative source of higher education statistical data worldwide."[53] UNESCO's "Education for All" program, which seeks to eliminate illiteracy, and to improve adult education, education for women, education in rural areas, and educational opportunities for disabled persons[54] has also been regarded as a beneficial and worthy program.[55] Although the education sector implements some worthy programs, the U.S. government has criticized it as being plagued by problems which seem to plague UNESCO on the whole.[56]

The eventual consequences for the Education Sector of U.S. withdrawal from UNESCO are momentous. Quite obviously, the most drastic effect to UNESCO will be the loss of U.S. funds. Also, UNESCO may lose the benefit of its interaction with the American professional community:

> This pool of competent [American] professionals has been, and continues to be, an invaluable resource for the work of organizations like UNESCO, for the recruitment of both staff and advisory and consulting personnel. In fields as complex as the relationship between education and the world of work, or the optimal use of appropriate educational technology, or the evaluation of new curricula, there is simply no substitute for solid professional competence — and this country, comparatively speaking, has an abundance of that competence. There is thus an important contribution to be made by this country's professional community to the quality of UNESCO's work — a

contribution which, incidentally, would in turn provide American professionals with new insights and experiences at an international scale.[57]

Withdrawal from UNESCO may also have some long range adverse affects on education in the United Sates. While certain alternatives to membership in UNESCO may provide the United Sates with some of the benefits of the Education Sector as well as those of other UNESCO sectors,[58] professional educators in the United States would suffer losses in their relationship to educational thought and practice in the rest of the world. To enrich education in the United Sates, we must keep open international channels of professional, educational communication. Failing to do so, withdrawal would therefore have consequences adverse to the interest of both the United States and UNESCO in the Education Sector.[59]

B. The Natural Sciences Sector

The Natural Sciences Sector provides numerous beneficial technical programs and access to important scientific information; it facilitates research; it allows nations to share the costs of international research facilities; and it provides a much-needed opportunity for international scientific cooperation.[60] The negative consequences of U.S. withdrawal include the following: the possible loss of scientific information, data bases and resources by the United States; the loss of funds which provided lesser developed nations an opportunity to establish and improve scientific research within their own countries; the potential loss of scientific exchange with countries with which the United States maintains limited contact; and the loss of U.S. membership in important international scientific organizations.

Looking at the Natural Sciences Sector in isolation, the negative consequences vastly outweigh its problems. The State Department characterized the problems as "organizational shortcomings," such as low quality of staff, unnecessarily high administrative costs, and other flaws which impede the quality of UNESCO projects. Once again, these criticisms appear to be no more than an echoing of the problems existing with the general framework of UNESCO, and go more to structure than to substance. By withdrawing, the United States has lost its ability to try to restructure UNESCO in order to eliminate the existing bureaucratic problems. It can be argued, and in fact is argued, that the U.S. can affect the inefficiencies in UNESCO most rapidly by reducing its budget by 25 percent. By leaving UNESCO in such a fashion, the U.S. only circumvents the problems and fails to work with other UNESCO member states to abrogate them.

C. The Social Sciences Sector

The Social Sciences Sector will also be eventually affected by the U.S. withdrawal. The United States, which has been very active in this sector, benefits from having access to foreign social science data and scholars, from UNESCO publications, and from social science research done in foreign countries. The greatest loss by far, is the U.S.'s voice in formulating the sector's programs and in shaping the nature of debate with regard to these programs. On the other hand, the United States would not lose its ability to receive UNESCO social science publications.[61] Thus, the losses to the United States from not participating in this sector would not be as numerous as in either the Education or Natural Sciences Sectors, but would still be important.

D. The Culture Sector

The Culture Sector of UNESCO has been the most successful Sector from the United States' perspective.[62] The major objectives of the Culture Sector's programs are 1) preservation of cultural heritage; 2) promotion of culture; 3) stimulation of intellectual and artistic activity; and 4) promotion and encouragement of endogenous cultural activities. The United States government has been satisfied with the work of the Cultural Sector, and has benefited from the research and training programs as well as UNESCO's financial assistance to other international non-governmental cultural organizations.

UNESCO's efforts in the Culture Sector also aided the United States government in helping to enact the Historic Preservation Act of 1966.[63] Prior to the passage of the Act, American officials went to study the private and government preservation practices in Great Britain, Germany, Poland, France, the Netherlands, Austria, Italy, and Czechoslovakia.[64] The trip resulted in UNESCO's publication of a book entitled *With Heritage so Rich*, which was used as support for enacting the Act.[65]

Although the Culture Sector has been relatively free of the problems that plague other UNESCO sectors, the United States could continue participation through the non-governmental international organizations to which UNESCO presently contributes.[66] The United States loses the benefit, however, of being a participant in the dialogue for international cultural issues, for which UNESCO is the best forum. As with every other Sector, the U.S. also loses its voice in supporting American and western-democratic views in the cultural field's only international forum. And although the U.S. can increase it support as a member of some of the non-governmental international cultural organizations,[67] it will not be eligible for membership in others.[68]

E. The Communications Sector

In the Communications Sector, the biggest problem from the United States' viewpoint is also the strongest reason why the U.S. needs to remain involved. The U.S. government has opposed from the outset the movement by some UNESCO member states to implement the New World Information and Communication Order (NWICO). NWICO, which has been a topic of great debate in UNESCO for years, is intended to correct the imbalance of access to and dissemination of information which exists between developed and lesser developed nations. The U.S. fears that NWICO would impede the free flow of information between countries and would amount to a censorship of the press and thus opposes the Order.

Although it is questionable whether NWICO will ever have enough support of the UNESCO member states to be implemented, the need for the U.S.'s voice for advocating the freedom of the press from censorship is a strong reason for the U.S. to rejoin UNESCO. Some UNESCO critics have argued that by remaining in UNESCO, the United States is tacitly legitimizing "anti-Western" beliefs such as the possibility of censorship of the press or curtailment of the free flow of information.[69] The risk that a failure to fight against proposals that reduce or eliminate "Western beliefs" may cause UNESCO to support them, however, far outweighs any risk the U.S. runs of appearing to tacitly approve such measures. The United States can affect neither other countries' positions nor UNESCO's positions on communication (and other) issues on a long-range basis from outside the organization.

V. Conclusions and Recommendations

The full effects of the U.S. withdrawal have not been felt, yet the U.S. must continually reassess the possible value of rejoining UNESCO. The problem to be resolved is not whether or not we should have withdrawn, but whether and when we should rejoin. The U.S. may well be able to reap many of the benefits of UNESCO outside of that organization. In fact, the U.S. could probably receive many of these benefits for much less than what it would contribute to UNESCO. A strictly economic evaluation of UNESCO membership, however, would fail to consider such intangible factors as maintaining this avenue of communication with UNESCO member countries and influencing UNESCO policies and programs. Additionally, by being a member of UNESCO, the U.S. can better combat certain problems it sees presently existing in that organization, particularly the amount of pure political, extraneous debate and the emphasis on states' rights rather than on individual rights.

Although withdrawal may not have been the best method by the United States to try to eliminate the problems existing in UNESCO, the United States should not rejoin the organization until some significant improvements in these areas are made. As an observer, the United States could work to see that UNESCO seeks to improve these areas. Having observer status would allow the U.S. a more active role in helping to bring about reforms in UNESCO; actively seeking to improve the situation is preferable, and to other countries looks much better, than waiting for UNESCO and its members to take the sole initiatives to bring about the improvements. Thus, observer status could be a useful means to the end — an improved UNESCO which the U.S. would be willing to rejoin.

The United States should also work more closely with the IMEC countries in causing positive changes in UNESCO. The greater cooperation would help all parties involved, for these countries have similar interests to promote in UNESCO, and also share discontents regarding UNESCO. Once improvements sufficient for a U.S. return are made, the U.S. should continue cooperation with IMEC countries to ensure that the interests of these countries and the U.S. are voiced clearly and responded to the UNESCO forum.

Although the U.S. should wait for some improvement in the UNESCO problem areas, it should not wait until the problems are eliminated. This recommendation is made for three reasons. First, the problems will never be completely eliminated due to the vulnerability of such an international forum to such problems. Second, the U.S. should not use its financial leverage to force others to bring about changes without some U.S. help. Third, great reductions in the levels of these shortcomings will take longer than the U.S. can afford to stay out without losing a strong voice and some credibility with other member countries.

As was true with the ILO experience, the United States should return to UNESCO if there are some strong initial improvements which illustrate, at the least, a good faith effort to eliminate the areas of U.S. discontent. By returning the United States would demonstrate its good faith in UNESCO. Furthermore, U.S. return at that point would also illustrate its intention to work toward eliminating the weaknesses in UNESCO, rather than using its contribution money as leverage to force others to bring about the improvements.

The ILO experience evinces another important step the United States should take with regard to UNESCO: improving the nature of its own participation in UNESCO. Much of the effort has been without direction, in part because the responsibilities regarding U.S. work in UNESCO are divided among various groups, with participation coming

from both the public and private sectors. As was needed with
the ILO, the U.S. needs to establish clearly its objectives in
UNESCO. By doing so, it can better monitor the problems it
sees in UNESCO. Such increased attention to UNESCO will
enable the United States to advocate its position more
effectively in that organization.

Because of the size of its contributions and because of
its position as a world leader, the United States was an
integral part of UNESCO. Additionally, the great level of
scholarship and intellectual resources in the U.S. is greatly
needed by, if not essential to, UNESCO. The efforts of both
UNESCO and the United States are necessary to make the
changes needed to warrant a U.S. return to UNESCO. The
U.S. withdrawal has provided the catalyst for improvements
in UNESCO. As was true with the ILO experience, a U.S.
return would further increase the improvements initially
brought about by withdrawal. The U.S. and UNESCO must
both work to make the changes necessary to allow a prompt,
necessary reunion.

NOTES

1.   UNESCO was founded in 1945 as a specialized
agency of the United Nations. As stated in Article I of the
UNESCO Constitution,

> The purpose of the Organization is to contribute to
> peace and security by promoting collaboration among
> the nations through education, science and culture in
> order to further universal respect for justice, for the
> rule of law and for the human rights and fundamental
> freedoms which are affirmed for the peoples of the
> world, without distinction of race, sex, language or
> religion, by the Charter of the United Nations.

UNESCO is structured such that its programs fall within
five sectors: education, social science, natural science, culture
and communication.

The UNESCO Constitution provides for an organization
composed of three organs: the General Conference, the
Executive Board and the Secretariat. The General Conference
is composed of the member states, of which there presently
are 100.   Also, there are three associate members, one

observer state and four national liberation movements with observer status. The General Conference's main function is to "determine the policies and the main lines of work of [UNESCO]." UNESCO Constitution, art. IV, cl. B, §2.

The Executive Board, the second organ, consists of fifty-one member states, with the President of the General Conference sitting ex officio as an advisor to the Board. The functions of the Board are to prepare the agenda for the General Conference, examine the program and budget submitted by the Director-General, and ensure execution of the program adopted by the General Conference.

The Secretariat, the final organ, consists of the Director-General and his staff as required. The Director-General is to submit periodical reports to the General Conference, as well as to submit a program and budget to the Executive Board. The present Director-General, Amadou-Mahtor M'Bow of Senegal, has held this position since 1974.

For a more detailed discussion of the structure and history of UNESCO, see R. Hoggart, *An Idea and its Servants* (1978); W. Laves & C. Thomson, *UNESCO* (1957); J. Sewell, *UNESCO and World Politics* (1975).

2.   On December 28, 1983, Secretary of State George Schultz had sent a one year notice of withdrawal letter to Director-General M'Bow [hereinafter referred to as Schultz letter]. In the Schultz letter, the Secretary of State outlined U.S. dissatisfaction with UNESCO and stated that if these problems were not sufficiently rectified within the one year notice period, the United Sates would withdraw effective December 31, 1984.   On this date, the U.S. made its withdrawal effective. For a reprint of the Schultz letter and Director-General M'Bow's reply, see *United States: Withdrawal from UNESCO,* 23 Int'l Legal Materials (1984).

3.   The United States contributed 25 percent of UNESCO's 1984-85 regular program budget, or $86.2 million. The second largest contributor is the Soviet Union, which contributed 10.41 percent ($35.9 million) of the budget. U.S. General Accounting Office, *Improvements Needed in UNESCO's Management, Personnel, Financial and Budgeting Practices 81* (1984) [hereinafter cited as G.A.O. UNESCO report].

4.   The ILO was established in 1919 by the Treaty of

Versailles. The formation of the ILO resulted from the belief held by many at the Versailles Peace Conference that an organization which would concern itself with international labor problems need be established.

Some of the guiding principles of the ILO are freedom of association, equal pay for equal work, and payment of adequate wages to maintain a reasonable standard of living. Other principles embodied in the Treaty of Versailles were that labor should not be regarded as a commodity or article of commerce, that a eight hour day or a forty-eight hour week was favorable, that there should be a weekly rest period of twenty four hours, that child labor should be abolished, and that each country should treat all workers equitably with regard to labor. To help ensure that these eight principles of member protection were achieved, the Treaty provided for the establishment of an inspection system.

Not only were some of the goals of the ILO formulated at the Versailles Peace Conference, certain leading ideas for the structure of the ILO also originated there. It was decided that the structure of the ILO would include a general governing body as well as a secretariat. It was also thought by those at the Conference that one of the main purposes of the ILO would be to supervise the observation of conventions by the countries which had ratified those conventions. This vision of the proper function of the ILO has materialized into one of the fundamental activities of the ILO — that of helping to ensure application of ratified conventions by ratifying countries. The ILO consists of three separate organs: the ILO Conference, the Governing Body and the International Labor Office. The ILO Conference meets each June in Geneva, Switzerland. The composition of the delegates to the ILO Conference is unique in that it is tripartite in nature. Each member country has four delegates to the ILO Conference. Two of the delegates represent the government while one each of the remaining two delegates represent workers and employers. The tripartite system of representation helps insure that the interest of governments, workers and employers are represented. The workers' delegate from the United States has been and still is the AFL-CIO. Prior to 1978, the employers' delegate was the U.S. Chamber of Commerce. Presently, the U.S. employer representative is the U.S. Council for International Business.

The ILO Conference serves many functions, the most important is its role as a policy-maker for the ILO. In its role as policy-maker, the Conference establishes labor standards and supervises the application of those standards by the member nations which have ratified them. The Conference is also responsible for the Budget proposed by the ILO Director-General, who heads the International Office.

The Governing body is the executive council of the ILO, which meets three times a year. The Governing Body consists of fifty-six delegates. Twenty-eight of the delegates are government delegates. There are fourteen workers delegates and fourteen employers delegates in the Governing Body. Thus, like the ILO Conference, the Governing body is tripartite in nature. Of the twenty-eight government seats, ten are permanently held by countries considered to be of great industrial importance. The other eighteen government members are elected from among countries which do not hold a permanent seat.

The International Labor Office, the third organ of the ILO, is the secretariat of the ILO. The Director-General heads the Office. The present Director-General, Francis Blanchard of France, has held this position since 1974. The work of the International Labor Office can be categorized into three principal areas of work. First, the Office implements the many technical programs of the ILO. Second, the Office provides for various regional services. Third, the Office controls and undertakes the ILO's research and publication activities.

For a more detailed discussion of the history, purpose and structure of the ILO, see A. Alcock, *History of the International Labor Organization* (1971); D. Morse, *The Origin and Evolution of the ILO and its Role in the World Community* (1969); W. Galenson, *The International Labor Organization: An American View* (1981).

5.   Rashin, *Struggle Over ILO Pullout*, N.Y. Times (Nov. 3, 1977), at 10, col. 1.

6.   See U.S. General Accounting Office, *Sustaining Improved U.S. Participation in the International Labor Organization Requires New Approaches*, Report to the Chairman, Senate Committee on Labor and Human

Resources (1984); U.S. General Accounting Office, *Need for U.S. Objectives in the International Labor Organization,* Report to the Senate Committee on Governmental Affairs (1977); U.S. General Accounting Office, *Numerous Improvements Still Needed in Managing U.S. Participation in International Organizations,* Report to the Congress (1974); U.S. General Accounting Office, *U.S. Participation in the International Labor Organization Not Effectively Managed,* Report to the Congress (1970).

    7. For example, a cabinet-level committee concerned with U.S. participation in the ILO was established and the Department of Labor did an intensive analysis of the ILO program and budget for 1982-83 in order to suggest changes in the 1984-85 budget. U.S. General Accounting Office, *Sustaining Improved U.S. Participation in the International Labor Organization Requires New Approaches* 18 (1984).

    8. "At the same time, we also recognized, and expressed our strong concern about, those pressures to divert UNESCO to politically-motivated ends which emanated from member states, rather than from within the organization itself.... We are convinced that [cooperation to achieve UNESCO's goals outside the agency] need not be diminished by the injection of political goals beyond its scope...." *United States: Withdrawal from UNESCO, supra* note 2, at 221-22.

    9. For example, politicization was cited as one of the reasons for withdrawal from the ILO.

    10. Politicization in most specialized agencies is kept within acceptable bounds by their specialized mandates. UNESCO's mandate, however, is unusually broad and vague, as a reading of its Constitution will show. It has therefore not been difficult to find some justification or rationale, however tenuous, for activities basically politically in purpose." State Department, *U.S./UNESCO Policy Review* 58 (1984).

    The language of the State Department, however, indicates that the scope of UNESCO's duties and objectives are broader than those of other specialized agencies and thus greater politicization should be tolerated where related to matters within its scope. Political matters wholly extraneous to UNESCO subject matters should not be condoned; however, the United States should not use the greater scope of UNESCO as a springboard to attack germane yet politically unfavorable debate or discussion.

11. *Id.* at 58. "The resulting system allows for the easy reflection of the shared orientation of the Secretariat and the majority in the Organization's program.... In giving many of UNESCO's programs a political start, the Secretariat and its supporting majority among member states have often ridden roughshod over minority points of view represented by democratic countries." *Id.*

12. *Id.*

13. The criticism that UNESCO should not concern itself with peace and disarmament issues was also raised by Gregory Newell, Assistant Secretary of State for International Organization Affairs. U.S. Withdrawal from UNESCO: Hearings Before the Subcomms. on Human Rights and International Organizations and on International Operations of the House Comm. on Foreign Affairs, 98th Cong., 2d Sess. 5-10 (1984) [hereinafter cited as Hearings], at 269-70 (statement of Edward Derwinski, Counselor, Department of State; accompanied by Gregory Newell, Assistant Secretary of State for International Organization Affairs).

14. Hearings, *supra* note 13, at 223-24 (Statement of Leonard R. Sussman, Executive Director, Freedom House, New York). *See also* Underhill, *UNESCO and the American Challenge*, 18 J. World Trade L. 381, 392 (1984). ("It seems somewhat unfair to make UNESCO the whipping boy of this state of affairs. There is scarcely a single UN organ or specialized agency which is not swamped by lengthy, bitter, protracted extraneous political debates. This applies even to regional organizations.")

15. Other western countries have criticized the increasing importance of collective rights and the de-emphasis of individual rights in UNESCO programs. E. Tholmann, the Swiss permanent delegate to UNESCO, stated that "[the Swiss] have the impression that individual becomes increasingly subjugated to collectivism which leads to a growing tendency of an instrumentalization of education, science, culture and communication at the service of the State." Underhill, *supra* note 14, at 384-85.

16. Department of State, *U.S./UNESCO Policy Review*, *supra* note 10, at 35.

17. *Id.*

18. Hearings, *supra* note 13, at 220 (Statement of Leonard R. Sussman, Executive Director, Freedom House, New York).

19. For example, *see* Hearings, *supra* note 21, at 321 (prepared statement by Samuel De Palma, Former assistant Secretary of State for International Organization Affairs).

20. *Id.* "Many societies which lack our heritage of individual freedoms, particularly those which are struggling for a national identity and a viable existence, are prone to think of peoples rights ahead of individual rights." *Id.*

21. *Id.*

22. Most important, peoples' rights, however defined, should encompass individual rights. They are not mutually exclusive. The Universal Declaration of Human Rights, since 1948, has set the global standard of *individual* freedom. The task now is to mesh the prerogatives of groups, however large, with the fundamental rights of all individuals within those groups.... Properly understood, peoples' rights can be seen as an integral part of the democratic tradition. We should not let the implication become accepted that because democracy begins with a consideration of the rights, it does not recognize as essential to their expression, collective institutions that secure these rights in a community or among communities of many individual with necessarily conflicting rights.

Hearings, *supra* note 13, at 222-23 (Statement of Leonard R. Sussman, Executive Director, Freedom House, New York).

23. As Samuel De Palma, Former Assistant Secretary of State for International Organization Affairs stated, "I cannot see how it would be in our interest to [withdraw from UNESCO] and leave it to others to define such rights for future generations." Hearings, *supra* note 13, at 321.

24. As Secretary of State George Schultz told UNESCO Director-General M'Bow; the U.S. government has been "concerned that trends in the management, policy, and budget of UNESCO were detracting from the Organization's effectiveness." *United States: Withdrawal from UNESCO, supra* note 2, at 221.

25. Department of State, *supra* note 16, at 52-53. Many

of the problems cited by the State Department were echoed by the General Accounting Office in a recent report on UNESCO. *See* U.S. General Accounting Office, *Improvements Needed in UNESCO's Management, Personnel, Financial, and Budgeting Practices*, Report to the House Committee on Science and Technology (1984) [hereinafter referred to as G.A.O. UNESCO Report].

26. *Id.*

27. *Id.* at 53.

28. *Id.* at 53-54.

29. *Id.* at 54-55.

30. *Id.*

31. *Id.* at 56.

32. Hearings, *supra* note 14, at 261 (Statement of Edward J. Derwinski, Counselor, Department of State).

33. According to the Department of State, other United Nations specialized agencies were better able to respond to the request for zero or near-zero proposed budget growth. For example, the ILO had a budget increase of 1.92 percent, the World Health Organization (WHO) had a decrease of 0.31 percent and the FAO had an increase of 0.5 percent. UNESCO's program increase was 2.5 percent (real growth increase of 3.7 to 4.3 percent). *See* Department of State, *supra* note 16, at 4 (Introduction).

34. Department of State, *supra* note 16, at 64.

35. G.A.O. UNESCO Report, *supra* note 25, at 71.

36. *United States: Withdrawal from UNESCO, supra* note 2, at 225.

37. Representative Jim Leach (D. Iowa) helped put the budget issue in perspective when he states: "[I]t is curious to note that while the Administration is correct in charging UNESCO with program growth, the Administration's budget figures show an actual decline of some 13 percent in UNESCO's 1984-85 biennium as calculated in nominal dollars. UNESCO has done a better job in restraining its budget in the last two years than the Reagan administration and Congress have our own." Hearings, *supra* note 13, at 8 (Statement of Rep. Jim Leach).

38. See generally, W. Galenson, *supra* note 4.

39. *id. supra* note 4, at 85.

40. The amendment adopted provided for the secret

ballot in the following instances: 1) when voting for the Conference President; 2) when a secret ballot is requested by 90 or more delegates; 3) when a secret ballot is requested by the chairman of a Group; or 4) when concurrent requests are made for record and secret votes.

41. W. Galenson, *supra* note 4, at 45-46.

42. W. Galenson, *supra* note 4, at 47.

43. W. Galenson, *supra* note 4, at 74.

44. *Id.*

45. *Id.* at 75.

46. See the discussion of attempts to amend Art. 17. W. Galenson, *supra* note 4, at 81-84.

47. W. Galenson, *supra* note 4, at 85.

48. Cuban and S. African apartheid policies.

49. W. Galenson, *supra* note 4 at 18.

50. *Id.*

51. For example, the ILO Conference passed several resolutions providing for the strengthening of the ILO's tripartite system.

52. In its U.S./UNESCO Policy Review, the State Department analyzed the problems existing in each UNESCO sector and provided alternative measures by which the United States could attain the benefits while remaining outside UNESCO. These alternatives will be discussed and analyzed in the text that follows.

53. The Education sector's staff constitutes 22 percent of UNESCO's staff. "The 19.5% of UNESCO's budget that goes to education compares to 5.9% for culture, 8.8% for science and technology, 7.2% for programs related to the human environment and its improvement, and . . . 3.7% for . . . communications." Hearings, *supra* note 4, at 103 (Statement of Hans N. Weiler, Professor of Education and Political Science, Stanford University).

54. Department of State *supra* note 16, at 5.

55. *Id.*

56. For example, the State Department felt that the education sector was plagued with top-heavy, ineffective management, with taking too theoretical of an approach in its programs, with being too slow to respond to new currents of thought, and with having too few Americans in key decision-making positions. Department of State, *supra* note 16, at 7.

It should be noted that these criticisms are vague, and run more to the structure of the sector rather than the substance of its programs.

57. Hearings, *supra* note 13, at 103-04 (Statement of Hans N. Weiler, Professor of Education and Political Science, Stanford University) and Department of State, *supra* note 16, at 5.

58. Department of State, *supra* note 16, at 8.

59. Some notable exceptions notwithstanding, the American professional community in education, for all its intellectual and organizational strength, is not particularly known for its international understanding and sophistication, and I say this as somebody who, for a major part of his life, has looked in on this country from the outside; working in a country as rich and varied as ours makes it easy to forget that there exist both important problems and significant ideas outside of our own boundaries. If anything, the majority of my colleagues in professional education in this country need the information and the inspiration that UNESCO can provide more rather than less; our students, the readers of our books, and the American public at large have a right to expect that we are, as educators, much more conversant with, and sophisticated about, the rich world of ideas outside of this country than we tend to be. What I am afraid of is that a professional community which already has a certain tendency towards insularity, ethnocentrism, and self-sufficiency would be removed yet further from the precarious and imperfect, yet remarkably effective network of communication and cooperation that UNESCO has over the years succeeded in building, especially between the rich and poor countries of this world.

Hearings, *supra* note 13 at 106-07 (statement of Haus N. Weber, Professor of Education and Political Science, Stanford University).

60. Department of State, *supra* note 16, at 10, 13. *See also* Hearings, *supra* note 13, at 177-78 (Statement of Walter A. Rosenblith, Foreign Secretary, National Academy of

Sciences).

61. Hearings, *supra* note 13, at 155-58 (Statement of Harold K. Jacobson).

62. Of the Culture Sector, the Department of State stated, "[t]here is a high degree of compatibility between the mandates and objectives of [the American cultural organizations] and those of UNESCO, and the United States has long been supportive of UNESCO's activities in the fields of preservation and conservation." Department of State, *supra* note 16, at 21.

63. *Id.*

64. Hearings, *supra* note 13, at 198 (Statement of Terry B. Morton, Chairman, U.S. Committee of the International Council on Monuments and Sites).

65. *Id.*

66. *Id.*

67. UNESCO is the only world organization that deals operationally with the cultural dimensions of socio-economic development. It will remain the focal point for dialogue on international cultural issues, and the central coordinating mechanism on cultural affairs and cultural polices. Withdrawal from UNESCO would mean that these central coordinating functions would no longer be as easily available to the U.S. Our participation in cultural affairs on a multilateral basis would diminish, as would our access to data now available to our cultural and academic communities. Department of State, *supra* note 16, at 26.

68. For example, withdrawal has made the U.S. ineligible to participate in the Intergovernmental Committee for Promoting the Return of Cultural Property to its Countries of Origin or Restitution in Case of Illicit Appropriation. Department of State, *supra* note 16, at 26.

69. Department of State, *supra* note 16, at 30.

Chapter X

The International Monetary Fund (IMF)

The International Monetary Fund (IMF) was founded at the Bretton Woods Conference in 1944. It went into operation in 1945, and currently the fund has 152 member countries and a Washington D.C. staff of 1652 people from 100 countries. Voting is weighted, with the Western nations (the "Group of Ten") holding a large percentage. The United States is particularly influential in this world financial institution, as it is in the World Bank. The IMF is financed by members' subscriptions and borrowing which, in 1989, totaled US$6.5 billion. The Fund's available resources were recently augmented by fifty percent in a replenishment program, which will allow for more Structural Adjustment Facility (SAF) Loans to developing countries. The IMF promotes monetary co-operation worldwide by way of collaboration and consultation. The IMF strives for stability and orderliness in exchange. It also aids the balanced growth of world trade and, thus, higher employment rates and higher real incomes. The fund assists in the ending of foreign exchange restrictions and aids members by providing temporary financial resources. The main goals of the IMF are, thus, financial stability and international co-operation. Third World countries have been quite critical of the IMF's "loan conditionality," which they view as detrimental to their economic and social development.

THE IMF UNDER FIRE

Jahangir Amuzegar

The global economic challenges of the 1980s — the colossal debt overhang, wild swings in exchange rates, and continued imbalances in external payments — have presented the International Monetary Fund (IMF) with the immense task of devising orderly and effective solutions. And they have focused unprecedented attention on the organization. Thrown suddenly and inadvertently into the epicenter of the world economic crises after the 1973-1974 oil price shocks, the IMF has gradually, and erroneously, come to be seen as the world's master economic trouble-shooter. A limited-purpose organization, conceived in 1944 to deal with 1930s-style exchange and payments problems, the Fund has recently been pushed by circumstances into becoming a superagency in charge of the global debt and development problems of the 1970s and 1980s — tasks for which it has neither adequate expertise nor sufficient resources.

The IMF still enjoys the support and respect of many multinational economic organizations, bankers, business leaders, government officials, and academics in both industrialized and developing countries. But misconceptions and unrealistic expectations have prompted harsh and often distorted criticisms from other quarters, especially the media.

Initially confined to some left-leaning fringe elements in the Third world, recent attacks on the Fund have been echoed by a curious coalition — including some U.N. Agencies — that defies both North-South and Left-Right divides.

Critics from the less developed countries (LDCs) and their supporters paint the IMF as a highly rigid, single-minded, biased institution dominated by a cabal of industrial countries. These critics accuse the Fund of following a narrow, free market approach to external imbalances and contend that the Fund shows little or no concern that its adjustment policies often cripple economic growth and further skew income distribution in Third World countries. They also think that the IMF is cruelly indifferent to the social and political consequences of its stabilization programs.

Fund detractors in industrialized countries criticize the IMF for being insufficiently market-oriented; for helping noncapitalist and anti-Western countries; and for progressively evolving into a softheaded foreign-aid agency.

Some observers from both sides of the North-South divide claim that fund-supported adjustment programs, by checking demand in many countries simultaneously, give a deflationary bias to the world economy as a whole.

Some skeptics see no useful role for the IMF under the present world economic order. A few believe that the Fund's existence blocks the Third World's economic interests; others argue that, in a world of floating exchange rates, the IMF — which was devised to ensure currency stability — has no part left to play. A hodgepodge of consumerists, religious activists,

and neoliberals oppose the Fund because the IMF allegedly
bails out big multinational banks, favors the rich, helps big
business, and supports dictatorial regimes.   Some old-line
conservatives and free-market ideologues disapprove of the
IMF because they generally oppose public intervention of any
kind in the economy.   And monetarist critics of the U.S.
Federal Reserve Bank would like to dismantle anything that
seems like an international central bank.

There are Western analysts who believe that Fund
programs and facilities — increasingly tailored for and used
by the LDCs — no longer benefit industrialized countries.
Other radical critics, such as the political economist Cheryl
Payer, believe that only a radical restructuring of the
international economic system will solve today's international
economic problems.   They believe that Fund assistance
frustrates the very type of economic discipline and financial
autonomy LDCs need to break out of "imperialism's grip."[1]

Many analysts, by contrast, urge major reforms of the
Fund.   Some conservatives want the IMF to be stricter with
borrowing countries.   Their liberal counterparts emphasize
creating a more Third World-oriented Fund.

Five aspects of the relationship between the IMF and
its LDC clients dominate the debate over the organization:
the Fund's philosophy and principal objectives; its approach
to economic stabilization in deficit countries; the conditions
attached to the use of Fund resources; the costs of domestic
economic adjustment; and the IMF's alleged biases in the
application of its policies and programs.

Critics accuse the IMF of deviating from its principles
and objectives as contained in its Articles of Agreement. They
include a call for "the promotion and maintenance of high
levels of employment and real income."   The Fund, they
argue, favors internal and external stability in deficit member
countries at the expense of economic growth and full
employment. Most LDC-oriented critics would like to see the
IMF facilitate capital flows and encourage stabilization and
expansion of trade in the primary commodities that many
Third World countries depend on for export earnings. Many
also would like to see more IMF control over the creation,
distribution, and management of global liquidity, and more
fund authority over worldwide capital flows, the domestic

policies of reserve-currency countries, and external debt issues. The positions taken by the Third World blocs in the United Nations Conference on Trade and Development, the U.N. General Assembly, and the Fund's Interim Committee and its annual meetings point in the same direction.

These critics argue that at its birth, the Fund was expected to deal with problems of the developed countries. Since no major industrial country currently uses Fund resources or is expected to tap them in the near future, the Fund should now cater to its new, Third World clientele.

The Fund staff rejects allegations of a vested interest in restoring external balances at the expense of other objectives such as employment and growth. The IMF maintains that its stabilization programs are designed to ensure domestic price stability and sustainable external balance, and are, in fact, the very ingredients of increased domestic production, more jobs, and larger incomes. By improving the allocation and use of internal resources like capital and labor, Fund programs help a country increase its productive capacity over the long term.

Additionally, the Fund has adapted its role and its policies to the perceived needs of its LDC membership by developing special facilities such as the buffer stock financing facility, the extended fund facility, the subsidy account, the supplementary financing facility, the cereal imports facility, the Trust Fund, and the latest structural adjustment facility.

Defining Responsibilities

The debate here seems largely a matter of nuance and emphasis rather than basic philosophy. The Fund's argument is that, within the Bretton Woods framework for postwar stability and development, its global task has been to serve as a monetary and financial agency, dealing with short-term gaps in external payments, exchange fluctuations, and capital flows. Its added responsibility for economic expansion and larger productive capacity in the Third world, the IMF emphasizes, must be achieved by encouraging balanced growth in international trade and by evening out short-term capital movements, not by dispensing aid.

Economic stabilization under the IMF's standard

"monetarist" model sees short-term external balance as a precondition for long-term growth. But many liberal critics insist that IMF programs must speed up economic growth and thereby achieve a viable balance of payments by stimulating supply instead of reducing demand. They believe that growth is a condition for adjustment.

According to these critics, the Fund's model subverts LDCs' development strategy in many ways. Essentially, they claim that the IMF view blames inflation on excess aggregate demand while the real culprits are structural bottlenecks in the agricultural, foreign trade, and public sectors; supply shortages due to unused capacity; and other nonmonetary problems common in developing countries. Thus combating inflation and external imbalances by choking off demand — by devaluing currency, reducing credit subsidies and imports, and raising taxes — results in depressing the economy instead. Economic stability requires removing supply bottlenecks by reallocating investment, cutting taxes, and somehow restraining prices and wages.

But the record of the IMF shows that as the nature and causes of the initial problems differ widely in different countries, so do the Fund's policy recommendations. A 1986 Fund staff study, *Fund-Supported Adjustment Programs and Economic Growth*, by Mohsin S. Kahn and Malcolm D. Knight, reiterates that Fund-supported adjustment programs comprise three distinct features: demand-side policies aimed at cooling an overheated economy, supply-side measures designed to expand domestic output, and exchange-rate incentives to improve a country's external competitiveness. For example, IMF programs in Gabon, Panama, Peru, and South Korea during the late 1970s and early 1980s did emphasize demand restraint. But similar programs in Burma and Sri Lanka encouraged an increase in the rate of public investment and the liberalization of imports. In Gabon, Panama, Peru, South Korea, and Sri Lanka, the objective was to increase supply by using excess capacity, improving external competitiveness, or boosting private or public investment.

According to a 1985 Fund report, *Adjustment Programs in Africa*, IMF staff members Justin B. Zulu and Saleh M. Nsouli show that IMF programs in 21 African countries strove to tailor each country's adjustment policies to that country's specific circumstances. While most programs aimed at increasing growth, reducing inflation, and improving balance of payments, considerable flexibility was shown with regard to budgetary deficits, credit expansion, inflation rates, and import volume. According to the same study, all stabilization programs in recent years have emphasized both supply- and demand-oriented policies. The former, addressing exchange rates, prices, interest rates, investment incentives, and efficiency of public enterprises, have all been conducive to growth.

A review of some 94 Fund-supported programs in 64 countries during the 1980-1984 period, prepared by Charles A. Sisson and published in the March 1986 issue of *Finance and Development*, shows a distinct variety of approaches to the adjustment problem and a wide range of policy measures. Although nearly all programs contained limits on credit expansion and government current expenditures, only 55 per cent included measures related to currency values and external trade liberalization; 41 per cent required a cap on or reduction in consumer subsidies; and a mere 28 per cent dealt with budgetary transfers to nonfinancial public enterprises. Even some of the Fund's more knowledgeable critics, such as the economist Graham Bird, clearly admit that "it is far too simplistic and inaccurate to claim that the Fund is a doctrinaire monetarist institution."[2]

Critics who concede that the Fund's primary objective is restoring short-term external balance still assail its approach to adjustment. They maintain that the Fund perceives LDC balance-of-payments deficits, foreign-exchange shortages, budgetary gaps, supply crunches, declining rates of productivity, inflation, and black markets to be largely of domestic origin — the result of economic mismanagement, overspending, exorbitant social welfare programs, and price controls. Domestic inflation and balance-of-payments deficits, in turn, are allegedly traced by the Fund to excessive consumption, insufficient investment, excessive import levels reflecting increased aggregate demand and caused by large budget gaps and loose credit, and anemic export earnings due to domestic inflation and overvalued currencies.

These critics maintain that LDC external imbalances

are in fact frequently caused by a host of other external factors beyond LDC control that have nothing to do with domestic waste or inflation: oil prices artificially stimulated rapid growth through easy credit, world-wide inflation, declining demand for commodities, deteriorating terms of trade and protectionism, rising real rates of interest on foreign debt, and poor harvests. The Fund is thus blamed for believing that deficits — no matter how they are caused — call for adjustment, and that adjustment must focus on the deficits, whether temporary or persistent.

The Fund is also often accused of identifying the adjustment's success with improvements in the trade or current account balance — an interpretation that the critics see not only as tautological but also as harmfully misleading. For improvements in the trade balance, they argue, result overwhelmingly from cuts in imports, not necessarily in big increases in exports. Such drastic and unsustainable cuts in foreign purchases not only limit LDCs' current and future output levels, they also hurt LDC trading partners, who end up losing markets. The real adjustment, say the critics, must be structural, involving such permanent changes as a shift in the composition of production and demand to boost export earnings and reduce dependence on imports.

The Fund's critics are right in claiming that it always insists on adjustment regardless of the nature or origin of the external balance. But the Fund also has an equally valid position in arguing that the need for adjustment is a pragmatic necessity, not the reflection of any dogma. In the March 1986 issue of *Finance and Development*, IMF managing Director Jacques de Larosière observes that countries with soaring inflation, enormous fiscal deficits, huge and wasteful public sectors, money-losing public enterprises, distorted exchange rates, and low interest rates are unlikely to mobilize domestic savings or attract foreign investment, and are bound to crowd out domestic resources in a way that will hurt growth. Without adjustment, writes Fund staff member Wanda Tseng, external and internal imbalances eventually will deplete the country's international reserves, erode its international creditworthiness, dry up access to foreign funds, and result in the stoppage of needed imports.[3]

With regard to the origin of external deficits, Fund critics seem bent on constructing a general thesis out of isolated cases. Some, but not all, balance-of-payments gaps are clearly caused by factors outside a country's control. In the case of Jamaica, for example, even one of the Fund's most astute critics admits that during the 1972-1980 period domestic policies and structural factors were the prime culprits behind the excess demand and the worsening payments position. Nor was imported inflation found to be a "major cause" of the island's deteriorating economy. In general, the authorities declined to adopt unpopular adjustment measures necessitated by their own profligate fiscal and monetary policies. Another IMF critic attributed Indonesia's 1965-1966 crisis mainly to hyperinflation between 1962 and 1966 resulting from government deficit financing. Even in Kenya between 1974 and 1981, where major external factors — mainly the two oil shocks — were at work, domestic monetary forces and the mismanagement of the coffee and tea boom had to bear their share of responsibility.[4]

The critics, however, seem to have a strong point in arguing that, for most of the deficit-ridden LDCs, the external shocks of the 1970s and the early 1980s almost totally altered the fundamental assumptions on which their medium-term economic planning was based. A completely different type and direction of adjustment was required for many of these countries, such as a much bigger shot of capital and much more stimulation of supply, instead of routine belt tightening.

IMF Biases

A much stronger and more vituperative attack is aimed at the Fund's conditions for making its resources available. The main condition — a "viable" payments position — is defined as a current account deficit that can be sustained by capital inflows on terms compatible with a country's development prospects without resorting to restrictions on trade and payments, which add to rather than correct the existing distortions.

Almost all critics agree on the need for some conditionality. The quarrel, then, is about the types of conditions needed. At the macroeconomic level, the IMF's

"draconian" approach and "shock treatment" are blamed for
hindering economic growth, raising unemployment, lowering
the already low Third World standards of living, ravaging the
poorest of the poor, and seriously undermining the country's
capacity for realistic adjustment.[5]   Even in countries
committed to adjustment and stabilization, the critics point
out, formidable constraints — internal political friction,
inadequate central financial control mechanisms, pressure
groups or broader public resistance, and bureaucratic
inefficiencies — make Fund measures hard to swallow.

Fund-prescribed   microeconomic   remedies   are
considered by the critics particularly ill-conceived, if not
downright harmful.   Devaluation is regarded as inherently
regressive because it raises the costs of essential imports,
leaves untouched exports subject to extremely low supply
elasticities, and adds to domestic inflation.   Higher interest
rates are judged irrelevant in the context of Third World
economies because so much credit goes to the public sector,
because private savers are usually few and insignificant, and
because capital flight has little to do with interest-rate
differentials.   Reduced real wages, lower subsidies for the
poor, and cutbacks on other social welfare programs are
regarded as the nemeses of sociopolitical stability.   Credit
restrictions are thought to reduce employment rather than
inflation.

The IMF responds by arguing that conditions are
neither rigid nor inflexible and that they are designed jointly
with the member country. IMF conditions are applied flexibly
as well, with varying socioeconomic circumstances taken into
account. The periodic review of Fund programs confirms the
agency's interest in ensuring sufficient flexibility. Further,
the IMF's approach to balance of payments does not work
only through demand deflation and real-income reduction.
The relationship between monetary factors and external
imbalances is important, but the IMF approach embraces all
aspects of economic policies, bearing on both demand and
supply conditions. Finally, although restoring the external
balance is admittedly a Fund objective, it is not the sole
purpose of adjustment. The IMF believes that adjustment
ultimately encourages high employment and long-term
growth by balancing aggregate demand and supply better.

Fund programs are also often blamed for their allegedly high social and economic costs. The critics argue that, despite its best efforts, the IMF can hardly avoid politics. National strikes, riots, political upheavals, and social unrest in Argentina, Bolivia, Brazil, the Dominican Republic, Ecuador, Egypt, Haiti, Liberia, Peru, Sudan, and elsewhere have been attributed directly or indirectly to the implementation of austerity measures advocated by the IMF.

The companion charge of undermining national sovereignty and political democracy in Third World countries follows from the social frictions and imbalances that austerity allegedly brings. LDC governments add that the Fund does not quite appreciate the political risks involved in applying the IMF recipe.

Conditionality is also thought to undermine fair income redistribution. The argument maintains that the Fund's adjustment programs almost always require a cut in both public and private consumption, in order to transfer resources to investment and the export sector. Critics frequently argue that the heaviest and most immediate burdens of adjustment are likely to be passed by the upper and middle classes to the poor. The Fund's alleged insistence on reducing or eliminating food and other consumer subsidies is further attacked on the ground that these policies are in fact a rational means of internal income redistribution in countries lacking an effectively progressive tax system or adequate social security schemes.

Fund supporters argue that blaming the IMF for fomenting political unrest merely confuses cause and effect. Many countries do not come to the IMF until the seeds of political turmoil are firmly rooted in their soil. Indeed, economics-related civil disturbances are hardly unknown in countries without Fund programs — witness Iran, Nigeria, South Africa, and Tunisia. And scores of countries adjusting with the IMF's assistance have been remarkably stable. Of the 67 countries that carried a stabilization program at some period between 1980 and 1983, critics can single out only the 10 mentioned previously as having experienced serious turmoil — not all of it Fund-related. Nevertheless, the unrest that can be blamed on the IMF must be considered a minus for adjustment policies.

Finally, the Fund is charged with harboring biases toward capitalism and against government planning and economic intervention.   Worse, it is called an agent of neocolonialization for the West. More moderate critics accuse the Fund of an ideological slant that results in the scrapping of public enterprises, the abandonment of price controls, the reduction of food subsidies and free medical and educational facilities, and the elimination of social services from already deprived populations.

The Fund is also alleged to discriminate in its treatment of poor and rich members.   LDC supporters claim that the Fund opposes as distortions of the free market such policies as exchange restrictions, wage-price controls, rationing, and subsidies when pursued by the developing countries.   Yet the IMF is virtually impotent in the fight against similar practices by its industrial members.   Critics additionally see a perceived asymmetry in treatment between reserve-currency centers (and surplus countries) on the one hand and the rest of the world on the other.   This asymmetry is considered not only inconsistent in itself, but also crucial in shifting the onus of adjusting external imbalance to deficit LDCs.   Reserve-currency countries like the United States, it is alleged, cannot be pressured by the IMF to adjust, and can continue their profligate ways year after year.

Finally, critics see an IMF political bias that is reflected in sympathy and leniency toward regimes pivotal to the economic, military, strategic, or geopolitical interests of the United States or other major Fund shareholders, and toward countries with international economic clout because of enormous debts that threaten the global monetary system.[6] To prove this political bias, critics such as staff members of the Center for International Policy claim that proposed IMF loans to "countries from the wrong side of the track," including Grenada before the U.S. invasion, Nicaragua, and Vietnam, have been vetoed by major shareholders for "technical reasons."   Credit for others, such as El Salvador and South Africa, is routinely approved.

Yet Fund members today include countries with distinctly nonmarket philosophies. Any penchant toward the market simply reflects the belief that market allocations are more efficient.   On the question of discriminatory treatment of the poor, the dividing line is not poverty but the balance-of-payments situation. Surplus or reserve countries may indeed escape the Fund's strict discipline. After all, they have no need for Fund resources. But this is a choice open also to poor countries, which can decide not to approach the IMF. Further, some of the rich deficit countries that have drawn on the Fund in the past, such as Great Britain, France, and Italy, have been similarly treated.

It is no secret that the IMF statutes and covenants expect the Fund to promote a world of free markets, free trade, and unitary exchange rates under a multilateral payments system. To allow any different course of action would place the IMF in violation of its legal mandate.

Yet not only do such centrally planned economies as China, Hungary, Romania, and Yugoslavia enjoy full IMF membership and make ample use of its resources without any encumbrances or impositions, but some left-of-center governments, in fact, have in the past benefited more from Fund assistance than supposedly favored regimes. By one key measure, Jamaica, under then Prime Minister Michael Manley's democratic socialist regime in 1979, was the world's largest recipient of Fund resources, receiving 360 per cent of its quota compared with only 64 per cent for other developing countries.[7]

The Fund adamantly maintains that its Articles of Agreement specifically prohibit political considerations for the use of its resources. Yet the charges of political bias deserve closer scrutiny. The Fund's ability to maintain absolute neutrality is, to be sure, affected by the interests of influential member governments, by the decisions of the executive board to grant or deny loans to a given country, and by the evaluation reports and recommendations of staff missions on a country's underlying economic conditions.

Major shareholding governments obviously have political, strategic, and economic interests in their own zones of influence or involvement and do not wish to separate economic from political and other considerations. The U.S. Congress, for example, explicitly requires that the American executive director at the Fund vote in a prescribed manner in regard to certain countries and regimes. Other major governments may have similar predilections, but are not quite prepared to legislate them.

The executive board has a mixed position. Its members are appointed or elected by developed or developing member governments, to whom they are beholden. They, too, cannot be purely apolitical robots. They lobby for their views among their colleagues; they try to win over management and staff; and they endeavor to protect the political and other interests of their constituencies. At the same time, board members are required and expected to uphold the Fund's basic objectives and to ensure the proper functioning of the international monetary system. In neither of these two capacities can the executive directors as a whole be found to be practicing a distinct, or immutable, political bias. The burden of proof is still on the critics to show that many IMF decisions are made deliberately   according   to   political   considerations. Significantly, the IMF staff has never been accused of partisan political bias.

The issue of inherent bias against the poor is more intractable.   In general, allegations that the Fund's reluctance to suggest specific national redistributive priorities is of no help to the poor and the powerless may have a certain moral validity. It is also true that the objective of better income distribution, or at least of proportionate sacrifices, is not explicitly included in a country's letter of intent as a condition for Fund assistance. But claims that the IMF is indifferent to such factors are grossly unfair.

More important, the critics' ardent contention that the cost of adjustment is always borne disproportionately by the poor has seldom been supported by any statistical evidence. Rather, there is usually an a priori presumption that Fund programs aggravate income inequities because the rich and the strong see to it that they avoid the effects of the stabilization measures. The arguments have been at best theoretical, and usually anecdotal. The countless books, articles, speeches, and statements critical of the Fund contain not a single piece of empirical information or statistical data showing that Fund-supported programs have, in a clear and convincing manner, aggravated internal income-distribution patterns.

Moreover, the impact of IMF programs on income distribution essentially depends on how the program is implemented by national authorities. In the Fund's view, any other approach would entangle the IMF directly in microeconomic policy measures closely related to a country's social and political choices. Such involvement probably would be vehemently resisted by most countries, and would also violate the Fund's own mandate and guidelines.

In addition, the Fund believes that changes in income distribution as such cannot be performance criteria in adjustment programs because this area is so difficult to quantify. The numbers can be affected by methods of classifying income recipients. Further, few programs last long enough to allow a comprehensive study of their distributional implications, particularly where necessary information on consumption, government transfers, nonmonetary sources of income, and personal income levels is inadequate or unreliable — as is generally the case in developing countries. Finally, the Fund maintains that any given domestic distributional system is the product of deep-rooted economic, social, political, and cultural phenomena going back decades, if not centuries. Fund programs, being of relatively limited scope and duration, cannot be expected to make much of a dent in the system.

In the absence of clear-cut evidence and good data, theoretical arguments do assume importance. In the short run, stabilization programs can worsen income distribution. But the story scarcely ends there. The distributional outcome of a cut in government outlays, for example, depends on where the specific reductions are made. A reduction of food subsidies to urban workers could help the rural poor by raising farm prices. A tax on urban services and amenities could likewise redistribute income from workers in modern industries — a minority in the labor force — to the rural poor. Moreover, a reduction in inflation itself tends to favor poorer groups because they can rarely adjust their incomes to rising prices.

A forthcoming IMF study, *Fund-Supported Programs, Fiscal Policy, and Income Distribution*, concludes, after presenting some case studies, that fund programs have not been directed against the poor; often, in fact, policies have been designed to protect low-income groups as much as possible. Even when total consumption has been reduced through prudent demand-management policies, high-income groups probably have been hit hardest. The elimination of large general subsidy programs has inflicted some hardships on the population as a whole, including the poor. But the study calls such programs "inefficient and ineffective" mechanisms for redistributing incomes.

Some Success Stories

Some Fund detractors are quick to denigrate the IMF's achievements in the Third World and cite Mexico's current crisis in particular as a blatant example of the failure of the adjustment formula. More moderate critics admit that Fund programs have succeeded in improving the balance of payments in several countries. But they contend that other significant benefits have not followed.

Yet the overall track record of IMF programs shows some noteworthy accomplishments. An independent 1984 study by the German Federal Parliament, *The Conditionality Policy of the IMF*, shows that although the current account deficits of all non-oil-developing countries (NODCs) tended to expand between 1970 and 1980, most Fund-assisted countries managed to close those gaps perceptibly. The inflation rate for all NODCs increased during that period, while the tempo in countries with adjustment programs was slower. Countries undergoing adjustment experienced sharper decreases in short-term growth than the group as a whole, but their long-term expansion rates were above average. Finally, the report noted, the increase in real consumption in program countries was only slightly less on average — 4.3 per cent as opposed to 4.7 per cent annually — than in the whole group.

According to the aforementioned 1985 IMF study of the 21 African countries where the IMF had an ongoing program from 1981 to 1983, economic growth targets were achieved in about one-fifth of the countries, inflation targets were reached in roughly one-half of the cases, and the balance-of-payments goals were reached in about two-fifths of these states.

At first glance, improvements under Fund-supported programs may show that the IMF's advice is often better suited to containing inflation and rectifying external imbalances than to fostering growth. But some short-term consolidation in the growth tempo may in fact be necessary for longer-term expansion. And although the success stories may not be numerous or seem spectacular or even truly impressive to the hostile critics, they nonetheless tend to contradict the allegations that Fund programs bring few, if any, benefits to LDCs. Moreover, these detractors frequently fail to ask where these countries would be without the IMF.

Still, it is disturbing that, despite its valiant rescue efforts across the Third World, the IMF is hard pressed to show more than a few clearly viable programs out of the roughly three dozen under its wing. Why haven't the programs done better?

One answer is that the IMF's latest perennial clients have been among either the poorest LDCs with large balance-of-payments disequilibriums, or the newly industrializing countries with gargantuan external debts. Adjustment has been made more difficult by outside factors such as high energy costs, high interest rates, world recessions, and protectionism.

Second, IMF programs often bring some concealed problems into the open, making partial success look like a setback and partial recovery like a retrogression. In a country living beyond its means, the real causes of payments difficulties — such as overvalued currencies, artificially low prices, and virtual rationing, as evidenced by shortages and black markets — are rarely acknowledged. When Fund programs begin to remove some of the existing distortions and dislocations through cost-price adjustments, the economic weaknesses that these policies hid or suppressed begin to emerge for all to see.

Third, the worse a country's problems, the harder it will be for IMF programs to succeed. The host government's cooperation is crucial as well. A 1984 Fund study showed a "striking" correlation between the success of IMF programs and the observance of policy measures by the governments concerned.[8]

Fourth, most of the Fund-assisted countries that have been less than successful are those that had long postponed adjustment efforts. As stabilization is delayed, distortions become solidified, and rectification becomes correspondingly costlier and more painful. It literally pays economically, socially, and politically to go to the IMF early.

In no other North-South debate has the so-called dialogue of the deaf been so evident as in that over the IMF. The biggest reason for the critics' persistence is surely the Fund's patchy track record. The increasing number of cases where disbursement of standby credits has been suspended because of noncompliance with Fund criteria, and the growing number of members declared ineligible for further assistance because of long overdue financial obligations, show that the path of the Fund-supported programs has been neither short nor smooth.

Indeed, in spite of prolonged use of Fund programs by certain members, economic imbalances persist for many internal and external reasons. Fund successes in other countries also have often been temporary.

But if the IMF cannot or will not influence domestic priorities, such as the size of military budgets or the pattern of income distribution, that have a major impact on the economy, why, the critics ask, impose an austerity program that skirts these problems? The same question is prompted by the IMF's inability to do much about external problems, such as protectionism or foreign recessions, that lie beyond the control of deficit LDCs and that can often make or break a country's prospects. If the IMF's conditional assistance produces no more than certain short-term improvements in the country's external balances and some temporary reductions in the rate of inflation at the cost of growth, full employment, social welfare, and self-reliance, is it worth the attendant sacrifices?

Convincing answers to these questions are not easy to come by because all these critical inquiries seem to miss two crucial points. First, what other choices do LDCs facing deteriorating debt and development problems have? Second, putting aside the merits of the critics' arguments or of the Fund's defense, are there other practical and effective policies that the IMF, as presently constituted, can pursue?

Debt-strapped countries incapable of paying their external bills and unable or unwilling to adopt Fund-supported adjustment programs have three alternatives: repudiate external debt altogether and seek to start afresh;

seek bilateral accommodations with bondholders; or go it alone.

An outright repudiation, or even a debt moratorium, obviously would release resources for more urgent outlays. But it might close off larger and more valuable access to foreign reserves, assets, credits, markets, and technology. For this reason, even the poorest African countries assembled for the July 1985 Organization of African Unity summit refused to endorse any suggestion of wholesale default. Nor did Cuban Premier Fidel Castro's similar proposal for Latin America attract any takers.

The second alternative is appealing, but except for a very few lucky and resourceful countries, foreign creditors usually ask LDC debtors to accept the Fund's discipline before engaging in debt renegotiations or extending new credits. The consequences of doing nothing, the third alternative, would be further economic deterioration and perhaps a need for stricter adjustment efforts. In the Fund's view, the cost of nonadjustment by any measure will probably greatly exceed those of adjustment.

The IMF, in its turn, can adapt to external realities and the critics' challenges in four ways: by increasing its resources and expanding both the scope and the number of its special LDC facilities to serve its Third World members better; by revising its rules and statutes to become more adjustment-oriented toward its developed members and comparatively more finance-directed toward LDCs; by abdicating its structural adjustment role in the LDC economies in favor or the World Bank; or by doing nothing.

A Fund with twice as much liquidity could accommodate its LDC members with less painful adjustment programs. The Fund also could revise its rules to improve more decisively its role in overseeing the exchange-rate system, its surveillance capabilities over the surplus and reserve-currency countries, and its management of international liquidity.

The Fund staff has already recommended improvements in the design of adjustment measures in favor of low-income groups. These include exchange-rate changes that provide adequate incentives for the agricultural sector dominated by small farmers, greater access to domestic credit markets, taxation of global income, expansion of tax bases, replacement of quotas by tariffs, and the provision of basic skills and vocational training for unemployables.[9]

In addition, the Fund could get out of medium-term or Extended Facility financing — an activity that may duplicate the World Bank's structural adjustment loans. This step would free the Fund to concentrate on its exchange-related functions and operations.

The fourth alternative — and perhaps the easiest — is for the Fund to do nothing. But the status quo includes the current and thorny problem of the repayment of the Fund's past loans, some of which are now technically in default. Without fresh efforts and initiatives, the number of countries in arrears will steadily rise. Further, the continued attacks on the Fund, if not properly dealt with, may further tarnish and distort the Fund's image, discourage some member governments from seeking badly needed IMF help because of domestic political opposition, and weaken and erode world public support for the Fund's surveillance, guidance, and assistance.

Meanwhile, the difficulty for the IMF in adopting any of the first three alternatives remains its members' inability to agree on either the need for fundamental revision of the current trade and exchange regime or the nature of critical procedural changes in the system's implementation. Most developed countries repeatedly have rejected such basic Third World proposals as a system of target zones for keeping major currencies in leash, a doubling of IMF quotas, larger LDC access to Fund resources, periodic issues of the Special Drawing Rights (SDRs), the IMF's reserve currency, a link between SDRs and development finance, a grant to LDCs of 50 per cent of the vote on all Fund decisions, the reactivation of the Trust Fund for fresh lending to poorer countries, and the establishment of a new interest-rate facility.

And the LDCs deem unacceptable such rich-country suggestions as giving greater publicity to the outcome of Fund consultations with members, extending the techniques of enhanced surveillance, assuring that commercial banks continue to play a big role in providing international reserves, and increasing World Bank-IMF collaboration in the design of conditionality.

No realistic compromise is yet in sight, except for possible elaboration of the Baker plan. Memories of the past create the uneasy feeling that, without a major new financial crisis, the Fund's principal shareholders and their bankers may not have enough incentive to accommodate poorer countries. Some concerned observers actually believe that such a crisis is already on the horizon. Averting disaster requires genuine debtor-creditor cooperation — no matter which side has a more valid position or better arguments.

Any new initiative must synthesize the positions of the two groups. The chances of reaching this consensus, in turn, would be greatly enhanced if the sparring partners could agree upon several fundamental postulates. First, LDC debtors must admit that the bulk of their credit needs must be reasonably conditioned. The debtors must also be willing, in exchange for fresh inflows of foreign credit, management, and technology, to adopt certain genuine domestic economic reforms.

The industrialized creditors must accept the fact that no matter how economically necessary adjustment conditions are, they must be politically palatable and operationally feasible and must offer a clear promise of growth in addition to economic stability. Also needed are improvements in the workings of the international exchange system, a multilateral trading regime where the handicaps of different players are properly reckoned with, and a system of resource transfers based on both country needs and global competitiveness. Such measures as multiyear reschedulings of debts, the reduction of interest rates, or some eventual debt write-offs might be part of the solution.

Serious North-South negotiations in the framework of the forthcoming meetings of the Fund's Interim Committee and the joint Bank/Fund Developments Committee — or a new global monetary conference — may offer new possibilities for such an approach. Without them, the expectations of critics and the Fund's capacity to meet these expectations will remain far apart. The persistence and poignancy of the attacks on the Fund — and eventually on the World Bank, once its inevitable conditionality begins to bite — will further damage the prestige and influence of both organizations at a time when their involvement in the Third World is more necessary than ever to ensure global economic stability and growth.

FOOTNOTES

1.   See for example, Cheryl Payer, *The Debt Trap* (New York: Monthly Review Press, 1975).

2.   Graham Bird, "Relationship, Resource Uses, and the Conditionality Debate," *The Quest for Economic Stabilization,* ed. Tony Killick (New York: St. Martin's Press, 1984), 179.

3.   Wanda Tseng. "The Effects of Adjustment," *Finance and Development* (December 1984), 2-5.

4.   Jennifer Sharpley, "Jamaica, 1972-80," Mary Sutton, "Indonesia, 1966-70," and Tony Killick, "Kenya, 1975-81," in *The IMF and Stabilization,* ed. Tony Killick (New York: St. Martin's Press, 1984).

5.   See Chuck Lane, "Dunning Democracy," *The New Republic* (4 June 1984), 9-12; and Richard E. Feinberg and Valeriana Kallab, eds., *Adjustment Crisis in the Third World* (Washington, D.C.: Overseas Development Council, 1984).

6.   See for example, Amir Jamal, "Power and the Third World Struggle for Equilibrium," *Banking on Poverty: The Global Impact of the IMF and World Bank,* ed. Jill Torrie (Toronto: Between The Lines. 1983); and Ismail-Sabri Abdalla, "The Inadequacy and Loss of Legitimacy of the IMF," *Development Dialogue,* no. 2 (1980), 25-53.

7.   Sharpley, "Jamaica, 1972-80," *IMF and Stabilization,* 160.

8.   Justin B. Zulu and Saleb M. Nsouli, "Adjustment Programs in Africa," *Finance and Development* (March 1984), 7.

9.   Charles A. Sisson, "Fund-Supported Programs and Income Distribution in LDCs," *Finance and Development* (March 1986), 36.

Chapter XI

International Maritime Organization (IMO)

The International Maritime Organization (IMO) was founded as a specialized United Nations agency in 1959, and currently has 133 member countries. The IMO budget is financed by contributions received from member states, and it totaled 21.6 million British pounds in 1988-1989. The organization encourages co-operation among states on technical matters related to international shipping. It is designed to create the highest possible standards of safety at sea and efficiency in navigation. The IMO also concerns itself with the protection of life at sea and the protection of the marine environment. This entails efforts to prevent pollution caused by ships and various other craft. The IMO also assists developing countries in maritime concerns that require technical knowledge and application. Related activities are the protection against sea piracy and terrorism, the facilitation of maritime traffic and assistance in legal matters.

The "New" International Maritime Organization and its Place in Development of International Maritime Law

Wilhelm H. Lampe

I. Introduction

Since May 22, 1982, "IMO" — for the "International Maritime Organization" — has been the new acronym of the former "IMCO," the "Inter-Governmental Maritime Consultative Organization." When in March, 1975 this author, on behalf of the Government of the Federal Republic of Germany, proposed to the Organization's Working Group on Amendments to the IMCO Convention that IMCO's name be changed to IMO,[1] that proposal and the reasons put forward to substantiate it met with general although not unanimous approval.

The Japanese delegation — otherwise often a supporter of the German Government's position — went into opposition, although no formal reason was given. Talks on a more personal level revealed the story behind it. The Japanese had no objections to the new name; quite the contrary, they thought it was a good and a correct one. But there was much consternation among the Japanese over that acronym — "IMO." When it was pronounced as a word — i:mou[2] — it was exactly the Japanese term for "hot potato." The Secretary-General soon came up with a solution to that problem. Care would be taken, he promised, that the acronym would not be pronounced as a word but rather as a three-letter abbreviation, viz. *ai-m-ou*, instead of *i:mou*. When in May of 1975 the Organization's Council recommended adoption of the name-change proposal, Japan joined in its unopposed adoption by the Assembly.[3]

This was, however, much more than a "cosmetic" change of the Organization's name, and the reasons for it reflect IMO's increasingly important role in implementing the developing body of international maritime law. This role was emphasized when, beginning in 1973, the Third United Nations Conference on the Law of the Sea Convention[4] made it plain that "competent international organizations" would have to take over numerous specific tasks, or at least the implementation of the various conventions with technical or maritime aspects they had been framing or would create in the future to serve as models or instruments for implementation of the new rules of the law of the sea.

The group of countries with special interest in shipping[5] — trying to keep the balance between protection of the marine environment and the freedom of navigation — were united in the opinion that only one organization of which all of them were members (and in which nine of them functioned as "Council" members) would be eligible for that purpose: IMCO. To the surprise of many delegates (the author included), there was one more thing they had to realize: IMCO was relatively little known, its importance was often underrated, and it turned out that the Organization overall was looked upon as being something which it was not.

Further investigation revealed that the misconceptions about IMCO were directly related to its name. The term "intergovernmental" met with distrust and suspicion, while the word "consultative" was interpreted to indicate the restricted powers and responsibilities of the Organization. Ideas of this kind were heard particularly in conversations with representatives of developing countries, and, because the above-quoted terms were an understatement of the Organization's scope and function, the principle that trade names must be true and correct was itself sufficient to require an amendment to the Organization's "label."

Indeed, the number of members had increased from 31 in the year of foundation, 1948, to 88 in 1975 (and has since reached 122[6]), plainly a size justifying the use of an adjective such as "international," even in the sense of "universal." Moreover, the Organization had by 1975 left the stage where it was engaged exclusively or predominantly in "consultative" activities. Its main function was no longer a free and friendly but non-committal exchange of opinions and experience, but rather that of an "umbrella" for comprehensive work in committees, subcommittees, and working groups undertaking to draw up a variety of multilateral instruments. The international conventions adopted by IMCO just in the first 15 years of its existence were quite impressive, both in number and in content.[7]

Study of the question of the Organization's name led to further review of its structure, so that, simultaneously with the change of name, a number of additions and other supplementations and modifications of the IMCO Convention[8] came into force. They were mainly related to the status of the "Legal Committee" and the "Marine Environment Protection Committee." Originally, both committees had been created by the IMCO Council, not through the Convention, so that they were considered more or less "dependent" upon the Council. Institutionalizing these two committees under the terms of the Convention was an obvious improvement that more clearly defined the relationship of the committees to each other and to the Council. The overall organizational structure chart on page 241 thus now reflects the following pattern:[9] four[10] committees "on equal footing" as the basic elements of IMCO's work, functioning under the coordinating and directive guidance of the Council. That new structure brought to the Organization the kind of internal order needed to avoid the friction and inefficiency inherent in overlapping spheres of responsibility and established an atmosphere conducive to achieving the best results in the Organization's work.

Consequently, the shortcomings of the Organization's original name and the aspects best conveyed in any replacement were almost self-evident by the time "IMO" was proposed in 1975. The subsequent changes in organizational structure adopted simultaneously in May of 1982 thus left IMO particularly well situated to fulfill its implementing role in the concurrently expanding field of international maritime law. What that role is now and is to become is a function of IMO's historical development, the primary areas of its current responsibilities and the already-apparent options for its future. It is these three topics that this article addresses.

II. IMO's Historical Development

A. Formation of the Organization

The history of the Organization, as such, began shortly after the Second World War, although the very foundations of well-organized, multi-national cooperation in the maritime shipping sphere dates back to the last years of the war. In 1944, ten of the Allies formed the so-called "United Maritime Authority," which carried on its work under the name of the "United Maritime Consultative Council" when the immediate burden of the war was no longer pressing.[11]   When discussions were underway for preparing the foundation of the United Nations Organization, they almost from the onset included the ways and means of international cooperation in the field of shipping.[12] In this context, it is significant that the question *whether* such cooperation through some sort of organization was useful and suitable was never posed; the matter was even then regarded as a self-evident necessity.

In the search for an answer to the question *how* that could be done, the means closest at hand was the Economic and Social Council of the United Nations ("ECOSOC"), which had commenced its work in early 1946. Several articles[13] of the U.N. charter gave ECOSOC competence in maritime-related matters with which this group soon occupied itself, and as early as at its meeting in London in February of 1946 established its initial contacts with the Consultative Council

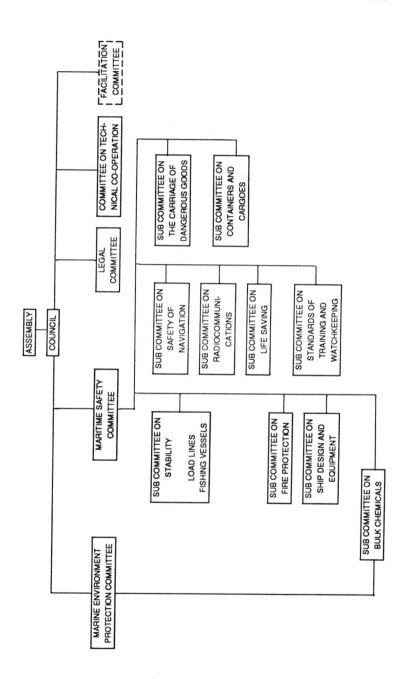

that was simultaneously meeting in that city. By the autumn of that year, the Consultative Council presented to its member-governments an initial program for an "Inter-Governmental Maritime Consultative Organization," including a draft convention establishing the Organization as a specialized United Nations agency, under Article 59 of the U.N. Charter, to be closely connected to the Economic and Social Council pursuant to Article 63 of the Charter. Looking back at the developments of the time, it is evident that the vigorous determination of many nations for international cooperation was the stimulus for such quick action.

The discussions of the draft constitution of the Organization within a specially-appointed working group focused on two main topics: the definition of the purposes of the Organization, on the one hand, and the responsibilities of its functional components (as well as their membership structure), on the other hand. From the outset of these discussions, there was unanimity among the members of the working group that the activities of the Organization should concentrate on matters of maritime safety, and they had no difficulty hammering out the finest details when it came to elaborating on the most comprehensive of definitions.[14]

The point where fundamental difficulties did arise, however, was in the discussion on the Organization's purposes and competences in the fields of shipping economics, commercial matters and the legal aspects of seaborne trade. The problem was solved through a compromise formula for Articles 1(b) and (c) of the Convention. That text — unchanged from the draft stage until today — specifies as one of the purposes of the Organization to encourage the removal of discriminatory action and unnecessary restrictions by member-governments with respect to seaborne trade, and also gives a carefully balanced description of such administrative measures that do not fall within that category.[15]

Nevertheless, a considerable number of member-governments expressed their opposition to this overall formulation by entering a reservation when they signed the Convention. It was by no coincidence that all the Scandinavian countries made a statement — and an unusually strong one — to the effect that they would consider a renunciation of the Convention if IMCO were to assume competence in matters of the kind mentioned in Articles 1(b) and (c). The Scandinavian countries (led by Norway), as well as Greece, have always been strong supporters of the principle of the freedom of international shipping, which, according to their philosophy, should be upheld through virtually unrestricted maritime shipping regulated by nothing but free and fair competition.

This is regarded as one of the binding principles by all member States of the Organization for Economic Co-operation and Development,[16] but it is an absolutely vital element of the day-to-day economic policy of those countries that have large merchant fleets but only a relatively limited volume of seaborne trade. These countries understandably had an almost allergic reaction to have even the mere terms of reference for a specialized agency of the United Nations include such matters. The obvious reason behind their reactions was the fear that the membership situation in an organization open to all states could produce majorities that would not support policies of the kind they considered an economic necessity.

A quarter of a century has elapsed since IMCO came into being. This should be time enough to measure the correctness of those political decisions by the yardstick of actual developments.

B. Intermediate Results of the Founding Premises

Since its founding, IMCO never made a serious effort to seize competence in matters bearing directly on the economic aspects of seaborne trade. Those who had originally favored such self-restraint have come to regret bitterly their attitude at the time, because the gap left open by IMCO was soon discovered and filled by the United Nations Commission on Trade and Development ("UNCTAD"), through its Committee on Shipping, which was founded in 1965 and became active in 1967. It soon became evident that the practice of UNCTAD (an organ of the United Nations Organization itself) to advance the often militant intentions and programs of developing countries with planned-economy policies was not at all what had been expected of a forum designed to draw up a "liberal" international shipping policy. By the time this pattern was perceived, it was too late for a change. The rare initiatives to bring about a change-over of responsibilities towards IMCO — for example, a submission by Venezuela to IMCO's XIth Assembly[17] — have all faltered in their early stages.[18]

Conflicts over competences in other areas were, however, numerous, and IMCO more often than it wanted to found itself in a defensive position. For example, an ECOSOC decision made in August of 1977[19] was meant to eliminate a certain overlap in the field of containerization by assigning the "primary responsibility" in these matters to UNCTAD. After a pertinent intervention by IMCO,[20] it was clarified that such assignment did not entail "exclusive responsibility." In the end, IMCO has restricted its own activities to the technical aspects, whereas UNCTAD has been dealing with the relevant problems of a commercial and/or economic nature.[21]

A similar dispute ensued when UNCTAD — although not requested to do so — offered its cooperation in the preparation of amendments to a number of long-standing conventions dealing with issues in the superior context of private and/or commercial maritime law.[22] No response has yet been made to UNCTAD's offer. Another sphere where such trouble had come up was the field of aid to developing countries, but a delineation of responsibilities has meanwhile been found along the lines mentioned above.[23]

IMCO also had teething pains with its own organizational structure. Up to 1967, there had been only two component groups, in addition to the Assembly, with decision-making authority: the Maritime Safety Committee, with its various sub-committees, and the Council. The former had 14 members, the latter 16. In accordance with the charter of the Organization, the membership of these groups was to represent primarily nations with interests in maritime shipping and commerce, respectively. As a result, they had basically the same membership structure; in either body the countries owning the largest merchant fleets constituted the majority. The original IMCO Convention had specified that in the Maritime Safety Committee "not less than eight [of its members] shall be the largest ship-owning nations," whereas the criterion for membership in the Council was defined with less clarity as the "six nations with the largest interest in providing international shipping services."[24]

In practice, the difference between the membership prerequisites for the two groups was negligible, since the six Council members were, as noted above, always among the eight Maritime Safety Committee members. Nevertheless, that difference was essentially the source of a question put before the International Court of Justice in 1959 by the first IMCO Assembly.[25]

As reformulated by the Court, the question to be considered was: "Has the Assembly, in not electing Liberia and Panama to the Maritime Safety Committee, exercised its electoral power in a manner in accordance with the provisions of Article 28(a) of the IMCO Convention?"[26] At the time, Liberia and Panama ranked third and eighth, respectively, in the world tonnage list.[27] The International Court of Justice therefore had to decide whether "election" to the Maritime Safety Committee under the terms of the tonnage criterion was limited to ascertaining the names of those eight members (according to their tonnage rank) or whether other circumstances would also have to be taken into account and, if so, which ones.

The two countries that believed they had been disadvantaged invoked their sovereign rights to register ships in accordance with their own legislation, a position supported by the United States, the country whose shipowners controlled the merchant fleets of those countries. The majority of member governments, on the other hand, felt that, in the context of the purposes behind the relevant article of the IMCO Convention, the concepts of "registration" in those two countries and "registration" elsewhere were ever so different. They argued that countries with flags of convenience — or "open registries" as the current term goes — had no right under international law to claim recognition as "ship-owning nations," as tonnage in their registries lacked the "genuine link" between ship and flag state — consisting mainly of control by the flag state of technical, social, and administrative matters related to a given ship — that should be a prerequisite for establishing a ship's nationality.[28]

The International Court of Justice did not adopt that view. In its majority-vote decision, it made reference, among other things, to the repeated use of "registered tonnage" as the criterion for certain legal effects, such as the entry into force of convention amendments and the apportionment among member states of contributions to the Organization. The Court's ultimate conclusion was that the term "registered tonnage" could not be applied in different ways, depending on the context.[29]

Since that time, Liberia has had her seat on the Maritime Safety Committee. Panama could not harvest the fruits of her success in the legal case, as she soon fell back to rank tenth on the tonnage list. In 1965 (effective from 1968), the number of members on the Committee was increased to 18; in 1974 (effective from 1978), all members of the Organization were admitted to the Committee, without, it should be noted, any substantial effect on the number of those countries actively involved in the work of the Committee. The same applies to the Council, with the exception that the number of its members was increased from 18 to 24 only as late as 1978. Its efficiency, however, was not noticeably augmented, unless the stronger representation of developing countries was in itself a contribution to an improved climate of discussions and, thereby, better results of the group's work.

III. Primary Responsibilities of IMO's Component Groups

The Council and the Maritime Safety Committee are not only the earliest, and thus oldest, but also the most important of IMO's component groups. More than ever before, the Council now functions as a central decision-making body that formulates the Organization's working program, its budget, and the major items of its day-to-day business. It goes without saying that, with an increase in the number of members from 30 to 122, of committees from one to four, and — last but not least — of Secretariat staff from about 25 to some 200, a strong and efficient central direction is of great advantage, particularly in coordinating work in the various committees.[30] In a period of increasing financial constraints, it is of utmost importance to provide for a smooth working machinery and to lay down a list of priorities. This is, in fact, the task now discharged mainly by the Council, as has lately been emphasized in an Assembly Resolution.[31]

The range of activities of the Maritime Safety Committee can best be gathered from the names of its many subcommittees, as set out in the organizational chart on page 241. The fine print of that portion of the original IMCO Convention establishing the Committee also gives a fair idea of its responsibilities:[32]

> The Maritime Safety Committee shall consider any matter within the scope of the Organization concerned with aids to navigation, construction and equipment of vessels, manning from a safety standpoint, rules for the prevention of collisions, handling of dangerous cargoes, maritime safety procedures and requirements, hydrographic information, log-books and navigational records, marine casualty investigation, salvage and rescue, and any other matters directly affecting maritime safety.

The results of the Committee's work are comprehensive and vary considerably in their form of presentation. There are sets of regulations by way of far-reaching conventions that are binding upon contracting parties,[33] resolutions of a merely advisory character and the so-called "Codes" that rank somewhere in between.[34] The Committee is always abreast of current developments in technical, and especially nautical matters, and keeps the regulatory texts issued under its leadership up to date and under constant review.

IMO's Codes, some of which are quite voluminous (the International Dangerous Goods Code, for example, comprises ten volumes), are held in high esteem by experts in the fields they cover, and it can fairly be said that they have become indispensable tools for the conduct of maritime shipping. As the language of the Codes is not subject to the formal restrictions used in wording conventions, the texts of the Codes are usually more descriptive than "regulatory" in the strict sense of the word, and they often present alternative solutions to a given problem. For this reason, the Codes are increasingly being used as testing grounds for regulatory concepts later to be incorporated into conventions which, in their turn, have a binding character.

Over the past few years, the continual review of the
International Convention for the Safety of Life at Sea
(SOLAS) was at the center of the Committee's work,[35] and it
has meanwhile become evident that such continuing
oversight is, in fact, a permanent task for the MSC. The
contents of the SOLAS Convention may best be outlined by
making reference to its various Chapters: construction of
ships, including subdivision, stability, and fire protection; life-
saving appliances; radiotelegraphy and radiotelephony; safety
of navigation; carriage of grain and dangerous goods; nuclear
ships; surveys and certificates. The Maritime Safety
Committee is not only the body to consider such matters but
also the one to make decisions when it comes to amendments
of a technical and especially nautical nature. A novel
procedure, provided in the Convention, for an accelerated
entry into force of amendments proposed by the MSC, is
considered to be a model for other international
instruments.[36]

Problems related to the quality of training of masters
and officers, as well as the minimum requirements for these
services, had for a long time been regarded as unsuitable for
regulation by way of international agreement. The
consideration behind this point of view was that, in order to
achieve satisfactory conditions for the success of such an
agreement, states would have to consent to giving away too
much of their sovereign rights, and also that the points from
which a start would have to be made seemed to be simply too
far apart ever to reach a common denominator. All the same,
IMO has overcome all those enormous difficulties by adopting
the International Convention on Standards of Training,
Certification and Watchkeeping of Seafarers, 1978.

The International Convention on Maritime Search and
Rescue, 1979,[37] is the first world-wide instrument to set up
standards for maritime search and rescue services, their
organization, and the cooperation in this respect among
states, especially on a regional basis. Thus, the Convention
provides the machinery that enables the system to work in
the first instance.

In the not too distant future, maritime search and
rescue will be vitally improved and facilitated through a

global maritime distress and safety system that will operate via satellites relaying distress calls combined with an indication of the position of the unit in distress. The system, including its satellites, is already operational for commercial radiocommunication. It is called the INMARSAT System and was created in 1976 through the Convention on the International Maritime Satellite Organization. This Convention had been prepared and concluded within the framework of IMCO, which also lent a helping hand in the build-up of that now independent organization.

The Marine Environment Protection Committee (MEPC) was IMCO's answer to the severe tanker casualties of the past decade or so; the names TORREY CANYON, ARGO MERCHANT, and AMOCO CADIZ may suffice to list those casualties that had the character of catalysts for action. The Committee took up the battle against oil pollution with great commitment and worked out the International Convention for the Prevention of Pollution from Ships, 1973, and the 1978 Protocol relating thereto.[38] As the latter is a non-self-contained instrument, the combined set of regulations is appropriately abbreviated "MARPOL 1973/1978."

This Convention, which tightens up on the essential provisions of the first such international convention of 1954, deals with marine pollution incidental to the operation of ships (i.e., the discharge of oil and oily mixtures), as well as with the disposal of garbage and the discharge of sewage. Its highly contextual provisions comprise an absolute ban on such practices in most areas, as well as its permission where and when their effects will be less harmful. Certain requirements for the construction and equipment of oil tankers were added to prevent and mitigate accidents and their consequences. While MARPOL is mainly meant to prevent oil spills, the so-called "Intervention Convention"[39] empowers coastal states to take such measures on the high seas as may be necessary to prevent imminent damage resulting from pollution. The above conventions are complemented, on the civil side of the law, by the International Convention Relating to Civil Liability for Oil Pollution Damage, 1969, and the International Convention on the Establishment of an International Fund for Compensation for Oil Pollution Damage.[40]

These last three conventions have been historic marks in maritime law. The Intervention Convention conferred upon coastal states, for the first time in history, under certain circumstances, sovereign rights-of-intervention powers on the high seas vis-à-vis foreign-flag ships; previously no state other than the flag state had been deemed to be so empowered. The two civil-law conventions, on the other hand, broke new ground, one by requiring an obligatory public liability insurance for certain vessels (1969 Convention), and the other by establishing an international compensation fund for the benefit of coastal states having sustained environmental damage (1971 Convention).

No description of IMO's activities in the field of environmental protection would be complete if it did not mention the preparation, adoption, and implementation of the so-called "London Dumping Convention," which should more appropriately be called the "Anti-Dumping Convention."[41] (The term "dumping" has come into use to designate all sorts of waste disposal at sea). The Convention contains different lists of substances the dumping of which is either prohibited, may be permitted on certain conditions and with certain restrictions, or is free of any limitations, as appropriate.

The Convention, which applies world-wide, is extremely important. This is true not only from the point of view of environmental protection, particularly with regard to the preservation of the living resources of the sea, but also from the point of view of the chemical industry, being at the root of any potential environmental disorder. Although this statement seems contradictory at first sight, there is a very simple explanation: when there is a conflict of interests, an objective and adequate compromise as the generally applicable and mandatory formula is in almost every case the best solution available.

The simple wording describing the purpose of the Legal Committee as "consider[ation of] any legal matters within the scope of the Organization"[42] requires no further clarification. Or does it, since the question immediately following will be, what, then, is a "legal matter"? The answer to this can be very different, depending on one's perspective. In actual practice, the differences between Continental and Anglo-American legal thinking play a most important part in such questions of delimitation. For example, if the Continental approach were the basis of evaluation for "legal matters," vital conventions such as SOLAS or MARPOL would have to be regarded as instruments of public law to a greater extent than is actually the case. However, if the Legal Committee were to take responsibility for such conventions, it would be forced into the entirely unintended role of a "super" committee. Thus, the view on the scope of the "legal matters" within this committee's competence is a practical blend of legal philosophies designed to avoid overlap with the substantive work of the other, more technically-oriented committees.

The "scope of the Organization" is defined in Articles 1 to 3 of the original Convention in terms sufficiently broad to avoid dispute on this score, although reference was made above to early questions of the Organization's competence vis-à-vis that of other U.N. bodies. Clearly, therefore, those conventions with an emphasis on maritime liability, referred to above in the context of IMO's mandate for protection of the marine environment, are indisputably among the "legal matters within the scope of the Organization." Other instruments falling within this category include a number of those known as the "Brussels Conventions."[43] These comprise such "standard" agreements as the Convention on Limitation of Liability for Maritime Claims, 1976, and the Athens Convention Relating to the Carriage of Passengers and Their Luggage by Sea, 1974. While neither of these conventions has yet come into force, both would supersede earlier "Brussels Conventions."

Yet another category of international instruments deals specifically with matters of liability in connection with the transport of dangerous goods, for example, the International Convention Relating to Civil Liability in the Field of Maritime Carriage of Nuclear Material, 1971.[44] Another regulatory instrument of this kind, the draft International Convention on Liability and Compensation in Connection with the Carriage of Hazardous and Noxious Substances by Sea, is currently under consideration in the Legal Committee and will be submitted to a diplomatic conference to be held probably in 1984.

The fourth and final of the IMO committees is the

Technical Cooperation Committee. As the nature of its work — aid to developing countries — suggests, this Committee deals not so much with normative rules and regulations but more with the planning and implementation of projects. The Committee's purposes according to the Convention[45] are quite comprehensive in this regard, and IMO is the only specialized agency of the United Nations that has incorporated in its constitution the task of providing technical cooperation.[46] Article 43 of the IMO Convention calls for this cooperation in the context of the "relevant United Nations programme," which is the "United Nations Development Programme" (UNDP) and which has been contributing two-thirds of pertinent IMO funds, a sum amounting to U.S. $1.5 million in 1982. The Technical Cooperation Committee thus engages in many wideranging projects and activities, such as quantitative analyses for the training of officers, recommendations for the purchase of training equipment, regional seminars on the handling of dangerous cargoes in ports and aboard ships, and assistance in preparing national maritime legislation or in setting up administrative organizations for maritime affairs.[47]

IV. Options for IMO's Future

Appropriate to the environment facing virtually every private and public organization today, a discussion of IMO's future may begin with reference to its budget, which overall amounted to $13.2 million for 1982 and amounts to $16.2 million for 1983 (excluding the budget for technical cooperation). It is noteworthy that IMO from 1982 to 1983 did without a budget increase in real terms, despite the fact that the new IMO Headquarters has been inaugurated during the biennium. That makes IMO one of the very few of the specialized agencies in the United Nations system to comply fully with the urgent appeal of the so-called "Geneva Group," a working group of ten major Western contributors to the United Nations budget, to eliminate spending increases.

There may, however, even be room for improvement. An alarmingly high percentage of the budget, about 20 percent, is being spent on costs for translation and other language services. This figure, revealed in a study undertaken by the Secretariat at the request of the Council,[48] does not take into account the flow of paper which rises enormously with each additional working language, nor does it reflect other such indirect costs. To be fair, it should be added that, compared to other specialized agencies within the United Nations system, with that percentage IMO ranks in the "upper middle class," while the International Civil Aviation Organization (ICAO) holds the top position, spending roughly a quarter of its budget on language services.[49] Costs even at the level experienced by IMO can have a paralyzing effect, and seem in any event excessive considering that English, the international language of shipping as well as of aviation, should do in either organization.

In a related but more fundamental vein, it would be worth any reasonable effort to investigate how much money member states would save if the two minor specialized agencies — the International Oil Pollution Compensation Fund and the INMARSAT Organization — with responsibilities that are most closely connected to those of IMO (and for which IMO has rendered many foster services) would be merged with IMO on the formal, financial, and administrative levels. There can be no doubt that quite considerable sums could be saved in the sector of general administration costs, both with regard to staff and office costs. Similarly, it may be fruitless to attempt to concentrate under one roof all 35 organs and specialized agencies of the United Nations (plus the numerous international fishery bodies) all of which claim "maritime" concerns and responsibilities.[50] Nevertheless, it may in the long term be the inevitable conclusion that significant financial and operational efficiencies could be achieved by amalgamating with IMO such organizations as the International Hydrographic Organization (IHO)[51] or the International Association of Lighthouse Authorities (IALA),[52] as both of them, taking an unbiased view, are nothing but virtual "departments" of the International Maritime Organization.[53]

Another area where progress has been made and can be improved upon is that of direct governmental relations. IMO has been entertaining close working relations with other international organizations having maritime responsibilities,

as well as with regional unions of a political and/or economic
character such as the Arab League, the Organization for
Economic Cooperation and Development, and the European
Economic Community (E.E.C.).[54]   Cooperation with the
E.E.C. has lately intensified, in that the E.E.C. Commission
has been assuming responsibilities in fields where IMCO-
sponsored conventions had formulated "framework"
conditions only. Thus, the Commission has been drawing up
sets of topic-related procedures and detailed regulations,
which are important for the effective implementation of
universal conventions in the legal and administrative practice
of states.

As the underlying conditions differ widely among the
states of the world, and also because many states —
especially those of the Third World — believe that the
practical application of international conventions is their sole
national competence and responsibility, most of those
international conventions are restricted to material
provisions and will, at the most, contain "outline" or
"framework" provisions for control and enforcement.
However, when it comes to combating effectively such
problems as sub-standard ships, uniform rules and
regulations are essential from the point of view of competition
between ports. This applies, in particular, to the situation in
the E.E.C. The problem was solved, quite satisfactorily, by
the conclusion of a memorandum of understanding between
the maritime authorities of the E.E.C. countries, the other
Scandinavian countries, and the two Iberian countries,
implementing uniform standards for allowing vessel entry
into ports of the signatory states.[55] Similarly, the E.E.C. has
uniformly implemented IMCO-sponsored conventions on
minimum requirements for tankers entering and leaving
Community ports and on the use of deep-sea pilots.[56]

On a related front is an increasingly customary practice
that should now affect IMO also, i.e., establishment of
diplomatic missions to international organizations, with their
personnel being exclusively accredited to the organization
concerned. Such missions have been opened by almost all of
the member states to the United Nations in New York and
Geneva, to supra-national organizations such as NATO and
the E.E.C., to the major multinational organizations such as

OECD, as well as to some of the specialized agencies such as UNESCO in Paris, IAEA and UNIDO in Vienna, and ICAO in Montreal. (In this last case, delegates are permanently stationed in that city).

At the insistence of the Soviet Union, IMO and the United Kingdom have recently amended and extended the "Headquarters Agreement"[57] to open the way for the establishment of permanent missions to IMO.[58] The Government of the United Kingdom did not declare its consent until a compromise had been reached for an accreditation procedure that will require the member government wishing to accredit a permanent representative to IMO to inform the IMO Secretary-General of the name and rank of such person before accreditation. The Secretary-General, in turn, must inform the Government of the United Kingdom of the nomination and obtain the views of the Government thereon. When it raises an objection, consultations must take place.

Most of the Western countries take the view that the traditional system — representation through the London embassy, in most cases by an official specifically appointed for that purpose — has been working well and they see no cause for modification. It seems quite certain, however, that before long the U.S.S.R. will establish an additional diplomatic mission in London to be assigned to IMO. Other Eastern Bloc countries are likely to follow suit, and a number of developing countries, too, have indicated such intentions. It remains to be seen whether this will become the trend and, if so, what will be its impact on the day-to-day work of IMO.

In closing, reference should be made to the long-term working program of IMO. Its main feature is that it calls for a period of consolidation and the implementation of the various IMO conventions amidst the practicalities of international relations and shipping circles. The XIIth Assembly has adopted a resolution that is quite impressive, not only for its serial number — "500" — but also because it states unmistakably that, following a period of great creative efforts,

> ...proposals for new conventions or amendments to existing conventions [should be entertained] only on the

basis of clear and well-documented demonstration of compelling need, taking into account the undesirability of modifying conventions not yet in force or of amending existing conventions unless such latter instruments have been in force for a reasonable period of time and experience has been gained of their operation, and having regard to the costs to the maritime industry and the burden on the legislative and administrative resources of Member States.[59]

It goes without saying that, despite this warning against new conventions or amendments to existing ones, the long-term working program does include a number of new projects, such as the improvement of radiocommunications at sea for the purposes of search and rescue and of navigational warning systems, safety requirements for mobile off-shore drilling units and for off-shore supply vessels, a convention on the removal of wrecks, another convention on the legal status of off-shore and other novel craft such as air-cushion vehicles, quite a number of highly beneficial projects in the field of facilitation of international maritime traffic (where developments have been somewhat behind the times as a result of procedural difficulties) and, to give one last example, a most interesting project from the point of view of international law, called "Uniform Interpretation and Application of the Provisions of MAR-POL 73/78."

Looking further ahead in time, IMO also will have to undertake those tasks and responsibilities that the United Nations Convention on the Law of the Sea will confer upon the Organization, both expressly and implicitly. It is an evident proof of the high reputation the Organization enjoys that the Law of the Sea Conference was increasingly willing to delegate responsibilities to IMCO and, on occasion, even conferred upon it the role of a mediator.[60] The technical, and especially the nautical standards adopted by IMCO and embodied in various conventions[61] and other instruments are being considered the yardstick of applicability for many basic provisions of international law and of the limitations on the lawmaking competence in the maritime field of individual, particularly coastal, states.[62]   In various instances, international regulatory competences have been conferred upon IMO.[63] It is true that IMCO/IMO is nowhere expressly named, but many years' discussions and negotiations have brought about a consensus that IMCO/IMO is in mind in connection with safety of navigation and protection of the marine environment whenever a "competent international organization" is referred to, at least when, significantly, "organization" is used in the singular.

NOTES

1. See IMCO Doc. WGIC I/2/2/ (1975).

2. Phonetic transliteration according to the system of the International Phonetic Association.

3. See IMCO Res. A.358 (IX) (1975), as amended by IMCO Res. A.371 (X) (1977). Unless otherwise stated, the IMO Convention is quoted in the version amended by these Resolutions.

4. See, e.g., ISNT (Informal Single Negotiating Text), U.N. Doc. A/CONF.62/W.P.8 (1975).

5. This group of countries included Australia, Belgium, Denmark, Finland, France, the Federal Republic of Germany, Greece, Ireland, Iceland, Italy, Japan, Liberia, the Netherlands, Norway, Poland, Sweden, Spain, the U.K., the U.S.A., and the U.S.S.R.

6. List of IMCO Members as of April 2, 1982: (Founding Members are marked *; Members having acceded as of 1975 are marked **).

Algeria**	Finland*	Lebanon*	Sierra Leone**
Angola	France*	Liberia**	Singapore**
Argentina*	Gabon	Libyan Arab	Somalia
Australia*	Gambia	Jamahiriya**	Spain**
Austria	German Democratic	Madagascar**	Sri Lanka**
Bahamas	Republic	Malaysia**	Sudan**
Bahrain	Germany, Federal	Maldives**	Surinam
Bangladesh	Republic of	Malta**	Sweden*
Barbados**	Ghana**	Mauritania**	Switzerland*
Belgium*	Greece*	Mauritius	Syrian Arab
Benin	Guinea	Mexico**	Republic**
Brazil	Guinea-Bissau	Morocco**	United Republic
Bulgaria**	Guyana	Mozambique	of Tanzania**
Burma**	Haiti**	Nepal	Thailand**

United Republic	Honduras**	Netherlands*	Trinidad and
of Cameroon**	Hong Kong**	New Zealand*	Tobago**
Canada*	(Associate	Nicaragua	Tunisia**
Cape Verde	Member)	Nigeria**	Turkey*
Chile*	Hungary**	Norway*	United Arab
China**	Iceland**	Oman**	Emirates
Colombia*	India*	Pakistan*	United Kingdom*
Congo	Indonesia**	Panama*	United States*
Costa Rica	Iran**	Papua New	Uruguay**
Cuba*	Iraq**	Guinea	U.S.S.R.**
Cyprus	Ireland*	Peru*	Venezuela
Czechoslovakia**	Israel**	Philippines**	Yemen Arab
Denmark*	Italy*	Poland*	Republic
Djibouti	Ivory Coast**	Portugal*	Yemen, D.R.
Dominica	Jamaica	Qatar	Yugoslavia**
Dominican	Japan**	Romania**	Zaire**
Republic*	Jordan**	Saint Lucia	
Ecuador**		Saint Vincent	
Egypt*	Kampuchea	and the	
El Salvador	Kenya**	Grenadines	
Equatorial	Korea,	Saudi Arabia**	
Guinea**	Republic of	Senegal**	
Ethiopia	Kuwait**	Seychelles	

7. International Convention for the Safety of Life at Sea (SOLAS), June 17, 1960, 16 U.S.T. 185, T.I.A.S. No. 5780, as amended IMCO No. 70.07.B (1966, 1967, 1968, 1969), IMCO No. 74.05.B (1971, 1973); International Convention for the Prevention of Pollution of the Sea by Oil, May 12, 1954, as amended, 1962, 1969, and 1971; Convention on Facilitation of International Maritime Traffic, Apr. 9, 1965, 18 U.S.T. 411, T.I.A.S. No. 6251, as amended; International Convention on Load Lines, Apr. 5, 1966, 18 U.S.T. 1857, T.I.A.S. No. 6331, as amended IMCO No. 72.06.B (1975), IMCO Res. A.411 (XI) (1979); International Convention on Tonnage Measurement of Ships, June 23, 1969, IMCO No. 70.01.B; International Convention Relating to Intervention on the High Seas in Cases of Oil Pollution Casualties, Nov. 29, 1969, 26 U.S.T. 765, T.I.A.S. No. 8068; International Convention on Civil Liability for Oil Pollution Damage, Nov. 29, 1969, U.N.T.S. No. 1409; Convention Relating to Civil Liability in the Field

of Maritime Carriage of Nuclear Material, Dec. 17, 1971, IMCO No. 72.11.B, U.N.T.S. No. 14120; International Convention on the Establishment of an International Fund for Compensation for Oil Pollution Damage, Dec. 18, 1971, U.N.T.S. No. 17146; International Convention for Safe Containers, Dec. 2, 1972, T.I.A.S. No. 9037; Convention on the International Regulations for Preventing Collisions at Sea (COLREG), Oct. 20, 1972, 28 U.S.T. 3459, T.I.A.S. No. 8587; Protocol Relating to Intervention on the High Seas in Cases of Maritime Pollution by Substances other than Oil, Nov. 2, 1973, IMCO No. 77.15.E; International Convention for the Prevention of Pollution from Ships (MARPOL), Nov. 2, 1973.

These conventions stipulated that the Organization be their depositary, with all its rights and obligations, i.e., for the consideration of proposed amendments and the convocation of Diplomatic Conferences for amending and extending conventions, or conferred upon it certain functions that might best be described as "administrative," such as the collection and evaluation of Casualty Reports and Deficiency Reports; further examples are given in IMCO Doc. WGI I/2/2 (1975). Consequently, it was part of the German initiative mentioned above to add the word "administrative" in Article 2 of the IMCO Convention (Convention on the Intergovernmental Maritime Consultative Organization, Mar. 6, 1948, 9 U.S.T. 621, T.I.A.S. No. 4044), then reading: "The function of the Organization shall be consultative and advisory."

However, it did not take long to see that terms such as "to administer"/"administration" would have had for many a representative — especially from Third World countries — a connotation like "to govern"/"government," and it was out of the question that they would run the risk of giving away any sovereign rights. So, in the end all that was done was to delete the word "consultative." When Article 2 was discussed again in the context of another set of amendments (IMCO Res. A.400 (X) (1977), it was decided to delete that provision altogether.

8. The original official title was "Convention on the Intergovernmental Maritime Consultative Organization," Mar. 6, 1948, 9, U.S.T. 621, T.I.A.S. No. 4044; the title was changed to "Convention on the International Maritime

Organization," Nov. 14, 1975, IMCO No. 68.01.B (entered into force May 22, 1982). Amendments to the IMCO Convention are as follows: Sept. 15, 1964, 18 U.S.T. 1299, T.I.A.S. No. 6285 (entered into force Oct. 6, 1967); Sept. 28, 1965; 19 U.S.T. 4844, T.I.A.S. No. 6490 (entered into force Nov. 3, 1968); Oct. 17, 1974, 28.4 U.S.T. 4607, T.I.A.S. No. 8606 (entered into force Apr. 1, 1978); Nov. 14, 1975, IMCO No. 68.01.B (entered into force May 22, 1982); Nov. 17, 1977, and Nov. 15, 1979 (neither of which has entered into force).

9.   The organizational chart anticipates the situation as it will be after the entry into force of the amendments embodied in IMCO Res. A.400 (X) (1977), which concern the institutionalization of the "Committee on Technical Co-operation" and consequential changes.

10. The "Facilitation Committee" has only limited functions (both in terms of competence and in terms of its life) related to the execution of the 1965 Facilitation Convention: consequently, it has not been established as a "full-fledged" committee.

11. The original members were Belgium, Canada, Denmark, France (Exile Government), Greece, the Netherlands, Norway, Poland, the U.K., and the U.S.A. In 1946, the following countries joined the group: Australia, Brazil, Chile, India, Yugoslavia, New Zealand, Sweden and South Africa.

12. See U.S. Dep't of State, Pub. No. 3196, *Toward a World Maritime Organization 5 et seq.* (1948).

13. See U.N. Charter arts. 55, 57, 59, 62, and 63.

14. See IMCO Convention, *supra* note 8, art. 1; the text in brackets contains the amendments adopted by Res. A.358 (IX), IMCO No. 68.01.B (1975):

The purposes of the Organization are:

(a) To provide machinery for co-operation among Governments in the field of governmental regulation and practices relating to technical matters of all kinds affecting shipping engaged in international trade; to encourage the general adoption of the highest practicable standards in matters concerning maritime safety, efficiency of navigation [and the prevention and control of marine pollution from ships; and to deal with legal matters related to the purposes set out in this Article;].

15. See IMCO Convention, *supra* note 8, art. 11:
The purposes of the Organization are:
(b) To encourage the removal of discriminatory action and unnecessary restrictions by Governments affecting shipping engaged in international trade so as to promote the availability of shipping services to the commerce of the world without discrimination; assistance and encouragement given by a Government for the development of its national shipping and for purposes of security does not in itself constitute discrimination, provided that such assistance and encouragement is not based on measures designed to restrict the freedom of shipping of all flags to take part in international trade;
(c) To provide for the consideration by the Organization of matters concerning unfair restrictive practices by shipping concerns in accordance with Part II.

16. Organization for Economic Co-operation and Development, Paris; the Organization's "Consultative Shipping Group" is a special forum for the discussion of questions related to the economic aspects of ocean shipping. The principle of "free and fair competition" has been, and continues to be, one of the fundamentals of OECD policy. See OECD Doc. C(61)95, Note 1 to Annex A, Code of Liberalization of Current Invisible Operations (1961).

17. See IMCO Doc. A/XI/WP.2 (1979).

18. It is not without delicacy to note the fact that the present Secretary-General of IMO, Mr. C.P. Srivastava, held in high esteem around the world, successfully chaired the most important UNCTAD conference on shipping matters, at which the draft Convention on a Code of Conduct for Liner Conferences was formulated, April 6, 1974.

19. See ECOSOC Res. 2098 (LXIII) (1977).

20. See IMCO Doc. C/SL/18(e) (1978) and IMCO Res. C.61 (XL) (1978); see also IMCO Doc. CXL/WP.1 (1978).

21. The International Convention for Safe Containers, *supra* note 7, has been dealt with by IMCO, whereas the international instrument dealing with the commercial aspects of containerization, The United Nations Convention on International Multimodal Transport of Goods, May 24, 1980, UNCTAD Doc. TD/MT/CONF./17, U.N. Sales No. E.81.II.D.7-Vol. I, was drafted under the auspices of UNCTAD.

22. These are the so-called "Brussels Conventions." For further explanation, see infra note 43; see also Docs. LEG XLIII/4 and 5 (1980).

23. See IMCO Docs. C/ES.IX5(b) (1977) and A/X/22 (1977).

24. The full texts of the relevant Articles (as in force until 1967 and 1968, respectively) read:

IMCO Convention, *supra* note 8, art. 17:

The Council shall consist of sixteen Members and shall be composed as follows:

(a) six shall be governments of the nations with the largest interest in providing international shipping services;

(b) six shall be governments of other nations with the largest interest in international seaborne trade;

(c) two shall be elected by the Assembly from among the governments of nations having a substantial interest in providing international shipping services; and

(d) two shall be elected by the Assembly from among the governments of nations having a substantial interest in international seaborne trade.

IMCO Convention, *supra* note 8, art. 28:

(a) The Maritime Safety Committee shall consist of fourteen Members elected by the Assembly from the Members, Governments of those nations having an important interest in maritime safety, of which not less than eight shall be the largest shipowning nations, and the remainder shall be elected so as to ensure adequate representation of Members. Governments of other nations with an important interst in maritime safety, such as nations interested in the supply of large numbers of crews or in the carriage of large numbers of berthed and unberthed passengers, and of major geographical areas.

25. The court has to give an "advisory opinion" in accordance with Article 96 of the Charter of the United Nations. The Asembly acted in accordance with Article 56 of the IMCO Convention, according to which the ICJ should decide upon legal points in the interpretation and application of the provisions of the IMCO Convention. See IMCO Res. A.12(I) (1959); First Assembly Resolutions, London, 1959.

26. See Simmonds, *The Constitution of the Maritime Safety Committee of IMCO*, 12 Int'l & Comp. L. Q. 56 (1963)

(hereinafter cited as "*Simmonds*").

27. See IMCO Docs. A/1/W.P.5 and Add. 1 (1959).

28. See, e.g., Convention on the Law of the High Seas, Apr. 29, 1958, art. 5(1), 13 U.S.T. 2312, T.I.A.S. No. 5200, which may be assumed to have become accepted as customary international law. The United Nations Convention on the Law of the Sea, Dec. 10, 1982, has taken over the "genuine link" requirements; see UNCLOS Doc. A/CONF.62/122 (1982). The questions related to the so-called "open registries," and thus to the "genuine link," have recently again become a topic of both national and international shipping policy. On the former level, the principal problem is the tendency of national shipowners to "flag out" ships; on the latter level, the upcoming UNCTAD conference on open registries will soon deal with the matter.

29. See Simmonds, *supra* note 26, at 73.

30. See IMCO Convention, *supra* note 8, arts. 22(a), 22(b), and 27.

31. See IMCO Res. A.500 (XII), paras. 1-3 (1981).

32. IMO Convention, *supra* note 8, art. 29(a).

33. Certain conventions, such as the Convention on the International Regulations for Preventing Collisions at Sea, Oct. 20, 1972, 28 U.S.T. 3459, T.I.A.S. No. 8587, may be assumed to legitimately claim to be instruments of customary international law.

34. For example, the International Maritime Dangerous Goods Code (IMDG Code), although not a formal convention, is a comprehensive set of regulations adopted by way of international consensus that can legitimately claim to have the character of a "standard," even with regard to countries that have not incorporated the Code into their national legislation. Other Codes dealing with the transport of dangerous goods in a broader sense include the "Bulk Chemicals Code," the "Gas Carrier Code," the "Bulk Cargoes Code," and the "Safety Recommendations on the Use of Ports by Nuclear Merchant Ships."

35. See *supra* note 7, for the titles of major conventions adopted as of 1973. SOLAS, 1960 was superseded in 1980 by SOLAS, 1974, T.I.A.S. No. 9700, which, in turn, was amended by the Protocol of 1978 Relating to SOLAS, 1974, IMCO No. 78.09.E., and the 1981 Set of Amendments.

36. See SOLAS, 1974, *supra* note 35, art. VIII(b). The SOLAS Convention does apply to passenger and cargo ships, including tankers. A similar set of regulations, but tailored to meet the specific purposes of fishing vessels, is the Torremolinos International Convention for the Safety of Fishing Vessels, April 2, 1977, IMCO No. 77.10.E.

37. International Convention on Maritime Search and Rescue, Apr. 27, 1979. IMCO No. 79.07.E.

38. Protocol Relating to the International Convention for the Prevention of Pollution from Ships, Feb. 17, 1978, IMCO No. 78.09.E.

39. See the International Convention Relating to Intervention on the High Seas in Cases of Oil Pollution Casualties and the Protocol Relating to Intervention on the High Seas in Cases of Maritime Pollution by Substances other than Oil, *supra* note 7.

40. International Convention on Civil Liability for Oil Pollution Damage and International Convention on the Establishment of an International Fund for Compensation for Oil Pollution Damage, *supra* note 7.   See also Protocol Relating to Civil Liability for Oil Pollution Damage, Nov. 19, 1976, IMCO No. 77.05.E, and Protocol Relating to the Establishment of an International Fund for Compensation for Oil Pollution Damage, Nov. 19, 1976, IMCO No. 77.05.E, which introduce Special Drawing Rights (SDR's) as the applicable units for measuring limitation of liability under the Civil Liability Convention and the size of the fund under the Fund Convention.

41. See the Convention on Pollution of the Seas by Dumping of Wastes and Other Matter, Dec. 29, 1972, 26 U.S.T. 2403, T.I.A.S. No. 8165, and the Resolution of the Third Consultative Meeting (of Contracting Parties to the Convention) on Incineration at Sea, oct. 12, 1978.

42. See IMO Convention, *supra* note 8, art. 34(a).

43. The so-called "Brussels Conventions" had been prepared by the Comité Maritime International (CMI), an international association comprising the national maritime law associations of most of the maritime countries, including the Maritime Law Association of the United States. They were later adopted at Diplomatic Conferences that regularly took place at the invitation of the Belgian Government, which

also assumed depository functions for these Conventions following their adoption. Conference activities have largely been taken over by IMCO, while CMI continues to fulfill highly valuable consultative functions. The most recent example of the co-operation between CMI and IMCO is the case of the Convention for the Unification of Certain Rules of Law Relating to Assistance and Salvage at Sea, Sept. 23, 1910, 37 Stat. 1658, T.S. 576, the revision of which is on the working programme of the Legal Committee. The 1981 CMI Conference, held in Montreal, adopted the draft of such a revised convention text.

44. IMCO No. 72.11.B, U.N.T.S. No. 14120.

45. IMO Convention, *supra* note 8, art. 43, as amended by Res. A.400 (X) (1977), *supra* note 9, will read as follows:

(a) The Technical Co-operation Committee shall consider, as appropriate, any matter within the scope of the Organization concerned with the implementation of technical co-operation projects funded by the relevant United Nations programme for which the Organization acts as the executing or co-operating agency or by funds-in-trust voluntarily provided to the Organization, and any other matters related to the Organization's activities in the technical co-operation field.

(b) The Technical Co-operation Committee shall keep under review the work of the Secretariat concerning technical co-operation.

46. See IMCO Doc. A/X/INF.4 (1977).

47. An excellent survey of the Committee's work is given in IMCO, *IMCO's Technical Assistance Programme* (1981).

48. See IMCO Doc. C/XLVI/WP.1 (1981).

49. See Report on the Implications of Additional Languages in the United Nations System, U.N. Doc. JIU/REP/77/5 (1977), prepared by the United Nations Joint Inspection Unit.

50. See the study prepared for the Third United Nations Conference on the Law of the Sea and entitled *Annotated Directory of Intergovernmental Organizations concerned with Ocean Affairs*, U.N. Doc. A/CONF.62/L.14 (1976).

51. All 47 member governments of the Organization, which has its headquarters at the International Hydrographic Bureau in Monaco, are IMO Members. The Organization's

main function is worldwide co-ordination of hydrographic survey work, publication of nautical charts, and navigational warning and information services.

52. The International Association of Lighthouse Authorities, with its headquarters in Paris, is an association uniting the representatives of the specialized technical authorities of 89 states, the governments of which are all members of IMO (with the exception of South Africa, which has been expelled from IMCO/IMO). Although IALA may not be considered an international "Governmental Organization" proper, it is, in fact, a semi-governmental institution, despite the many features of private law in its constitution. Its main function is the worldwide co-ordination of work in the field of aids to navigation, lights, and buoyage systems. It is an important forum for the exchange of relevant information.

53. The same basically applies to the International Oceanographic Commission (IOC), which is connected with UNESCO. A permanent liaison officer from IMO is stationed there even now.

54. Besides its relation to governmental organizations, IMO's co-operation with so-called Non-governmental Organizations ("NGO's") deserves mentioning. Numerous associations, delegating highly qualified technical experts to the appropriate IMO (sub) committees, not only provide their advice on particular problems or take over a whole complex of preparatory work, but they also promote the implementation of convention provisions following their adoption. Among these NGO's are such well-known organizations as the International Chamber of Shipping, the International Union of Marine Insurance, the International Radio Maritime Committee, the International Federation of Shipmasters' Associations, the International Association of Classification Societies, and the Oil Companies' International Marine Forum. Organizations may officially be granted "consultative" status; prerequisites include an application to that effect and formal admission procedures. Of course, as IMCO kept growing, it was inevitable that among the applications received by the Organization were some coming in from associations that had mainly an interest in adding a line in their letterheads referring to their consultative status, or from associations that barely concealed downright business

interests behind their names. A set of guidelines for the granting and withdrawal of consultative status (IMCO Doc. C/XL/20(a) (1978) tightened up on earlier rules of admission and made it easier to turn down applications. It was on the strength of those guidelines that the Organization could recently be relieved of a number of useless would-be consultants.

55. See Memorandum of Understanding on Port State Control, Jan. 26, 1982 (entered into force July 1, 1982).

56. See O.J. Eur. Comm. (Nos. L 33/32 and L 33/33) (1979).

57. See Agreement between the Government of the United Kingdom of Great Britain and Northern Ireland and the Inter-Governmental Maritime Consultative Organization Regarding the Headquarters of the Organization, Nov. 28, 1968, published in IMCO, Basic Documents II (1969).

58. See IMCO Doc. C/XLVI/11 (1981).

59. IMCO Doc. A XII/Res. 500 (1982).

60. For example, an amendment proposed by the United Kingdom to change the draft of Article 60(3) (calling for only partial instead of, as drafted, total removal of drilling rigs after exploitation had been given up) was not acceptable to a majority of delegates until it was agreed that IMCO/IMO would adopt the necessary criteria for the safety of navigation applicable to such cases.

61. See *Supra* note 7.

62. The relevant terms are "generally accepted (applicable) international rules (standards)." They refer to: Coastal State laws and regulations concerning innocent passage of foreign vessels through the territorial sea (Art. 21(2) and (4)), transit passage through straits used for international navigation (Arts. 39(2)(a) and (b), 41(3) and 42(1)(b)), the laws and regulations for the prevention, reduction and control of pollution of the marine environment from vessels (Art. 211(2) and (5)), as well as their enforcement (Art. 220(2) and (3)).

63. For example, IMCO has been empowered to recommend sea lanes and traffic separation schemes in the teritorial sea (Art. 22(3)(a)), in straits used for international navigation (Art. 41(4)), and in archipelagic waters (Art. 53(9)), and to recommend safety zones around artificial

islands (Art. 60(5)). In the case of straits and archipelagic waters, the states concerned must refer proposals to the Organization which, under certain conditions, may adopt them.   Wherever, in the field of marine environmental protection, states are obliged to establish international rules and standards to prevent, reduce or control pollution of the sea by deep sea mining (Art. 209), dumping (Art. 210) or from vessels (Art. 211), they are recommended or even required to "act through the competent international organization."

Chapter XII

International Telecommunications Union (ITU)

The International Telecommunications Union (ITU) was founded in 1865, and it became a United Nations specialized agency in 1947. It has 166 member states and a staff of 425 people at its Geneva headquarters. The budget for 1990 is 115 million Swiss francs. The ITU strives to "maintain and extend international co-operation between all members of the union for the improvement and rational use of telecommunications of all kinds." The union also endeavors to promote and provide technical assistance in developing countries in the field of telecommunications. ITU encourages the establishment of technical facilities, and their efficient operation, in developing countries in hopes that this will increase efficiency, usefulness and accessibility of telecommunication services for the public. This increased use of telecommunications, particularly in the realm of satellite communication, is hoped to facilitate peaceful relations between countries and promote international co-operation. ITU maintains three boards or committees to regulate and facilitate growth in the various fields of communication. These are the International Frequency Registration Board (IFRB), the International Telegraph and Telephone Consultative Committee (CCITT), and the International Radio Consultative Committee (CCIR).

Financing Development Assistance in the ITU

George A. Codding, Jr.

The problem of helping the developing countries of the world establish a viable domestic telecommunications system is a difficult one. Because of an overwhelming need and the recommendations laid down in *The Missing Link*, many proposals are bound to be made to the Nice Plenipotentiary to increase the amount of technical assistance provided by the ITU. This paper examines the history of the debate over development assistance in the ITU, the structures of the ITU for development assistance activities, and the funding of technical assistance. It concludes that there is a serious threat of the ITU's overall effectiveness becoming weakened if it is forced to stretch too far its resources in funding special development funds.

Except for the election of the International Telecommunications Union's top officials, and the countries to be represented on its Administrative Council, development assistance will be one of the most time-consuming subjects to be addressed at the 1989 Plenipotentiary in Nice.[1] This was the case at the 1959, 1965, 1973 and 1982 plenipotentiaries. And, unless something extraordinary should occur at Nice, it will be one of the major subjects of concern of plenipotentiaries in the future.

The basic issue is, of course, how best to finance the high cost of helping the developing countries become effective partners in the world telecommunication network. Should financing be left to outside organs such as the United Nations Development Program and the World Bank, or should additional help be given by the ITU itself? And if the ITU is to be involved, what portion of its resources should be devoted to this cause, and how should it be administered?

As a reference point, it should be noted that the celebrated Maitland Commission in its 1984 report estimated that the developing countries of the world would need a 'total investment of $12 billion a year' in order to reach the Commission's objective of bringing their inhabitants 'within easy reach of a telephone by the early part of the next century.'[2]

The Debate

The history of the debate over development assistance in the ITU is primarily the history of the rise in influence of the developing countries and their increased ability to use their voting power in an attempt to make the ITU better reflect their special needs and desires.

The 1952 and 1959 Plenipotentiaries

Albeit with some reluctance, the ITU became affiliated with the United Nations Expanded Program of Technical Assistance in 1952 with the approval by the Buenos Aires Plenipotentiary of an Administrative Council resolution. This resolution requested that the United Nations include telecommunications among the subjects for which technical assistance funds were allocated, and signalled the ITU's willingness   to   undertake   the   task   of   reviewing telecommunications assistance projects, helping recruit experts for such projects, and advising the UN on the training of telecommunication experts from the developing countries.[3]

Participation in the UN programme became a major item of discussion at the 1959 Geneva Plenipotentiary. In the words of the chief US delegate to that conference, 'the tremendous interest of the new or developing countries in technical assistance [was] the most significant single trend noted at this conference.'[4]

A number of resolutions were passed in 1959 designed to increase the effectiveness and extent of the ITU's participation in the United Nations' ongoing technical assistance activities, including a decision to participate in the UN's new Expanded Program of Technical Assistance. In addition, over the objections of some of the developing countries, a new clause was added to the section of the ITU Convention which detailed the more specialized purposes of the Union, stating that: the ITU shall 'foster the creation, development, and improvement of telecommunication equipment and networks in new or developing countries by every means at its disposal, especially its participation in the appropriate programmes of the United Nations.'[5]

The 1959 plenipotentiary also added a section to the ITU Convention requesting its semi-autonomous international consultative committees to 'pay due attention to the study of questions and to the formulation of recommendations directly connected with the establishment, development, and improvement of telecommunications in new or developing countries in both the regional and international fields.'[6]

The 1965 Montreux Plenipotentiary

By 1965 the membership of the ITU had increased from 96 to 124, the majority of the newcomers being from recently independent developing countries. This group was vocal in its criticisms of the amount of assistance being offered by the United Nations and the administration of that assistance by the ITU and the UN.

Several proposals, quite radical for the time, were offered by the developing countries to remedy the situation.

One was a request for the creation of a special ITU technical assistance programme to be funded through the ITU's regular budget. Not only would such a programme provide additional help to the developing countries, according to the proponents, but being under the ITU auspices it would be better attuned to the real telecommunication needs of the countries involved. Another proposal involved the establishment of regional ITU offices to help developing nations with their telecommunications projects, and a third was to create a new ITU technical assistance organ similar to the ITU's international consultative committees, with its own elected director to provide expert help to developing countries with telecommunications projects.

All three proposals were turned down by the delegates mainly on the basis of the additional costs that would be involved and the need for coordination of technical assistance activities by an agency, such as the United Nations Development Program (UNDP), which could look at all of the needs of developing countries rather than one sector such as telecommunications.[7]

The developing countries did, however, succeed in expanding the ITU's commitment to development assistance by obtaining the passage of three more limited, but nevertheless important, proposals. The first was the decision to recruit four 'telecommunication specialist engineers' competent in the fields of 'network planning, preparation of specifications, and evaluation of systems' for the ITU General Secretariat to work 'with the technical staff of the specialized secretariats of the International Consultative Committees and of the International Frequency Registration Board in providing information and advice of a practical nature on subjects of importance to new or developing countries for the planning, organization, and development of their telecommunications systems.'[8]

The second and third were resolutions asking the Secretary-General to begin a study of methods for training the telecommunications personnel of developing countries and to arrange for seminars to provide the technicians of developing countries with information concerning the latest developments in telecommunications.[9]

The importance of these decisions lay in the fact that

they provided for a purely ITU effort, carried out under its own authority and financed from its regular budget, rather than as part of an overall UN technical assistance effort.

The 1973 Malaga-Torremolinos Plenipotentiary

The 1973 Malaga-Torremolinos Plenipotentiary was dominated by the developing countries and their concern for help in creating viable national telecommunication networks. By 1973 membership in the ITU had increased to 135 and the developing country majority was correspondingly stronger.

One of the most controversial proposals was the revival of that submitted in 1965 to establish an ITU technical assistance fund to be financed through the regular ITU budget. After violent opposition was expressed by delegates from several of the developed countries, notably the USA, and the method of financing was changed to one based on voluntary contributions, the conference created a Special Fund for Technical Cooperation to be 'based on voluntary contributions in any currency or in some other form, to meet the needs of the developing countries who submit urgent requests for assistance to the Union.' All member countries were urged 'to make the resources required to meet the needs of the developing countries more effectively.'[10]

It is important to note, in regard to the proposal to finance the special ITU technical cooperation fund from the regular budget, that the Malaga-Torremolinos Plenipotentiary also saw a move on the part of several developing countries to change the ITU contribution system from the voluntary class unit system that it has used in the past to the UN system where the size of the contribution is fixed by a committee. Under the voluntary class unit system, the major countries all paid approximately 7% of the expenses of the ITU. Under the UN system the proportion paid by the major countries would have risen considerably. In the case of the USA it would rise from about 7% to 25% of the annual budget. After an extensive debate in a plenary meeting, and after strong objections from the USA, the USSR and other developed countries, that proposal was rejected by a vote of 48 for, 67 against, with 3 abstentions.[11]

The regional offices proposal was also revived at

Malaga-Torremolinos and came close to being accepted. The proposal was first defeated in committee in an open vote by 36 for, 36 against, and 4 abstentions. When submitted to a secret vote, however, it passed by 47 to 42, with one abstention. The proposal finally lost in a plenary meeting, in a secret ballot, by a vote of 45 for, 68 against, and 4 abstentions.[12]

The Malaga-Torremolinos Plenipotentiary also passed a number of additional resolutions dealing with the needs of the developing countries, many of which were extensions or updates of recommendations passed in 1965, but with some innovations including Resolution 19 requesting the Secretary-General to review the problems facing the 'least developed countries' as identified by the United Nations, and to propose concrete measures to bring improvement in their conditions 'through the Special Fund for Technical Cooperation and from other sources.'[13]

The activities of the delegates from developing countries in these and other matters prompted the US delegate to comment that, 'The obtaining of more funds from the major contributions to the ITU seemed more important to many of the developing countries than furtherance of the basic purposes of the Union.' and further:[14]

> We think, as did many of the developed countries, that this approach of the developing countries, placed in doubt the continuing usefulness of the ITU as an international regulatory agency for telecommunications. In this regard, it was openly discussed among the principal developed countries, Members of the Union, whether the developed countries should continue to finance and participate in the Union.

The 1982 Nairobi Plenipotentiary

The developing countries renewed their efforts to obtain additional development assistance at the Nairobi Plenipotentiary Conference. The most conspicuous success in this regard was the decision to make the following paragraph the first in the list of the primary purposes of the ITU:[15]

to maintain and extend international cooperation between all Members of the Union for the improvement and rational use of telecommunications of all kinds, as well as to promote and to offer technical assistance to developing countries in the field of telecommunications.

The Nairobi Plenipotentiary also saw a renewal of the proposals to finance an ITU technical assistance programme from the regular budget[16] and to create an ITU regional presence. The developing countries achieved success in the latter and a limited success in the former.

The debate on an ITU regional presence ended with a compromise by which no specific number of regional offices was to be established, but rather an attempt would be made to achieve 'a strengthened regional presence which will be as economical as possible and at the same time improve the effectiveness of the Union's activities.'[17]

The discussions over financing technical assistance activities directly for the regular ITU budget covered many of the arguments that had been put forward at Malaga-Torremolinos. A number of delegates from the developing countries argued that a fund was needed to bring some countries up to standard, and that such a fund existed in other international organizations. Several delegations, including those of West Germany and the USSR, argued that not only was it unnecessary, but there was a possibility that such an action would be illegal.[18]

The results of the debate at Nairobi were similar to those at Malaga-Torremolinos. It was decided not to establish a development assistance fund to be financed through the regular budget, but rather to create a new voluntary plan to replace that which had been created in 1973. The new fund, to be called the Special Voluntary Program for Technical Cooperation was to be based 'on contributions in currency, training services, or in any other form to meet as much of the telecommunication needs of developing countries as possible,' and member countries were urged to participate.[19]

Perhaps the most important action was the passing of an omnibus resolution, designed to reinforce the ITU's technical assistance efforts, that included the following list of activities which 'could possibly be taken into consideration for funding from the ITU's own resources':[20]

- Services of the Group of Engineers.
- Services of the Training Division, including the CODEVITAL activity (Training Standards).
- Short-term missions — specialists and Group of Engineers.
- Logistic support for seminars.
- Fellowship programme to participate in ITU seminars (eg IFRB seminars) and in CCI Study Group meetings.
- Regional presence.
- Services of the Head of the Technical Cooperation Department and his office.
- Logistic support for the Voluntary Programme of Technical Cooperation.
- Special assistance for the least developed countries.
- Provision of common services for technical cooperation activities.
- Identification of benefits of telecommunications for development.
- Follow-up action on the recommendations and decision taken by conferences and meetings of the ITU for the benefit of developing countries.
- ITU publications.
- World Communications Year.
- Review of ITU technical cooperation and assistance activities.
- Resources to promote technical cooperation among developing countries.
- Any other activities that the Administrative Council considers appropriate.

The Nairobi Plenipotentiary also passed a number of other resolutions which were extensions or updates of recommendations that had been adopted in Malaga-Torremolinos including a plea to UNDP to 'give greater appreciation to the importance of telecommunications in the development process,' and a decision to establish an ITU training fellowship programme.[21]

The decision of the Nairobi Plenipotentiary that

received the most publicity was the creation of a Commission for World-Wide Telecommunications Development. At a point in the deliberations when it seemed that the conference might become deadlocked over the issues of financing a special ITU technical assistance programme from the regular budget, and the proposal to adopt the UN system of financing, a group of delegates from both developed and developing countries presented a proposal calling for the establishment of a commission made up of members 'of the highest international reputation' to:

- Examine the issue of technical cooperation and identify the best methods of transferring resources for that purpose.
- Recommend methods for stimulating telecommunication development in the developing world.
- Consider how the ITU can best stimulate and support telecommunications development activities.[22]

The Maitland Report

The International Commission for World-Wide Telecommunications Development, dubbed the Maitland Commission after the name of its chairman, submitted its report in December 1984. As might be expected, it concluded that telecommunications are essential to the cultural growth and economic well-being of nations and that much of the developing world was deficient in telecommunications. And, as stated earlier it also estimated that some $12 billion a year would be needed to bring the developing countries up to an acceptable level of development.[23]

Among the Commission's many suggestions to remedy the situation was one to create a Center for Telecommunications Development, to cost $10 million a year, to:

- 'Collect information about telecommunications policies and experience...[and] make the results available to developing countries to help them formulate policies for the evolution of their own networks.'
- 'Advise developing countries on creating and operating an effective telecommunications system.'

- 'Provide specific assistance including preparation of
  plans; preparation of specifications for projects;
  assistance with manpower planning and training;
  management assistance; assistance in research and
  development, and so on.'[24]

The cost of the centre would be met from various sources such
as 'setting aside a small proportion of revenues from calls
between industrialized and developing countries,' regular
contributions, and contributions in kind from 'operating
entities in industrialized countries and other interested
parties including manufacturers and suppliers of telecommunications services....'[25]

   While this new centre would have a semi-independent
existence within the ITU in its initial phase, the Commission
saw that eventually it would be merged with the ITU General
Secretariat's Telecommunication Cooperation Division.

   The Center for Telecommunications Development came
into being in 1985 with the activation of its Advisory Board by
the ITU Administrative Council.[26]

   From this short history, several conclusions seem to
emerge. First, the developing countries have been able to
implant the concept that the ITU should have the provision of
development assistance as one of the major functions solidly
in the ITU's basic documents. Second, they have been able to
write into the Convention and its Recommendations various
ways that the organs of the ITU should help them in their
attempts to improve their telecommunications networks.
Third, they have been able over time to have many of these
efforts funded from the regular ITU budget. Fourth, they
have been able to initiate voluntary technical cooperation
funds. And fifth, so far they have been unable to obtain their
aim of setting up a technical cooperation fund financed from
the regular budget.

Structures for Development Assistance

The ITU's structures for development assistance activities
reflect its overall federal structure. As has been discussed, all
four of the ITU's permanent organs are involved to a certain
extent in activities that could be classified as technical

assistance. The major burden, however, clearly falls on the
General   Secretariat   and   its   Technical   Cooperation
Department.

The Technical Cooperation Department

The hard-working Technical Cooperation Department
is made up of six general divisions and four specialized units.
The six general divisions include four geographical units: the
Africa Division; the American Division; the Asia and Pacific
Division; and the Europe and Middle East Division. These
are supplemented by an Administrative Division and a Field
Personnel Service.

The ITU divides its development assistance work into
three sectors: the development of regional telecommunications networks, such as PANAFTEL, which is designed to
interconnect the countries of Africa without the need to
transit outside the continent; the strengthening of national
telecommunications technical and administrative services;
and the development of human resources through the
establishment of training centres and the awarding of
fellowships to obtain training.

The specialized units include: a Training Division; the
Group of Engineers; a Telecommunications Economic Unit;
and a Voluntary Program Unit.

The Group of Engineers is involved in such tasks as
providing assistance for the review of telecommunications
master plans and technical specifications for switching
equipment, assistance for tender evaluation of digital
switching equipment, and help in planning satellite systems.
The Training Division was active in various training
activities including the CODEVTEL project, workshops on
training standards, and missions to give advice on training
questions.

The objectives of the Telecommunication Economics
Unit are:

• 'To conduct and promote research on the impact of
  telecommunications in development.'
• 'To apply economic techniques to problems of
  developing countries.'

- 'To disseminate information, advice and training to developing countries.'[27]

Examples of its work include a report on information, telecommunications and development and one on investing in telecommunications.

And finally, the Voluntary Program unit administers projects financed by the Special Voluntary Program for Technical Cooperation.[28]

As of 15 May 1987, there were 101 employees in the six major divisions and 30 in the four specialized units.[29] All of the employees in the six major divisions and five in the Fellowship Section of the Training Division were paid through the technical cooperation budget (UNDP reimbursement funds), while all others were paid out of the ITU's ordinary budget.

In addition, there were four Senior Regional Representatives, one for Africa (Addis Abbaba), one for Latin America (Bogota), one for Asia and the Pacific (Bangkok) and one for the Arab States (Bahrein). All four senior representatives and a small staff are a part of the Office of the Secretary-General and are paid out of the regular ITU budget.[30]

The International Consultative Committees

The two International Consultative Committees, the International Telegraph and Telephone Consultative Committee (CCITT) and the International Radio Consultative Committee (CCIR), have been involved in helping the developing countries since being asked to do so by the 1959 Plenipotentiary.[31]

Probably the most important effort in this respect is the handbook, dealing with general aspects of telecommunications, drawn up especially for developing country administrations, produced by their joint Special Autonomous Groups (GAS). There are five such groups in existence at present including:

- GAS 3, Economic and technical aspects of the choice of transmission systems.

* GAS 7, Rural telecommunications.
* GAS 9, Economic and technical aspects of the transition from analogue to digital telecommunication networks.
* GAS 10, Planning data and forecasting methods.
* GAS 11, Strategy for public data networks.[32]

Recent examples of handbooks include *Economic Aspects of the Choice of Transmission Systems,* Volumes I and II, by GAS 3 published in 1986, the 1985 edition of *Rural Telecommunications* by GAS 7 published in 1986, and *Economic Aspects of the Transmission from Analogue to Digital Telecommunications* by GAS 9 published in 1985.

The work of the joint CCIR/CCITT plan committees is also of importance to the developing countries. They include the World Plan Committee, whose job it is to devise a general plan for the development of an international telecommunication network, and the African, Latin American, Asian and the European plan committees whose task it is to develop plans for regional telecommunication networks.[33]

Each committee also claims certain activities in support of general ITU development assistance by its director or members of its specialized secretariat, and miscellaneous publication as part of their annual contributions to development assistance.[34] Both Committees have also discussed methods by which they can expand their efforts to help developing countries.[35]

The International Frequency Registration Board

Probably the least important of the ITU's permanent organs with respect to technical assistance activities is the International Frequency Registration Board (IFRB). However, there are three activities of the Board that could be included if the definition were stretched far enough.

The first activity are the measures taken under the Board's mandate in the ITU Convention to take special cognizance of the needs of 'members requiring assistance, the specific needs of developing countries, as well as the special geographical situation of particular countries' when furnishing advice on the rational use of radio frequencies and the geostationary satellite orbit.[36]

The second involves the preparation of the Tentative High Frequency Schedules. The Radio Regulations provide that in their preparation:

> At the request of administrations, particularly those of countries in need of special assistance and which have no suitable listings in the Master Register, the Board shall give special consideration to the requirements of those administrations in preparing the Tentative Schedule.[37]

Third, the IFRB is required by the Convention to help the other permanent organs of the ITU in preparing for administrative radio conferences. The Board shall also 'provide assistance to the developing countries in their preparations for those conference.'

Funding of Technical Assistance

In the end, the proof of the effectiveness of the different recommendations made by the various plenipotentiary conferences and the changes that they have made in the Convention in favour of technical cooperation lies in the actual funding that results. In this section we attempt to sort out just how much funding has been made available from three major sources: the United Nations Development Program, the ITU's regular budget, and special voluntary funds. Mention is also made of the contributions of the World Bank and the International Development Agency.

The United Nations Development Program

Over the years the allocations from UNDP have been the primary source of funds for the technical assistance programme administered by the ITU. With these funds the ITU carries out various tasks for the UNDP including the administering of 'experts' missions, fellowships, purchase of equipment, and related contract arrangements, seminars, etc.'[38]

Since the exact amount that is allocated to telecommunications is determined by the countries requesting the assistance and the financial resources made available to UNDP, the ITU has little if anything to say about how large that portion should be. As we have noted, there have been complaints in the past concerning both the amount that has been allocated by UNDP to telecommunications, but to little avail. Table 1 shows the allocations by UNDP to telecommunications project administered by the ITU for the period 1974-1987:[39]

Table 1: UNDP allocations for telecommunications technical assistance (1974-1987)[40]

Year	Amount in $ millions
1974	11.1
1975	18.8
1976	20.2
1977	17.1
1978	21.6
1979	26.1
1980	33.3
1981	40.3
1982	31.9
1983	28.3
1984	23.6
1985	26.3
1986	27.2
1987	27.4
Total	353.2

The ITU Ordinary Budget

The only item that appeared in the ordinary budget before the Nairobi Convention came into force was that for the support of the Group of Engineers which came to about 300,000 Swiss francs a year. Starting in 1983, however, when the Administrative Council began implementing the decisions of the 1982 Plenipotentiary, there was a dramatic increase as shown in Table 2.[41]

Two additional items must be added to this amount: the cost of the four Senior Regional Representatives who work out of the office of the Secretary-General, and the cost of amortizing   the   expenses   incurred   by   the   ITU   in

administering UNDP projects that have not been covered by
reimbursements from that UNDP.

As regards the latter, while fields costs of the UNDP
programme are accounted in US dollars, because of the
location of the ITU's headquarters administrative costs are
incurred in Swiss francs. Each year between 1973 and 1979
the UNDP reimbursed the ITU for any shortfall due to the
fluctuation of the dollar *vis-a-vis* the Swiss franc on an *ad hoc*
basis.

In 1980, however, the Governing Council of UNDP
decided to fix the reimbursement for agencies participating in
the UNDP programme at 13% of the annual project
expenditures. As a result of the continued decline in the US
dollar, 'despite the determined efforts of the Secretary-
General to keep costs to the minimum,' the shortfall in the
special accounts of the ITU's Technical Cooperation
Department has continued to grow. In 1986: the continuing
decline in the value of the dollar with respect to the Swiss
Franc has meant that the income accruing to Section 21 [the
reimbursement from UNDP] of the ITU budget is less by
almost SFr. 2 million than in 1985 — a drop of twenty three
and a half per cent.[42]

Table 2: Ordinary budget items charged to technical cooperation
(1974-1987)

Year	Amount in Swiss francs
1974	103,228
1975	299,539
1976	280,000
1977	301,494
1978	299,665
1979	300,000
1980	300,456
1981	328,451
1982	310,000
1983	2,371,348
1984	3,851,835
1985	5,423,128
1986	5,480,112
1987	5,432,532

When the UNDP Governing Council refused to refund any portion of the shortfall, the ITU's Administrative Council decided in 1985 that it thus had to amortize the accumulated shortfall from the Union's own resources. The allocation for this purpose in 1986 amounted to SwFr 3 251 422.47 and in 1987 SwFr 1 877 000.

Table 3 demonstrates the manner in which the amount of the shortfall has accumulated over the past five years.[43]

Table 3: Accumulated shortfall in UNDP reimbursement to the ITU for administrative costs (1981-1987)

Year	Amount in Swiss francs
1981	21,985.17
1982	263,401.27
1983	2,207,463.67
1984	6,419,560.94
1985	7,400,973.38
1986	6,029,537.63a
1987	7,402,306.25a

[a]After deduction of the amortization payment.

Unless changes are made in the system, or unless the US dollar strengthens a great deal in comparison to the Swiss franc, it is likely that this item will be seen in future ITU budgets.

Special ITU Voluntary Technical Cooperation Funds

The third source of income for ITU related telecommunication technical cooperation projects is the voluntary technical cooperation fund. So far there have been two, the Special Fund for Technical Cooperation established by the Malaga-Torremolinos Plenipotentiary, and the Special Voluntary Program for Technical Cooperation created by the Nairobi Plenipotentiary. As shown in Tables 4 and 5, neither has been a prime source of income.[44]

The Center for Telecommunications Development

Although a few projects have been initiated, the new

Center for Telecommunications Development has not as yet generated a great deal of income for development assistance. The situation in which the centre finds itself is clearly expressed in the following excerpt from the ITU's 1986 Annual Report.[45]

Table 4: Special Fund for Technical Cooperation (1974-1983)

Year	Cash contributions (in Swiss francs)	Other contributions
1975		Germany (West) & Japan: 4 generators and 2 transceivers.
1976		Holland: 12,000 in Dutch guilders. Belgium: 5 fellowships. Germany (West): portable cable measuring set & HF radio equipment.
1977	186,097	Belgium: 4 fellowships. Austria, Belgium, & France, 6,700 telephones and 160 teleprinters.
1978	16,463	Belgium: 5 fellowships.
1979	50,243	Belgium: 4 fellowships.
1980	25,230	
1981	26,388	Sweden: 150 telex machines.
1982	27,230	Sweden: 400 teleprinters. Belgium: 4 fellowships. Various Pacific countries: $1,000,000 worth of assistance in kind.
1983	33,358	Belgium: 4 fellowships.

Table 5: Special Voluntary Program contributions (1984-1987)

Year	Cash contributions $	Cash value of other contributions $
1984	2,700,000	
1985	1,995,200	230,000
1986	1,497,414	86,000
1987	1,249,825	174,230

In fact, the campaign to mobilize resources was launched as long ago as 1985; however, the level of contributions pledged to date falls far short of the expectations of the Independent Commission and still gives rise to serious concern, and even disappointment. Theoretically, the situation should improve when the CTD has proven its effectiveness in its activities and in specific field projects.

It should be noted that if the centre does not do better in fund raising before the 1989 Plenipotentiary, there may well be a move at that conference to merge it with the General Secretariat's Technical Cooperation Department as provided for in the Maitland Commission's Report.

World Bank and the International Development Agency

The World Bank remains the major international source of funds for upgrading domestic telecommunications networks. It should be noted, however, that although the ITU maintains close contact with the bank and its affiliate, it has even less control over the projects that are funded and the amount allocated for telecommunication projects than it has in relation to UNDP. In fact, the amount loaned for telecommunication projects by the bank and the International Development Agency (IDA) is a small portion of the funds they make available to developing countries. It should also be noted that only the credits made available by the IDA are long term and low interest. Table 6 covers bank loans and IDA credits for the period 1975-1985.[46]

The UNDP programme has been the mainstay of the ITU's technical cooperation activities. In addition, over the years the developing countries have obtained some technical assistance financed through the regular ITU budget. These two sources of funds have been augmented to a certain extent by the two voluntary technical cooperation funds.

However, even if one includes the amounts allocated to telecommunications by both the World Bank and IDA, and figures in a dollar equivalent for the work of the IFRB and the CCI's which could be considered as technical assistance, the total amount available falls far, far short of the $12 billion annual figure produced by the Maitland Commission.

Table 6: World Bank group telecommunications loans and credits in
$ millions (1975-1985)

Year	World Bank	IDA	Total
1975	96.0	103.0	109.0
1976	59.0	5.2	64.2
1977	140.0	0.0	140.0
1978	168.1	53.0	221.1
1979	110.0	14.5	124.5
1980	0.0	65.0	65.0
1981	66.0	329.2	395.2
1982	87.5	40.5	128.0
1983	250.8	49.0	299.8
1984	166.5	22.0	188.5
1985	59.6	62.0	121.6
1986	24.5	25.9	50.4
1987	552.5	6.0	558.5 (planned)
Totals	1,780.5	775.3	2,555.8

Conclusions

The problem of helping the developing countries of the world
establish a viable domestic telecommunications system is a
difficult one.

The need is overwhelming. As a result of that fact, and
the recommendations of Maitland Commission, there will
doubtless be many proposals submitted to the next
plenipotentiary to increase the amount of technical assistance
provided by the ITU. There could well be demands for more
help from the ITU's permanent organs, financed through the
regular ITU budget. There is also a strong possibility that
there will be proposals to create a new ITU
telecommunications assistance fund. In view of the rather
weak performance of the past two ITU voluntary technical
assistance funds, however, there is likely to be a renewal of
the proposal to finance this fund from the regular ITU budget
rather than relying on voluntary contributions. Further, such
a proposal may well be accompanied by a proposal for the ITU
to adopt at the same time as the UN system of financing.

How far the ITU can go in meeting this need is a
difficult question to answer. The statement by the US

delegate to the Malaga-Torremolinos Plenipotentiary, and the opposition of developed countries from East and West to the financing of a special fund from ITU resources, are strong indications that the ITU many already be reaching its limits in this endeavour.

Attempts to obtain significantly more at Nice could have a consequence that none of the members of the ITU really want — a serious weakening in the ITU's overall effectiveness.

NOTES

1. The plenipotentiary conference is the ITU's supreme organ with power to make any changes it wishes in the ITU's basic documents. The ITU has held five such conferences since its reorganization in 1947: Buenos Aires, 1952; Geneva, 1959; Montreux, 1965, Malaga-Torremolinos, 1973; and Nairobi, 1982.

2. See ITU, Report of the Independent Commission for World-Wide Telecommunications Development, *The Missing Link* (Geneva: December 1984), 5, 57.

3. See ITU, *Resolutions of the Administrative Council of the International Telecommunication Union, 7th Session, Geneva, April-June 1952* (Geneva: 1952), 134. See also the account of the discussions at the 1952 Plenipotentiary in Jean-Luc Renaud, *The Changing Dynamics of the International Telecommunication Union: an Historical Analysis of Development Assistance,* Michigan State University PhD Dissertation (1986), 64-6.

4. As quoted in George A. Codding Jr. and Anthony M. Rutkowski, *The International Telecommunication Union in a Changing World* (Dedham, MA: Artech House, Inc., 1982), 285.

5. ITU, *International Telecommunication Convention Geneva, 1959,* Geneva 1960, Art 4, para 2, d. See also Resolutions 24 through 29.

6. *Ibid,* Art 13, para 1, (3).

7. See Codding and Rutkowski, 285-6.

8. ITU, *International Telecommunication Convention,* Montreux, 1956, Geneva, circa 1966, Resolution No 29.

9. *Ibid,* Resolutions Nos 31, 34.

10. ITU, *International Telecommunication Convention, Malaga-Torremolinos, 1973*, Geneva, 1974, Resolution No 21.

11. See the record of the discussions in US, Department of State, Office of Telecommunications, *Report of the United States Delegation to the Plenipotentiary Conference of the International Telecommunication Union, Malaga-Torremolinos, Spain, September 14 - October 25, 1973*, TD Serial No 43, Washington, DC, 1973, p 10.

12. See op cit, Ref 4, 287-8.

13. See op cit, Ref 10, Resolution No 19.

14. Op cit, Ref 11, 26-8.

15. ITU, *International Telecommunication Convention, Nairobi, 1982*, Geneva, 1983, Art 4, para 1, a).

16. As at the 1973 Plenipotentiary it was accompanied by a move to adopt the UN system of financing.

17. See op cit, Ref 15, Resolution No 26.

18. See the discussion of these issues in US Department of State, *Report of the United States Delegation to the Plenipotentiary Conference of the International Telecommunication Union, Nairobi, Kenya, September 28-November 6, 1982*, Washington DC, 1982, 28-9.

19. Op cit, Ref 15, Resolution No 19.

20. Ibid, Resolution No 18. It was also agreed, however, that any resulting increase in the regular budget of the ITU 'that will occur from expansion of technical cooperation and assistance activities should be found, whenever possible, by affecting economies elsewhere in the budget.'

21. Ibid, Resolutions Nos 24, 30.

22. Ibid, Resolution No 20.

23. See op cit, Ref 2, 57.

24. Ibid, 53-5.

25. Ibid, 55.

26. In 1986 Dietrich Heinrich Karl Westendoerpf of West Germany was named its Executive Director and Ahmed Laouyane of Tunisia its Deputy Executive Director. See ITU, Press Release, ITU/86-12, 25 June 1986, Annexes 2, 3.

27. See *Report on the Activities of the International Telecommunication Union in 1986*, 142.

28. Ibid, 135-43.

29. ITU, *General Secretariat*, 15 May 1987, 8.

30. The tasks of the Senior Representatives are to act as

a liaison with the administrations and international organizations in their regions, to represent the ITU at conferences and meetings that are held in their regions, and to report back items of interest. Op cit, Ref 27, 122.

31. The bulk of the work of the international consultative committees is carried out by individuals seconded for this task by home administrations or recognized private operating agencies. Most of the participants in the work of the committees come from the developed countries.

32. See ITU, CCITT, *Red Book* 1 (Geneva: 1985), 7.

33. The European Plan Committee also includes the Mediterranean Basin.

34. See op cit, Ref 30, 89-90, 101.

35. The CCITT also devotes one of its four Plenary Assembly standing committees to the study of ways in which the CCITT can participate more fully in the ITU's technical assistance efforts. See op cit, Ref 32, 50-2, 259-70, and *Recommendations and Reports of the CCIR, 1982*, 218-20. For further information on the work of the CCIs in the area of technical assistance see Jean-Luc Renaud, 'The ITU and Development Assistance: North, South and the Dynamics of the CCIs,' *Telecommunications Policy* 11, no. 2, (June 1987), 179-92.

36. Op cit, Ref 15, Art 10, 4, c). Note should also be taken of the IFRB's periodic seminars on frequency management.

37. ITU, *Radio Regulations, Edition of 1982*, Geneva, 1982, para 1759 and Resolution 103, 'Relating to improvements in Assistance to Developing Countries in Securing Access to the HF Bands for their Fixed Services and in Ensuring Protection of their Assignments from Harmful Interference.' See also Art 10, 4, e).

38. Op cit, Ref 27, 117.

39. See United Nations, Joint Inspection Unit, *Report on Technical Cooperation Activities of the International Telecommunication Union*, Geneva, 1986, 17; *Report of the Activities of the International Telecommunication Union in 1985*, Geneva, 1986, 246; op cit, Ref 27, 239; and ITU, Administrative Council, 43rd Session, Geneva, June-July 1988, Addendum 3 to Document 6734-E (CA 43-51), 10 June 1988, An 5/24.

40. The ITU also participates in the Funds in Trust Program and the Associate Expert Program. In 1987, for instance, the Funds in Trust Program provided an extra $4,075,067 and the Associate Experts Program $598,511.

41. *Report on the Activities of the International Telecommunication Union in 1974*, 132; *1975*, 116; *1976*, 104; *1977*, 126; *1978*, 114; *1979*, 126; *1980*, 144; *1981*, 156; *1982*, 192; *1983*, 182; *1984*, 158; *1985*, 198; *1986*, 188; and Addendum 1 to Document 6734-E (CA43-38), 7 June 1988, An 2/2.

42. Op cit, Ref 27, 117, 119.

43. See *Report on the Activities of the International Telecommunication Union in 1982*, 198; *1983*, 184; *1984*, 160; *1985*, 200; *1986*, 191; and Addendum 1 to Document 6734-E (CA43-38), 7 June 1988, An 2/4.

44. *Report on the Activities of the International Telecommunication Union in 1975*, 77; *1976*, 67; *1977*, 80-81; *1978*, 69; *1979*, 82; *1980*, 100; *1981*, 110; *1982*, 155; *1983*, 138; *1984*, 123; *1985*, 256; *1986*, 261; and Addendum 3 to Document 6734-E (CA43-51), 10 June 1988, An 5/46.

45. Op cit, Ref 27, 146.

46. World Bank, *World Bank Group Telecommunications Loans and Credits*, 8 December 1986.

Chapter XIII

United Nations Conference on Trade Aid and Development (UNCTAD)

The United Nations Conference on Trade, Aid and Development (UNCTAD) was established as an autonomous United Nations agency in December 1964. It has 159 U.N. members and 9 others, for a total of 168 member states. The expense of the Geneva-based Conference is borne by the regular budget of the United Nations, and the 1988-1989 budget totaled US$77 million. UNCTAD is charged with the role of "promoting international trade, particularly that of developing countries, with a view to accelerating economic development." UNCTAD is the instrument of the General Assembly, and thus, developing countries, in the field of international trade. It serves as the developing world's counterpart to the developed world's GATT. The UNCTAD Conference is held every four years in different member states, and it was most recently convened in Geneva in 1987. Between Conferences, UNCTAD work is carried out by the Trade and Development Board. UNCTAD serves to ensure stable and fair prices for the commodities upon which most developing countries depend for export earnings. UNCTAD also attempts to aid developing countries in expansion and diversification of exports, particularly into the realm of manufactured products. This is performed chiefly through the Generalized System of Preferences (GSP), which guarantees preferential tariff treatment for a certain percentage of the developing world's exports to the developed world. UNCTAD works diligently in the transfer and development of technology in the developing world, thus helping these countries to increase their international trading participation. UNCTAD's work has resulted in the negotiation of several conventions, such as the UN Convention on a Code of Conduct for Liner Conferences. It has also resulted in the passage of the UN Convention on International Multimodal Transport and the 1987 Conference agreement recognizing the need for flexibility in rescheduling of debts, even though the developing world failed to persuade the developed to increase debt relief. UNCTAD has, thus, been an advocate of the developing world, though it has failed to bring about any part of the desired New International Economic Order (NIEO).

An Assessment of UNCTAD's Effectiveness as an Instrument to Promote the Interests of the Third World

Ron Sanders

> It is imperative to build a new order with a view to solving the serious problems of trade and development that beset the world, especially the problems that affect the developing countries.
>
> *Raul Prebisch*[1]

> UNCTAD was conceived nearly twenty years ago to deal with those trade matters as well as other aspects of co-operation of the centres with developing countries.   A very strenuous effort indeed! However, very little has been gained.
>
> *Raul Prebisch*[2]

Those two statements, made seventeen years apart, by the first Secretary-General of the United Nations Conference on Trade and Development (UNCTAD) sum up, in large measure, the effectiveness of the organization as an instrument to promote the interests of developing countries. So far it has failed to produce the results developing countries want. This is not to say that UNCTAD has achieved nothing for developing countries. It will be shown here that UNCTAD played a valuable role in formulating and enunciating the principles which became the basis of the Third World's demands for a New International Economic Order (NIEO); its work had a systemic effect in the institutions of the United Nations and, thereby, was influential in gaining wider acceptance of certain principles of benefit to developing countries, in international economic relations.   Further, UNCTAD was effective in exerting pressure for concessions from developed countries to the Third World on matters such as the Generalized System of Preferences (GSP).   What is more the work of UNCTAD placed the legitimacy of aid from rich to poor countries firmly on the agenda of international discourse. However, these observations apart, when analysed in terms of promoting what the developing countries themselves posited as their fundamental interests, UNCTAD has not proved to be effective.

This paper will set out the interests of the developing countries as expressed by their representatives in key meetings before and after the establishment of UNCTAD. These interests will be examined in the context of the changing international economic environment and the interests of the Western developed states who were the dominant group. UNCTAD's effectiveness, as an instrument for promoting the interests of developing countries, will then be measured by the extent to which it was able to alter the prevailing international economic system to achieve benefits for developing countries.

The International Environment for UNCTAD's Creation

UNCTAD, in the words of one analyst, 'was a child of the era of decolonization — the first institutional response in the economic sphere to the entry of the Third World on the economic scene.'3 As they became independent, Third World states immediately began to question not only the economic order into which they had emerged, but also how it was being managed. The order had been created by the Western states at the Bretton Woods Conference in 1944, and they had a vested interest in its maintenance. As Javed Ansari observes:

> This international economic system has made possible the unquestioned leadership of the USA, on the one hand, and the spectacular economic recovery of Europe and Japan, on the other. The Third World played little part in the management of the international economic order, and any move to redress this imbalance was likely to affect adversely the position of the West within the system.4

The economic order was founded on the corner stones of the International Monetary Fund (IMF) and the International Bank for Reconstruction and Development (IBRD) in which the Western powers enjoy 'weighted voting.' The third foundation stone of the Order was the General Agreement on Tariffs and Trade (GATT) which is firmly committed to an organizational ideology of a liberal trading system. The Third World saw this ideology as inimical to their aspirations for expanded trade on a basis which discriminated in their favour so that they could 'catch up' in the development process, and which corrected the inequities they suffered. Against this background, developing countries agreed that there should be one organization which would deal with all the trade, aid and international finance issues involved in promoting their economic development. Specifically, they wanted a body in which their voting power would have meaning.

As early as April 1955, at the Asian — African Conference held at Bandung, 24 Third World countries voiced their concerns about the international system, recommending 'collective action...for stabilizing the international prices of, and demand for, primary commodities through bilateral and multilateral arrangements.'[5]   By the time that the first Summit Conference of Non-Aligned countries was held in Yugoslavia in September 1961 with the participation of 25 member countries and three observers, Third World concern about the international economic order had become wider; their communique declared that they

> ...consider it necessary to close, through accelerated economic, industrial and agricultural development, the ever widening gap in the standard of living between the few economically advanced countries and the many economically less developed countries.... They further agreed to demand just terms of trade for the economically less developed countries and, in particular, constructive efforts to eliminate the excessive fluctuations in primary commodity trade and the restrictive measures and practices which adversely affect the trade and revenues of the newly developing countries.[6]

Less than a year later 36 developing countries, including eight Latin American states, gathered in Cairo for a 'Conference on the Problems of Economic Development.' The conference was 'notable for the active participation of Raul Prebisch, the Argentinian Economist who had recently been the Secretary-General of ECLA.'[7] At ECLA — the Economic Commission for Latin America — Prebisch had begun to formulate a new doctrine for development, and at Cairo he worked to forge 'some identity of purpose between Latin America and Afro-Asians.'[8]   Having recognized that 'the economic development of countries is meeting with increasing difficulties due partly to some international factors beyond their control and to tendencies which might have the result of perpetuating past structures of international economic relations,' the Conference declared itself 'resolutely in favour of the holding of an international economic conference'[9] at an early date in 1963.   The force of this declaration was considerably enhanced by the admission, in 1960 alone, of 17 newly independent states to membership of the United Nations Organization.   Thus, the developing countries, knowing that the Bretton Woods institutions were controlled by the Western powers in their own interests, succeeded in shifting their struggle 'to the UN system where their numerical preponderance would ensure them a hearing.'[10]

The first United Nations Conference on Trade and Development (UNCTAD) convened in March 1964.   But between 1962 when it was agreed in the UN Economic and Social Council (ECOSOC) to hold the conference and its actual opening the division between the developed and developing countries polarized.[11]   There had been several meetings of a Preparatory Committee in 1963, and while the Western developed countries 'had agreed to the Conference on trade and development it was repeatedly emphasised by them that they did not wish to see a new organisation set up...they preferred to rely on such instruments as GATT and ECOSOC.'[12]

Part of the reason that the Western countries went to UNCTAD I rested in 'fear that the Soviet Union would reap political gains.'[13]   The cold war between the East and West had only just begun to thaw in 1964, but the residue of suspicion still influenced thinking on both sides.   The Eastern bloc countries had themselves been calling for a trade conference to focus on East-West trade, and while their calls fell upon deaf Western ears, they supported Third World requests for such a conference.   Engaged with the Eastern bloc countries in a battle for influence in the Third World, the Western countries were determined not to leave them a clear field.   As it turned out, by the time UNCTAD became functional, 'the ideological sharpness of the East-West

cleavage diminished, marking the apparent beginnings of a
United States-USSR detente.'[14]   What is more, the active
participation of the Eastern bloc countries in pressing their
own case for normalization of East-West trade was not
encouraged by the Third World. The developing countries
were already concerned that the Eastern bloc countries were
enjoying a greater share of the value of world exports than
they did. At the First Ministerial Meeting of the group of 77
(which is what the developing countries in UNCTAD came to
be called), they drew attention to their concern by saying:

> While the value of exports of manufactures from
> industrialised countries increased between 1953/54 and
> 1965/66 by 65 million dollars and from Socialist
> (Eastern bloc) countries by 10 million dollars, the
> increase from developing countries amounted to only 3
> billion dollars.[15]

The developing countries, therefore, were unwilling to help
promote East-West trade at the expense of their own
exports.[16]

UNCTAD and Third World Unity

In the months leading up to, and including, UNCTAD I, a
remarkable unity was fashioned amongst the countries of
Latin America, Africa and Asia — the three regional groups of
developing states. They had enjoyed little previous contact
with each other since each had been colony to a metropolitan
centre, and while there was much contact between the centres
and the countries on the periphery, there were very few links
between the peripheral countries themselves. In the case of
the Latin American countries, although they had attained
their independence from European powers much earlier than
the countries of Africa and Asia, the USA became the
dominant centre of their international life. Thus, the one
thing the countries of the three regions shared in common
was a condition of underdevelopment and a determination 'to
remove economic imbalance inherited from colonialism and
imperialism.'[17]

At UNCTAD I, the 77 developing countries present

overcame differing positions on a number of issues to manifest a unified position in their negotiations with the Western developed countries. Many analysts have observed that this unity was really a consensus position in which every concern of the developing countries was included. A Commonwealth Experts group, examining the process of negotiations in UNCTAD, states that after agreements are reached between the three regional groups in the Group of 77,

> ...the balance struck in establishing the group's position is...inherently fragile and introduces a significant measure of rigidity into negotiations. Reluctance to endanger internal compromises pre-empts effective bargaining and militates against optimal and creative solutions.[18]

Nonetheless, it was in the face of that unity that developed countries agreed, in 1964, to the establishment of UNCTAD as a permanent organ of the UN. Not surprisingly at the end of UNCTAD I, the developing countries hailed their own unity 'as the outstanding feature of the conference.'[19] And, having expressed the 'conviction that there is a vital need to maintain and further strengthen this unity in the years ahead,' they declared it to be 'an indispensable instrument for securing the adoption of new attitudes and new approaches in the international economic field.'[20] But the Conference was not a great practical success. The work of six committees was mostly exhibitions of confrontation between the developed and developing countries. In the end, the Western developed countries opposed or abstained from many of the Conference's sixty major resolutions which, in any event, were diluted from their original form as presented by the developing countries.[21]

The Third World's success in establishing UNCTAD was not welcomed by the Western countries. The unity of the Third World has come 'as a shock to'[22] them, and they determined that UNCTAD would never become the 'negotiating' forum which the Third World envisaged; for them, UNCTAD would be no more than a 'forum for discussion' of the broad problems of trade and development. Thus, from the beginning UNCTAD was a handicapped organization.

Interests of Developing Countries

Against this background, we could conclude that the specific interests of the developing countries at the birth of UNCTAD focused on removing inequitable terms of trade particularly for commodities. However, over time, their interests expanded beyond reform to the establishment of a new order. The formal call for a NIEO was made in the Non-Aligned Movement (NAM). The call came in the wake of the action of the Organization of Petroleum Exporting Countries (OPEC) in 1973-74 not only to raise oil prices, but to impose an embargo against supplying oil to certain Western countries, especially the USA. Encouraged by the new-found Third World strength displayed by OPEC, the Chairman of the NAM, Algerian President Houari Boumedienne, called for a special session of the UN General Assembly devoted to the problems of raw material and development. At the Sixth Special Session in 1974, Third World countries secured the adoption by consensus of two documents: 'The Declaration on the Establishment of a New International Economic Order' and a 'Programme of Action on the Establishment of a New International Economic Order.' Later that same year, the Twenty-Ninth Session of the UN General Assembly, by majority vote, also adopted the 'Charter of the Economic Rights and Duties of States.' The adoption of these documents by the UN General Assembly was the impetus for UNCTAD's work on restructuring.

Later UNCTAD Conferences

It is generally agreed that UNCTAD II in 1968 was a failure. Its only achievement was the setting up of an intergovernmental group to develop a workable scheme for generalized preferences. A third UNCTAD was held in Santiago in 1972, but that too was regarded as ineffectual. Four more UNCTADs have since been held in 1976, 1979, 1983 and 1987, but none of them has been regarded as successful. Throughout the last four UNCTADs, the dominant theme was the need for an Integrated Programme for Commodities (IPC) with the establishment of a Common Fund as a key component.[23] These will be considered in greater detail later. Suffice to record at this point that while at the end of some of these conferences, a few Third World representatives and members of the UNCTAD Secretariat claimed success, much of this was exaggerated. The IPC is still to become a reality and the Common Fund, agreed in 1979, was ratified by the required number of countries only as recently as 1988 and is not yet functional. However, a proposal for a Generalised System of Preferences (GSP) was implemented after UNCTAD II, although not in the form that developing countries desired. Similarly, a proposal for a complementary financing facility, proposed at UNCTAD V in 1979 and designed to provide loans to developing countries experiencing export shortfalls, had an influence on the expansion of an existing compensatory financing facility in the IMF.

In effect, developed countries succeeded in foiling developing countries in their attempt to make UNCTAD a negotiating forum, limiting it instead to a 'largely deliberative role.'24

How UNCTAD Operates

Before we proceed to analyse UNCTAD's effectiveness in promoting the interests of developing countries which they have themselves identified, account has to be taken of three important factors in its operations.

(i)   Resolutions are adopted in UNCTAD on the basis of one state, one vote; and the majority vote prevails. However, decisions made in UNCTAD are not legally binding on any member state.
(ii)   Negotiations within UNCTAD are conducted on a group basis.
(iii)   The UNCTAD Secretariat has much influence in determining the agenda for discussion within the organisation and for much of its life, it has been biased toward the Third World.

The first of these three factors is self-explanatory and requires no further elaboration. However, the remaining two are discussed in greater detail below.

System of Negotiating in UNCTAD

The membership of UNCTAD is broken into groups with the Eastern bloc countries in Group D, the Western developed countries in Group B, the African and Asian countries in Group A and the Latin American countries in Group C. China is not a member of any group and participates in negotiations on its own. From the outset, the African, Asian and Latin American states combined their two groups under the umbrella of the Group of 77, and this led the Western developed countries to strengthen their own coordination and prior consultation.[25] To a great extent the Secretariat of the Organisation for Economic Co-operation and Development (OECD) coordinates the position of the Western developed countries, and the Eastern bloc countries organize their stance within the Council for Mutual Economic Assistance (CMEA).

Much has been made of the unity of developing states under the umbrella of the Group of 77, but there is a danger of misunderstanding the nature of that unity and placing more importance on it than it deserves. Therefore, some explanation is needed. Obviously, the developing countries are not an entirely homogeneous group; they are at different stages of development with some in competition with others for markets. Therefore, their interests are not identical, and, in some cases, they even conflict. Their joint positions within UNCTAD are reached in intra-group negotiations in which every country has to be satisfied. Thus, in the words of Marc Williams theirs was 'not an organic solidarity.'[26] Indeed, their unity was fragile at the best of times, and its maintenance was dependent on the inclusion of almost every demand in consensus positions.

The Western developed countries adopted a similar method of reaching agreement. Consequently, their Group position was governed by the countries which were determined to concede the least to the Group of 77. But, it is worth noting that the Western developed countries seldom made proposals. As one former Director of the UNCTAD Secretariat notes, 'they do not take the initiative of presenting their own proposals but wait for the Group of 77 proposals to be tabled. As a general rule (with rare exceptions) proposals made by Group B are a response and reaction to the Group of 77 proposals.'27

This aggregation of interests between the main protagonists — the Western developed states and the developing countries — resulted in a situation in which 'rigid maximal demands confront rigid minimal concessions.'28 And that has been UNCTAD's negotiating character; a character that could effect little compromise and even less agreement.

UNCTAD's Organizational Ideology and the Role of the Secretariat

At the inception of UNCTAD the Group of 77 was very much under the influence of Raul Prebisch, the organisation's first Secretary-General. As has been mentioned earlier, he was a moving light for Third World solidarity at the 1962 Cairo Conference and his ideas formed the basis for the organizational ideology of UNCTAD. The elements in the organizational ideology included Third World unity, the portrayal of the world as divided into a developed centre and an underdeveloped periphery, the need for compensatory programmes, and new principles of international economic organization which took account of the needs of less developed countries.29 But Prebisch went even further. He made the Secretariat virtually the servant of the Group of 77 by producing papers, advising on negotiating strategies against the Western states, making partisan alliances and even arbitrating disputes between developing countries.30 The Secretariat adhered to the organizational ideology set by Prebisch even after his retirement, and over time a special relationship between the Secretariat and the Group of 77 became established. For instance, since 1971 a liaison office has been in existence in the Office of the Secretary-General 'to provide a channel of communication and to facilitate liaison between the G77 and the Secretariat.'31

There is no doubt that the help given by the Secretariat to the Third World was necessary. Only less than half of the Group of 77 states have resident missions in Geneva, where UNCTAD is headquartered, and most of them are under-staffed and have limited expertise.32 Therefore, they depended on the Secretariat to help them to formulate and enunciate their concerns about the international economic order. The Secretariat did this by producing position papers and technical studies which developing countries adopted as their own.[33]   There were undoubted benefits in this arrangement. For instance, as Kenneth Hall observes, work in UNCTAD, resulting from the help given to the Group of 77 by the Secretariat, has led to 'a measure of agreement on principles of sovereignty in the context of natural resources, equitable distribution to the benefits of economic expansion, technological progress and the accumulation of knowledge, and fair participation by developing countries in the international decision making process.'[34]   Also, some concepts created within UNCTAD became accepted principles throughout the UN system, and there was spill over even into organizations such as the World Bank. An example of this is the report of a Commission on International Development, set up by the Bank under the chairmanship of former Canadian Prime Minister Lester Pearson.[35] That report submitted in 1969 contained many of the ideas on aid and development being advanced within UNCTAD at the time.

However, it is now arguable that while the UNCTAD Secretariat's assistance was invaluable, it went on for too long. A mechanism to prepare the developing countries for negotiations should not have continued to be linked to the Secretariat of an international organization, financed mainly by Western countries who were the adversaries in the Third World's negotiations, particularly as the negotiations were expected to take place within that same organization. Yet, on at least two occasions the Group of 77 spurned the idea of establishing their own Secretariat. In 1977 a Working Group rejected this idea,[36] and in 1979 the Foreign Ministers of the Group of 77 turned down a recommendation for the setting up of a small technical support unit,[37] preferring to continue the relationship with the UNCTAD Secretariat. This decision was undoubtedly influenced by the hierarchy of the Secretariat itself, for their own alliance with the Third World gave them considerable influence over the work of the organization, and expanded their bureaucracy. But, this situation was bound to lead to mistrust of the Secretariat by the Western countries, thereby rendering it unsuitable as an honest broker. Western countries were bound to turn on the Secretariat, demanding that it adopt a less partisan stance, and threatening to withdraw from the Organization, particularly as a major consideration in their agreement to participate in the first place had been removed, i.e. fear of the Eastern bloc making gains in the Third World. And once the Secretariat complied with this demand, the Third World countries would view the Secretariat with suspicion. Both these events came to pass as we shall see later.

UNCTAD's Effectiveness for the Third World

An examination of the areas of UNCTAD's work, which have been hailed as achievements, provides a basis for measuring the organization's effectiveness in promoting the interests of the Third World. Below is a list of achievements generally agreed by sympathizers of UNCTAD:[38]

- the Set of Multilaterally Agreed Equitable Principles and Rules for the Control of Restrictive Business Practices;
- cancellation of official debt of the poorest countries;
- the establishment of a Code of Conduct for Liner Conferences;
- the incorporation in Part IV of the GATT of the idea of special and preferential treatment for the Third World;
- the implementation of the Generalized System of Preferences (GSP);
- the expansion of the Compensatory Financing Facility in the IMF; and
- agreement on the establishment of the Common Fund.

It is difficult to see what practical benefit the Principles and Rules for the Control of Restrictive Practices have brought to the Third World, particularly as they are not enforceable. As a set of principles, they represent a code of conduct which is desirable, but which has been breached far more often than it has been respected. And Third World countries, desperate for foreign investment, have had to turn a blind eye to such breaches.

   The cancellation of the debt of the poorest countries in

1978, and the establishment in 1983 of the Code of Conduct for Liner Conferences were clearly achievements for UNCTAD as an institution, and they both served the interests of developing countries. In the former case, over 40 developing countries had more than $3 billion worth of official debt written off by a large number of Western developed countries,[39] and in the latter, developing countries with shipping lines were able to claim 40 per cent of the transport of their own trade.[40] However, two points should be noted about these agreements: first, they were negotiated outside the rigid group system within UNCTAD — the developed and developing countries concerned negotiated directly; and second, negotiations within UNCTAD for further official debt relief and private debt relief have achieved no success. In fact, some of the larger debtor developing countries displayed little enthusiasm to discuss private debt within UNCTAD.[41]

The remaining achievements claimed for UNCTAD do little more than tinker with the institutions which are the cornerstones of the existing international economic system. They have not served Third World interests by altering the economic order in any meaningful way, nor have they prepared solid ground for change. In this connection, UNCTAD has not been effective in promoting the Third World's interests in establishing a NIEO.

Western countries made two concessions on the NIEO — both were to hold conferences. The first was a Conference on International Economic Cooperation (CIEC). The Second was a Summit Conference of representative Heads of Government of Cancun, Mexico in 1982. The Cancun Conference was an abject failure and with its conclusion came the end of the NIEO which, to all intents and purposes, has been dead ever since. The CIEC, held from 1975 to 1977, was somewhat more promising, but in the end equally non-productive. Originally, the Western countries wanted the conference restricted to energy matters, but with the support of the OPEC countries, the Third World insisted that the agenda include commodities of concern to them. Twenty-seven countries participated, 19 from the Third World and eight from the Western group (although the European Community countries negotiated through the European Commission). Midway through the negotiations, a

Ministerial Meeting of the Group of 77 held in Manila in 1976 decided to establish a liaison group to transmit the views of the Group of 77 to the 19 negotiating countries, but there is no evidence to suggest that this formal contact ever took place. The conference bogged down on demands by developing countries for indexation of the price of raw materials, and a moratorium on repayment of debt. The Western countries, led by the USA, refused to budge. Then, in 1977 the USA agreed to participate in a Common Fund to stabilize the prices of raw materials 'dependent on Third World demands being dropped.'[42] As one observer concluded, the conference 'ended without results except for impetus it gave to on going negotiations within UNCTAD on (the) Common Fund.'[43]

The Common Fund itself was then negotiated between 1977 and 1979 in the context of an Integrated Programme for Commodities (IPC) proposed in UNCTAD. But these negotiations, conducted in the atmosphere of maximum demands and minimal concessions that had become typical of UNCTAD, produced a compromise concept which did not satisfy Third World expectations. The more influential Western countries, particularly the USA and West Germany, rejected many of the Group of 77's demands concerning the structure of the Fund and the amount of money it should have. The Group of 77 wanted $6 billion; the Western countries insisted on $470 million in direct contributions and $280 million in voluntary ones. In the end, it was agreed to set up two windows — the first to finance international buffer stocks and internationally coordinated national stocks of commodities, and the second to finance activities such as research and development and marketing.[44] Left with accepting the Western developed countries' position or nothing, the developing countries were forced to go along with it. In 1980 the articles of agreement for the Fund were adopted, but ratification by at least 90 countries accounting for not less than two-thirds of the Fund's directly contributed capital was not reached until July 1988.[45] But, the Fund is yet to become operational and this may be due, in part, to the recognition by developing countries that its resources are too small to have a meaningful impact on stabilizing commodity trade, and on research, development and marketing.

With regard to the IPC itself, Third World negotiators suffered from what has been described as 'a chronic lack of basic information on the issues under negotiation.'[46] The original 1976 UNCTAD resolution had proposed inclusion of 18 commodities, but only one new one (natural rubber) was negotiated and four existing ones (cocoa, coffee, sugar and tin) re-negotiated with some difficulty.[47] The tendency now is for producer and consumer countries to negotiate commodity agreements outside UNCTAD. In the context of negotiating beneficial commodity agreements, therefore, UNCTAD had not proved to be effective for developing states.

This brings us to a consideration of whether UNCTAD's achievements have been successful in the other stated area of Third World interest, namely terms of trade. The single substantial attempt at institutional change was the incorporation in Part IV of the GATT of the idea of special and preferential treatment for the Third World. But, 'qualifications make the section non-binding, an expression of a goal and a series of recommendations but not a commitment to take action.'[48]

With regard to the GSP, which was an early preoccupation of developing countries in UNCTAD, Prebisch himself has concluded that its 'clearly restrictive nature considerably limits its practical value.'[49] The GSP was put into effect after UNCTAD II in 1968, but it demonstrated the limited role of UNCTAD as a negotiating forum. For while developing countries had pushed for the GSP within UNCTAD, it was the Western developed countries which unilaterally determined its 'design' implementation and execution.'[50] The final form was not what developing countries wanted. As they saw it, the GSP would provide non-reciprocal preferences for the manufactured exports of developing countries. But, what the Western countries agreed to was a system that is not permanent and has no provision for international consultation before the exemption of any product from GSP. In fact, only about 8 per cent of trade from developing countries actually qualifies for preferences under the GSP.[51]

This leaves only the expansion of the Compensatory Financing facility within the IMF. It stretches the imagination somewhat that this should be hailed as an achievement of UNCTAD, for once again what actually happened highlights the organization's ineffectiveness as a negotiating forum. The idea of a complementary financing facility was mooted at UNCTAD V as a means of compensating developing countries for shortfalls in earnings on commodity exports. The Western industrialized nations opposed it 'on the grounds that a compensatory facility was already in operation through the IMF.'[52] The arguments of developing countries that the IMF facility was inadequate and its terms 'unduly conditional on domestic policy changes,'[53] produced no major shift in the position of the developed countries; they merely expanded the IMF facility 'to some extent to meet the demands for greater support for depressed earnings.'[54] And as a Group of Commonwealth Experts concluded, 'the facility does not have a commodity focus; the support it provides is limited by IMF quotas; and its conditionality appears recently to have hardened.'[55]

Thus, it can be seen that the achievements claimed by UNCTAD's sympathizers have produced little practical benefit for developing countries. Yet, for almost two decades it was the single international organization concerned with economic issues in which the Third World had a strong voice, and this undoubtedly sustained their commitment to it. However, by the 1980s even that political commitment began to evaporate.

Decline of Third World Solidarity

As part of a retreat from multilateralism, and an assault on the UN and its agencies, the government of the USA launched an attack on UNCTAD in the early 1980s for its partisanship. The then Secretary-General Gamani Corea shifted the emphasis of the Secretariat's work trying to find a middle ground which could satisfy everybody and declaring, 'I wish to emphasise that UNCTAD is not the Secretariat of the Third World.'[56] This movement away from the key element for the Third World in UNCTAD's organizational ideology considerably weakened their support for the institution. As one study notes the Group of 77 had already become 'suspicious of the UNCTAD Secretariat and this suspicion is not allayed by the fact that most of the staff come from

Groups B and D.'[57]

But, even before the retreat from multilateralism and the frontal assault on the UN system began, the West had already begun to chip away at Third World unity. As Carol Geldart and Peter Lyon observe, from the mid 1970s, 'the approach of the leading Western industrialised countries towards the developing countries has been based on the general philosophy seen as divisive by G 77, namely that different policies are required for different groups of G 77 countries.'[58] A resurgence of bilateralism placed some Third World countries in a situation of greater dependency on major developed states. It also led to a widening gap in the levels of development among the developing countries themselves, and thus created a situation in which agreement between them for changes in the international economic environment became more difficult. A series of vertical linkages on a regional basis which offered trade and tariff preferences to some regions served to further weaken Third World solidarity. Among the vertical linkages were European Community agreements with African, Caribbean and Pacific (ACP) countries on trade and aid, US adoption of the Caribbean Basin Initiative (CBI) giving Caribbean and Central American countries preferential access to the US market, and special trade agreements between Japan and countries in Asia.

A combination both of suspicion of the UNCTAD Secretariat and either their new found strength (in the case of the newly industrialized developing countries) or their renewed dependency (in the case of those who were the focus of Western bilateral aid and trade schemes) led to a fracture of the always fragile unity of the Group of 77, and to a moving away from their earlier closeness to the UNCTAD Secretariat. Thus, R. Krishnamurthi, writing when he served as Special Adviser to the UNCTAD Secretary-General in 1983, records 'the relative failure of the developing countries to utilise the UNCTAD machinery'[59] in relation to the Tokyo Round of the Multilateral Trade Negotiations (MTNs) which began in the GATT in 1973. Indeed, he goes further to state that 'developing countries themselves have not utilised the UNCTAD machinery lest their negotiating chances in the MTNs should be jeopardised.'[60]

A Constipated Organization?

UNCTAD did much to help formulate and enunciate Third World concerns for change in the international economic order; but, measured by the interests which the Third World countries themselves identified, it has not turned out to be an effective instrument for promoting those interests. From its inception the organization was handicapped by the confrontational stance adopted by its member states. The group system employed by UNCTAD was also unhelpful to the process of genuine negotiation. For as the Brandt Commission observed, 'genuine progress in international relations depends on painstaking negotiations to reach agreed principles on legal instruments; only these processes can produce a common language to provide a basis for action.'[61]

Paradoxically, the original bias of the UNCTAD Secretariat toward the Third World also militated against the organization's effectiveness, for the Secretariat operated as the Secretariat of the Third World. Apart from attracting the hostility of the Western developed nations and thereby limiting UNCTAD's suitability for genuine negotiations, this created a dependence by the Third World on the UNCTAD Secretariat. And once the Secretariat shied away from this role under attack from powerful Western states, the Third World's capacity to formulate and implement policy was considerably weakened.

Undoubtedly, developing countries required a Secretariat to help them to coordinate their positions, to provide good technical studies, and to assist in the bargaining process, but it now seems clear, as a number of analysts have observed, that what is needed is an independent Secretariat to prepare the Third World for negotiations in much the same way that the OECD Secretariat helps to prepare the Western states.[62] And an important part of the activity of such a Third World Secretariat would be to re-establish the unity of the Group of 77 which has fractured in the last few years. An independent Commission, called the South Commission, and made up of leading Third World thinkers under the chairmanship of former Tanzanian President Julius Nyerere, was set up in 1987. Its task is to produce an 'analysis of the formidable economic, social and political challenges confronting the nations of the Third World, and of the ways to meet these.'[63]   Among the 'ways' it is considering is the possibility of establishing a Third World Secretariat. One of their biggest headaches will be a governing body for such a Secretariat, and no doubt the Group of 77 will be a prime candidate for the task.   But, the laborious and virtually unworkable system of consensus decision-making within the Group of 77 has demonstrated that it is not a suitable organ to oversee any Secretariat which might be established in the future.   By the same token the Non-Aligned Movement (NAM), which itself lacks a Secretariat and continues to widen membership of its Coordinating bureau (now more than 60 members) insisting that meetings should be open-ended,[64] is also not a viable alternative.

An efficient management group for such a Secretariat could be established on the basis of 19 representatives from the three regions, with the countries of each region electing their quota of representatives every two years. This biennial election would be consistent with existing procedures relating to governing bodies within the UN system, and the number would correspond with the group which negotiated for the Third World at the CIEC. Such a Secretariat could provide technical studies and negotiating briefs for the Group of 77, and other Third World coalitions, not only in UNCTAD, but also at meetings of the IMF, the World Bank and the GATT. In this way, UNCTAD could become a genuine negotiating forum and its Secretariat would be free to carry out its legitimate function as an honest broker for all its members states. However, it may well be that the heterogeneity of the developing countries has now become so pronounced that no Third World Secretariat may be possible, and UNCTAD will continue to limp along, a forum for little more than talk. Developing countries, meanwhile, will continue to be without an effective instrument for the promotion of their interests.

NOTES AND REFERENCES

1.   Raul Prebisch, *Towards a New Trade Policy for Development* (New York: Report by the Secretary-General of the United Nations Conference on Trade and Development, UN, 1964).

2. Raul Prebisch, 'Capitalism: the Second Crisis' text of the Second Third World Lecture delivered in New York on 2 April 1981, in Altaf Gauhar, ed, *South-South Strategy*, Third World Foundation (London: 1983), 7.

3. Michael Zammit Cutajar, ed, *UNCTAD and the North-South Dialogue: The First Twenty Years* (Oxford: Pergamon Press, 1985), vii.

4. Javed A. Ansari, *The Political Economy of International Economic Organization* (Brighton: Wheatsheaf Books, 1986), 188.

5. Final Communique of the Bandung Conference, 24 April 1955, in Philippe Braillard and Mohammad-Reza Djalili, *The Third World and International Relations*, Francis Pinter (London: 1986), 61-62.

6. Declaration from the First Conference of Heads of State or Government of Non-Aligned Countries, Belgrade, 1-6 September 1961, in Philippe Braillard and Mohammad-Reza Djalili, op. cit., Ref. 5, 112-113.

7. Carol Geldart and Peter Lyon, 'The Group of 77: A Perspective View,' *International Affairs* (London: January 1981), 83.

8. *Ibid*, 84

9. Cairo Declaration of Developing Countries from Conference on the Problems of Economic Development, Cairo, 9-18 July 1962, in Philippe Braillard and Mohammad-Reza Djalili, op. cit., Ref. 51, 204-209.

10. James Mayall, 'Post War Economic Co-operation,' in A. I. R. Groom and Paul Taylor, eds., *International Institutions at Work* (London: Pinter Publishers, 1988), 72.

11. See Marc A. Williams, *The Group of 77 in UNCTAD: Anatomy of a Third World Coalition*, Doctoral Thesis (London: London School of Economics, University of London, 1986), 101.

12. Carol Geldart and Peter Lyon, *op. cit.*, Ref. 7, 85.

13. Joseph S. Nye, UNCTAD: poor nation's pressure group,' in Robert W. Cox and Harold K. Jacobson, eds., *The Anatomy of Influence: Decision Making in International Organization* (New Haven: Yale University Press, 1973), 360.

14. *Ibid.*, 359.

15. *Charter of Algiers*, First Ministerial Meeting of the Group of 77, Algiers, 10-25 October 1967, in Philippe

Braillard and Mohammad-Reza Djalili, *op. cit.*, Ref. 5, 183.

16. See Sidney Dell, 'The origins of UNCTAD,' in Michael Zammit Cutajar, ed, *op. cit.*, Ref. 2, 21.

17. Declaration from First Conference of Heads of State or Government of Non-Aligned Countries, *op. cit.*, Ref. 6.

18. *The North-South Dialogue: Making it Work*, Report by a Commonwealth Group of Experts (London: Commonwealth Secretariat, 1982), 54.

19. Joint Declaration of the 77 developing countries made at the conclusion of the United Nations Conference on Trade and Development, 15 June 1964, in Philippe Braillard and Mohammad-Reza Djalili, *op. cit.*, Ref. 5, 215.

20. *Ibid.*

21. See A. I. MacBean and P. N. Snowden, *International Institutions in Trade and Finance* (London: George Allen and Unwin, 1981, 100.

22. Joseph S. Nye, *op. cit.*, Ref. 13, 335.

23. See A. I. MacBean and P. N. Snowden, *op. cit.*, Ref. 21, 101.

24. *The North-South Dialogue: Making it Work, op. cit.*, Ref. 18, 29.

25. Joseph S. Nye, *op. cit.*, Ref. 13, 335.

26. Marc Williams, *op. cit.*, Ref. 11, 470.

27. R. Krishamurthi, cited in Thomas G. Weiss, *Multilateral Development Diplomacy in UNCTAD* (London: Macmillan Press, 1986), 53.

28. Robert S. Walters, 'International Organizations and Political Communication: The Use of UNCTAD by Less Developed Countries,' *International Organization* (Autumn 1971), 832.

29. See Joseph S. Nye, *op. cit.*, Ref. 13; for a full elaboration of UNCTAD's organizational ideology from which this paper draws.

30. Anindya K. Bhattacharya, 'The influence of the International Secretariat: UNCTAD and Generalized Tariff Preferences,' *International Organization* (Winter 1976), 82.

31. Marc A. Williams, *op. cit.*, Ref. 11, 246.

32. Kenneth O. Hall, with a note from Ismail-Sabri Abdalla, 'The Group of 77: Strengthening its Negotiating Capacity,' *Third World Forum*, Occasional Paper No. 11 (1979).

33. Thomas G. Weiss, *op. cit.*, Ref. 27, 53.

34. Kenneth O. Hall, *op. cit.*, Ref. 32.

35. *Partners in Development*, Report of the Commission on International Development (New York: Praeger Publishers, 1969).

36. See L. Searwar and V. A. Lewis, *Proposals for Central Technical Support Unit*, Report prepared in 1979 for Ad Hoc Committee of 21 of the Group of 77 in 1979, typescript.

37. See Lloyd Searwar, *North-South Negotiations: Institutions and Processes*, memorandum prepared for the South Commission, typescript (September 1988).

38. See Chakravarthi Raghavan, 'UNCTAD and the Group of 77 at Twenty-one: Hope or Uncertainty?,' *Third World Affairs 1985* (London: Third World Foundation, 1985), 54; also Raul Prebisch, 'Two Decades After,' Michael Zammit Cutajar, ed., *op. cit.*, Ref. 3; also Gwyneth Williams, *Third World Political Organizations* (London: Macmillan Press, 1987).

39. Iqbal Haji, 'Finance, Money, Developing Countries and UNCTAD,' Michael Zammit Cutajar, ed., *op. cit.*, Ref. 3, 155.

40. Thomas G. Weiss, *op. cit.*, Ref. 27, 114.

41. Iqbal Haji, *op. cit.*, Ref. 39, 156.

42. Gwyneth Williams, *op. cit.*, Ref. 38, 105.

43. Chakravarthi Raghaven, *Improving the Capacity of the South*, a paper delivered in Malaysia in March 1988, typescript, 5.

44. A. I. MacBean and P. N. Snowden, *op. cit.*, Ref. 21, 126.

45. *International Development Policy No. 32*, October-December 1988, Commonwealth Secretariat.

46. John W. Sewell and I. William Zartman, 'Global Negotiations,' *Third World Quarterly* 6, no. 2 (April 1984), Third World Foundation, 385.

47. *The North-South Dialogue: Making it Work, op. cit.*, Ref. 18, 37.

48. Joan Edelman Spero, *The Politics of International Economic Relations* (London: George Allen and Unwin, 1985), 236.

49. Raul Prebisch, 'Two Decades After,' Michael Zammit

Cutajar, ed., *op. cit.*, Ref. 3, 5.

50. Marc A. Williams, *op. cit.*, Ref. 11, 359.

51. Joan Edelman Spero, *op. cit.*, Ref. 23, 237-238.

52. Alfred Maizels, 'Reforming the World Commodity Economy,' in Michael Zammit Cutajar, ed., *op. cit.*, Ref. 3, 110.

53. *Ibid.*

54. *The North-South Dialogue; Making it Work*, op. cit., Ref. 18, 38.

55. Ibid.

56. Gamani Corea, in Altaf Gauhar, ed. *Talking about Development* (London: Third World Foundation, 1983), 92.

57. Kenneth O. Hall, op. cit., Ref. 28, 20.

58. Carol Geldart and Peter Lyon, op. cit., Ref. 7, 96.

59. R. Krishnamurthi, 'Multilateral Trade Negotiations and the Developing Countries,' in Altaf Gauhar, ed., *South-South Strategy*, (London: Third World Foundation, 1983), 168.

60. Ibid., 169.

61. *North-South: A Programme for Survival*, The Report of the Independent Commission on International Development Issues under the Chairmanship of Willy Brandt (London: Pan Books, 1980, 262.

62. See Gerry K. Helleiner, 'An OECD for the Third World,' *Quarterly Bulletin of the Institute for Development Studies* 7, no. 4, University of Sussex; also, Shridath S. Ramphal, 'Not by Unity Alone,' *Third World Quarterly* 1, no. 3 (July 1979) (London: Third World Foundation, 1979); also, Robert L. Rothstein, 'Is the North-South Dialogue Worth Saving,' *Third World Quarterly* 6, no. 1 (January 1984) (London: Third World Foundation, 1984).

63. Report of the Second Meeting of the South Commission, Kuala Lumpur, Malaysia, 1-3 March 1988, South Commission.

64. Lloyd Searwar, *op. cit.*, Ref. 31.

BIBLIOGRAPHY

Mangat Ram Aggarwal, *New International Economic Order, Independence and Southern Development* (London: Oriental University Press, 1987).

William R. Cline, ed., *Policy Alternatives for a New International Economic Order: An Economic Analysis* (New York: Praeger Publishers, 1979).

Jock A. Finlayson and Mark W. Zacher, 'The Politics of International Commodity Regulation; The Negotiation and Operation of the International Cocoa Agreements,' *Third World Quarterly* 5, no. 2 April 1983 (London: Third World Foundation, 1983).

Albert Fishlow, et. al., *Rich and Poor Nations in the World Economy* (New York: McGraw-Hill, 1978).

Colin W. Lawson, 'The Future of East-South Trade After UNCTAD VI,' *Third World Quarterly* 6, no. 1, January 1984 (London: Third World Foundation, 1984).

Matthew Martin, 'The G77 and a Third World Secretariat,' *The Round Table*, no. 299 (July 1986).

Robert Ramsay, 'UNCTAD's Failures: The Rich Get Richer,' *International Organization* 38, no. 2 (Spring 1984).

John Ravenhill, 'Aid Through Trade: The Least Developed,' *Third World Quarterly* 8, no. 2 (London: Third World Foundation, 1986).

Robert S. Walters, 'International Organization and Political Communication: The Use of UNCTAD by Less Developed Countries,' *International Organization* (Autumn 1971).

Chapter XIV

The United Nations Industrial Development Organization (UNIDO)

The United Nations Industrial Development Organization (UNIDO) began operations in 1967 as an autonomous organization within the UN Secretariat. It became a specialized agency in 1986. Currently the membership of UNIDO is 152 member states. The General Conference meets every two years and it last met in Vienna in the fall of 1989. There are 1,257 staff members in the UNIDO Secretariat. An additional 1,910 experts were engaged to provide technical assistance. The biennial budget for 1988-89 was 154.3 million Swiss Francs. In addition to the General Conference, two other important UNIDO organs are the Industrial Development Board and the Program and Budget Committee.

The primary objective of UNIDO is the promotion of industrial development in developing countries in line with the recommendations of the "1975 Lima Declaration and Program of Action." The target set at that time was an increase to 25% of the world's industrial output by the developing countries.

In 1988 UNIDO carried out 1,784 projects at a cost of $119,780,000. UNDP provides the main source of funding for UNIDO technical co-operation activities. Since its inception UNIDO has carried out 13,500 technical assistance projects in 179 countries. Examples of UNIDO assisted technical assistance are: developing a fish skin leather industry in Kenya, modern wooden fishing boats for Indonesian fishermen, assisting Mozambique in developing a bread baking industry and aiding Turkey in the establishment of an herbal medicine industry. UNIDO has established Investment Promotion Offices in several major world cities to publicize investment opportunities and to provide information to potential investors in developing countries.

Realizing the Goals of the "Lima Declaration": UNIDO and the Industrial Development of the Third World

Robert N. Wells, Jr.

UNIDO is the third UN Agency which was created in response to developing countries' initiatives. In 1964

318

UNCTAD was established to improve the position of the developing countries in world trade and developments. In 1974, in response to the recommendations of the World Food Conference, IFAD was created to address long term food needs of the poorest developing countries and improve the food production in rural areas. It took twenty years for UNIDO to achieve specialized agency status. A major boost to UNIDO's goal was the 1975 "Lima Declaration and Plan of Action" of UNIDO's Second General Conference. Improving the industrial capability of the Third World was also an objective of the "New International Economic Order."

There was resistance among developed countries to making UNIDO a specialized agency. Like UNCTAD, UNIDO was viewed as a UN agency which was primarily responsive to, and supportive of, developing countries objectives. It also had the strong endorsement of the Socialist countries. The western, free enterprise countries had concerns about UNIDO's financial cost, economic orientation and political direction. These questions were ultimately resolved and UNIDO became a specialized agency in 1986. It currently has 152 members and a biennial budget of 154.3 million Swiss Francs.

A key responsibility of UNIDO is to coordinate all activities of the UN system relating to industrial development. Since 1975 UNIDO has been concerned with raising the developing countries' share of the world's industrial output. UNIDO also supports the attainment of self-reliance of the developing countries in the development of local human and material resources. In line with this objective it has encouraged small scale industrial development and the use of appropriate technology.

Similar to other specialized agencies, UNIDO is a major contractor for UNDP. It has over 80 senior and junior Industrial Development Field Advisors working along with UNDP Resident Representatives in developing countries. In the most recent reporting year UNIDO was involved in 1,784 industrial development projects. Nineteen hundred project personnel were appointed to assist UNIDO in providing technical assistance to third world industrial development projects. The cost of those projects was 119.7 million dollars.[1]

The direction of UNIDO is set by the General

Conference which meets every two years. The General
Conference elects the Director General, the Industrial
Development Board (53 members), and the Program and
Budget Committee (27 members) and sets the program
budget for the biennium. There are five major departments
in the secretariat: Program and Project Development;
Industrial Operations; Industrial Promotion, Consultations
and Technology; External Relations, Public Information,
Language and Documentation Services; and Administration.
There are 1,257 staff members in the secretariat, of which 423
are professionals.

Geographically, the two major areas of UNIDO's
technical cooperation activities are Africa (32%) and Asia and
the Pacific (36.7%).   Latin America receives only 9% of
UNIDO's technical assistance.   The cost of technical
cooperation is primarily personnel costs.   In 1988 71% of
UNIDO's technical assistance budget was for project
personnel and subcontracts to obtain technical expertise. The
next largest expenditure was for training and fellowships for
recipient countries.[2] Most UNIDO projects are not large. Of
the 1,784 projects in 1988, 1,599 were under a million dollars
and 1,031 of that number were under $150,000.

UNIDO provides its largest support to the chemical
industry sector ($31.4 million). The total for the three next
largest sectors; engineering, agro-industry and metallurgy, is
$33.3 million. UNDP provides the main source of finance for
UNIDO's technical cooperation activities.   Other sources
include the UNIDO Industrial Development Fund ($50
million annual goal), the Industrial Development Decade for
Africa and UNIDO's regular program of technical assistance.
The United States has urged UNIDO to draw upon private
sector capital and expertise to meet developing countries'
needs, particularly in the agro-industrial sector.

Similar to other specialized agencies, UNIDO has
recently had to cope with hiring freezes, travel reductions,
cutbacks in conferences and program curtailment. The 1990-
1991 biennium budget is a zero growth budget. This was a
result of a United States sponsored resolution in the General
Conference to set a resource ceiling for the next biennium
budget. At United States urging, the Industrial Development
Board, in October 1988, directed the Director General to

undertake a management review of the organization's staff and structure. Its recommendations are to be examined by the Program and Budget Committee.

UNIDO Technical Cooperation

Under UNIDO's leadership and technical support a number of innovative and viable industrial enterprises have taken off in developing countries. An early UNIDO success was the development of a roofing tile industry in Mexico. All the tiles were produced from local materials (clay) by local people. Recently UNIDO has supported several programs which have received international recognition.

In Kenya, UNIDO has aided the Kenyan Industrial Research and Development Institute (KIRDI) to develop a synthetic leather industry from perch fish skins. Finished leather products are one of Kenya's main exports. However, recent bans on the killing and exporting of endangered animal hides had hindered the Kenyan leather export business. With the assistance of a one million dollar grant from West Germany, Kenya was able to build a modern tanning and finishing plant for the new fish skin and leather industry. Kenya now exports over four million hides and skins with a greater value added because of the new processes. By processing the hides up to the finished state, as opposed to semi-processing, it adds 150% to the value.

As a result of the Kenyan fish skin and leather tanning project UNIDO was able to launch a $20 million enterprise to overcome the waste of rawhides and skins brought about by substandard slaughtering and flaying techniques, inadequate tanning and other poor capacity utilization. The project will cover over fourteen countries in East and West Africa and the potential savings will run hundreds of millions of dollars. UNIDO's experience with applying environmentally sound techniques to leather tanning in Brazil may have valuable applications in projects in Africa and other developing countries. The process focuses on effluent treatment and disposal of waste from leather tanning. In Brazil alone, tanning has resulted in discharge of 10-20 million cubic metres of effluents annually.[3] With an $819,000 contribution from Italy, UNIDO cooperated with the Brazilian Tannary

School in 1981 to put a demonstration effluent treatment plant into operation. The new treatment plant removes 40-60% of organic matter and up to 91% of biological effluents. As a result of this new process over one hundred tanneries in Brazil have benefited from this technique. The impact of this project reaches beyond Brazil as the Brazilian Tanning School is sharing its knowledge about environmentally clean tanning with other Latin American states.

Fishing is a major industry for Indonesia which is an island archipelago. Over two million Indonesians are employed in the extensive fishing industry. With the financial assistance of the Dutch Government UNIDO has been able to undertake a project to modernize the world's largest wooden fleet of boats, the majority of which are used for fishing and trawling. The one-half million officially registered Indonesian vessels are traditional wooden craft with a short life span and high running costs. With UNIDO's help Indonesia has embarked upon a project to prefabricate components in production centers and then send these parts in kit form to local shipyards. The materials were constructed from laminated wood and marine plywood. The median size of these prefabricated wooden vessels is fifteen metres in length and twenty tons in registered weight.

Experience gained in Indonesia has spread to Papua New Guinea and Africa. One spinoff of the boat building project in Indonesia is that laminated wood is being introduced to replace traditional wood working techniques. The result is a considerable saving in timber resources for Indonesia.

In Argentina UNIDO has assisted the iron and steel industry in becoming more efficient and profitable. With UNIDO's technical assistance the Argentine Institute of Iron and Steel is revamping the national iron and steel industry. The project has boosted production by some $38 million annually while saving some $40 million in raw material imports. The project has been both a financial and technological success. With a grant of $1.4 million from UNDP, UNIDO's sponsored steel research center at San Nicolas was able "to investigate domestic raw material inputs, energy management, optimization of technological processes and development of new types of steel."[4] Argentina now has a revitalized iron and steel industry, operating on modern standards and capable of serving Argentina's modernization needs. One of UNIDO's most unique technical assistance programs is the herbal medicine project in Turkey. This is part of a larger project of UNIDO to make low cost herbal drugs an available alternative to costlier conventional pharmaceutical drugs manufactured in developed countries. By reducing its dependency on foreign pharmaceuticals Turkey could reduce its importation of foreign drug raw materials by almost half. Of the 120 pharmaceutical companies in Turkey, only a very few manufacture drugs based on medicinal plants. With over 10,000 plant species Turkey has a long history of medicinal plant herb medicine. To move Turkey to greater use of medicines the government turned to UNIDO in 1983 for assistance. With a $275,000 grant from UNDP, UNIDO set up a pilot plant and a quality control laboratory for the development of medicinal plant based pharmaceuticals. By 1986 both were operational and providing information to help local pharmaceutical firms. With this development Turkey now has the solid research and quality control center to move forward on the expansion of medicinal plant based pharmaceuticals.

Two additional projects illustrate the scope and diversity of UNIDO's program of technical cooperation; a program in Chile to provide bacterial leaching of copper ore and the development of new production techniques for "pandai besi" (small colonies of blacksmiths) in Java. In Chile the goal was to reduce the amount of sulphides in copper ore. As more copper ore is mined the amount of sulphides in the deeper ore increases. Ore with sulphides is more difficult to process and the cost goes up and productivity down. With a grant of $400,000 from UNDP, UNIDO has helped to develop a process of scientific bacterial leaching of copper ore to remove the insoluable sulphates. Traditional means of smelting are not as effective and are more expensive. Also by bypassing smelting sulphur dioxide will be eliminated, an environmental plus. Because of UNIDO's involvement in the biological leaching of copper/sulphate ore, Chile is in the forefront of a new technology in copper mining.

For years the blacksmiths of Java have been producing

tools for the farmers and cottage industries of Java. What they have not been able to do is to keep up with modern technology or demand for more and better basic farm and construction tools. As part of Indonesia's goal to strengthen small scale industry it requested assistance from UNIDO. A $2.4 million multi-sector project funded by UNDP will provide the technology and know-how for the "pandai besi" to retool their industry and meet new demands. The approach to this problem was to pursue appropriate technology solutions provided they were low cost and simple to understand.[5]

P.K. Sandell, a UNIDO expert, designed a pedal-operated grinding machine which was both light and sturdy. This new implement is quickly replacing traditional blacksmith techniques to produce tools. The basic cost of prototypes was less than $3,000. This innovation has modernized the farm tool industry in Java, increased production to respond to increased demand and raised the earning power of the "pandai besi."

UNIDO has filled an important gap in development assistance: industrial development. It is the one sector in which the developing countries still lag substantially behind. What UNIDO provides is expertise, investment, technology and appropriate solutions to third world industrial needs. It has been responsive to developing countries industrial requirements and UNIDO has served as an important link between first world know-how and investment capital, and third world industrial development goals. Its emergence as a specialized agency has allowed UNIDO to expand its capacity to serve developing countries and solicit expertise and resources from the industrialized countries. Even its most ardent critics would concede that UNIDO has filled an important void in development assistance.

FOOTNOTES

1. *UNIDO Information*, September 1989, p. 1.
2. Ibid., p. 2.
3. *UNIDO in Action*, March 1989, p. 3.
4. Ibid., p. 8.
5. Ibid., p. 15.

BIBLIOGRAPHY

Imber, Mark. *The USA, ILO, UNESCO, and IAEA: Politicization and Withdrawal in the Specialized Agencies.* New York: St. Martin's Press. 1989.

UNIDO in Action. Vienna, Austria. March 1989.

UNIDO Information. Vienna, Austria. September 1989.

United Nations Handbook. New Zealand Ministry of External Relations and Trade. Wellington: Government Printer. 1989.

"United Nations Industrial Development Organization — UNIDO," *The Europa World Yearbook,* 1:81, 1990.

United States Department of State, "United States Participation in the United Nations," Report by the President to the Congress (annual).

Williams, Douglas. *The Specialized Agencies and the United Nations.* London: Hurst. 1987.

Chapter XV

Universal Postal Union (UPU)

The Universal Postal Union (UPU) holds a Congress every five years to revise its constitution, and currently it abides by the provisions of the 1984 Hamburg Congress. Twenty such Congresses have been held, and the most recent took place in Washington, D.C. in 1989. UPU has 169 member countries, and its headquarters is in Berne, Switzerland. The budget is financed by contributions from member countries, and in 1987 it totaled 22.2 million Swiss francs, about 2 million Swiss francs less than the 1988 budget. The purpose of UPU, according to its 1964 Vienna Constitution, is "to secure the organization and improvement of the postal services and to promote in this sphere the development of international collaboration and undertake, as far as possible, technical assistance in postal matters requested by member countries." UPU serves to integrate the countries of the world into a single postal territory, thus facilitating more efficient transfer of mail and electronic mail. UPU promotes international collaboration and provides technical assistance. One issue of current concern is the need for a more rational terminal dues structure, allowing for more efficient and fair international compensation for mail handling. The realization that the international market for document and goods transfer is expanding presents a challenge for UPU in the near future. The United States has been assuming a growing role as a UPU leader, serving as 1989 host and chairman, and prospective chairman for 1989-1994. Through its Consultative Council for Postal Studies (CCPS), UPU has been looking into issues such as productivity in mail service, high-speed mail delivery, improvement of standards in mail delivery and computerization world-wide.

The Universal Postal Union

Ursula Wasserman

In 1971, there were about 550,000 post offices in the world. They employed 4,500,000 persons who handled more than 250,000 million postal items. The co-ordination of this international public service was, is and has been in the hands of the Universal Postal Union for nearly 100 years. It is one of the oldest inter-governmental organizations in existence.

While taken for granted as long as it works reasonably well, few of us realize that even though nearly a hundred years old, postal service still represents a relatively modern institution. Not many centuries ago, the dispatch of letters depended exclusively on the messenger service of royal and other noble households, universities and religious orders. The first international postal service was set up in the sixteenth century and constituted an exchange of mail between Austria, Germany, the Netherlands, Italy, France and Spain, governed by bilateral agreements which were adapted to the specific situation of each country. This resulted in a vast variety of different postal rates, calculated in various currencies according to different units of weight and measurement.

In the nineteenth century, as means of transport — such as railways and steamships — became faster, postal administrations began to feel the need for standardized charges and a simplification of formalities. The introduction of a single rate, the penny postage, where before there had been 1,200 different rates, and the introduction of the postage stamp by Rowland Hill in 1840, opened up new horizons.

In 1863, at the initiative of Montgomery Blair, Postmaster-General of the United States, a conference was held in Paris which was attended by delegates from fifteen European and American countries. This conference established the general principles recommended to administrations as a basis for mutual agreements. However, it soon became clear that bilateral agreements were no longer sufficient and that a single convention was needed to regulate postal relations between states. At the request of Heinrich von Stephan, a high-ranking official of the Postal Administration of the Confederation of Northern Germany, the Swiss government, in 1874, convened a conference at Berne, which was attended by representatives of twenty-two states. On 9 October *a Treaty concerning the Establishment of a General Postal Union* — commonly known as the *Berne Treaty* — was signed. This was the forerunner of the multilateral Convention governing the international postal service, which came into force on 1 July 1875. In 1878, the General Postal Union became the *Universal Postal Union*.

The basic Act of the Union is its constitution, under

which member countries are considered to form "a single postal territory for the reciprocal exchange of letter-post items." From this derives the principle of freedom of transit, under which intermediary administrations are obliged to transport correspondence delivered to them in transit by another postal administration. Other fundamental principles concern standard rates and weight steps and the non-sharing of postage for letter-post items. Since 1875 the Administrations of origin have retained the entire charges levied by them and the administrations of destination were no longer remunerated for the distribution of items. This led to great simplification and savings both for the administrations and the public. However, the 1969 Tokyo Congress of the UPU agreed to one important exception to this principle: an administration which, in its exchanges with another administration, receives more letter-post items than it sends, has the right to collect from the dispatching administration by way of compensation a flat-rate payment for costs incurred through the conveyance, sorting and delivery of any such excess international mail received.

Certain common rules applicable to the international postal service and the provision governing letter-post services are contained in a *Convention*, supplemented by *Detailed Regulations*. The concept "letter post" applies to five categories of items: letters, postcards, printed matter, literature for the blind, and small packages; the convention fixes the rates, weight and size limits and the conditions of acceptance.

In addition, the convention prescribes methods for calculating and collecting postal charges for mail passing through the territories of several countries. It also establishes regulations for the dispatch of registered correspondence, air-mail correspondence, and such objects as require special precautions — perishable biological substances and radioactive substances.

The constitution and its *General Regulations*, as well as the convention and its detailed regulations are binding on all member countries which by 1970 numbered 143, covering practically the entire population of the world. The UPU's decision, on 18 May 1972, to recognize the representative of the People's Republic of China as the only representative of

China brought about no change in membership; China had long been a member of the organization and any change effected merely a replacement of Taiwan by Peking.

Apart from binding agreements, there exist a large number of optional agreements, governing the operation of postal services as regards the handling of insured values, parcels, postal orders, transfers, reimbursements, collection, savings and, lastly, subscriptions to newspapers and periodicals.

Membership of the UPU is open to any member of the United Nations. Sovereign countries which do not belong to the U.N. may, however, request admission to the UPU and are admitted if their request is approved by at least two-thirds of UPU members. The Union's expenses are borne jointly by all member countries, divided into seven contribution classes. A five-year budget is fixed by its Congress, with the Executive Council determining the Union's annual budget approved by the Supervisory Authority — the Swiss government.

Congress, the supreme authority of the Union, meets every five years. Its main function, so as to keep abreast of technical advances and their impact on the postal field, is to study and revise the Acts of the Union; revisions are based on proposals put forward by member countries, the Executive Council or the Consultative Council for Postal Studies (CCPS). The Executive Council, composed of thirty-one members, is elected by Congress and meets each year, as does the CCPS, which is composed of thirty members, and is responsible for studies on major problems affecting postal administrations in all UPU member countries, in the technical, operational and economic fields and in the sphere of technical co-operation. The CCPS also deals with teaching and training problems in the new and developing countries.

Since the establishment of the Union, a central office, known as the International Bureau, has functioned in Berne. The Bureau is responsible for the co-ordination, publication and dissemination of all types of information concerning international postal services. At the request of the parties concerned, the Bureau will give opinions on disputes. It considers requests for amendments to Acts of the Union, gives notice of changes adopted, and prepares the work of Congress.

It acts as a secretariat for all UPU bodies and promotes technical assistance of all types. The UPU's only official language is French.

Transport and Trade

In many countries postal vehicles assure the conveyance of passengers and goods. Thus, in Sweden, the post has made a large contribution to the development of the northern part of the country by providing bus services throughout the year. To this end, the postal administration has from the outset assumed responsibility for keeping the roads clear of snow. In Switzerland, 38,140,000 passengers travelled by postal bus in 1968, or an average of six trips per inhabitant. The establishment of postal automobile lines in some alpine regions has greatly helped to check de-population.

Moreover, the post is a major user of non-postal transport services. Letters and small parcels are the ideal freight for aircraft. To give some examples: In 1968, Air France made as much from the conveyance of 1 ton-kilometre of postal freight as it did from the conveyance of 1.2 ton-kilometres of passengers. During the same year, Pakistan International Airlines earned 13,544,675 rupees for mail conveyance out of a total freight earnings of 69,002,000 rupees. According to the International Civil Aviation Organization (ICAO), total freight traffic carried on scheduled airlines in 1968 amounted to 37,450 million ton-kilometres, with mail accounting for 2.420 million ton-kilometres. The airlines of ICAO contracting states in that year realized receipts amounting to U.S. $12,500 m., 4.5 per cent of which was derived from postal traffic. The post paid 28 cents per ton-kilometre, while only 18 cents was charged for the "freight" category. For a number of airlines conveyance of mail is a vital budget item, bringing in receipts in excess of the average 4.5 per cent figures. Thus Air Ceylon and Air India (8.6 percent), Aerolineas Argentinas (6.4 per cent), Qantas (10.9 percent), Canadian Pacific (6.7 per cent), Air New Zealand (8.5 per cent), BOAC — £15.5 m. or 10.2 per cent. Pan American earned $108 m. from air-mail conveyance in 1967, or 11.5 per cent of its total revenue. This figure is higher than total receipts of about 90 other individual airlines.[1]

In terms of domestic trade, mail order sales play an important role, especially in countries or areas with a predominantly rural population. But even in urban areas, especially in new towns and outlying suburbs, mail order sales have helped solve the problem of insufficient commercial facilities within easy reach. In the United States, the mail order industry grew from a modern effort to serve rural customers at the turn of the century into a huge business now grossing an average of over $6,000 m. a year or about 8 per cent of the total turnover of the various distribution services. Corresponding figures in the Federal Republic of Germany, Great Britain and Sweden are around 5 per cent.[2]

In terms of international trade, the parcel-post service may play an important part in encouraging the export trade: In Britain in 1965 exports to the value of over £100 m. were sent by parcel-post.[3] By using the post, exporters are relieved of the necessity of booking space on ships or aircraft — an important factor for smaller firms — and in many cases the importer is relieved of arranging customs clearance. Moreover, even where goods are sent abroad by means other than by post, the relevant shipping and other documents are still sent on by postal means.

A Means of Development

In most of the developing countries, the majority of the population still lives in the countryside. Here the post provides services which make rural areas less isolated. Until after the second world war, rural delivery service was the exception rather than the rule. Since then there has been a massive increase in the number of post offices. In India, for example, this number rose from 22,116 in 1947 to 101,033 at the end of 1968. Needless to say, this increase has been costly, as many new post offices — especially in rural areas — operated, and still at times operate, at a loss. However, with 82 per cent of the population still living in the countryside, this policy was essential in the attempt of breaking down isolation and making for national cohesion. Moreover, as

postal traffic gradually increases, the operating deficit
decreases. In Pakistan, there has been a similar, if slower
development. The number of post offices increased from
6,474 in 1947 to 13,046 in 1967. Emphasis has been on the
development of rural post offices, with the postal
administration authorized to open a post office in the public
interest without regard to immediate profitability. The
objective is to open a post office in each village or group of
villages having a population of 2,000 or more. This long-term
plan is being realized in phases.

The physical establishment of postal facilities in itself,
however, will not guarantee efficient service. A study of Latin
American postal services carried out in the late sixties stated,
"It is a well-known fact that in many countries of the area
these services do not meet the needs of the population and the
nation's economic activity. This situation leads to manifold
losses, compels the users to resort to unusual methods, causes
delays and at times impedes business transactions, and tends
to create a climate of insecurity and lack of confidence that
has an effect on all aspects of national life. If these losses
could be converted into a monetary equivalent, they would
undoubtedly reach a very high figure."[4]

The volume of postal traffic is a sound indication of
economic development, as shown by the following table for
1965:

Country	Gross domestic production per inhabitant (U.S.$)	Average postal traffic per inhabitant, excluding postage-free items
Canada	2,179	228
Federal Republic of Germany	1,918	167
Italy	822	106
Netherlands	1,550	200
Switzerland	1,758	181
United States	3,185	353

Source: UPU: *Memorandum on the role of the Post as a factor in economic and social development.*

Yet, despite the ready acceptance of an efficient postal
service for economic and social development, many of the

major institutions in development planning have ignored or minimized postal development. The World Bank has made no loans in this field. Apparently, the principal reason has been that the postal system as a rule has a high ratio of labour cost to capital investment, with development planners too often thinking in terms of capital investment as the prime essentials for economic growth. Physical resources normally take precedence over human resources, with national and international development institutions concentrating on such capital projects as road construction — one essential aspect, of course, for postal development — but ignoring the development of human resources in terms of postal personnel. As a consequence, developing countries often obtain the physical facilities necessary for an effective postal system, but not the skills needed to use these plants.

Technical Co-operation

Even though the major development planning bodies may have been slow in promoting postal development, the UPU itself has long realized the need for technical assistance and training. Aid rendered as a rule takes three forms: recruiting and supplying experts, awarding fellowships for basic or advanced vocational training, and furnishing minor equipment as well as training or demonstration material. The Union endeavours especially to encourage joint projects on a regional or inter-regional basis for the more rational and economic solution of problems in any given area — such as vocational training, for example. There exists also a tradition among UPU member countries to provide bilateral technical assistance which may prove very effective. It consists mainly in receiving postal officials from other countries, making available experts, exchanging information, documentation and the results of new experiments.

Since 1963, the UPU has participated in the U.N. Enlarged Programme of Technical Assistance which, on merging with the U.N. Special Fund, resulted in the U.N. Development Programme. The UPU administers postal projects submitted by beneficiary countries and approved by the UNDP's Board. The aim of these projects is to develop and modernize postal services in developing countries, as well as to introduce new fields of postal activity. During the U.N. Second Development Decade, it is hoped to enable postal administrations:

- to serve through one post office on an average either an area of 20-40 sq. km. or 3,000-6,000 people;
- to deliver priority items on the day after posting within a radius of 500 km., under normal conditions of transport;
- to introduce — where they do not already exist — financial services (savings bank, giro, etc.);
- to increase progressively, up to 30 per cent of the total number, the percentages of parcels forwarded by air in the international postal service.

In addition to participating in UNDP programmes, the UPU is also in close contact with the International Telecommunications Union and assists in preparing and implementing joint technical assistance projects, especially in the vocational training field. UPU naturally also co-operates with other specialized agencies, such as ICAO on the development of air-mail traffic, with the International Atomic Energy Authority (IAEA) on methods relating to the postal conveyance of radioactive substances, and with the World Health Organization (WHO) regarding the transport of perishable biological substances. The UPU is proud of the fact that the post knows no frontiers. Distances no longer count, with mail being flown from one continent to another at great speed. Any postal item, the Union states, "must reach the addressee regardless of his social status, political views, religion or race."

FOOTNOTES

1. Universal Postal Union: *Memorandum on the role of the Post as a factor in economic and social development,* Berne.
2. UPU, *Ibid.*
3. UPU, *Ibid.*
4. *Union Postale,* No. 1/68.

Chapter XVI

World Health Organization (WHO)

The World Health Organization (WHO) was founded in 1948. It has 166 members, and its headquarters are in Geneva, Switzerland. WHO's goal is "the attainment by all peoples of the highest possible level of health," and its slogan is "health for all by the year 2000." This means that resources for health will be more evenly distributed among the peoples of the world. It calls for access to essential health care for all, not the final elimination of disease and suffering. WHO's regular budget is financed by contributions of member states according to assessments similar to those of the United Nations, and for 1990-1991 it totals US$653.7 million. Additional funds earmarked for special projects are provided by voluntary donations from members and other sources. WHO acts as director and coordinator for the world's health work programs. The organization also strives to ensure technical co-operation between nations, to promote research, and to establish standards in a variety of fields. Prevention is the central theme for WHO. Immunization for the six main communicable childhood diseases (diphtheria, measles, polio, tetanus, tuberculosis and whooping-cough) is the jewel in the WHO preventative medicine crown. WHO was in the vanguard of the world effort that eradicated smallpox; today it is spearheading the global fight against AIDS. AIDS is changing from a disease of the industrial world to a disease of the developing world. By the year 2000, two-thirds of all HIV infections and AIDS cases will be in the developing world. This presents a tremendous challenge for WHO, which must focus its efforts on the Third World if it hopes to combat this new and formidable menace to the health of all peoples.

Codes of Conduct for Transnational Corporations: The Case of the WHO/UNICEF Code

Kathryn Sikkink

On 25 January 1984 one of the world's largest food corporations, Nestlé, signed an unprecedented agreement with its nongovernmental critics. Nestlé pledged to implement fully the WHO/UNICEF International Code of

335

Marketing of Breast-milk Substitutes, which the World Health Assembly had adopted in May 1981. In return the company's critics, represented by the International Nestlé Boycott Committee (INBC), recommended a suspension of the seven-year international consumer boycott of Nestlé products.[1]

The agreement was the culmination of an often novel interaction among international organizations, transnational corporations, national governments, and a transnational grass-roots movement of church groups, health workers, political activists, and consumer organizations. The WHO/UNICEF code is one of the few successful efforts to date to get an international code, and the final joint agreement between Nestlé and the INBC is even more unusual: a formal agreement between a corporation and its non-governmental critics by which the corporation guarantees to abide by a voluntary code of conduct worked out in an international organization.

In the political economy literature of the 1980s it has become unfashionable to speak about "codes of conduct" for transnational corporations (TNCs); codes seem the vestiges of an unrealistic optimism about a New International Economic Order. Indeed, the literature on the issue reveals that very little has been written recently about ongoing efforts to regulate the international operations of TNCs.[2] Declining interest in codes may have resulted in part from the stagnation perceived in two of the largest and most visible efforts at codes: the general code of conduct being negotiated by the UN Commission for Transnational Corporations, and the transfer of technology code considered within UNCTAD. However, codes in more narrowly defined issues, such as the WHO/UNICEF code and the subsequent agreement for the code's implementation, may provide insights into future patterns of TNC regulation.[3] In this article I shall examine the WHO/UNICEF code, emphasizing its implications for other international code efforts.[4]

1. Codes of Conduct and an Emerging Investment and TNC Regime

Theories of the formation and transformation of international regimes, which focus on behavior and expectations that converge around a common set of principles, norms, rules, and procedures, provide a useful framework to examine this issue. Regime theories have been used to study international arrangements on trade, money, oceans, debt, food, and energy, but rarely has the body of theory been brought to bear on questions of international investment and transnational corporations. The WHO/UNICEF code will be discussed as an instrumentality developed within an emerging regime for investment and transnational corporations.[5] I shall argue that the code is a high-water mark for agreements possible within the current normative consensus because of a convergence of conditions favorable to its adoption.

While new regimes for both trade and monetary issue areas emerged after 1945, as part of the Bretton Woods system, new principles, norms, rules, and procedures to govern international investment or the activities of international firms attracted little attention (excluding the stillborn ITO Charter). By the late 1960s and early 1970s, however, this attitude was changing as Third World countries (and some developed countries) began to demand increased national and international control over TNCs.[6]

An active and sustained interest in TNCs on the part of the United Nations has been a feature of the 1970s and 1980s. The most significant UN resolution on the subject, passed in 1972 in ECOSOC, formally recognized the importance of TNCs for the United Nations and recommended the formation of a group of eminent persons to study the issue and make recommendations. This ECOSOC resolution laid the groundwork for subsequent UN actions on TNCs, among them the opening of negotiations on codes of conduct.[7] After the Group of Eminent Persons issued its report in 1974, a plethora of code efforts was initiated both inside and outside the UN system. A few have already been adopted; most are still being discussed or are under negotiation. The various efforts to regulate TNCs through codes of conduct fall into four main categories. First, industry codes, adopted either by a single company or more often by an industry or sector, are often "preemptive codes" — responses to criticism of industry practices, they attempt to ward off external regulation by showing that the industry is capable of regulating itself.

Examples include the International Council of Infant Formula Industries (ICIFI) code on infant food marketing, adopted in 1975, and the code of the International Federation of Pharmaceutical Manufacturers Associations on the marketing of pharmaceutical products. At a more general level, both the International Chamber of Commerce (in 1972) and the U.S. Chamber of Commerce (in 1975) have published voluntary codes of conduct designed to guide the operations of their member companies.[8]

Some industries are making efforts short of actual codes to respond to their critics by means of "dialogue groups" aimed at developing guidelines for corporate behavior. One such group, for example, has been discussing the export and marketing of pesticides.[9]

Second, regional governmental codes are efforts by groups of countries to develop common policies and harmonize existing practices with regard to the treatment of foreign investment or the behavior of corporate actors. Such codes include all rules on investment and TNCs involving more than bilateral agreements and yet less than global organization.[10] The two best-known examples are the Andean Investment Code and the OECD Guidelines for Multinational Enterprises.

Third, international codes of narrow scope often address a single industry or even a specific aspect of a particular product. While the best-known example is the WHO/UNICEF code on baby foods, a similar code for the marketing of pharmaceutical products has also been discussed. Work is also going forward, in the Food and Agriculture Organization, on a draft international code for the distribution and use of pesticides.[11]

Finally, international codes of broad scope set standard for TNCs as a group rather than for specific industries or sectors. These codes are characterized by general (often vague) language and provisions. The broadest is the code currently being negotiated in the Commission on Transnational Corporations, which include provisions for most aspects of TNC as well as governmental behavior. Other broad-scope codes include the ILO Tripartite Declaration of Principles Concerning Multinational Enterprises and Social Policy; the UNCTAD Set of

Multilaterally Agreed Equitable Principles and Rules for the Control of Restrictive Business Practices; and the Transfer of Technology Code under consideration in UNCTAD. These various attempts at international regulation share sufficient characteristics that one can envision them as components of a new investment/TNC regime. Most national and international efforts to regulate TNCs stress not "delinking" but rather the need to "harmonize" the activities of corporations with the economic and development goals of states. They seek to limit the potentially harmful aspects of TNC activity and ensure a higher net benefit for host countries. In this sense the underlying principle of the emerging TNC regime resembles the principles that have characterized the trade and monetary regimes — reconciliation of the needs of the capitalist international economic system with domestic social and economic policy. The compromise involved is what John Ruggie has called "embedded liberalism."[12] A multilateral, negotiated framework for TNCs and investment within which to resolve problems is still being constructed.

While the emerging regime provides an overall normative structure, the particular form and nature of attempts at regulation — the instrumentalities adopted in each issue area — are not predetermined by the general framework. Outcomes (specific agreements) thus depend on process-level factors that vary from one issue to another. The agreements that develop within regimes can be explained in part by factors that modify the cost-benefit calculations of important actors.[13] The WHO/UNICEF code is perhaps the most detailed and restrictive agreement possible within the current normative consensus, because the convergence of favorable conditions created a significant demand for its adoption among key actors.

The favorable factors that contributed to the adoption of the WHO/UNICEF code can be divided into broad categories of issue, actor, and setting. Among the issue characteristics, the specificity of the issue and the high level of consensual knowledge contributed to code development. Among actor characteristics, I shall focus on three groups of actors: governments, industry, and nongovernmental organizations (NGOs) that criticized industry's marketing

practices.   What is especially significant in the baby food
debate is that from the beginning a group of relatively unified
and well-informed NGOs was heavily involved in the issue
and in the code process. Most previous work on regimes has
virtually ignored the role of nonstate actors in the formation
and transformation of regimes. The baby food case illustrates
the opportunities for nonstate actors (in this case,
transnationally organized nongovernmental, nonprofit
organizations) to alter the incentive structure for major actors
and help create a demand for new agreements within the
regime.   The characteristics of the baby food industry in
general, and Nestlé Corp. in particular, made these
companies more susceptible to public pressure and, in the
case of Nestlé, to a consumer boycott. Characteristics of the
setting and timing of debate, in particular the speed of the
code-building process, the commitment of WHO/UNICEF
staff, and the extensive involvement of all interested parties
in consultation and negotiation but not in actual drafting,
also contributed to the successful completion of a detailed
code.

        In subsequent sections, after discussing the background
to the WHO/UNICEF code, I shall discuss each of these
characteristics in greater detail.   I then examine the influence
of some of these same factors on the code's implementation.
Finally, I shall discuss some implications of the baby food
issue for the general development of codes of conduct for
transnational corporate activities and for the specific
possibilities for a similar code for pharmaceuticals.   The
WHO/UNICEF code is significant not only because it is one of
the few successful code efforts to date but also because, within
some business and government circles, it is being discussed as
a harbinger.[14]   Kenneth L. Adelman, when U.S. deputy
representative to the United Nations, wrote that "it appears
that the infant formula drive was just the opening skirmish
in a much larger campaign.... And this larger campaign could
reach beyond regulation of pharmaceuticals to encompass
United Nations codes on hazardous chemicals, transborder
data flow, and an array of so-called consumer protection
activities."[15]

        One business service that monitors international
organizations has warned its clients that "unless chemical

and pharmaceutical [corporations]...carefully monitor developments in hazardous substances policy in the interim and deftly work to counter their growing critics, they may be faced...with the sort of fast-paced, hard-hitting, emotional code building exercise that confronted infant formula manufacturers."[16] An examination of the baby food code and a possible pharmaceutical code will help us to evaluate whether such sweeping judgments are justified.

2. The Background of the WHO/UNICEF Code

Infant formula was developed as a consumer product to respond to changing life-styles and high incomes in the developed world. As birth rates in the developed world declined, however, markets expanded only slowly, and producers began to export to and market in the Third World. They gave little thought to the impact of their product in a new context. But illiteracy, poverty, contaminated water, and the absence of facilities to sterilize and refrigerate transformed a product relatively safe in the First World into a potentially hazardous substance in the Third.[17] Despite mounting scientific evidence and criticism of the impact of corporate marketing, industry refused to acknowledge responsibility for what seemed at times an inevitable misuse of the product it was aggressively promoting.

Although some infant formula TNCs began to locate production facilities abroad, subsidized milk production and export subsidies for dried milk exports in the European Economic Community (EEC) led many to maintain production units in Europe and the United States, supplying Third World markets through exports. These firms competed for market share primarily through minor product differentiation and intensive marketing and advertising, including mass media campaigns, free samples, free gifts to doctors, and donations of supplies and equipment to hospitals and clinics. Sales personnel attired as nurses, the so-called "mothercraft nurses," promoted infant formula directly to new mothers in hospitals, clinics, and home visits.[18]

The issue first came to public attention in the early 1970s when health workers in Third World countries began to document significantly higher morbidity and mortality rates

among bottle-fed as compared to breast-fed infants.[19]
International organizations were actively involved in the
issue from the outset. In the early 1970s the UN Protein
Calorie Advisory Group warned that poverty, unsanitary
conditions, and illiteracy could lead to abuse of infant
formulas.   It recommended careful supervision of the
marketing and use of breast-milk substitutes. The Twenty-
Seventh World Health Assembly, in 1974, passed a resolution
that urged "member countries to review sales promotion
activities on baby foods and to introduce appropriate remedial
measures, including advertisement codes and legislation
where necessary."[20]

     Although international organizations had embraced the
infant formula issue before activist groups became involved,
the involvement of nongovernmental organizations (NGOs)
speeded up and strengthened activity and ensured more
complete implementation of the code once adopted. Church
and consumer organizations helped generate public debate.
They began to publicize the issue, focusing on the role of
Nestlé, a company that accounted for approximately 40
percent of infant formula sales in developing countries. The
British development organization War on Want published a
pamphlet in 1974 entitled *The Baby Killers*, which the Swiss
Third World Action Group translated into German and
retitled *Nestlé Kills Babies*.   Nestlé inadvertently provided
the activists with a prominent public forum when it sued the
Third World Action Group for defamation and libel.[21]

     In 1977 a U.S. group, the Infant Formula Action
Coalition (INFACT), was formed and initiated a consumer
boycott of Nestlé to pressure the company into changing its
marketing practices. Increased domestic concern led Senator
Edward Kennedy (D.-Mass.), chairman of the U.S. Senate
Subcommittee on Health and Scientific Research, to call
hearings on "The Marketing and Promotion of Infant Formula
in the Developing Nations." At a meeting in 1978 between
Senator Kennedy and representatives of the infant formula
industry, all parties agreed that an international approach
should be taken; they requested a World Health Organization
meeting.

     The joint WHO/UNICEF consultative meetings on the
issue, held in Geneva in 1979, included not only

representatives from governments and international organizations but also industry executives, health experts, and NGO and consumer activists. In May 1980 the World Health Assembly gave the WHO secretariat a mandate to prepare a code of conduct regulating industry behavior. Twelve months later the World Health Assembly adopted the Code of Marketing for Breast-milk Substitutes prepared by the secretariat. The vote was 118 in favor, 3 abstentions, and one (the United States) against.

The code, adopted as a recommendation nonbinding on member governments, is a fairly specific, detailed set of guidelines. It restricts the more aggressive forms of marketing and advertising but does not limit the sale of infant formula. It calls for a prohibition on the use of mothercraft nurses to promote formula, bans direct advertising of breast-milk substitutes, prohibits distribution of free samples to mothers, and requires product labels to acknowledge the superiority of breast feeding and warn about the dangers of improper preparation. The code forbids the use of health care facilities for the promotion of baby food and limits company donations and gifts to hospitals and health care personnel. In addition, it specifies that companies shall not pay employees any commissions or bonuses on sales of infant formula.

NGO field monitoring has determined that, although significant violations still occur, industry marketing of baby foods and hospital feeding practices for infants have changed substantially since the code was adopted.[22] One activist referred to the result as a "minor revolution in infant feeding practices in the Third World."[23] Mothercraft nurses and mass media advertising have been virtually eliminated, while gifts, free sampling, and blatant misrepresentation of the benefits of formula feeding are much rarer than they used to be.[24]

Almost three years after the adoption of the code, Nestlé and its NGO critics signed a joint agreement that expressed Nestlé's commitment to abide by four final aspects of code implementation: a limit on the supply of free formula to hospitals, no personal gifts to health professionals, hazard warnings on labels, and no written materials to mothers and health care staff that omit the hazards of formula feeding and the benefits of breast feeding.

The WHO/UNICEF code, while extremely limited in scope, is one of the most successful code efforts to date, in terms both of the detail of its provisions and the degree of its implementation.   Why should this particular attempt at regulation have proved so successful?

3. Explanations for the Code's Success

The emerging regime for international investment and international enterprises may have created the general context for the code debate.   But it was the special convergence of favorable characteristics of issue, actor, setting, and timing that resulted in a detailed code being successfully completed and implemented.

a. Issue Characteristics: Consensual Knowledge

The infant formula issue had several unique characteristics that help explain how the code developed. First, the issue was inherently emotional, and it was posed in such a way as to highlight the conflict between increased corporate sales and the well-being of infants in developing countries.   Industry sources believed that the emotional nature of the issue colored the dispute.   "Once an issue reaches the emotional plane (as when infant formula manufacturers were accused of killing babies) facts tend to become secondary and even the most brilliantly compiled scientific evidence has little or no impact on public opinion," said one *Business International* article.[25]

More interesting than how emotionalism skewed the debate away from "facts" is how an industry that had long cultivated the image of "mother's helper" was put on the defensive for endangering the health of infants.   The issue shows that debates and actions within the UN system have the potential to delegitimize previously accepted practices and to create new consciousness about problems, especially where a high level of consensual knowledge exists.[26] In this sense, industry's intransigence when faced with an increasing level of consensual knowledge on the part of health professionals and NGOs contributed to the move toward an international code.[27]

Public health experts uniformly agreed that breast feeding is far superior to bottle feeding and that improper bottle feeding contributes to infant mortality and malnutrition.[28] Prestigious pediatricians estimated that in 1978 about ten million cases of infant malnutrition were occurring yearly in developing countries as a direct and indirect result of mothers ceasing to breast-feed their children. Improper infant feeding practices resulted in one to three million infant deaths per year. In addition, breast feeding was on the decline, and there was significant agreement that one important reason for that decline was misleading sales promotion of formula.[29] Industry representatives argued that although breast feeding was superior, no clear scientific evidence linked advertising to changes in infant feeding practices — but they found little support from health experts familiar with conditions in developing countries.

The high level of consensual scientific knowledge contributed to WHO/UNICEF action on the issue, swelling the ranks of industry critics with medical and scientific groups. When the companies refused to change marketing practices, organizations such as the American Public Health Association, the Ambulatory Pediatrics Association, and the National Council for International Health became endorsers of the WHO process and the Nestlé boycott. But it is not enough to say that consensual knowledge contributed to the development of the WHO/UNICEF code. Rather we need to ask how the political struggle surrounding the issue permitted a role for knowledge and learning within the debate. Not only was there a greater degree of consensual knowledge in the infant formula debate than in many code negotiations, but the interests that favored a code were able to introduce code-supporting knowledge.[30]

The perception of WHO as a technical and professional organization with low "politicization" increased the impact of consensual scientific knowledge from credible health sources in the case of the baby food debate. Moreover, scientific consensus had begun to form before the debate began providing a substantial base of information that shaped a highly charged dispute.

All parties presented scientific material, but industry positions generally relied on in-house or industry-sponsored research. Critics of industry practices, on the other hand, were able to draw on a wide variety of independent scientific sources.[31] NGOs also reprinted and distributed material originally produced by international organizations, such as the seminal article on the issue which had first appeared in the *WHO Bulletin*.[32] Robert Rothstein has pointed out that bureaucrats often serve as key conduits or bridges between producers and users of knowledge. In the infant formula debate not only bureaucrats but also NGOs diffused, publicized, and dramatized the information that supported the code effort.[33]

In the development and adoption of the code delegates clearly "learned" about the role of advertising in infant nutrition — learning that many of them did not possess before the debate began. But consensual knowledge and learning had a wider significance in the issue. Learning, on the part of such nongovernmental institutions as hospitals as well as of governments, was also important in the implementation of the code's provisions.

b. Actor Characteristics

i. Industry and market structure. The major companies involved in the baby food debate derived only a fraction of their total sales from infant formula, and the code's marketing limitations actually affected only a fraction of infant formula sales. In 1978 worldwide sales affected only a fraction of infant formula sales. In 1978 world wide sales of formula amounted to approximately $1.5 billion, of which an estimated $600 million were in the developing world. Nestlé's global sales in 1978 approached $10 billion, of which formula accounted for approximately $400 million.[34] Critics confronted a relatively small number of companies that devoted only a portion of their activities to the marketing of infant formula in developing countries.

Moreover, despite increasing limitations on company advertising, the baby food market continued to expand throughout the controversy. James Post estimates that by 1983 the global market for infant formula products probably exceeded $4 billion, with developing nations accounting for about 50 percent of the total. Since 1978 the total market had more than doubled. "This growth does not mean that the WHO Code has failed," Post argues. "Rather, it simply means that there has been continued population and market growth while, at the same time, there has been an improvement in the quality of competitive conduct."[35] It seems likely that regulating an industry in a constantly increasing market will be easier than regulating an industry whose market is shrinking. In the baby food case, increased regulation may have slowed market expansion, but it caused no absolute decline in sales.

The companies lobbying against the code often did not agree on strategy. Early in the campaign one U.S. formula producer, Abbott Laboratories, refused to join the International Council of the Infant Food Industry and criticized the ICIFI code of ethics as weaker than the Abbott code of marketing. Later Nestlé would exceed the marketing changes of other companies as a result of pressures from the infant formula campaign and agreements with boycott leaders.

Nestlé, the leader in the industry, held approximately 40 percent of the infant formula market in developing countries. Certain characteristics made the company particularly vulnerable to one of the strategies chosen by the consumer critics — a consumer boycott of Nestlé products. (The boycott began and was always strongest in the U.S. market but eventually spread to nine other industrialized countries.) Most of Nestlé's products are food products, many of them clearly identifiable not only by brand but also by parent company (Nescafé, Nestea, Nestlé Crunch, Nestlé Tollhouse Chips, etc.) and easily replaceable with alternative products. Nestlé had also invested heavily in a corporate image based on high-quality products, which accusations that the company's products led to increased infant mortality in the Third World obviously threatened with long-term damage.

Before the boycott, Nestlé had targeted the United States as the primary market for corporate growth. The corporation intended to double sales and increase U.S. operations until they were approximately 30 percent of worldwide sales, both through expanding existing market lines and, in particular, through mergers.[36]   There are indications that Nestlé eventually reached agreement with its critics not only because its sales were directly hurt but also because a new senior management team wanted to turn its attention to more pressing business problems, in particular mergers and acquisitions in the U.S. market.[37]

   ii. The role of nongovernmental organizations.   The important NGO actors in the baby food debate included the Inter-Faith Center on Corporate Responsibility (ICCR), the organization that had initiated work on the issue in the United States through stockholders' resolutions by its church members; the International Organization of Consumers Unions (IOCU), an umbrella organization based in The Hague for consumer organizations around the world; and INFACT, the U.S. organization that organized and coordinated the Nestlé boycott.   In addition, these three groups helped form and worked with the International Baby Food Action Network (IBFAN), which eventually brought together 100 groups working in 65 countries on issues of infant nutrition.   The International Nestlé Boycott Committee, formed by INFACT and the U.S. National Council of Churches and representing 87 of the 120 national organizations that had endorsed the boycott in the United States and Canada, took responsibility for negotiations with Nestlé.   U.S. and Canadian churches and religious orders were especially active in the committee and in ICCR.

   The resources of NGOs working on the infant formula issue were severely limited.   INFACT, for example, began in Minneapolis, Minnesota, as a group of twenty volunteers and one paid staff member.   Though INFACT grew in size and sophistication over the years, its total budget for the seven-and-one-half-year period it waged the boycott probably never exceeded $3.5 million.[38]

   The NGO coalition supporting the boycott was loosely knit, bringing together groups and individuals of various political persuasions and interests.   Some elements had limited goals, others saw the infant formula campaign as one part of a larger political change.   The number of full-time core activists was small, and the coalition relied heavily on volunteers, church groups, and the networks of endorsing organizations to spread news of the boycott.

The strengths of NGO actors were fourfold. First, they strengthened and used to their advantage the emotional and consensual characteristics of the issue. Second, the organization of a loose but nonetheless effective transnational network enabled them to gather and disseminate information internationally and to organize different forms of resistance to company policies in different settings. Third, they had the capacity to bring economic, moral, and political pressure to bear on TNCs in order to change their interest calculations and engage them in making and implementing international rules. Fourth, they were able to hold a disparate coalition together for over seven years of boycott, to present a unified front, and to prevent significant defections.

NGOs operated both inside and outside the UN system. They made their positions felt effectively within WHO and UNICEF, through participation in meetings, lobbying of delegates and officials, and the publication and distribution of materials. But it was activities outside the United Nations, especially the Nestlé boycott, stockholders' resolutions, and publicity campaigns, that proved decisive in getting a final agreement. The combination of NGO activities inside and outside international organizations was particularly productive.[39]

The single most effective tactic of these groups was their ability to alter the interest calculations of companies and some national governments. Changes in TNC behavior on the infant formula issue were motivated more by increasing activism than by concerns over national law or WHO censure. For example, the industry group, ICIFI, was formed and adopted its voluntary marketing code of ethics in 1975 only a few days before the beginning in Switzerland of Nestlé's suit against the Third World Action Group over the pamphlet *Nestlé Kills Babies*. In December 1977 the Bristol Myers Company announced changes in its marketing of infant formula as a result of a two-year court battle, with church groups owning shares of its stock, over alleged false and misleading statements in the company's proxy material.

Perhaps the most powerful incentive for the industry to change was the Nestlé boycott. Although Nestlé has never revealed how much damage the boycott inflicted, its actions indicated that it took the boycott very seriously. Nestlé's main antiboycott strategist, Rafael Pagan, conceded that "it is hard to quantify the effects of a prolonged controversy of this nature on the bottom line. However, we estimate that the implementation of the WHO Code alone will cost Nestlé $10-20 million. The cost in executive time and effort has been high. The impact on employee morale and on the corporation's image was quite substantial."[40] Boycott leaders argued that the boycott succeeded because it increased the costs for Nestlé while a Third World campaign simultaneously reduced the benefits that Nestlé received from violating the code.[41] According to one source, the boycott was the most "devastating attack [ever mounted] on corporate advertising in the Third World." *Business International* warned that consumer movements need to be taken seriously; they are developing effective international networks that allow them to draw world attention to single issues and spread information about regulations in the industrial world to other regions.[42]

Industry approached first voluntary codes and then action in international organizations as ways of diffusing public criticism and avoiding economic boycott. Initially both Nestlé and the American companies supported the idea of an international code of marketing. The infant food industry itself, after consultations with Senator Kennedy, requested international action on the baby food issue. Moreover, the issue was taken to WHO as a result of an industry decision, not of a request from governments or NGO lobbyists. Industry, it seems clear, saw the movement into international forums as an alternative to responding to activists' attacks.[43]

During WHO negotiations, industry representatives stressed privately to the U.S. delegation that their major concern was not host-country regulation but increased activism. A State Department telegram records a conversation with Nestlé executive Geoffrey Fookes:

> Fookes revealed a most interesting industry perspective. According to Fookes, industry is not really worried that any countries will in fact try to implement the Code in its entirety or as a minimum standard. They believe that countries necessarily will have to use

great flexibility in implementing the Code. Industry's concern about many of the specific parts of the Code and about the strong wording in the resolution relates almost entirely to their relations with the critics and consumer activists. They believe that if the Code and the resolution are not crystal clear on the need for flexibility in implementation, either can be used for further direct criticism of industry in the public fora, that industry would be held to the highest apparent standards even though some countries may choose not to implement the Code exactly as the critics understood the words.[44]

The industry put considerable effort into its attempts to influence the code.[45] Nestlé officials initially told the U.S. delegation in Geneva that there was a consensus in ICIFI not to oppose the code but rather to shape the resolution in an acceptable fashion.[46] As soon as the infant formula TNCs realized that they could not control the WHO process, and that the code would be much more detailed and stricter than they had anticipated, they began working to undercut it. One U.S. government memorandum reported that "some companies find the Code unacceptable; in particular, the three major U.S. manufacturers are currently considering a consolidated position against the Code."[47] U.S. industry found a sympathetic ear in the new Reagan administration, and their lobbying efforts were responsible for the U.S. "no" vote.[48] Nestlé, the corporation subject to the widest public criticism, worked behind the scenes to undermine the code, but its public pronouncements stressed support for the principle if not the letter of the code, which remained the only alternative to negotiations with its NGO critics.

The behavior of the baby food industry during negotiations and after the adoption of the code made it clear that its primary concern was its critics, and in particular the U.S. groups and consumers involved in the Nestlé boycott. In 1981 Nestlé set up a Nestlé Nutrition Center in Washington, D.C., to present Nestlé's point of view to policy makers and the public. The center became the headquarters for Nestlé's response to its critics. From 1981 to 1984 Nestlé held five press conferences to announce changes in its marketing practices. Each of these conferences was held in Washington rather than at company headquarters in Switzerland. In 1982 Nestlé formed the Nestlé Infant Formula Audit Commission (NIFAC), to monitor Nestlé compliance with its marketing guidelines. The commission, headed by former U.S. secretary of state Edmund Muskie, was clearly a U.S. affair: its members all lived in the United States, where it met and held all of its press conferences. After the signing of the joint agreement to end the Nestlé boycott, NIFAC stopped holding quarterly press conferences even though Nestlé and Muskie had always asserted that the commission was not a response to the boycott.

   iii. Government positions. The strength of the code vote (118 in favor, 1 against, and 3 abstentions) underlined the seriousness with which many countries, especially in the Third World, viewed the problem. Third World governments faced general demands to protect their domestic economies and societies from destabilizing forces and to reassert national control over TNCs' activities. More specifically, a consensus existed that breast-milk substitutes contributed little to national economies, used scarce foreign exchange, and by increasing infant morbidity and mortality generated unnecessary health care and hospital costs.

   At the WHO Executive Board meeting in January 1980, and at the World Health Assembly in May 1980, government representatives from both less developed and developed countries passed a consensus resolution calling for an international code for marketing for breast-milk substitutes. They requested that the director general prepare such a code "in close consultation with member states and with all other parties concerned."

   The initial U.S. position at the May 1980 assembly opposed the development of a baby food marketing code. Domestic NGO lobbying pressured the U.S. government to reconsider its position during the assembly meeting, and eventually the United States supported the final resolution calling for a draft code. Subsequently the United States developed an interagency taskforce, chaired by the Department of Health and Human Services and including the State Department, the Agency for International Development, the National Institute of Health, and ACTION, the umbrella agency incorporating the Peace Corps and VISTA, to develop U.S. recommendations for the code. The taskforce gave priority to the health issues involved; it participated in building the code, although not totally in accordance with NGO recommendations. The eventual U.S. position was in part a result of top officials' commitment to the health aspects of the issue[49] and in part a response to more "strategic" concerns. On the strategic level one U.S. government memo pointed out that "it is clear that virtually all of the 156 member nations of the WHO are intent that there will be a code.... Key Europeans and developing countries [feel] that any weakening of the Code is unacceptable." The memo's author raised the concern that the "U.S. would be completely isolated in its position which could have deleterious effects in terms of support we would need (from such countries as Mexico, Nigeria, Algeria, India, Norway, Sweden, Kenya, and Jamaica) on other important issues, such as those involving Egypt and Israel."[50]

The active support of such European countries as Sweden and Norway and the acquiescence of all of the other Western nations was important in the code's adoption. The Netherlands and Switzerland, both major exporters of baby food, supported a code. West Germany, the United Kingdom, France, Australia, and Canada offered little opposition to the code's content, but they believed strongly that the code should be adopted not as a regulation but as a recommendation. The Third World used regulation vs. recommendation as a bargaining tool. Fred Sai of Ghana, the highly respected professional who helped chair the preliminary meetings, warned that if the World Health Assembly saw the issue as a contest between a West that wanted to protect its industry and the South, the code would certainly be adopted as a regulation.[51]

The WHO secretariat, aiming for a code based on a consensus of member governments, made efforts throughout the code-building process to accommodate the demands of the United States and other countries. The new Reagan administration sent its assistant secretary of state for international organizations, Elliot Abrams, to Geneva to discuss the code with WHO's director general, Hafdan Mahler. Abrams told Mahler that the United States would vote for a recommendation to member governments, and

WHO went on record favoring a recommendatory code.[52] As a result of industry lobbying, however, the Reagan administration reversed its decision at the last minute and cast the sole vote against the code. This reversal caused some resentment among code supporters who felt that they had bent over backward to incorporate U.S. concerns. In retrospect, the episode was an early indication of what would become, during the Reagan administration, characteristically abrupt and confrontational U.S. behavior in international forums.

c. Setting Characteristics

WHO and UNICEF's reputations as technical agencies, as mentioned above, created greater receptivity for the body of scientific data that tended to support regulation. Staff in the two organizations were concerned with the problem and committed to finding a solution. Once the process was underway, they helped move the code along quickly.

Timing also was important to the success of the code. The WHO/UNICEF code took only eighteen months from initial conceptualization to final vote. Speed prevented extended lobbying that might have diluted code provisions. The pace resulted from the initial convergence of almost all the major actors around the idea that a code was desirable. In addition, the process was accelerated by the practice of WHO and UNICEF staffers drafting the code and negotiators modifying the prepared text. By the time that industry and the new U.S. administration began to have serious misgivings, they were too late to block the momentum for a code.

The WHO/UNICEF code was developed in a process that allowed full participation to governments, experts, industry, and critics.[53] The extensive involvement of all major actors in negotiations contributed to the development of detailed, meaningful regulations. WHO and UNICEF ensured the participation and consultation of all interested parties while limiting the actual drafting to the secretariats. The result was rapid and relatively consensual.

The final negotiations between Nestlé and the INBC were carried out at UNICEF in New York. Although UNICEF denies that it served as a mediator or arbitrator,[54] its presence in the negotiations clearly provided a face-saving way for Nestlé to reach an agreement with groups that the company had previously characterized as "irresponsible." UNICEF's role as a facilitator of the negotiations and the final agreement between Nestlé and its critics was also a departure from the customary activities of international organizations.[55]

The final joint agreement between Nestlé and the INBC guarantees that the corporation will abide by a voluntary code of conduct worked out in an international organization. The only parallel cases might be found where trade unions work to have references to codes of conduct included in their contracts with companies.[56] In both cases the activities of nongovernmental organizations create opportunities to implement a code beyond those envisioned when the codes were adopted.

It is important to stress this interaction of characteristics. The international forum, WHO, was more open to an issue characterized by a high level of consensual knowledge; the NGO actors used to their advantage both the emotional and the consensual characteristics of the issue and the susceptibility of corporate actors to public pressure; the speed of the process prevented key actors, especially a new U.S. administration, from undermining the negotiations.

4. Code Implementation

The adoption of the code was no guarantee, of course, that actual behavior would change at a national level. Initial evidence suggests, however, that governments, health professionals, and TNCs have begun significantly to modify their behavior (though often for very different reasons). Some of the factors that contributed to the adoption of the code also helped in implementing it, especially the role of consensual knowledge and continued NGO pressure on industry.

The implementation of the code at the level of the health ministry, the hospital, and the individual health worker or doctor often resulted from an increased availability of information about the dangers associated with the misuse of breast-milk substitutes. Such information was generated and disseminated by the WHO, UNICEF, and NGOs as a by-product of building a code. Medical professionals had

previously received much of their information on infant
feeding practices from TNC employees. The process in the
WHO raised the salience of the issue and provided a
countersource of information for health workers. Health
ministry officials, hospital administrators, and other health
professionals in Panama, Costa Rica, and Nicaragua,
interviewed in early 1982, constantly referred to infant
feeding in terms of "before" and "after" the code. Even health
professionals who were not aware of the exact contents of the
WHO/UNICEF code reported that they were much more
conscious than previously of the dangers of bottle feeding and
the need to promote breast feeding.

a. Implementation by Industry

Continued activist pressure on the baby food producers
also contributed to practical implementation of the code by
Nestlé. Three times in the two years following the code's
adoption Nestlé publicly announced changes in its marketing
strategy designed to bring it into accord with the code. On
each of these occasions the critics, represented by INFACT
and INBC, found that Nestlé policy still fell short of the code
and refused to lift the boycott. What was significant about
each of these marketing changes, however, is that Nestlé was
taking concrete steps to translate the code's provisions into
specific instructions to its managers around the world. This
translation from code language to company instruction is
crucial to the effectiveness of any code of conduct for TNCs.

In 1983 INFACT spearheaded a new strategy to bring
Nestlé to the negotiating table. It focused the boycott on one
of Nestlé's best-known and most profitable products —
Taster's Choice instant coffee — and reinvigorated the boycott
at the grass roots by opening new local action centers in
Chicago and Boston. In December 1983 INFACT and INBC
made four final demands at a Washington press conference
and announced an international conference by baby food
activists to be held in Mexico in early 1984. Nestlé recognized
an opportunity to negotiate an end to the boycott and asked
UNICEF to facilitate negotiations with boycott leaders. After
rapid and intense final negotiations Nestlé and its activist
critics hammered out a joint agreement to end the boycott.

In that agreement both Nestlé and the INBC stated their firm commitment to see the International Code of Marketing for Breast-milk Substitutes implemented by governments and all parties concerned.[57] On the basis of the agreement, the INBC suspended the boycott. Progress would be evaluated in the autumn of 1984, and a final decision would then be made regarding the termination of the boycott. In October 1984 boycott activists examined monitoring reports from fifteen countries and verified a significant change in Nestlé's marketing practices. They officially ended the Nestlé boycott. Critics have since turned their attention to other baby food companies in the United States and Europe, because field reports indicate that they lag behind Nestlé in implementing the code.[58]

b. Implementation by Governments

By July 1984 the international code in its entirety was in effect as law in only seven countries. In another thirty-seven countries it had been recommended as national law but awaited enactment. Some national law exceeds the provisions of the international code. In India, for example, the national code prohibits all distribution of free samples, directly or indirectly, where the WHO/UNICEF code permits free samples to doctors for professional evaluation.[59] Legislation, rules, or regulations have been passed in twenty-four additional countries that incorporate some but not all of the provisions of the international code. Of 134 countries surveyed by the International Organization of Consumers Unions in July 1984, only four (the United States, the Maldives, Tonga, and Vanuatu), planned no action to regulate baby food marketing. In the other 130 countries either the government directly controlled distribution and marketing, or at least some form of voluntary or legal regulation was under discussion, awaiting implementation, or already implemented.[60]

5. Implications of the WHO/UNICEF Case

Can the baby food code provide a model for codes for TNCs? Certain attributes of the process may be reproducible in other forums and issue areas, but the baby food code may nonetheless be a special case.

Collaboration between actors in the case was largely the result of the focused and consensual nature of the issue and the ability of nongovernmental groups to change the interest calculations of industry. One can argue that related events were largely responsible for the success of the UNCTAD code on restrictive business practices. There also, consensual knowledge was important — most participants, governments and industry alike, agreed that restrictive business practices had negative economic effects. Moreover, U.S. law already held American companies to standards higher than the code's in their overseas operations, giving U.S. business and the U.S. government an incentive to work for the adoption of international norms. In the absence of such norms, U.S. businesses felt that they would be at a significant disadvantage vis-à-vis competitors based in other countries.

One determinant of future code efforts will be the business community's experience with these early codes. Indeed, many business groups view the WHO/UNICEF code and subsequent agreements as important precedents for UN regulation of TNCs. Opinion within the business community ranges from alarm (codes are an unacceptable encroachment on a firm's freedom of operation) to moderation (codes provide both opportunities and problems for TNCs).

The pharmaceutical industry in particular is on the defensive because it believes itself targeted for the next round of regulation.[61] Moderate attitudes have led some industry groups to meet criticism early in the hope of diffusing demands for strong codes in the future. In October 1983, for example, the Agricultural Chemicals Association Dialogue Group, composed of industry and NGO representatives, negotiated the Guidelines for Advertising Practices in the Promotion of Pesticides Products in Developing Areas of the World.

More generally, however, it is puzzling that corporate response has been so strong to a relatively minor code on an extremely narrow topic, especially when the infant formula industry initially supported the code. The solution to the puzzle lies in the nature of the modern corporation.

Flexibility in export and marketing strategies is one of the essential requirements of a corporation, and the detailed, specific marketing regulations of the WHO/UNICEF code, applied to a wider range of TNC products and exports, could seriously hamper the TNC's ability to organize its activities globally.

The ability to organize worldwide depends in part on the maintenance of legitimacy or ideological hegemony.[62] The emerging TNC regime rests on a compromise between domestic stability and an open economy, the balance between the two based in part on a continuing belief in the overall benefits of an open international system and the specific benefits of TNC activity. TNCs increasingly view attacks as cutting into the legitimacy of their operations, which they believe will undermine their flexibility and scope. They take the struggle for political legitimacy very seriously; a token of that seriousness is the title of a session at a recent corporate conference — "The War of Ideas: The Struggle for Moral Legitimacy."[63]

6. What Chance for a Pharmaceutical Code?

The export and marketing of potentially dangerous drugs has been on the UN agenda since 1978, when the World Health Assembly gave WHO a mandate to develop a code of marketing practices under the Action Program on Essential Drugs. The proposal for code building has met with resistance. In 1981, for example, U.S. government lobbyists succeeded in excluding a specific reference to a possible international code from a General Assembly resolution on unsafe pharmaceutical and chemical products. And many developed countries opposed a proposal made to UNCTAD's Trade and Development Board in 1984 to circulate the International Federation of Pharmaceutical Manufacturers Associations code on marketing practices and the draft proposal for an international code on pharmaceuticals by Health Action International (an international consumer activist group modeled after IBFAN) to state members of UNCTAD for comments.

However, a resolution at the 1984 World Health Assembly to convene a meeting of experts on pharmaceutical marketing practices with consumer and industry participants (similar to the expert meeting that preceded the WHO/UNICEF code effort), which would report to the 1986 assembly, passed in spite of opposition from Canada, the Netherlands, the United Kingdom, and the United States. In December 1984, after a disastrous gas leak at Bhopal, India, caused the deaths of more than 2,000 people, the UN General Assembly voted 147 to 1 (the United States) to expand a directory listing 500 potentially dangerous products that are banned or restricted in member countries.[64] Nevertheless, the development of a detailed, stringent pharmaceutical code will be more difficult than the development of the WHO/UNICEF code, because issues, actors, setting, and timing are all significantly different.

As regards issue characteristics, for example, there is less consensus about what is a dangerous or an unsafe pharmaceutical product. The WHO/UNICEF code dealt with a small group of products; the pharmaceutical issue area, by contrast, covers thousands of products, many of them with tremendous life-saving capacity. Many important life-saving drugs, such as antibiotics, can be dangerous when used incorrectly.[65] The most obvious targets for regulation are dangerous and unnecessary products and inadequate labeling and information. However, the pharmaceutical products that most profoundly affect general health care in the Third World may well be the relatively harmless tonics and vitamins that account for a significant portion of the drug market there. Aggressive marketing of such products can lead to a misallocation of national and personal health budgets that may be more detrimental to health than the more occasional but shocking deaths caused by dangerous drugs.

Activists have recognized the complexity of the pharmaceutical issue. As a Health Action International publication points out, "The rational use of medicines is a complex issue to research and campaign on. It is not clearcut, especially since literally thousands of products are involved. Some are essential, life-saving drugs; others are useless or dangerous; many more are inappropriate or wasteful.... There are many grey areas."[66]

The complexity and ambiguity of the issue has caused critics to develop multiple strategies for dealing with misuse of pharmaceuticals. Some groups stress aspects that were important in the infant formula issue, such as the reckless marketing of inappropriate products. Other consumer groups and many international organization officials stress the adoption of rational health policies at the national level and such programs as the WHO Action Program on Essential Drugs rather than the development of a code of conduct for pharmaceutical marketing. While the numerous consumer groups have produced significant changes in industry marketing practices, no comprehensive campaign has yet convinced major industry actors of the desirability of an internationally negotiated code of conduct for pharmaceutical marketing.

Characteristics of the pharmaceutical industry will also make it difficult to bring pressure to bear on it. The value of world production in pharmaceuticals is estimated to have reached $84 billion by 1980.[67] According to one industry source, the world market will reach $150 billion by 1990 and $270 billion by the year 2000; much of this anticipated growth will come in the markets of developing countries.[68] Because most drugs are sold in developed countries only by prescription, moreover, a consumer boycott of pharmaceutical companies would be much more difficult to organize.

In addition, the pharmaceutical companies have learned from the experience of the infant formula issue. (Many pharmaceutical companies such as Abbott Laboratories and the Bristol-Myers Corporation are also important producers of infant formula.) They appear to be more willing to make early, preemptive changes in marketing practices to avoid exacerbating the controversy. For example, in the face of criticism from Health Action International and the International Organization of Consumers Unions, the Ciba-Geigy Company agreed in early 1985 to remove two brands of its highly criticized drugs, clioquinol and systemic oxyphenbutazone, from the market.

The slow progress toward a pharmaceutical code is also due in part to the position taken by WHO. At a recent Trade and Development Board meeting of UNCTAD, J. F. Dunne of WHO made it clear that his organization would not take up what he referred to as "marginal controversial issues." The Action Program on Essential Drugs was crucial, he argued, and the organization was deeply concerned lest pressure for a marketing code divert attention from essential drugs. In his view it was up to governments to control the use and marketing of drugs, with WHO assistance if needed.[69]

Dunne's comments appear to imply the pressure that WHO faces on the code issue. The essential drug program and the tropical drug research program both depend heavily on the cooperation of the drug industry. In addition, approximately 25 percent of the WHO working budget comes from the United States. Both the drug industry and the U.S. government may have threatened to withdraw support for current programs should WHO move on proposals for a pharmaceutical code of conduct.[70] Thus an issue linkage may be at work causing an international organization to limit progress on a pharmaceutical code in order to protect other crucial programs.

While it will be more difficult to reach a strong, detailed code on pharmaceuticals than it was on breast-milk substitutes, unexpected developments could alter the context. In the case of hazardous chemicals, for example, the poisonous gas tragedy of December 1984 created new awareness about the dangers of certain chemicals and may facilitate new attempts to draw up international regulations. The Bhopal disaster may also lead to a reevaluation of corporate interests, changing the cost-benefit analysis by increasing emphasis on longer-term business risks.[71]

7. Conclusions

The baby food debate indicates, more than anything else, that blanket statements about the future of codes of conduct are not possible. Nevertheless, the case alerts us to certain factors that may be common to other cases. First, it seems clear that too little attention has been given to nonstate actors and their impact in building codes. Most codes not only address nonstate actors (TNCs) but also depend on nonstate actors as well as states for implementation and monitoring. In the case of the WHO/UNICEF code the activities of nongovernmental groups, in particular transnational activist groups, were essential to the final outcome.

International organizations, WHO and UNICEF, played crucial roles in building the code, as arena, as grantor of legitimacy, creator of consciousness, and center of debate. Their importance to this case has been recognized even by the severest critics of the United Nations. Adelman points out, critically, that "the drive for international regulation of infant formula and pharmaceuticals surely would exist in a world without the U.N.... But it would not have an institutional, concrete locale. It is the U.N.'s organization and resources that give substance to what might otherwise be merely an abstract wish."[72] Other conservatives have also focused on the baby food case because it illustrates the UN capacity to open a space for new ways of thinking about problems and to generate momentum toward solutions to these problems. The WHO/UNICEF code is a fait accompli, however; it has set in motion a global reordering of infant feeding practices and transnational marketing schemes. The debate over the WHO/UNICEF code emphasizes some of the opportunities for action within the UN system, action that can save children's lives, modify global marketing strategies, and alter national health care practices. The case illustrates not only the potential for action but also the potential for creating or removing legitimacy.

Progress toward the international regulation of TNCs and negotiated agreements at the international level is bound to be slow and difficult. To ensure that international regulation actually leads to different TNC and state behavior will be even more difficult. The special conditions that led to an agreement on infant formula are unlikely to be duplicated. Still, opportunities exist within the UN arena for unexpected and vital developments on the regulation of transnational corporations.

FOOTNOTES

1. World Health Organization, *International Code of the Marketing of Breast-milk Substitutes* (Geneva, 1981); "Joint Agreement, International Nestlé Boycott Committee and Nestlé," 25 January 1984, signed by Carl Angst, executive vice president of Nestlé, S.A., and William L. Thompson, stated clerk of the United Presbyterian Church,

representing the International Nestlé Boycott Committee.

2. Exceptions include John Robinson, *Multinationals and Political Control* (New York: St. Martin's, 1983), and Bart Fisher and Jeff Turner, eds., *Regulating the Multinational Enterprise: National and International Challenges* (New York: Praeger, 1983). In addition, legal journals have given considerable attention to codes, for example, the special issue of the *American Journal of Comparative Law 30* (Autumn 1981) devoted to an examination of codes of conduct.

3. Often called the Infant Formula Code, the code applies to "any food being marketed or otherwise represented as a partial or total replacement for breast-milk, whether or not suitable for that purpose." I thus refer to it as the WHO/UNICEF code and to the entire debate as the baby food debate rather than the infant formula debate.

4. For other aspects of the baby food controversy, see Wolfgang Fikentscher, "United Nations Codes of Conduct: New Paths in International Law," *American Journal of Comparative Law* 30 (Autumn 1982), 590-93, on legal implications. Prakash Sethi, *The Righteous and the Powerful: Corporations, Religious Institutions and International Social Activism — The Case of the Infant Formula Controversy and the Nestlé Boycott* (Marshfield, Mass.: Pitman, 1985), examines the issue in relation to the business literature. See also James E. Post, "Assessing the Nestlé Boycott: Corporate Accountability and Human Rights," *California Management Review* 27 (Winter 1985), 113-31.

5. Regime theorists have never shown how specific agreements relate to the larger regime. In this case it seems absurd to speak of an "infant feeding regime," though in the future it may be possible to speak of a "hazardous substances regime" of which the Infant Formula Code is a part. For the time being it is more useful to think of all current code efforts for transnational corporations as specific instrumentalities or agreements within the normative framework of the emerging regime for investment and TNCs.

6. In the late 1960s many countries began to assert increased control over the TNC activities. Nationalization is the most dramatic, but not necessarily the most characteristic, form of host-country control, which can also

involve policies, legislation, and provisions on such basic issues as monitoring and screening investors, ownership, and divestment, technology transfer, taxation, disclosure, investment guarantees, and dispute settlement. One survey reveals that of 29 less developed countries, 22 adopted regulations on transnational corporations during the period 1967-80; seven had legislation relating the TNCs prior to 1967; and only one has no such regulation. See United Nations, Centre on Transnational Corporations (UNCTC), "National Legislation and Regulations Relating to Transnational Corporations" (New York, 1981).

7.   See Werner J. Feld, *Multinational Corporations and U.N. Politics: The Quest for Codes of Conduct* (New York: Pergamon, 1980), 18.

8.   International Chamber of Commerce, "Guidelines for International Investment" (Paris, 29 November 1972); U.S. Chamber of Commerce, "Elements of Global Conduct for Possible Inclusion in Individual Company Statements" (Washington, D.C., January 1975).

9.   "Guidelines for Advertising Practices in the Promotion of Pesticides Products in Developing Areas of the World," (Washington, D.C.:   Prepared by the Agricultural Chemicals Association Dialogue and accepted by the National Agricultural Association,October 1983).

10.   Robert Grosse, "Codes of Conduct for Multinational Enterprises," *Journal of World Trade Law* 16 (September-October 1982), 147.

11.   FAO, "Draft International Code on the Distribution and Use of Pesticides" (Rome, February 1984).

12.   John Ruggie, "International Regimes. Transactions, and Change: Embedded Liberalism and the Postwar Economic Order," *International Organization* 36 (Spring 1982).

13.   Cf. Robert O. Keohane, "The Demand for International Regimes," *International Organization* 36 (Spring 1982).

14.   Adopted UN codes includes UNCTAD's Set of Multilaterally Agreed Equitable Principles and Rules for the Control of Restrictive Business Practices, adopted by the UN General Assembly in 1980 (TD/RBP/CONF/10/Rev.1); the Tripartite Declaration of Principles Concerning Multinational

Enterprises and Social Policy, passed in November 1977 by the ILO Governing Body; the WHO/UNICEF Code for the Marketing of Breastmilk Substitutes; and the FAO/WHO Code of Ethics for International Trade in Food, adopted by the Codex Alimentarius Commission in 1979.

15. Kenneth L. Adelman, "Biting the Hand That Cures Them," *Regulation* (July-August 1982), 16.

16. International Organization Monitoring Service, Bulletin 82-102 (11 January 1982), 6.

17. See, for example, D. Surjano et al., "Bacterial Contamination and Dilution of Milk in Infant Feeding Bottles," *Journal of Tropical Pediatrics* (1979).

18. James Post and Edward Baer, "Demarketing Infant Formula: Consumer Products in the Developing World," *Journal of Contemporary Business* 7 (Autumn 1978), 22; Andy Chetley, *The Baby Killer Scandal* (London: War on Want, 1979), pp. 94-95.

19. S.J. Plank and M. Milanesi, "Infant Feeding and Infant Mortality in Rural Chile," *WHO Bulletin* no. 48 (1973), p. 48; H. Kananneh, "The Relationship of Bottle Feeding to Malnutrition and Gastroenteritis in a Pre-Industrial Setting," *Environmental Child Health*, December 1972; D.B. Jellife, "Commerciogenic Malnutrition," *Nutrition Review* 30 (1972).

20. Resolution WHA27.43, *Handbook of Resolutions and Decisions of the World Health Assembly and the Executive Board*, 4th ed. 2, (Geneva, 1981), 58.

21. From case materials prepared by Professor James E. Post of Boston University, "Nestlé Boycott (A)" (Graduate School of Business, Stanford University, 1981), 9.

22. See INFACT, *Monitoring Report: Infant Foods Industry*, July-August 1984: "Thirteen Nation Field Data and Analysis of the International Babyfood Industry Marketing Activity with Reference to Industry Obligations under the International Code of Marketing of Breast-milk Substitutes." I have also used my field interviews, conducted in Central America December 1981-January 1982.

23. Interview with Edward Baer (New York: Interfaith Center on Corporate Responsibility, 15 April 1982).

24. Post, "Assessing the Nestlé Boycott," 121.

25. "Lessons from the Anti-Infant Formula Campaign," *Business International* (5 February 1982), 8.

26. See Inis L. Claude, Jr., "Collective Legitimation as a Political Function of the United Nations," Leland M. Goodrich and David A. Kay, eds., *International Organizations: Politics, Process* (Madison: University of Wisconsin Press, 1973), 209-21.

27. Ernst Haas has defined consensual knowledge as "a body of beliefs about cause-effect and end-means relationships among variables (activities, aspirations, values, demands) that is widely accepted by the relevant actors irrespective of the absolute or final truth of these beliefs." Quoted in Robert Rothstein, "Consensual Knowledge and International Collaboration: Some Lessons from the Commodity Negotiations," *International Organization 38* (Autumn 1984).

28. A study by the Sao Paulo School of Medicine in 1979, for example, monitoring babies of low-income families, found that 32% of bottle-fed babies suffered from malnutrition compared to 9% of breast-fed babies; 23% of the bottle-fed babies and none of the breast-fed babies had to be hospitalized. Research in Chile has shown that Chilean babies who were bottle-fed during the first three months of life suffered three times the mortality rate of those who were exclusively breast-fed. Reported in *Washington Post* (21 April 1981).

29. D. B. Jellife and E. F. P. Jellife, *Human Milk in the Modern World* (Oxford: Oxford University Press, 1978). See also Ambulatory Pediatrics Association, "Statement by the Board of Directors on the WHO Code of Marketing of Breast-milk Substitutes," *Pediatrics* 68 (September 1981).

30. "The political implications of the consensual knowledge (especially interpretations of its effect on national interest) and the specific bargaining configuration must interact in a fashion that permits or facilitates diffusion and subsequently agreement on new policies." Rothstein, "Consensual Knowledge," 755.

31. For a summary of scientific literature distributed by activists, see Interfaith Center on Corporate Responsibility (ICCR), *Breast Is Best* (New York, n.p., n.d.), and Infant Formula Action Coalition, "Policy vs. Practice: The Reality of Formula Promotion" (Minneapolis, May 1979). The latter juxtaposes quotations from scientific studies and health

professionals with baby food company statements.

Other NGO publications and flyers that served to
32. Plank and Milanesi, "Infant Feeding," 203-10.
33. Other NGO publications and flyers that served to highlight, publicize, and circulate authoritative information on the issue include ICCR, "What the International Health Agencies Recommend about Baby Formula Promotion: Excerpts and Recommendations" (n.d.); "What Health Personnel Say about Infant Formula Promotion in the Third World" (n.d.); and "Excerpts from Documents: WHO/UNICEF Meeting on Infant and Young Child Feeding, Geneva, Switzerland, October 9-12, 1979," *ICCR Brief*, January 1980.
34. Post, "Assessing the Nestlé Boycott," 121, and Robert Ball, "Nestlé Revs up its U.S. Campaign," *Fortune* (13 February 1978), 80-90. In 1978 Nestlé employed more than 140,000 persons in fifty plants and operated in more than fifty nations. Worldwide sales approached $10 billion — 47% in Europe, 20% in the United States, 20% in the Third World. The company ranked 19th of *Fortune's* foreign 500.
35. Post, "Assessing the Nestlé Boycott," 121.
36. By the mid-1970s Nestlé had nearly $2 billion in sales in the United States, and company plans called for a doubling of U.S. sales to $4 billion by 1982 (from over 20% to over 30% of Nestlé worldwide sales), by a combination of internal growth and energetic acquisitions. Post, "Nestlé Boycott," and Ball, "Nestlé Revs up."
37. Post, "Assessing the Nestlé Boycott," 124.
38. "Nestlé Boycott Being Suspended," *New York Times* (27 January 1984).
39. Thierry Lemaresquier, "Beyond Infant Feeding: The Case for Another Relationship between NGOs and the U.N. System," *Development Dialogue* (1980), 120-25.
40. Rafael D. Pagan, Jr., president, Nestlé Coordination Center for Nutrition, Inc., "Issue Management: No Set Path," before the Issues Management Association (Roosevelt Hotel, New York City, 7 November 1983).
41. Interview with Douglas Johnson, executive director of the Infant Formula Action Coalition (New York: 5 December 1984).
42. *Business International* (17 October 1980).
43. Some in the business community feel that codes of conduct will continue to proliferate and that corporations

must get involved in their development. John Kline, for example, argues that "a carefully structured participatory role [in code exercises] could turn challenge into opportunity, benefiting both individual corporations and the broader objective of an open international economic system." Kline, "Entrapment or Opportunity: Structuring a Corporate Response to International Codes of Conduct," *Columbia Journal of World Business* 15 (Summer 1980), 6.

44. U.S. Department of State, telegram from U.S. Mission in Geneva (no. 02652), March 1981, 1.

45. Two internal Nestlé documents leaked to INFACT and later published in the press in mid-1980 outline the tactics used by Nestlé and other infant formula companies to influence the code and discredit the activists. These tactics included lobbying top-level WHO officials (to spearhead this effort, an ex-assistant director general of WHO, Stanislaus Flache, was hired as secretary general of the infant formula industries association, ICIFI) and using "third party rebuttals of the activists' case." Nestlé and other infant formula producers funded the Ethics and Public Policy Center at Georgetown University, headed by Ernest W. Lefever, when they discovered that Lefever was sympathetic to their position. They also circulated a *Fortune* article favorable to Nestlé that accused proboycott groups of being "Marxists marching under the banner of Christ." See *Washington Post*, 4 January 1981. Lefever, a member of the Reagan administration transition team, was nominated as deputy assistant secretary of state for human rights. During Senate confirmation hearings it was revealed that Lefever's research center had received $35,000 from Nestlé, which was one of the factors responsible for the rejection of his nomination.

46. U.S. Department of State, telegram from U.S. Mission in Geneva (no. 02652), March 1981.

47. U.S. Department of Health and Human Services (DHHS), Memorandum, "WHO Code of Marketing of Breastmilk Substitutes — Decision" (October 1980), 3.

48. *Washington Post* (18 March 1981).

49. To protest the U.S. "no" vote, two senior AID officials resigned. They were Stephen Joseph, a pediatrician and the highest-ranking health professional at the agency, and Eugene Babb, deputy assistant administrator for food

and nutrition.
    50. DHSS, memorandum, 3.
    51. U.S. Department of State, telegram from U.S. Mission in Geneva (no. 12065), September 1980.
    52. Post, "Assessing the Nestlé Boycott," 120.
    53. Lemaresquier, "Beyond Infant Feeding," 120.
    54. Interview with Kathleen Cravero, UNICEF (New York: 10 Janaury 1985).
    55. As a result of the negotiations between INBC and Nestlé, UNICEF and WHO were requested to clarify a portion of the code which states that infant formula companies could donate supplies to hospitals for infants who "have to be fed on breastmilk substitutes." WHO argued that the code was written and adapted by governments, and thus only the governments could further interpret it. Eventually, however, WHO developed a plan, presented by Dr. David Tejada, assistant director general of the organization, whereby WHO and UNICEF agreed to give technical advice to governments who would in turn develop the requested definitions based on that advice. Both Nestlé and the INBC agree to cooperate fully in the implementation of the Tejada Plan. See Minutes of the Joint Press Conference between Nestlé and INBC to announce the termination of the Nestlé Boycott, 4 October 1984 (Mayflower Hotel, Washington, D.C.).
    56. On the role of labor and trade unions in the adoption and implementation of codes at the regional and international level, see Robinson, *Multinationals and Political Control*.
    57. See Minutes of Press Conference (4 October 1984).
    58. INFACT, *Monitoring Report: Infant Foods Industry* (July-August 1984).
    59. Annelies Allain, "Toward a Better Code," IBFAN/IOCU (mimeo, April 1984).
    60. Reported in "International Code of Marketing of Breast-milk Substitutes, Update on Implementation," UNICEF *Ideas Forum* no. 19 (1984).
    61. Harry Schwartz, "Perspective on the Third World," *Pharmaceutical Executive* (March 1982), 13-16.
    62. Robert Cox, "The Crisis of World Order and the Problem of International Organization in the 1980s," *International Journal* 35 (Spring 1980), discusses the role of international organization in the institutionalization of

hegemony — the universalization of norms proper to a structure of world power — and also the possibility that international institutions may become vehicles for the articulation of a coherent counterhegemonic set of values.

63. Public Affairs Council, Program for Conference, "Activist Groups at the International Level" (Hilton Hotel, New York City, 21-22 April 1982).

64. *New York Times* (19 December 1984).

65. See UNCTC, "transnational Corporations in the Pharmaceutical Industry in Developing Countries" (New York, 1983), 27-28.

66. Virginia Beardshaw, *Prescription for Change: Health Action International's Guide to Rational Health Projects* (The Hague: International Organization of Consumers Unions, 1983), 9.

67. UNCTC, "Transnational Corporations in the Pharmaceutical Industry," 1.

68. *SCRIP* no. 509 (28 July 1980), 10.

69. *Health Now* (17 May 1984).

70. Heritage Foundation, "The World Health Organization: A Policy Assessment," draft, (Washington, D.C.: November 1984)

71. *New York Times* (6 December 1984)

72. Adelman, "Biting the Hand," 16.

I am indebted to John Ruggie for his assistance and encouragement. I also acknowledge the helpful comments and criticisms of Glenn Adler, Margaret Keck, and two anonymous reviewers, and the skillful editing of Roger Haydon.

Chapter XVII

World Intellectual Property Organization (WIPO)

The World Intellectual Property Organization (WIPO) was established in 1970 and became a specialized agency of the United Nations in 1974. It has 123 member states, and its headquarters is in Geneva, Switzerland. The WIPO budget is financed by members' assessments, and for the biennium 1988-1989 it totaled 107.1 million Swiss francs. WIPO ensures the protection of intellectual property throughout the world. The principal unions established to guarantee this protection are the Paris Union, which has protected industrial property (inventions, industrial designs) since 1883, and the Berne Union, which has protected literary and artistic work (copyrights) since 1886. These two unions have independent memberships which are not identical, but the members of both converge to form WIPO. The United States is a member of the Paris Union, the Berne Union, and WIPO. A second purpose of WIPO is to provide administrative co-operation between the intellectual property unions of which it is comprised. WIPO strives to encourage creative intellectual activity and facilitates the transfer of technology to the developing countries in order to accelerate the social, economic and cultural growth of the world.

WIPO'S Involvement in International Developments

Michael K. Kirk

Dean Stevenson has been credited with awakening Albany Law School to the issue of intellectual property and the growing importance of that topic. This is happening all over the United States. It is not just here in the Capital City area, but everywhere. Intellectual property protection is becoming recognized as a critical issue in the future of the United States. More and more, we are seeing that in trade talks, bilateral discussions, and multilateral discussions, intellectual property is coming to the fore.

I am sure that Emory Simon[1] mentioned the efforts of the United States to strengthen and expand the rules of international trade in the new round of trade negotiations that the United States is seeking and hopes to get. One of the critical areas that the United States hopes to include on the agenda of any new round is a discussion of intellectual property. The attention that the United States is bringing to bear on intellectual property is having an impact not only in the General Agreement on Tariffs and Trade (GATT), but also in a number of international organizations around the world. A voice is finally being heard for intellectual property. There is a new urgency with respect to intellectual property in many international intergovernmental organizations.

The organization that I would like to talk about today, because it is perhaps the main international organization dealing with intellectual property issues, is the World Intellectual Property Organization (WIPO). I would like to address one activity that WIPO is presently pursuing, perhaps reflecting the United States efforts in GATT. WIPO is a specialized agency of the United Nations and is headquartered in Geneva, Switzerland. It is responsible for about two dozen international intellectual property treaties. The two major treaties that you may have heard about during your earlier sessions are the Paris Convention for the Protection of Industrial Property, a 100-year-old patent and trademark treaty, and the Berne Convention for the Protection of Literary and Artistic Works, a copyright treaty. WIPO's activities center around these two treaties and are important for the United States because the United States remains the world's leading holder of intellectual property. Therefore, the more aggressively WIPO acts to protect intellectual property, the greater the benefit to United States' nationals.

The topics I will address fall under the heading of harmonization. The activities that WIPO has pursued most aggressively in the last year involve the question of harmonization. It has established a Committee of Experts for the Harmonization of Certain Aspects of Patent Laws. This really grows out of an initiative that the United States started some three years ago with the European Patent Office, the Japanese Patent Office, and, of course, the United States Patent and Trademark Office. This trilateral activity, as we call it, was started to foster the development of the automated system that Commissioner Quigg just described.[2] This activity resulted in attention being turned to the harmonization of substantive laws, and we started thinking about such areas as biotechnology, the administrative practices before the agencies, and some of the specialized patent rules. WIPO, seeing this flurry of activity among three of the world's major offices, decided to play a more central role. Also, the increased activity in GATT, reflecting an unhappiness with the lack of activity in WIPO, has spurred WIPO to respond aggressively on a number of fronts.

A number of topics were discussed at a meeting which I attended last week dealing with harmonization. I would like to share them with you because I think they are going to have an impact on the future of patent protection in the United States. One of these areas has already been touched on by Ralph Oman,[3] and involves the extension of process patent protection to the resulting product. A WIPO proposal would require countries to extend process patent protection to the resulting products. Japan and many European countries already do this, and the United States is, therefore, more the exception to the rule in this area. There is presently some congressional activity, and I would personally speculate that we will see the law change in this Congress.[4] But the only protection available today in the United States to reach the product of a patented process coming from abroad is through International Trade Commission proceedings. Of course, these proceedings have some limitations in their effectiveness.

The WIPO proposal requiring that all countries extend process patents to cover the resulting products would also create a presumption that a product, if it is a new product, was made by the patented process. This is obviously helpful with respect to products coming from abroad where the difficulty of establishing proof of how the product was actually made would make it very difficult to obtain any real relief. The defendant is clearly in a much better position to establish, or to have a supplier establish, that the product did not come from the patented process.

Another topic that is going to be very controversial in the United States deals with the question of the "prior art effect" of a previously filed, but not yet published, patent application. "Prior art effect" means the use of a patent as a reference against an invention covered in a later-filed patent application to determine whether that later-filed application covers an invention that is new and unobvious. In this area the United States law differs substantially from that in most other countries.

Under the Paris Convention, you are entitled to the filing date of your first-filed application for purposes of obtaining patents in other member countries as long as you file within one year in these other countries. Filing within the year results in the first filing date being considered the constructive date of the filing, called a priority date, in subsequent countries. While the United States recognizes the Convention's priority date for purposes of obtaining a patent, it does not recognize this date for patent-defeating purposes. For patent-defeating purposes, the United States recognizes only the date on which the application is actually filed in the United States. Most other countries recognize the Convention priority date for establishing the date of first filing and for patent-defeating purposes. The WIPO proposal presently under consideration would require that all countries recognize the Convention priority date as the effective date for patent-defeating purposes.

Another aspect of the proposal may be even more controversial. Under many foreign patent laws, an unpublished patent application has a prior art effect as of its filing date only for purposes of establishing that a later-filed patent application is not new. The filing date is not considered with respect to whether or not the invention is unobvious or involves an inventive step. United States patent law considers the filing date of patent applications for both purposes: to determine novelty and unobviousness. The WIPO proposal would require a change, requiring countries to apply unpublished patent applications for patent-defeating purposes only with respect to whether or not subsequent applications cover a new invention. It would thus not reach the unobviousness of the invention. This will obviously require a substantial change in our law. I would speculate that this will be considered quite controversial in the United States.

Another harmonization proposal that WIPO is considering involves the international grace period. In most countries, the publication or disclosure by an inventor of his invention prior to filing a patent application creates a bar to his being able to obtain a patent. A grace period gives the inventor a period of time, after he has disclosed his invention, to file a patent application with no loss of rights. In the United States an inventor has one year after disclosing his invention in which to file his application. But while the grace period protects an inventor in this country, it is a trap with respect to filing abroad. If an inventor discloses in the United States prior to filing, he is precluded from obtaining a patent in any foreign country that does not have a grace period. Thus, the purpose is to try to convince all countries to adopt a grace period, but a grace period somewhat different from the grace period we now have.

This grace period would be effective for a disclosure in the United States for a certain period of time prior to filing here. The United States would also be required to reciprocate by recognizing that a disclosure or publication in a foreign country by an inventor within a certain period of time prior to his filing in that country would not defeat his right to get a patent in this country. In other words, rather than being tied to the United States filing date, the grace period would be tied to the inventor's Convention priority date. This would eliminate substantial problems, particularly for the scientific community in this country, where it is normal to publish or perish. While this would be a very positive change in the law, one which I feel should be supported, there is resistance in some European countries, particularly in Scandinavia. Further, the French and the Dutch delegates also appear a bit reluctant, so the outcome is not certain.

Other topics that are to be discussed are the drafting of a patent application, the number of claims that may be included in a patent application, and the number of inventions that may be covered in a single patent application. The number of inventions in one application is referred to as the "unity of invention" concept. A federal district court recently decided that the United States practice regarding unity of invention was not in compliance with the requirements of the Patent Cooperation Treaty.[5] There is a strong interest here and abroad that the United States relax its practice in this area and follow something more in line with that decision.

There are some highly controversial areas of concern that will not be discussed at these meetings and will thus have to wait for later meetings. One is the permissible exclusion of categories of inventions from patent protection. What is at issue here is when a country can say it is not going to grant patent protection to a category of inventions. This could include pharmaceuticals, chemical compounds, microorganisms, and other subject matter. This would be a very positive development for the United States.

Another positive development is the interpretation of patent claims. This area has the potential for a lot of mischief. For example, in attempting to enforce a patent in some countries, you are limited to the specific examples of chemical compounds or processes disclosed in your patent. Thus, if someone comes in with a slight modification, your patent claims will not cover this new product. I am hopeful that the WIPO proposal will give greater breadth to the interpretation of patent claims.

Another topic is establishing a uniform minimum term or duration for patents. There are many very unfair and short patent terms around the world. An example is India which only has a seven-year patent term for pharmaceuticals.

Another topic of discussion that will be very controversial in the United States is determining the basis of awarding patents. Should the basis be the first to file an application or the first to invent? Every country except the United States, Canada, and the Philippines operates on a first-to-file basis.

Harmonization is a give and take proposition, and we are going to try to argue and defend those areas of our law that, although different, we believe are best for the United States. WIPO is pushing this particular activity on a fast track. It is going to have three additional meetings followed by a diplomatic conference: one more meeting in November of this year, two next year, and the diplomatic conference tentatively scheduled for 1988.

The WIPO effort should prove helpful to the United States in the context of the new round of multilateral trade negotiations. This is because one of the purposes for the United States putting intellectual property on the agenda for the new round is to raise the standards. There is probably no area where the standards need to be raised more than in the patent field. The Paris Convention has precious little in the way of minimum standards. It has national treatment; it has a right of priority; it has some very limited restrictions with respect to compulsory licensing of patents, and that is about it. There is no mention in the Convention of subject matter coverage, term, and many other standards related to these items. WIPO is, therefore, presently developing standards, or minimum standards, that will augment this lack of standards in the Paris Convention. The resolution will be what is referred to as a special treaty under Article Nineteen of the Paris Convention. This will probably be a limited convention with about fifteen or twenty substantive articles. It will be negotiated and available for signing by Paris Convention member countries. Assuming that it can be negotiated in a way that we believe is in our best interest, we could adhere to it. The real question is: How do we get the other countries, whose standards are much too low, to adhere? I think this is where GATT may be able to provide trade-based incentives to encourage countries to adhere to such a treaty. This approach looks both promising and exciting.

WIPO is also becoming involved in the question of counterfeiting, a question with which GATT is concerned. The United States is continuing its efforts to develop an anti-counterfeiting code within GATT. This would require nations to seize imported counterfeit trademarked goods and not return those goods to the importer; taking the fun and profit out of counterfeiting. To delay this effort in GATT, Brazil and India raised the notion of studying counterfeit goods in WIPO, arguing that WIPO is the appropriate forum for considering intellectual property issues, not GATT. The first WIPO meeting on this topic was held in Geneva in early May. Great interest was displayed as thirty-seven countries and an equal number of private organizations attended. Three topics were considered. First, do the provisions of the Paris Convention deal effectively with the counterfeiting of trademarked goods? The answer is obviously either A) they don't; or B) they do, and everybody's in violation.

Secondly, WIPO proposed draft model law provisions to deal effectively with counterfeiting that they would ultimately recommend to member countries. This would augment what is going on in GATT. The GATT proposal would protect trademark owners at the border, and the WIPO model law would permit them to attack counterfeiting at the source.

The third item they considered was whether to hold informational meetings to try to bring the glare of publicity on those countries that refuse to act against counterfeiting. I think that this effort by WIPO will also be put on a relatively fast track. We are hopeful that we will at least have a model law. We are pressing very hard to have meetings to bring more publicity on those nations that do not adequately protect intellectual property.

Ralph Oman mentioned that the United States is assuming the leadership in developing a treaty for the protection of semiconductor chip designs.[6] Even if this treaty should unfortunately, get mired in United Nations-style debating, the Semiconductor Chip Protection Act of 1984 has had a very strong and harmonizing effect on the development of national laws in this area. Specifically, the Act grants protection only to nationals of countries having laws providing similar protection to our nationals. I am totally convinced that these reciprocity provisions are why Japan adopted a law in one year and why the thirteen other countries which Ralph Oman mentioned yesterday[7] are aggressively moving to adopt similar laws.

Another area of great interest to us is biotechnology. This is an area in which the United States is clearly the world leader. The protection of biotechnological inventions is found to vary from country to country. It seems that the attitudes of countries, when this is discussed, are directly proportional to the size of their industrial activity in this field. The matter is further complicated because there are several treaties covering related aspects of this subject matter; the European Patent Convention and the International Convention for the Protection of New Varieties of Plants are examples.

WIPO has held three meetings to develop information in this area. The Organization for Economic Cooperation and Development (OECD) has published a study of national practices with recommendations for change in these national practices. This February, WIPO held its third meeting on this topic and decided to develop and transmit questionnaires to learn what is going on at the national level with respect to protection of biotechnological inventions. These rather detailed questionnaires will be reviewed by WIPO shortly. Two questionnaires will be circulated. One will be sent to governments and is voluminous. The second one, a shorter one, is being sent to private organizations seeking their attitudes and ideas on what ought to be done in this area. This is an extremely important and complex area. For example, locating an expert in the United States who is knowledgeable about both biotechnology and its protection in the United States and abroad is very difficult. There are less than two dozen people who are currently experts. It is really a new, difficult, and very important area.

A few comments about the Berne Convention, to which we do not adhere. This Convention, administered by WIPO, is a higher level convention than the Universal Copyright Convention (UCC) administered by the United Nations Educational, Scientific and Cultural Organization (UNESCO), a convention to which we are a party. The Berne Convention is, if you will, a "premier" convention. Recent events in both the United States and the world have encouraged us to look toward the Berne Convention with a new interest. The first event is the United States withdrawal from UNESCO. While this does not directly affect our participation in UCC, it does reduce the United States' ability to control what happens with respect to the copyright activities in UNESCO.

Secondly, the United States has been going around the world speaking with countries about stronger protection for intellectual property rights. We lose some of our high ground when we say "We think you should have stronger protection for intellectual property rights," and it is known that we are not a member of the premier copyright convention, the Berne Convention. Under these circumstances, our arguments have a slightly hollow ring. Consequently, the President endorsed an Economic Policy Council recommendation that the United States work toward joining the Berne Convention.

A major problem in the United States' adherence to the Berne Convention is the issue regarding the extension of the manufacturing clause. This clause in our copyright law denies copyright protection to English language books and magazines of United States authors if they are not printed in the United States or Canada. The manufacturing clause dates back to 1891, and was a blatant protectionist measure adopted to protect what was, at that time, an infant printing industry. We believe that it has no place in our present law. It was to expire in 1982 but was extended over a Presidential veto for four years. It is again set to expire June 30th. There is a very strong effort in the Congress to extend the clause, either indefinitely or for another four years. We believe it is extremely important that this effort be resisted and the clause be permitted to expire. It is protectionist, a clear violation of our obligations under GATT, and constitutes an impediment to our adherence to the Berne Convention. Demonstrating the strong feeling of the Administration on this point, a panel consisting of the Secretary of Commerce, Malcolm Baldrige; the United States Trade Representative, Clayton Yeutter; and Undersecretary of State, W. Allen Wallis testified before a congressional committee opposing extension of the manufacturing clause. It is impossible to predict what is going to happen, but certainly the next three or four weeks will show us.[8]

The last area I will touch on deals with trademarks. There are two treaties administered by WIPO on the international protection of trademarks. These are the "Madrid Agreement," concerning the International Registration of Marks and the "Trademark Registration Treaty" (TRT). The United States is not a member of either treaty. The Madrid Agreement is older and has twenty-eight members. TRT is the more recent, and it has five members.

The United States considered joining the Madrid Agreement in the late 1960's but found two features unacceptable. These features are referred to as "dependence" and "central attack." Dependence refers to the fact that under the Madrid Agreement trademark owners must first register their trademark in their home country, before they can apply under the Agreement in other countries. This was considered unacceptable to the United States because we have a rigid examination system for registering marks while many foreign countries have no examination at all; they simply register. Thus, requiring a United States trademark owner to first register in the United States would put him at a disadvantage.

Central attack is a shorthand phrase referring to a provision in the Madrid Agreement which says that if your home country registration fails during the first five years, your registrations in every other Madrid Agreement country will also fail. This provision therefore puts you at great risk for five years.

Due to the unwillingness of the members of the Madrid Agreement to change these provisions, the United States negotiated the second treaty, TRT, that was concluded in 1973. Unfortunately, the final version of TRT would have required a fundamental change in United States trademark law in order for the United States to adhere. United States law generally requires use in commerce before a trademark application can be filed. There is some relaxation on this requirement with respect to foreign origin marks that I will discuss. Under TRT, the United States would not be able to require use until three years after filing, and this was considered, particularly by the trademark bar, to be an unacceptable provision. The United States was thus not able to ratify this treaty, and trademark owners still have to seek registration in each of as many as 150 separate jurisdictions.

WIPO is presently trying to develop a treaty that would be attractive to both the United States and to a larger number of countries than currently adhere to the Madrid Agreement and TRT. There were two meetings of experts last year. There is one this November, and WIPO is proposing some alternatives for consideration by the involved countries. At one extreme is a simple filing arrangement under which a single application could be filed and have the effect of filing in a number of countries. At the other end of the spectrum there would be an agreement where a filing in one country would actually result in registration of your mark in designated countries. Obviously, this latter approach would require considerably more changes to our national law.

We will continue to follow these efforts, reflecting the interest of United States industry, and to try to develop an acceptable trademark filing arrangement for the United States.

Thank you.

FOOTNOTES

1. Simon, U.S. *Trade Policy and Intellectual Property Rights*, 50 ALB. L. REV. 501 (1986).
2. Quigg, *The Patent System: Its Historic and Modern Roles*, 50 ALB. L. REV. 533 (1986).
3. Oman, *Technology and Intellectual Property: The View from Capitol Hill*, 50 ALB. L. REV. 523 (1986).
4. *See, e.g.*, S. 1543, 99th Cong., 1st Sess. (1985); H.R. 4899, 99th Cong., 2d Sess. (1986).
5. Caterpillar Tractor Co. v. Commissioner of Patents and Trademarks, 231 U.S.P.Q. (BNA) 590, 591 (E.D. Va. 1986).
6. Oman, *supra* note 3.
7. Id.
8. Legislation to extend the clause was not enacted during the 99th Congress. The clause therefore expired.

The World Intellectual Property Organization: Its Recent Past and its Future Plans

Arpad Bogsch

The World Intellectual Property Organization — WIPO — is what is called an intergovernmental organization. Its members are States, and there are 81 of them today, including the United States of America.

Those States, or certain of them, meet from time to time in sessions of the Governing Bodies of WIPO. Those bodies represent one of the two kinds of constitutional organs through which WIPO can express itself.

The other one is the Secretariat of WIPO, which is also called the International Bureau of WIPO. The two terms — Secretariat and International Bureau — designate one and the same thing, namely, the 200 or so persons who form the staff of WIPO under the direction of the Director General. Whereas the Director General is elected — usually for terms of 6 years — by the Member States, each member of the staff is appointed by the Director General.

This staff, this Secretariat, this International Bureau, serve not only WIPO but also the various other associations — generally called by the venerable name "Unions" — of States constituted for special purposes. The two principal Unions are the Paris Union for the Protection of Industrial Property (patents, trademarks, etc.) and the Berne Union for the Protection of Literary and Artistic Works (copyright). The reference to Paris and Berne in the titles of these Unions is an allusion to the cities where the Conventions establishing them were concluded: the first in Paris in 1883, the second in Berne in 1886. Thus, each of them is nearing its centenary.

The member States of WIPO are not necessarily the same as those which are members of the Paris and Berne Unions. Any State may belong to WIPO and/or the Paris Union and/or the Berne Union. Their total number at the present moment is 106.

The United States is a member of the Paris Union and of WIPO. It is not a member of the Berne Union.

Members of the Paris Union may also be members of any of the sub-Unions created for international cooperation in specific fields of industrial property. Whether they are, in fact, is a matter of choice on the part of the States concerned and depends on their own decision. Among these Unions are the Union created by the Patent Cooperation Treaty — the PCT — the Unions for the international registration of trademarks and industrial designs, called respectively the Madrid and the Hague Unions, and three Unions that take care respectively of the international classification of inventions, of goods and services to which marks apply, and of goods in which industrial designs are incorporated. There are eight such sub-Unions which are operational. Five others have been created in recent years but are not yet operational.

Each of these Unions has its own independent budget and program, independent probably for the very reason that membership in each of them is not the same.

In the field of copyright, the situation is somewhat different. There is, of course, the Universal Copyright Convention — open to any State, just like the Berne Convention — but the States party to the Universal Copyright Convention do not constitute a Union. The Universal Copyright Convention — UCC — provides neither for a program nor for a budget. It has no governing body in which all States would have a vote. It does, however, have a Committee — called the Intergovernmental Copyright Committee — consisting of selected States party to the UCC and with mainly advisory functions. The Secretariat of that Committee is furnished by the United Nations Educational, Scientific and Cultural Organization — Unesco — with headquarters in Paris. WIPO, although statutorily represented on the Intergovernmental Copyright Committee, has no role as a secretariat in connection with the UCC. Any program that Unesco has in the field of copyright is not decided by the 70 or so States that are party to the UCC, but by the 145 or so members of Unesco in the General Conference of Unesco, which also decides, as part of Unesco's budget, what expenditures Unesco may incur for its activities in the field of copyright.

Contrary to the Paris Convention, the Berne Convention has no sub-Unions. However, there are, in the field of neighboring rights, two multilateral treaties — the Rome Convention for the Protection of Performers, Producers of Phonograms and Broadcasting Organizations and the Geneva Convention for the Protection of Producers of Phonograms Against Unauthorized Duplication of Their Phonograms — which have close ties with WIPO. Each of these treaties created an intergovernmental committee, and the secretariat of the former is provided for by WIPO, Unesco and the International Labour Office, whereas the secretariat of the latter is provided for principally by WIPO.

The foregoing enumeration of all the treaties administered by WIPO, though somewhat tedious, might prove to be useful when we come to the discussion of the activities of the intergovernmental organs, since such activities are all anchored in those treaties.

I said a little earlier that WIPO and the Unions had two kinds of constitutional organs: the Governing Bodies and the Secretariat. There are no fewer than twenty Governing Bodies at the present time, and their number will increase if and when treaties already concluded, but not yet in force, come into effect. These Governing Bodies act when they meet, deliberate and decide. Their members are representatives of governments. But theirs are not the only meetings held under the aegis of WIPO. There are also a number of committees and working groups — some having a permanent existence, others ad hoc. The total number of such meetings in recent years was in the neighborhood of sixty a year with an average duration of one week for each meeting. The composition of such committees and working groups, created by or with the approval of the Governing Bodies, varies between those wholly manned by government representatives and those whose members act in a personal capacity, without government instructions and without binding their governments.

In recent years, the growing tendency has been that in meetings organized by WIPO, between the sessions and during the meetings themselves, countries consider themselves as belonging to one of three groups, each of which holds separate private meetings. The three groups are, in United Nations parlance, "Group B," the "Group of 77" and "Group D." Group B is the group of market economy or capitalist countries. They are all "industrialized" or "developed," to use two other words taken from the terminology of the United Nations. The "Group of 77" is the group of developing countries, or the Third World. Their total number is now well over a hundred. The figure 77 in their description dates from the time when their total number was 77. Finally, "Group D" is constituted by the Soviet Union and those Socialist countries of Eastern Europe with which the Soviet Union maintains the closest ties. There are rare cases where, at least in WIPO, a country belongs to two groups. For example, Cuba can be seen in the meetings of both Group 77 and Group D. Finally, one country belongs to none of the groups, and that is China.

A delegation to any given meeting usually consists of government officials. But some government delegations also include persons who are not government officials. The United States delegations in particular, quite frequently have members who come from what is called the private sector.

Representatives of the private sector have direct access to most of the WIPO meetings dealing with substantive matters — as distinguished from administrative and budgetary matters — through international, private or non-governmental organizations, such as the International Publishers Association or CISAC, in the copyright field. It is a pity that, in the field of copyright, there is no international non-governmental organization comparable to AIPPI or FICPI — the *Association internationale pour la protection de la propriété industrielle*. When I say "comparable" I mean comparable in respect of the number of its members and the very active participation of lawyers and other specialists in the United States, since, of course, there are, in the copyright field, smaller organizations of this kind, in particular ALAI, the *Association littéraire et artistique internationale*. Perhaps, one day, the United States Copyright Society could give thought to the creation of something with ALAI which would increase the direct participation of American copyright lawyers in the private sector at WIPO meetings.

The direction taken by any meeting on substantive questions is, naturally, mainly influenced by the professional background of the delegates. WIPO deals primarily with the protection of what in most countries is private property:

private property in the fields of copyright, patents, trademarks, etc. That is why it is so important that the representatives or the owners of such private property should exert their full influence. And that is why I am so anxious to see the private international organizations or associations participate in all WIPO work dealing with substantive matters, and why I consistently seek the authorization of our Governing Bodies to associate the representatives of private interests in our substantive meetings or, when I can act without such authorization, I consistently invite and encourage such participation.

Let me turn now to the Secretariat of WIPO. Constitutionally, the Secretariat merely serves the Governing Bodies, which make the decisions. But because these decisions must be prepared — in the form of drafts or suggestions — and because this preparation frequently has some influence on the outcome, the policy attitude of the Secretariat is not a matter devoid of relevance.

At the present time, the Secretariat consists of some 200 persons, 60 of them being in what are called "professional" posts. The desire of the Member States to see the Secretariat include the greatest possible number of different nationalities — and at the proper level — is extremely strong. I consider this desire absolutely legitimate. A wide "geographical distribution" — yet another expression taken from United Nations terminology — in the staff is indispensable to sense and to interpret the aspirations and wishes of the various countries. It is also extremely useful for me in conveying my thoughts to each country with the advice and/or active participation of the staff best informed in respect of that country. In this way, I have a better chance than I would otherwise have to communicate WIPO's views, advice or suggestions in any given situation.

Although geographical distribution is characteristically a matter where the ideal can never be obtained, and where no Member State is ever entirely satisfied, WIPO's staff has, I think, a reasonably good record. We have staff members from over forty different countries. I have three Deputies and, by virtue of a decision made by the supreme Governing Body of WIPO, one of them must be a national of a developing country, one of them must be a national of a Socialist country and one of them must be a national — so the decision says — of "another" country. At the present time, this national of "another" country comes from the Federal Republic of Germany, whereas the Socialist national is a citizen of the Soviet Union, and the one from a developing country comes from the Ivory Coast.

Having briefly enumerated the treaties in which WIPO's activities are anchored and having mentioned the *dramatis personae* or the human factor, both among the delegates and the staff, I come to the activities themselves.

One may classify them in many different ways. I shall try a simple distinction between two kinds of activities: on the one hand, action through treaty relations among States and, on the other, action through relations between States and the Secretariat. The distinction is perhaps somewhat arbitrary and the two kinds of activities are in some instances superimposed on each other. Nevertheless, the distinction may allow of an easier definition and of a schematic picture of what WIPO stands for and does.

First, then, treaty relations among States. One can distinguish between two kinds of treaties. The first kind are those which guarantee to the nationals of any Member State that they will enjoy protection in other States for their literary and artistic works, inventions and other subject matters of copyright and industrial property. I shall call them the substantive treaties. They are the Berne Convention, the Rome Convention, the Phonograms Convention and the Paris Convention. The other kinds of treaties, for the moment existing only in the field of industrial property, may be called administrative treaties. They serve the administration of industrial property rights, mainly through international registration, deposit and classification systems. They are not only useful but absolutely indispensable for the survival of the protection, in international relations, of inventions, etc., because, without such treaties, relations would be so complicated and cumbersome that, for all practical purposes, protection would cease to be viable.

The existing treaties require constant adjustment to changing needs, and new needs call for the conclusion of new treaties. In the last fifteen years — that is, during the period in which I have been directly involved in these matters since I joined the International Bureau in 1963 — all the treaties then existing have been revised at least once, and some of them, including the Berne Convention, twice, whereas ten new multilateral treaties have been adopted during the same period. The changing needs or the new needs may stem from technological developments (as we well know in the field of copyright and neighboring rights), political developments (such as the emergence of the developing countries), or simply changes in the socio-economic outlook.

I know, of course, that reflecting these changes in the form of the revision of existing treaties or the creation of new ones is not received with uniform favor. Yet, I find it indispensable for the survival of the protection of intellectual property on the international level since, failing the reflection of the changes in the said treaties, these treaties would no longer be respected and, for all practical purposes, would become a dead letter.

Now we come to the second kind of activities, namely, those which go on between the States and the Secretariat. Naturally, these activities are based on treaty provisions which prescribe the tasks of WIPO and the Unions and, in particular, the tasks of the Secretariat. Among these tasks, a distinction could be made between those of primary interest to developed countries and those of primary interest to developing countries.

The search for solutions to the problems created by new technological developments are of primary interest to the countries in which those new technological developments originate, that is, the developed countries. Among the well-known examples of new questions raised by new technology are protection of computer software, protection against unauthorized use of protected works in computer input and output, protection of computer-created works (if there is such a thing), cable television, video-cassettes, and inventions involving microorganisms. WIPO — in some cases together with Unesco — is then the forum in which experiences are reported upon and ideas for solving the legal questions of protection are put forward and discussed.

If such solutions include solutions by treaty provisions, the matter comes under the treaty-making or treaty-revision activities. But, frequently, this is not the case, and the international meetings organized by the Secretariat of WIPO serve as warnings and solutions ought rather to be found on the domestic level.

The tasks of the Secretariat of WIPO *vis-à-vis* developing countries are numerous and varied. First, there is the task of explaining what copyright and industrial property are and the reasons for which they should be protected by a developing country both domestically and internationally. This is done by giving introductory courses to nationals of developing countries, training them, mainly in developed countries, holding seminars in and sending missions to interested developing countries. The Secretariat of WIPO, alone or in cooperation with one or more developed countries, organizes such courses, traineeships, seminars and missions. To give an idea of the volume of the training, I might mention, for example, that WIPO's fellowships program in 1978 provided for fellowships for over 100 persons. Also, in recent years, we have been trying to organize training for nationals of developing countries in other — relatively more developed — developing countries, thereby increasing the chances that the training will be closer to the real needs of such countries and increasing the overall credibility of the operation.

A second field in which the Secretariat assists developing countries is their legislation on intellectual property. If they ask for our advice when they are about to introduce or modernize their legislation, we give it willingly and pay particular attention to the need for such legislation to be compatible with the various treaties to which the country is — or may in the future become — a party.

The third field of assistance to developing countries which I think is worth mentioning is that of assistance in institution building or modernization. The tasks in this field are particularly clear-cut in industrial property: the setting up of a government office for the granting of patents, the registration of marks, the deposit of industrial designs, the recording of certain transactions in the corresponding titles of protection. In the field of copyright, there are no corresponding activities, formalities being taboo under the Berne Convention. But, the contacting of and contracting

with copyright owners, the setting up of copyright royalty
collecting and distributing mechanisms, and the furnishing of
advice as to how to operate them, are very real and very
practical problems in most developing countries, and we do
our best to assist them.

Last, but not least, WIPO's Secretariat considers that
its paramount duty is to demonstrate to and convince
developing countries, where they are not yet fully convinced,
that the protection of copyright and industrial property, both
on the domestic level and in international relations, as
indispensable for encouraging their own authors and
inventors. All the activities just mentioned — training,
legislation, institution building — focus on this central aim,
the respect of intellectual property. The fact that the advice
we give, in order to be useful and accepted, is not a carbon
copy of what exists in the United States or other developed
countries may cause some disapproval in some of those
developed countries, but it is unavoidable because of the
simple fact that developing countries are not developed
countries and, consequently, their needs in certain cases and
to a certain extent, may be different — but not
fundamentally.

In my view, the Secretariat of WIPO can do for the
respect of intellectual property no greater service, in the long
term, than to try to introduce and, where it already exists,
maintain such *respect* in the developing countries, since the
role of those countries in international relations is so
important that their cooperation is a *conditio sine qua non* of
the survival of the aims for which WIPO was founded and for
which it stands.

Chapter XVIII

World Meteorological Organization (WMO)

In 1950 the World Meteorological Organization (WMO) replaced the International Meteorological Organization, which was formed in 1873. The charge of this new specialized agency was to "improve the exchange of weather information and its applications," and there are currently 161 member states. The Geneva Secretariat employs 296 people. The WMO budget is financed by contributions from members on a proportional scale of assessments, and the 1988-1991 budget is 170 million Swiss francs. WMO encourages co-operation between countries in the establishment of stations to provide weather observation and services. The organization promotes the creation and maintenance of communication systems capable of rapid information exchange, as well as the standardization of observation and statistics. WMO deals with meteorology as it relates to shipping, aviation, water problems, agriculture and various other programs and activities. Hydrology is one operation with which WMO is intimately related, and the organization endeavors to increase international co-operation between meteorological and hydro-meteorological services. WMO must also foster research and training in meteorology in order to stay on the cutting edge of weather technology. WMO maintains three main scientific and technical programs. The first, and best known, is the World Weather Watch (WWW), which maintains a global observation system, a telecommunication system, and a data-processing system. Second is the World Climate Program (WCP), which maintains a climate date program, a climate application program, and a climate research program. WCP is an attempt to use climate information "to alleviate some of the major problems of mankind." Third is the WMO hydrological services program.

The World Climate Program: Collaboration and Communication on a Global Scale

Eugene W. Bierly

ABSTRACT: This article discusses the rationale and history of the World Climate Program (WCP) as a prime example of gains in scientific knowledge achievable only through collaboration and communication on a worldwide basis. The WCP is managed jointly by the World Meteorological Organization and the United Nations Environmental Program, both of which are specialized agencies of the United Nations, and by the International Council of Scientific Unions. This unique arrangement has both given strength and presented problems in getting governments and scientists from all over the world to work together in the pursuit of program goals. Vital to this work are the tools made available by contemporary communications technology, particularly supercomputers and satellites. Nevertheless, the availability and usefulness of those tools does not supplant the more basic groundwork that has to be laid and maintained in order to conduct global research. The necessary groundwork requires intra- and intergovernmental collaboration, and also continued progress in the underlying science base. The WCP is composed of the World Climate Data Program, the World Climate Applications Program, the World Climate Impact Program, and the World Climate Research Program.

The World Climate Program (WCP) represents many elements of a science program that is composed primarily of the physical sciences but is composed also of elements from the social and biological sciences. Progress is being made in the WCP because of cooperation between nearly a dozen U.S. government agencies and several agencies of the United Nations. These represent the governmental input to the program. The nongovernmental input comes via the National Academy of Sciences, within the United States, and the International Council of Scientific Unions (ICSU), representing other academies of science around the world. The WCP already can point to some successes; however, as ultimate success will be determined only if the science base needed to answer many of the issues that confront human beings and their environment is used carefully by decision makers so that legal circumstances and administrative decisions are in concert with scientific results.

Background and History of the WCP

The WCP is a natural outgrowth of the Global Atmospheric Research Program (GARP), whose original planning began in the late 1950s.[1] GARP was designed to study the physical processes in the troposphere[2] and in the stratosphere[3] that are essential for an understanding of (1) the transient behavior of the atmosphere as manifested in large-scale fluctuations that control changes of the weather[4]; understanding this behavior could lead to increasing the accuracy of forecasting over periods from one to several weeks; and (2) the factors that determine the statistical properties of the general circulation of the atmosphere; understanding these factors would lead to better understanding of the physical basis of climate.[5] The GARP field programs that were designed to provide the data required for the design of theoretical models and the testing of their validity now have been completed; however, analyses are proceeding still and will continue for some years.[6]

The Rise of Public Concern

The second objective of the original GARP concept concerning climate did not receive much attention immediately. In later years, during the early 1970s, however, climate became an important public issue. The early 1970s witnessed a number of climatic events that had disastrous consequences. The Sahel region of Africa suffered a five-year drought that brought famine and death on a large scale. In 1972 the Soviet Union had a significant drought and had to buy grain from the United States. That same year there was an El Niño, a warm current off the coast of Peru, that destroyed the anchoveta fishery. The year 1974 brought a severe monsoon to India that reduced food production. Cold weather reduced Brazil's coffee crop in 1975. Cold weather in Europe in 1976 caused widespread economic dislocation. An unusually cold winter in the United States the same year caused many industrial and school closings. Thus the attention of the public was drawn to the extremes of climatic variability.

U.S. Government Reactions

Was there any reaction to these disasters? There was indeed. Several agencies of the U.S. government established programs to study the dynamics of climate. The Climate Dynamics Program established in 1974 by the National Science Foundation is one result of that reaction. The U.S. Congress passed the National Climate Program Act of 1978, which set up an interagency office to coordinate the U.S. government's activities and to begin new ones where needed.[7] This office was established within the National Oceanic and

Atmospheric Administration, and it was responsible for
reporting to the Congress via the administrator of the
National Oceanic and Atmospheric Administration, the
secretary of commerce, and the president. The National
Climate Program Office was responsible for writing the initial
five-year plan laying out programs that were needed and
keeping them within the framework of ongoing budgets of
various agencies that were involved. There have been eight
reports sent to Congress since 1979 describing the on-going
program and citing any needs, administrative or budgetary,
that might be felt.[8]

International Reaction

        Meanwhile, activities were taking place internationally,
under the auspices of the World Meteorological Organization
(WMO). The Joint Organizing Committee for GARP, a
committee composed of 12 scientists selected jointly by WMO
and ICSU to give guidance to GARP, realized as early as 1973
that the second objective of GARP deserved some attention.
This concept was not readily acted on by most of the scientific
community because a great deal of effort was being expended
in those days on the implementation of the major GARP
experiment, the Global Weather Experiment, held in 1978
and 1979. Nevertheless, the Joint Organizing Committee
proceeded to call the Study Conference on Climate, which was
held in Stockholm, Sweden, in July of 1974. This study
conference set the state for all later activities under the
ICSU-WMO banner.[9] The conference was supported also by
the United Nations Environmental Program.
        The Joint Organizing Committee continued to discuss
climate at its meetings and in fact identified early on two
important components of a climate program that deserved
attention. Those components were ocean dynamics — that is,
the interaction between the atmosphere and the oceans'
surface — and the effect of clouds on long-wave and short-
wave radiation. Both of these topics were discussed
extensively, and plans were laid to identify how these
components could be studied so that the results would be
useful to modeling the general circulation of the atmosphere
successfully. From the very beginning the WMO was

envisioned as the scientific leader for the climate program. This was so primarily because WMO had a broad cross-section of member countries, it had the key to governmental action as evidenced by GARP, and, through its connection with ICSU, it also had a way to call on the academicians of the world.

By 1977 the Executive Committee of the WMO decided to request the Secretary-General of the WMO to make specific proposals regarding the establishment of the WCP within the WMO. In addition the Executive Committee decided to convene a high-level scientific and technical World Climate Conference in early 1979 to be attended by physical and social scientists as well as experts from climate-sensitive branches of national economies, including agriculture, energy, water resources, fisheries, and health. The main purposes of the conference were to review knowledge of climatic change and variability, due to both natural and anthropogenic causes, and to assess possible future climatic changes and variability and their implications for human activities. There were more than 350 attendees at the conference. The assembled group heard papers from users of climate information, researchers, politicians, and gatherers of climate data. It was a diversified group, many of whom had had interests in climate studies for years and other who were just beginning to understand that climate played an important role in the life and welfare of human beings.[10]

The World Climate Conference outlined, in general, the problems of climate studies and did something even more important. It discussed some of the interfaces between climate and human activities. These areas could be referred to as impact studies, depending upon whether there was an impact on policy considerations or, at least, on applications of climate information to selected problems. The major interfaces were with regard to climate's relation to food, water, energy, and urban planning. Although many important issues were discussed at the conference, it was May 1979, when the WMO's Eighth Congress met, before the WCP really came into being.

Components of the WCP

Eventually, the WCP was structured to have four
components: the World Climate Data Program (WCDP), the
World Climate Applications Program (WCAP), the World
Climate Impact Program (WCIP), and the World Climate
Research Program (WCRP). One of the unique facets of the
WCP is that the responsibility for managing its several
components was not all vested in the WMO. The first two
areas became the responsibility of the WMO because the
WMO is the international agency responsible for observing,
collecting, and disseminating meteorological data. Those data
serve as the basis for weather forecasting, but they also serve
as the basis for climate studies. In addition, the WMO was
given the responsibility to direct, oversee, and coordinate the
entire WCP.

Responsibility for the WCIP was given to the United
Nations Environmental Program. The WCRP responsibility
was assigned to WMO in cooperation with ICSU.

An International Governmental-Nongovernmental Alliance

The alliance between WMO, an intergovernmental
group, and ICSU, a nongovernmental group, had worked
successfully during GARP, so it was thought that such an
alliance could work again for climate studies even though it
was recognized that studies of climate would be much more
difficult and complicated than GARP had been. Such an
alliance brings together the funding, planning, and other
attributes of governments and the intellectual power of the
world's academic community. Thus scientists anywhere in
the world, whether in government or not, had a mechanism
that would allow them to work together.

The actual working mechanism that allows WMO and
ICSU to work together is the Joint Scientific Committee
(JSC), composed of about 12 well-recognized scientists who
were selected from throughout the world as individual
scientists and not as representatives of their governments.
The JSC is the equivalent of the Joint Organizing Committee
for GARP. Its responsibility is to lay out in general terms
plans for the WCRP. The JSC meets about every nine

months to discuss how present programs are proceeding and what future ones should be planned. If a new program is selected, then the JSC gives general guidelines on how that program is to be implemented. The reports of JSC meetings are disseminated widely so the community of interested parties can be aware of the JSC's deliberations and plans.

Oceanographic Participation

Because oceanography is such an important part of the WCRP, the oceanographic community established a coordinating Committee on the Climate of the Oceans to plan the oceanographic aspects of the WCRP. The committee is similar to the JSC in that it is composed of scientists from the Scientific Committee for Oceanographic Research of ICSU and the International Oceanographic Commission of the United Nations Educational, Scientific, and Cultural Organization. Thus it has the ability to blend governmental views from the International Oceanographic Commission and academicians' views from the Scientific Committee for Oceanographic Research. It works closely with the JSC due to close staff liaison and sometimes overlapping membership on the two committees.

The World Climate Data Program

The WCDP is truly the foundation of the WCP. All of the aspects of the WCP are dependent on the availability of relevant climate data. In order to manage, plan, and carry out programs within the WCP, it is necessary to have long time-series of the necessary data with sufficient spatial coverage. Thus the purpose of the WCDP is to ensure reliable climate data from the atmosphere, oceans, cryosphere, and land surfaces including the biosphere. These data have to be easily accessible and exchangeable in an acceptable format.
The long-term objectives of the WCDP are to

• improve national systems for climate data management and the availability of referral information on station networks, data sets, and publications;
• coordinate existing data exchange systems and

consolidate requirements for observations and data exchange;
- assist nations in building data banks to serve their needs; and
- develop a monitoring, diagnostic, and dissemination system to highlight climatic events that may effect activities of human beings.

The following is a description of projects that are part of the WCDP.[11]

Projects Within the WCDP

Improvement of climate data management systems and user services. Data are being rescued by microfilming original manuscripts before they deteriorate. Technical guidelines are being prepared on observing networks, data quality control, data processing and management, organization of data banks, and user services. Reference climatological stations will be established, and data sets, inventories, and catalogs of existing data will be compiled. Computerized procedures will be initiated at centers. Education and training workshops plus seminars will be held to aid in molding the data requirements to national needs. Coordination between countries and regions will be promoted.

Transfer of technology in climate data management and user services. The climate computer (CLICOM) project has as its goal the transfer of technology in climate data management and user services through the provision of comprehensive specifications for microcomputer systems. The CLICOM is a package concept that includes computer hardware, user-friendly software, and training. Within ten years it is hoped that all meteorological services throughout the world that desire such equipment will have a CLICOM system. An important component involves the application of climatic data to problems in agriculture and water resources management.

Consolidation of climate data requirements and improvement of data exchange. Climate applications and monitoring require time series and the operational exchange of monthly and daily data that have sufficient spatial density.

A composite observing system using satellite remote sensing and a surface-based network is planned. It will be necessary to increase the exchange of data from one to ten stations per 250,000 square kilometers, and, as requirements change, more data and parameters may need to be observed and exchanged. A reference climatological station network will be established, and the exchange of daily precipitation data will be improved using the Global Telecommunications System.

Implementation of the climate data referral system. There is a need for concise information on climate data. Specifically, information is needed on the availability of data sets, data summaries, and station networks. Initial catalogs have been published, as have input and output formats and access codes for computerized retrieval and storage of information. Information on data centers and their holdings are included as well as cross-references to WMO, ICSU, International Oceanographic Commission, and United Nations Environmental Program centers.

Development of global and regional climate system data sets. Global data sets must be available in order to pursue climate diagnostic studies and climate prediction research. For the WCP, a variety of data sets will be required comprising regular observations of surface and upper-air meteorological variables — including remote-sensed parameters — as well as marine, oceanographic, cryospheric, land-surface and subsurface, vegetation, soil, topography, and other variables. Use of image processing, enhancement, and overlay techniques will aid studies.

Development of a climate system monitoring capability. The capability to monitor climate systems is needed to provide nations with information on large-scale climate system fluctuations and to facilitate the interpretation of anomalous climatic events. These aims are accomplished through monthly bulletins, special advisories, and annual summaries. Data and processed information for the climate system monitoring come from many sources in several countries such as the Climate Analysis Center of the National Oceanic and Atmospheric Administration within the United States, the University of East Anglia, in the United Kingdom, the Bureau of Meteorology in Australia, and the Hydrometeorological Service of the USSR.

The World Climate Applications Program

The real payoff to nations is the WCAP, for it is from this program that the uses for climate information will be identified and applied to the many problems that exist around the world. The WCAP has four subprograms: WCAP-Food, WCAP-Water, WCAP-Energy, and WCAP-Other Applications. Many of the activities within the WCAP are conducted with U.N. agencies such as the Food and Agricultural Organizations and the United Nations Educational, Scientific, and Cultural Organization, and with other components of the WMO.

Projects Within the WCAP

Definition of user information requirements for specific climate applications. It is anticipated that by 1995, 95 percent of the nations of the world will have defined their requirements for major climate applications.

Description of climate effects on food production. Past, present, and future purpose-oriented forecasts will be used to determine the influence of climate on the productivity of specific crops, forests, pastures, and animals.

Determination of climate implications for water resources management. A better understanding of the impact of climate, climate variability, and climate change in water resources will be developed.

Determination of climate implications for energy. What information is useful, how it will be collected, and how it will be presented will be determined.

Implementation of climate applications in other human activities. The effects of climate on buildings and human settlements will be documented in a report called Urban and Building Climatology. The specification of user requirements, creation of data formats, making of special observations, production of guidelines, and development of computer data bases will be undertaken.

Assistance in employing existing practical methodology. National climate application programs will be developed, and information on economic benefits of climate applications will be exchanged.

Combating effects of drought. Studies of observational network density, preparation of drought probability maps and guidelines on the use of climate data to combat the effects of drought, and studies on the assessment of semiarid zones for the support of human activities will be undertaken.

Development of a Climate Applications Referral System (CARS). The upgrading and completion of CARS-Food, the completion of CARS-Solar and Wind Energy, and the beginning of CARS-Water, Urban and Building Climatology, and Climate and Human Health will be accomplished.

Promotion of the development of new climate application methods. The use of satellite information will be promoted. New ways to present data and information and new methods to use statistical and real-time data for the formulation of application-oriented forecasts will be developed.

The World Climate Impact Program

The purpose of the WCIP is to bring climate information into the consideration of policy alternatives and to warn of economic, political, and social impacts that climate change and variations might bring forth. This program is very sensitive because expectations are high, yet what can be delivered credibly is much less. Thus there is frustration with the scientific community because important questions cannot be answered. There also is frustration on the part of the scientific community itself because of the impatience of users and the knowledge by scientists that the answers desired will take years before they are available, if ever.

Projects Within the WCIP

Assessment of the role of CO_2 and other radiatively active gases in climate variations and their impact. The assessment of effects on the atmosphere of changing greenhouse gas[12] concentrations in the atmosphere and the effects of the resulting climate change on human beings and their environment will be undertaken about every five years, with particular emphasis on the socioeconomic aspects.

Dissemination of information on the greenhouse

gas/climate change issue. Through guidelines, brochures, and audiovisual materials, nations and individuals will be sensitized to the issue of greenhouse gas and climate change.

Regional assessment of impacts of climate change. Six regional assessments will be carried out, three in developed regions and three in developing regions, to aid in national decision making.

Assessment of the impact of sea-level change. Analysis of the impact of sea-level change on environmental sectors and on human socioeconomic sectors will be undertaken, consistent with greenhouse-gas-induced warming of coastal, estuarine, and river delta regions.

Advisory group on greenhouse gases. The determination of the need for guidelines for a global framework convention for the protection of the tropospheric climate will be pursued.

Dissemination of knowledge and methods of climate impact assessment. Handbooks on climate impact assessment will be developed, and demonstration projects will be carried out.

Study of impacts of drought in developing countries. Support will be given to the African Centre of Meteorological Applications for Development. Support will also be devoted to research on the socioeconomic impact of droughts and to the development of strategies for the prevention, mitigation, and avoidance of adverse impacts of drought.

Monitoring of the impacts of the El Niño Southern Oscillation events and other teleconnections. Information will be exchanged on the impacts of climatic events on climatically sensitive sectors such as agriculture, fisheries, and water resources.

International network of climate impact studies. National and regional climate impact studies will be identified and national climate programs invited to exchange information. An inventory of climate impact studies will be made. A bibliography and directory of scientists and institutions will be published.

Establishment of national impact studies programs. The development of national climate programs that have as a component climate impact studies will be encouraged. Once developed, they will become a part of the climate impact studies network.

Support to national climate impact studies. Special climate impact studies will be undertaken when gaps in knowledge are identified or when sufficient resources are not available in a region where such studies are needed.

The World Climate Research Program

The research component of the WCP has as its goal the improvement of our knowledge of climate, climate variations, and the mechanisms that might bring about climate change so one can determine the extent to which climate can be predicted and the extent of human influence on climate. Such a program consists of studies of the global atmosphere, oceans, sea and land ice, and the land surface. The development of models to simulate the climate system so that the sensitivity of climate to natural and man-made influences can be determined is an important aspect of this work.

Projects Within the WCRP

Global climate analysis and model development. Progressive improvement of the formulation of all significant physical processes in the climate system will be undertaken through numerical experiments and comparison with global climatological data or detailed observations during intensive field studies of specific processes. Global estimates of derived quantities such as surface fluxes of momentum, energy, and water will be produced through three-and four-dimensional analyses of the primary meteorological fields.

Research on climate processes. A refining of the formulation, in terms of climate model parameters, of the physical processes that are significant in determining the mean state of climate and its variations is needed. Cloud-radiation feedback, atmospheric boundary layer exchanges, and hydrological processes over the land surface are priority areas for all aspects of climate research and for long-range weather prediction on time scales of one to two months. A fully interactive treatment of sea-ice processes in the polar oceans and studies of polar ice sheets and glaciers also are needed.

Study of the tropical ocean and global atmosphere (TOGA). Prediction of the evolution of the coupled system comprising the tropical oceans and the overlying atmosphere is important to the study of the mechanisms that determine the interseasonal and interannual variability of global large-scale monsoon flow.

World ocean circulation experiment (WOCE). Understanding the world ocean circulation and its relation to climate is necessary. Emphasis will be on the large-scale average heat and fresh water fluxes and their annual and interannual variations, the variations of the space-averaged ocean circulation on a time scale of months to years and the statistics of smaller-scale motions, and the volume and location of water masses with a ventilation time scale of 10 to 100 years.

Study of climate forcings. Determining the sensitivity of climate and climate variations to possible causal factors such as changes in solar radiation, composition or particulate matter loading of the atmosphere, land vegetation, and other earth environmental or external factors will be undertaken.

Study of global change. How the earth's land, sea, and atmosphere interact through the combination of physical, chemical, and biological processes and how ecosystems function to absorb, buffer, or generate changes on the global scale are important aspects of global change. An extension of the quantitative modeling methods used in earlier studies will be used to incorporate global or large-scale ecosystems using suitable parametric representations. Ecosystems will be characterized by expressing fluxes of the energy and chemicals that they absorb or yield, in quantitative terms, based on global surveys of large ecosystems using fast data acquisition techniques such as satellite remote sensing.

Conclusion

The WCP has addressed some important communications problems in very unique ways. It has brought in the U.S. scientific community through the National Academy of Sciences and has allowed the various federal agencies to work together through several interagency committees. Internationally, it has built upon an earlier relationship between WMO and ICSU, extended it to the climate research area, and continues to bring together the world's academicians and government scientists to make it work.

The WCP is grounded upon sound scientific principles and a successful set of global-scale experiments that were carried out under the aegis of GARP. The WCP is a logical extension of this work. It incorporates much more oceanography into the research because the time scale of the predictions is months to years, and on those time scales, the oceans play a major role in storing, transporting, and distributing the energy received from the sun at the Earth's surface.

The JSC, jointly sponsored and supported by ICSU and WMO, is the mechanism that lays out the scientific program for the WCRP. Members of the JSC are selected on the basis of their scientific credentials and not on political considerations. Nevertheless, there is a balance maintained on the JSC between the superpowers and other countries that can contribute to the scientific efforts of the WCRP.

Credible data drive the WCP. Accurate and timely observations, made at the proper places, disseminated through the WMO, and archived in an acceptable format are now available. This achievement is due to the long history of exchanging meteorological data among countries of the world. All countries can make observations. Thus there is a real way for all countries to participate in a program like the WCP even though a given country might not be able to bring sophisticated instrumentation to an experiment or provide a modeling facility.

The availability of personal computers, software, and a data base composed of the country's own observational records provides the infrastructure for making excellent use of the climate data to help irrigation, design dams, and address other water resource management problems. The CLICOM will be in use in about 100 countries by the early 1990s. This project, which began as a U.S. idea, is now being funded by the United Kingdom, France, Finland, and the United States.

Policymakers and scientists working together can accomplish a great deal, as scientific issues have a way of becoming policy issues demanding solutions. The greenhouse effect, stratospheric ozone depletion, and climate change are specific examples. Policymakers and scientists alike must recognize that there always will be some scientific uncertainty involved in such issues. They must not let this uncertainty impede the decision-making process. Through the WCIP, it is anticipated that decision makers and policymakers will be able to work with scientists for the common good. That will be a very difficult task, however.

The WCP will continue for decades. Field experiments such as that concerning the tropical ocean and global atmosphere (TOGA) are long-term efforts that are scheduled to last for at least ten years. Analyses and interpretation will take another ten years, so some investigators conceivably could spend their entire research life on the project. A completion date for the WCP has not been set. The program is, in a sense open-ended; moreover, it is still evolving and projects are being designed and formulated even today.

The WCP is one of the building blocks for the future ICSU program known as the International Geosphere-Biosphere Program: A Study of Global Change. From the WCP will come a cadre of interdisciplinary scientists who have global horizons, an understanding of problems well beyond their own discipline, and experience in communicating internationally, independent of politics. The future is bright for the success of the WCP and the International Geosphere-Biosphere Program but it will take many years before the harvest is gathered.

FOOTNOTES

    1. Julie G. Charney, *The Feasibility of Global Observation and Analysis Experiment*, A Report of the Panel on International Meteorological Cooperation to the Committee on Atmospheric Sciences, National Academy of Sciences-National Research Council, 1965. This report is reprinted in *Bulletin of the American Meteorological Society*, 40 (3), 200-220 (Mar. 1966).
    2. The troposphere is the lower portion of the Earth's atmosphere extending from the surface to 10 to 20 kilometers. The troposphere is characterized by decreasing temperature with height, appreciable vertical wind motion, appreciable

water vapor content, and weather.

3. The stratosphere is the layer of the atmosphere above the troposphere extending to 20 to 25 kilometers. The stratosphere is characterized by stability and persistence of circulation patterns. Ozone concentrations are highest in this layer.

4. Weather consists of short-term — minutes to weeks — variations of the atmosphere, popularly thought of in terms of temperature, humidity, precipitation, cloudiness, visibility, and wind.

5. World Meteorological Organization and International Council of Scientific Unions, Report of the Study Conference on the Global Atmospheric Research Program, jointly sponsored with the International Union of Geodesy and Geophysics, Geneva, 1967. Climate comprises the long-term — ranging from months to eons — manifestations of weather. The climate of a specified area is represented by the statistical collective of its weather conditions during a specified interval of time.

6. Jay S. Fein, Pamela L. Stephens, and Kristyne S. Loughran, "The Global Atmospheric Research Program: 1979-1982," *Reviews of Geophysics and Space Physics* 21, no. 8 (June 1983), 1076-96.

7. Public Law No. 95-376, 95th Cong., 2d sess. (17 Sept. 1978), 92 Stat. 601-5.

8. *Annual Report National Climate Program* (Rockville, MD: U.S., Department of Commerce, National Oceanic and Atmospheric Administration, National Climate Program Office, 1979-86).

9. *The Physical Basis of Climate and Climate Modelling*, Report of the International Study Conference in Stockholm GARP Publications Series no. 16 (Geneva: World Meteorological Organization, 1975).

10. *Proceedings of the World Climate Conference*, WMO — No. 537 (Geneva: World Meteorological Organization, 1979).

11. The description of WCDP projects and of projects of the other WCP component programs later in this article are based on World Meteorological Organization, "The World Climate Program 1988-1997," *Second WMO Long-Term Plan* 2, pt 2 (Geneva: World Meteorological Organization, 1987).

12. Greenhouse gas is a gas that traps solar energy in the atmosphere, thus contributing to the warming of the Earth. Examples of such gas are carbon dioxide, methane, nitrous oxide, and chlorofluorocarbons.

NOTE: This article was written while the author was employed by the government, and is in the public domain. The ideas and opinions expressed in this article are those of the author and do not necessarily represent the views of the National Science Foundation or the government of the United States.

World Meteorological Organization — Demonstrated Accomplishments and Strong Plans for the Future in Applying Space Technology

John A. Leese

a. Background

The World Meteorological Organization (WMO) is a specialized agency of the United Nations which has a membership of 159 States and Territories. Three of the purposes of the organization are particularly pertinent to the topic:[1]

- facilitate world-wide co-operation in the establishment of networks for making meteorological, as well as hydrological and other geophysical, observations and centres to provide meteorological services;
- To promote the establishment and maintenance of systems for the rapid exchange of meteorological and related information;
- To promote standardization of meteorological observations and ensure the uniform publication of observations and statistics.

The constituent bodies of the WMO consist of the following:

The *World Meteorological Congress* is the supreme body of the Organization. It brings together the delegates of all Members once every four years to determine general policies for the fulfilment of the purposes of the Organization;

The *Executive Council* is composed of 36 directors of national Meteorological or Hydrometeorological Services serving in an individual capacity; it meets once a year to supervise the programmes approved by Congress;

Six Regional Associations are each composed of

Members whose task is to co-ordinate meteorological
and related activities within their respective regions;
Eight Technical Commissions, composed of experts
designated by Members, are responsible for studying
meteorological and hydrometeorological operational
systems, applications and research.

The *WMO Secretariat*, located at Geneva, Switzerland,
is composed of an international scientific, technical and
administrative staff under the direction of the Secretary-
General. It undertakes technical studies and is responsible
for the numerous technical co-operation projects in
meteorology and operational hydrology throughout the world
aimed at contributing to economic development of the
countries concerned. It also publishes specialized technical
notes, guides, manuals and reports and in general acts as the
link between the meteorological and operational hydrological
services all over the world.

For more than 25 years, WMO has played a continuing
role in international co-ordination for the development of the
network of meteorological satellites. In 1959, the Third
Meteorological Congress of WMO,[2] recognizing the potential
value of meteorological measurements from artificial
satellites, requested the WMO Executive Council..."to arrange
for a continuing review to be made of the uses of artificial
satellites for meteorological purposes and to keep Members
informed of interesting developments in this field." The
Executive Council has carried out this continuing request
through its Panel of Experts on Satellites.

Resolutions were adopted at the sixteenth (1961) and
seventeenth (1962) sessions of the General Assembly of the
United Nations on International Co-operation in the Peaceful
Uses of Outer Space.[3] In particular, the General Assembly
recommended that WMO study how the developments of
outer space could be used to advance the state of atmospheric
science and technology. The WMO responses to these
resolutions led to the establishment of the World Weather
Watch and also set forth the necessary conditions for the
optimum use of meteorological satellite systems.

b. Meteorological Satellites in the Context of a Global
    Network

The first meteorological satellite was launched in April
1960 and the decade of the 1960's witnessed the development
of the meteorological satellite as an unprecedented tool for
observing broad-scale atmospheric phenomena. By the end of
the 1960's, the meteorological satellite had grown to be a
highly sophisticated platform which could provide global
coverage of cloud observations and was beginning to provide
quantitative measurements of pertinent meteorological
parameters. During the 1970's there was an evolutionary
development of a co-operative international network of
meteorological satellites. This effort culminated in 1979 with
the contribution to the Global Weather Experiment (FGGE)
by a nearly complete global network of meteorological
satellites. In the present decade of the 1980's, we are seeing a
stabilizing of the global network of meteorological satellites in
terms of sensor data and services. There is now a more
intensive effort in the processing and applications of satellite
data in order to increase the information obtained.

The advent of meteorological satellites gives a new
dimension to meteorology both from a technical viewpoint
(more or less permanent watch over the globe rather than a
network of individual locations) and also from a policy
viewpoint through the co-ordinated free access of all WMO
Members to raw or pre-processed satellite data. The
operational use of these data are summarized in a WMO
publication.[4]

Meteorological satellites have become a critical source
of data used in the preparation of weather forecasts and
warnings of severe weather over land and sea. The existing
network of meteorological satellites, forming part of the
Global Observing System of the World Weather Watch,
regularly produces real-time weather information. This
information is acquired several times a day, through direct
broadcast from the meteorological satellites, by more than
1000 stations located in 125 countries.

There are two major components in the current
meteorological satellite network. One element is the various
geostationary meteorological satellites which operate in an

equatorial belt and provide a continuous view of the weather
from roughly 70°N to 70°S. At present there is a satellite at
0° longitude (operated by the European Space Agency), a
satellite at 74°E (operated by India), a satellite at 140°E
(operated by Japan) and satellites at 135°W and 75°W
(operated by the U.S.A.). A satellite is planned to be added by
the U.S.S.R. at 76°E. The Co-ordination of Geostationary
Meteorological Satellites (CGMS) is an informal international
body made up of countries and agencies which are operating
or have firm plans to operate geostationary meteorological
satellites.   This presently consists of the European Space
Agency (ESA), India, Japan, USA and the U.S.S.R. WMO has
participated in the activities of CGMS from the first meeting
in 1972. Results from CGMS have produced a network of
geostationary satellites which operate in a well co-ordinated
manner.

The second major element comprises the polar-orbiting
satellites operated by the U.S.S.R. and the U.S.A.   The
"Meteor-2" series has been operated by the USSR since 1977.
The polar satellite system, operated by the U.S.A., is an
evolutionary development of the TIROS satellite first
launched in April 1960.[5] The NOAA series, based on the
TIROS-N system, has been operated by the USA since 1978.
These spacecraft provide coverage of the polar regions beyond
the view of the geostationary satellites and fly at altitudes of
850 to 900 km. Additionally, they are able to acquire certain
data not presently available from geostationary altitude.

Together,   the   geostationary   and   polar-orbiting
satellites constitute a truly global meteorological satellite
system. Further details about these meteorological satellites
and the future plans are available in WMO Publications.[6,7]

c. Applications in the Major Programmes

The main features of WMO's activities relating to outer
space occur within the major programmes through which the
work of the Organization is conducted. Information about
these programmes with specific reference to their long-term
goals and objectives are given in the WMO Long-term Plan.[8]

The *World Weather Watch (WWW)* serves as the basic
programme of the WMO, supporting other programmes and

activities of the Organization. Co-operation in operational meteorology among WMO Member nations is the cornerstone of the WWW, especially since modern developments in technology over the last 15 to 20 years have brought about some rather remarkable changes in the way weather services operate. The observation of weather by satellites and the use of electronic computers in weather-date processing and telecommunications have had a significant impact for national services on the methods of producing and exchanging weather observations and weather analyses and forecasts.

The WWW is an integrated system which functions on the global, regional and national levels. The WMO Congress decides on general directives for the structure and operation of the WWW; other appropriate bodies of the Organization are concerned with the organizational and procedural details. Planning at the national level is, of course, left to individual Members.

The primary objective of the *Tropical Cyclone Programme* is to mitigate cyclone disasters through improvements in all aspects of a tropical cyclone warning system. This Programme is being implemented partly through transfer of technology: for example, through reports prepared by small groups of experts on specific subjects such as meteorological satellites, cyclone forecasting, flood risk evaluation, storm surge prediction and community preparedness. It is also being implemented partly by means of programmes organized regionally. In the latter category, the activities are organized through four regional cyclone bodies.

The Eighth WMO Congress in 1979 established the *World Climate Programme (WCP)* and further decided that this main programme should comprise the following four components:

- World Climate Applications Programme (WCAP)
- World Climate Date Programme (WCDP)
- World Climate Research Programme (WCRP)
- World Climate Impacts Programme (WCIP).[9]

The first two components are the primary responsibility of the WMO. The WCRP is a joint programme between WMO and the International Council of Scientific Unions (ICSU). The UN Environmental Programme (UNEP) has the primary responsibility for the WCIP.

The WCAP is concerned, amongst other matters, with the development and improvement of methodologies for the application of meteorological (especially climatological) information in such fields as energy, land use and human settlements, engineering and building, human well-being (especially health and disease), tourism, industry, transportation (especially on land) and communications, economic and social planning.

The purpose of the WCDP is to ensure timely access to reliable climate data which are exchangeable in acceptable format to support climate applications, impact studies and research. The scope of the WCDP includes climate data from the entire climate system composed of the atmosphere, oceans, cryosphere and land surface.

The main objectives of the WCRP are to determine to what extent climate can be predicted and the extent of man's influence on climate. The WCRP's highest priority requirement is for consistent, long time series of global data.[10] For this reason, the WCRP relies heavily on operational programmes which provide systematic observations of the atmosphere and the oceans. Meteorological satellites and the oceanographic satellites now being developed are essential elements of the WCRP in order to obtain a long series of consistent observations.

One of the objectives of the *Agricultural Meteorology Programme* is to provide Members with guidance material on satellite information that can be used in agriculture, forestry and the combat of desertification. Activities are mainly concerned with the use of remote sensing techniques for obtaining agrometeorological information and the application of satellite techniques to agrometeorology. Present projects include (i) compilation of practical satellite applications in agrometeorology, (ii) guidance material on aspects of satellite applications to agrometeorology, and (iii) training courses on remote sensing techniques in agrometeorology. WMO has been involved since 1977 in the presentation of international training courses in satellite applications to agrometeorology and rural disaster preparedness. The courses are designed primarily for personnel from developing countries.

The *Aeronautical Meteorology Programme* has space-related activities in the following main areas:

(i)   Use of satellite data for the preparation of information required for flight operation;

(ii) Direct use of satellite imagery and other satellite data for short range weather forecasting;

(iii) Satellite support to the World Area Forecast System.

These activities are directed essentially at the efficiency and safety of air operations.

Space activities within the *Marine Meteorology Programme* occur in two main areas:

(a) The use of satellite remote-sensing instrumentation to measure a variety of meteorological and oceanographic parameters;

(b) The use of satellites in marine telecommunications for the collection of meteorological data from ships and ocean buoys and for the distribution of meteorological service products to shipping.

These activities are directed essentially at the safety and efficiency of ocean-based and ocean-dependent activities such as maritime transport, fisheries, offshore mining and related activities, coastal engineering works, marine pollution detection and control, etc.

Under the Integrated Global Ocean Services System (IGOSS), WMO and the Intergovernmental Oceanographic Commission (IOC) co-operate in formulating requirements for satellite observations of various ocean parameters and in establishing international procedures for the exchange of these data for both operational and scientific research uses.

Applications of space technology are a common feature of the *Hydrology and Water Resources Programme* and will continue having a significant impact on the activities of national hydrological services of WMO Members. The long-term objectives give priority to promoting applications of remote-sensing techniques to hydrology to cope with existing deficiencies and to meet new requirements through more

extensive use of observational and communication
capabilities of satellites in the design and operation of
networks of hydrological observing stations, and by use of
advanced interpretation techniques to derive qualitative and
quantitative areal values for hydrological elements.

The successful implementation of the aforementioned
programmes of WMO depend to a large extent upon the
strengthening of national meteorological and hydrological
services, particularly in the developing countries. For this
reason, the organization's *Education and Training
Programme* continues to be regarded as a matter of high
priority. The transfer of knowledge in the area of
management and applications of satellite data is being
covered by this programme through the organization and
implementation of several international training events in all
of the WMO Regions. This programme has close collaboration
with other agencies of the UN system and international
organizations. The organization is also engaged in the
preparation of syllabi and corresponding training materials
for the education of meteorological personnel in satellite
meteorology and in the provision of fellowships for training in
meteorology and operational hydrology.

The applications of satellite technology in meteorology
and operational hydrology form an important element of the
Technical Co-operation Programme of WMO. Activities are
undertaken generally with assistance either from the
Voluntary Co-operation Programme (VCP) or the United
Nations Development Programme (UNDP).

Each year several projects are completed under the
VCP for the provision of direct satellite read-out stations.
Support is also given under the VCP for training personnel in
the operation and maintenance of such stations. During the
period 1977 to 1985, a total of 54 direct read-out stations have
been installed with the support of the VCP.

d. Considerations for Long-Term Continuity

During the last several years there has been increasing
concern about the reliability and continued operation of the
global meteorological satellite network. The WMO Executive
Council session in 1980[11] urged Members to explore

possibilities for future international or multilateral collaboration and an appropriate method for financing operational systems in order to help assure continuity of satellite data. In 1982, the Executive Council stated that the overall value of the global satellite network to operational meteorological, hydrological and oceanic services had increased to such an extent that extraordinary steps may have to be taken to assure continued operation and that the loss of one or more satellites due to economic, technical or whatever reasons should be avoided if at all possible.[12]

The question of the operational meteorological satellite system was discussed in several sections of the UNISPACE-82.[13] The Conference recommended that the WMO undertake a study on how to better assure the continuous availability of and access to meteorological satellite data.

The Ninth World Meteorological Congress[14] endorsed this recommendation. It considered that the continued operation of meteorological satellites, both polar-orbiting and geostationary, in their observation, data collection and dissemination roles is essential and must be ensured if the World Weather Watch system and the related applications are to be preserved. The Executive Council requested its Panel of Experts on Satellites to complete this study in a timely manner for incorporation of the major results in the next WMO Long-Term Plan for 1988-1997 which is to be presented to the Tenth WMO Congress in 1987.

FOOTNOTES

1. Anon., Basic Documents No. 1, *WMO No. 15*, (1983).
2. Anon., Third World Meteorological Congress — Abridged report with resolutions, *WMO No. 88*, (1959).
3. Anon., Resolution 1721 (XVI), Annex I, Section C and Resolution 1802(XVII), Annex II, Section III on International Co-operation in the Peaceful Uses of Outer Space.
4. *WMO No. 585*, "Satellites in Meteorology, Oceanography and Hydrology," (1982) (Prepared by Arnold I. Johnson).
5. A. Schnapf, "The Development of the TIROS Global Environmental Satellite System" *Meteorological Satellites* —

Past, Present and Future, NASA Conference Publication 2227, (1982) 7.

6. *WMO No. 411*, "Information on Meteorological Satellite Programmes Operated by Members and Organizations" (1975 with supplemental updates).

7. D. S. Johnson, Satellites Capabilities to 1995 for Meteorology and Operational Hydrology, *SAT-2; WMO/TD-No. 56*, (1984).

8. Anon., First WMO Long-term Plan, Part I: Overall Policy and Strategy 1984-1993, *WMO No. 616* (1983).

9. Anon., Eighth World Meteorological Congress. Abridged report with resolutions, *WMO No. 533* (1979).

10. Anon., Scientific Plan for the World Climate Research Programme, *WCRP Publication Series No. 2, WMO/TD-No. 6* (1984).

11. Anon., Thirty-second session of the Executive Committee — Abridged report with resolutions, *WMO No. 556* (1980),

12. Anon., Thirty-fourth session of the Executive Council, Abridged Report with Resolutions of the Thirty-fourth Session, *WMO No. 599*, Geneva (1980).

13. United Nations — A/Conf. 101/10, Report of the Second United Nations Conference on the Exploration and Peaceful Uses of Outer Space (UNISPACE 82) Vienna (1982).

14. Anon., Ninth World Meteorological Congress. Abridged report with resolutions, *WMO No. 615*, Geneva, (1983).

The views expressed in this paper are those of the author and not necessarily the views of the World Meteorological Organization.

NOTES ON CONTRIBUTORS

Michael J. Allen is an Associate of the law firm Keck, Mahir and Cate, Chicago, Illinois.

Jahangir Amuzegar, a former executive director of the IMF, is an international economic consultant.

Jack Barkenbus is Deputy Director of the Energy, Environment and Resource Center, University of Tennessee. He is currently involved in a study of an international role in Arms Control Verification, Knoxville, Tennessee.

Eugene W. Bierly is Director of Atmospheric Sciences, Directorate for GeoSciences, National Science Foundation.

Arpad Bogsch is the Director General of the World Intellectual Property Organization.

George A. Codding, Jr., is Professor in the Department of Political Science, University of Colorado at Boulder, Boulder, Colorado.

Victor-Yves Ghebali is Lecturer at the Institut de Hautes Etudes, Geneva, Switzerland.

John Andrews King served as Senior Operation Officer of IFAD's Project Management Department from October 1978 to January 1982.

Michael K. Kirk is Assistant Commissioner for External Affairs, U.S. Patent and Trademark Office.

Wilhelm H. Lampe, Ministerial Counsellor, is Director, Office of Maritime Law, Ministry of Transportation, Federal Republic of Germany.

John A. Leese is a Senior Scientific Officer in the World Meteorological Organization, and is responsible for meteorological satellite activities. He has worked on the development of meteorological satellites since 1959.

H. Wayne Moyer is Professor of Political Science at Grinnell College, Grinnell, Iowa.

Ron Sanders is a visiting Fellow at Queen Elizabeth House, Oxford University. He served as High Commissioner in London (1984-87) and Ambassador to UNESCO (1983-87) for Antigua and Barbuda. He was also Deputy Permanent Representative to the UN (1982-83).

Jonathan E. Sanford is an analyst in international political economy at the Congressional Research Service, Library of Congress, Washington, D.C.

Kathryn Sikkink is Assistant Professor of Political Science, University of Minnesota at Minneapolis, Minneapolis, Minnesota.

Eugene Sochor is a member of the secretariat of the International Civil Aviation Organization, Montreal, Canada.

Ross B. Talbot is Professor of Political Science at Iowa State University of Science and Technology, Ames, Iowa.

The late *Ursula Wasserman* was a frequent contributor to *The Journal of World Trade Law* and a former permanent member of the United Nations Secretariat.

Joachim Zietz is Associate Professor of Economics at the University of Detroit, Detroit, Michigan.

BIBLIOGRAPHY

The United Nations Specialized Agencies

United Nations Publications
(records of meetings, reports, research studies and communications from governments and other international agencies)

"Annual Report of the Secretary-General on the Work of the United Nations," 1946- .

Demographic Yearbook, United Nations, 1948- .

Everyone's United Nations (previous title: Everyman's United Nations), 1st-8th ed., 1948-1968, 9th ed., 1979- .

Statistical Yearbook, United Nations, 1948- .

Treaty Series, United Nations, 1946- .

Yearbook of the United Nations, 1946- .

Government Publications

Documents to the People (quarterly).

Government Information Quarterly.

Government Publications Review (bi-monthly).

International Bibliography, Information, Documentation (quarterly).

"Symposium on the Role of the United States in Specialized International Organizations," Hearings before the

Government Publications (cont.)

Committee on Government Affairs, United States
Senate, 95th Congress, 1st Session, June 15, 1977.
Washington, D.C.: Government Printing Office, 1977.

United States Department of State, "United States
Contributions to International Organizations," Report to
the Congress for Fiscal Year (annual), 1951- .

United States Department of State, "United States
Participation in the United Nations," Report by the
President to the Congress (annual), 1948-1977.

U.S. Department of State Bulletin (monthly), 1939-1989.

U.S. Office of the Federal Register Weekly Compilation of
Presidential Documents, 1965- .

Reference Sources

Clive, Archer. *International Organization.* Winchester, MA:
Allen and Unwin. 1983.

Europa Year Book. London: Europa Publications. 1959- .

Goodrich, Leland M., Hambro, Edward, & Simons, Anne P.
United Nations Charter: Commentary and Documents
(3rd ed.). New York: Columbia University Press. 1969.

International Conciliation. 1907-1972.

International Organization (quarterly). 1947- .

Issues Before the General Assembly of the United Nations.
Annual Volumes. New York: United Nations
Association of the United States of America. 1977- .

United Nations Chronicle. 1975-. (previous title: *UN
Monthly Chronicle* 1964-1975).

Worldmark Encyclopedia of the Nations, 1, *The United Nations* (6th ed.). New York: John Wiley and Sons, Inc. 1984.

Yearbook of International Organizations. 1985-86 (22nd ed.). Brussels: Union of International Associations. 1985.

General References

BOOKS

Ahlurvalia, Kuljit. *The Legal Status, Privileges and Immunities of the Specialized Agencies of the United Nations and Certain Other International Organizations.* New York: International Publishing Services. 1964.

Alexandrowicx, Charles H. *Law Making Functions of the Specialized Agencies of the United Nations.* Text Ed. Littleton, CO: Rothman. 1973.

Ameri, Houshang. *Politics and Process in the Specialized Agencies of the United Nations.* Aldershot, Hants: Gower. 1982.

Ansari, Javed. *The Political Economy of International Economic Organization.* Boulder, CO: Reinner. 1986.

Bissell, Richard E. *Apartheid and International Organizations.* Boulder, CO: Westview. 1977.

Claude, Inis L., Jr. *The Changing United Nations.* New York: Random House. 1967.

Cox, Robert W. (ed.). *The Politics of International Organization: Studies in Multilateral Social and Economic Agencies.* New York: Praeger. 1970.

Cox, Robert W., & Jacobson, Harold. *The Anatomy of Influence: Decision Making in International Organization.* New Haven, CT: Yale University Press. 1974.

Donnelly, Jack. *The Concept of Human Rights.* New York: St. Martin's Press. 1985.

Dormael, Armand van. *Bretton Woods: A Birth of a Monetary System.* New York: Holmes & Meier. 1978.

Eichelberger, Clark Mell. *Organization for Peace: A History of the Founding of the UN.* New York: Harper & Row. 1977.

Ferris, Elizabeth, G., ed. *Refugees and World Politics.* New York: Praeger. 1985.

Forsythe, David P. *Human Rights and World Politics.* Lincoln, NE: University of Nebraska Press. 1983.

Goodrich, Leland M. *United Nations in a Changing World.* New York: Columbia University Press. 1974.

Groom, A. J. R., & Taylor, P. (eds.). *Functionalism.* London: University of London. 1975.

Haas, Ernst B. *Beyond the Nation State: Functionalism and International Organization.* Stanford, CA: Stanford University Press. 1964.

Hajnal, Peter I. *Guide to UN Organization, Documentation, and Publishing for Students, Researchers, Librarians.* Dobbs Ferry, NY: Oceana Publications. 1978.

Henkin, Louis, ed. *The International Bill of Rights: The Covenant on Civil and Political Rights.* New York: Columbia University Press. 1981.

Hill, Martin. "The Administrative Committee on Co-ordination," in *The Evolution of International Organizations.* Evan Luard (ed.). New York, NY: Praeger. 1966.

Hill, Martin. *Toward Greater Coordination, Order, and Coherence in the UN System.* New York: UNITAR, Res. Rept. 20, 1975.

Hill, Martin. *The United Nations System: Coordinating its Economic and Social Work.* New York: Cambridge University Press. 1978.

Hovet, Thomas, & Chamberlain, Waldo. *The Chronology & Fact Book of the UN, 1941-1979.* Dobbs Ferry, NY: Oceana. 1979.

Hufner, Klaus. *The UN System International Bibliography.* New York: Verlag Documentation. 1976-1979.

Imber, Mark. *The USA, ILO, UNESCO, and IAEA: Politicization and Withdrawal in the Specialized Agencies.* New York: St. Martin's Press. 1989.

Jacobson, Harold K. *The USSR and the UN's Economic and Social Activities.* Notre Dame, IN: University of Notre Dame Press. 1963.

Jacobson, Harold K. *Networks of Interdependence: International Organizations and the Global Political System.* New York: Knopf. 1979.

Kay, David A. *The Changing UN: Options for the U.S.* New York: Praeger. 1978.

Kirgis, Frederick L., Jr. *International Organizations in their Legal Setting: Documents, Comments & Questions.* Anaheim, CA: West Publications. 1977.

Luard, Evan. *International Agencies: The Emerging Framework of Interdependence.* London: Macmillan. 1977.

Luard, Evan. *The UN: How it Works & What it Does.* New York: St. Martin's Press. 1979.

Meron, Theodore, ed. *Human Rights in International Law*. 2 vols. Oxford: Clarendon Press. 1984.

Mitrany, David. *The Progress of International Government*. New Haven, CT: Yale University Press. 1933.

Mower, A. Glenn, Jr. *International Cooperation for Social Justice*. Westport, CT: Greenwood Press. 1985.

Nicholas, H. G. *The United Nations as a Political Institution*. Fairlawn, NJ: Oxford University Press. 5th ed. 1975.

Osakwe, Chris. *Participation of the Soviet Union in Universal Organization: A Political Analysis of Soviet Strategies and Aspirations Inside ILO, UNESCO, and WHO*. Atlantic Highlands, NJ: Humanities Press. 1973.

Plano, Jack C., & Riggs, Robert E. *Forging World Order: The Politics of International Organization*. New York: Macmillan. 1967.

Richards, J. H. *International Economic Institutions*. Fort Worth, TX: Holt, Rinehart & Winston. 1970.

Robertson, Arthur H. *Human Rights in the World: An Introduction to the International Protection of Human Rights*. New York: St. Martin's Press. 1982.

Sachs, Moshe Y. *United Nations: A Handbook on the UN: Its Structure, History, Purposes, Activities & Agencies*. New York: Wiley. 1977.

Schorr, Alan E. *Government Documents in the Library Literature*. Ann Arbor, MI: Pierian Press. 1977.

Sewell, James P. *Functionalism and World Politics*. Princeton, NJ: Princeton University Press. 1966.

Sharp, Walter R. *The United Nations Economic and Social Council*. New York: Columbia University Press. 1969.

Shih-Tsai Chen, Samuel. *Basic Documents of International Organization.* Dubuque, IA: Kendall-Hunt. 1978.

Taylor, Paul, & Groom, A. J. R. (eds.). *International Institutions at Work.* London: Pinter. 1988.

United Nations Handbook. New Zealand Ministry of External Relations and Trade. Wellington: Government Printer. 1989.

Williams, Douglas. *The Specialized Agencies and the United Nations.* London: Hurst. 1987.

Yoder, Amos. *The Evolution of the United Nations System.* New York: Taylor and Francis. 1989.

ARTICLES

Bergsten, C. F., "Interdependence and the Reform of International Institutions," *International Organization,* 30:361-72, Spring 1976.

Bienen, H. S., & Gersovitz, M., "Economic Stabilization, Conditionality, and Political Stability," *International Organization,* 39:729-54, Autumn 1985.

Burki, S. J., & M. ul Haq., "Meeting Basic Needs: An Overview," *World Development,* 9:167-82, Feb 1981.

Geidart, C., & Lvon, P., "Group of 77: A Perspective View," *International Affairs,* 57:79-101, Winter 1980, 1981.

Ghebali, Victor-Yves, "The Politicization of UN Specialized Agencies: A Preliminary Analysis," *Millennium: Journal of International Studies,* 14:317-33, Winter 1985.

Gold, Joseph, "Developments in the Law and Institutions of International Economic Relations," *American Journal of International Law,* 68:687-708, Oct 1974.

Gowa, Joanne, "Hegemons, IOs, and Markets: The Case of the Substitution Account," *International Organization*, 38(4):661-84, Autumn 1984.

Haas, Ernst, "Regionalism, Functionalism, and Universal International Organization," *World Politics*, 238-63, Jan 1956.

Helleiner, G. K., "An Agenda for a New Bretton Woods," *World Policy Journal*, 1(2):361-76, Winter 1984.

Hoole, F. W., "Appointment of Executive Heads in United Nations Treaty-Based Organizations," *International Organization*, 30:91-108 & 75-90, Winter 1976.

Hoole, F. W., "Evaluating the Impact of International Organizations," *International Organization*, 31(3):541-63, 1977.

Johnson, B., "The United Nations Institutional Response to Stockholm: A Case Study in the International Politics of Institutional Change," *International Organization*, 26:255, 1972.

Kaufmann, Johan, "The Capacity of the United Nations Development Program: The Jackson Report," *International Organization*, 25(4):938, 1971.

Kotchnig, Walter M., "The United Nations as an Instrument of Economic and Social Development," *International Organization*, 22:16-43, 1968.

Luard, Evan, "Functionalism Revisited: The UN Family in the 1980s," *International Affairs*, 59:677-92, Autumn 1983.

Lyons, G., Baldwin, D., & McNemar, D., "The Politicization Issue in the UN Specialized Agencies," *Proceedings of the Academy of Political Science*, 32(4):81-92, 1977.

McLaren, Robert, "Mitranian Functionalism: Possible or Impossible?," *Review of International Studies*, 11:139-52, April 1985.

Meltzer, R. I., "Restructuring the United Nations System: Institutional Reform Efforts in the Context of North-South Relations," *International Organization*, 32:629-39, Autumn 1980.

Miller, A. J., "Consensus and Conflict in Functionalism: Implications for the Study of International Integration," *Canadian Journal of Political Science*, 4(2), June 1971.

Nicol, Davidson, & Renninger, John, "The Restructuring of the UN Economic and Social System: Background and Analysis," *Third World Quarterly*, 4:74-92, Jan 1982.

Pallaczek, G., "UN and Specialized Agencies," *American Journal of International Law*, 49:592-619, July 1946.

Pendley, R., Scheinmen, L., & Butler, R. W., "International Safeguarding as Institutionalized Collective Behavior," *International Organization*, 29(3):585-616, 1975.

Righter, R., "Battle of the Bias," *Foreign Policy*, 34:121-38, Spring 1979.

Rothstein, R. L., "Regime Creation by a Coalition of the Weak: Lessons from NIEO and the Integrated Program for Commodities," *International Studies Quarterly*, 28:307-28, Sept 1984.

Sathyamurthy, T. V., "Problems of the Central and Regional Coordination in Functional International Organization," *Midwest Journal of Political Science*, 267-76, Aug 1964.

Skjelsbaek, Kjell, "The Growth of International Nongovernmental Organization in the Twentieth Century," *International Organization*, 25(3), Summer 1971.

Spector, Leonard, "Silent Spread," *Foreign Policy*, 58:53-78, Spring 1985.

Steele, D. B., "The Case for Global Economic Management and UN System Reform," *International Organization*, 39:561-78, Summer 1985.

Stewart, Frances, "Alternative Conditionality," *Development: Seeds of Change*, 1:64-76, 1984.

Thorpe, Paul A., Jr., "Transnational Enterprises and International Regulation: A Survey of Various Approaches in International Organization," *International Organization*, 30:47-73, Winter 1976.

"Trade Winds That May Blow Fair," *Economist*, 306:80-81, Feb 20, 1988.

Wallace, Michael D., & Singer, J. David, "Intergovernmental Organizations in the Global System, 1815-1964: A Quantitative Description," *International Organization*, 24:239-87, Spring 1970.

Williamson, R. S., "The United Nations: Some Parts Work," *Orbis*, 32:187-97, Spring 1988.

Wolf, Peter, "International Organization and Attitude Change: A Re-Examination of the Functionalist Approach," *International Organization*, 27:347-71, Summer 1973.

Food and Agriculture Organization

BOOKS

Talbot, Ross B. *The Four World Food Agencies in Rome*. Ames, IA: Iowa State University Press. 1990.

ARTICLES

Jorden, Robert, & Weiss, Theodore, "Bureaucratic Politics
and the World Food Conference: The International
Policy Process," *World Politics*, 28(3):422-39, April
1976.

Riggs, R. E., "FAO and the USDA: Implications for
Functionalist Learning," *World Politics Quarterly*,
33:314-29, Sept 1980.

"The UNs Food and Agriculture Organization: Is it Dead on
Arrival?," *Society*, 25:4-41, Sept/Oct 1988.

General Agreement on Tariffs and Trade

BOOKS

Baldwin, Robert E. *Trade Policy in a Changing World
Economy.* New York: Harvester/Wheatsheaf. 1988.

Camps, Miriam, & Diebold, William, Jr.   *The New
Materialism: Can the World Trading System be Saved?.*
New York: Council on Foreign Relations. 1983.

Dam, Kenneth W. *The GATT: Law and International
Economic Organization.* Chicago, IL: University of
Chicago Press. 1970.

Evans, John W. *Kennedy Round in American Trade Policy:
The Twilight of the GATT?.* Cambridge, MA: Harvard
University Press. 1971.

Glick, Leslie Alan. *Multilateral Trade Negotiations: World
Trade After the Tokyo Round.* Lanham, MD: Rowman &
Allanheld. 1984.

Hathaway, Dale E. *Agriculture and the GATT: Rewriting the
Rules.* Washington, DC: Institute for International
Economics. 1987.

Hudec, Robert E. *The GATT Legal System and World Trade Diplomacy.* New York: Praeger. 1975.

Jackson, John Howard. *The World Trading System: Law and Policy of International Economic Relations.* Cambridge, MA: MIT Press. 1989.

Kock, Karin. *International Trade Policy and the GATT: 1947-1967.* Stockholm, Sweden: Almquist and Wilsell. 1969.

Snape, R. H., ed. *Issues in World Trade Policy: GATT at the Crossroads.* New York: Macmillan Press Ltd. 1986.

Tussie, Diana. *The Less Developed Countries and the World Trading System: A Challenge to the GATT.* New York: St. Martin's Press. 1987.

ARTICLES

Balassa, Bela, "The Tokyo Round and the Developing Countries (How the Tariff Reductions in the Multilateral Trade Negotiations Affect the Export Products of Developing Countries)," *Journal of World Trade Law,* 14:93-118, March/April 1980.

Barcelo, John J., III, "Subsidies, Countervailing Duties, and Antidumping After the Tokyo Round (Focuses on the Trade Agreement Act of 1970)," *Cornell International Law Journal,* 13:257-88, Summer 1980.

Bergsten, C. Fred, "Reforming the GATT," *Journal of International Economics,* 7:1-18, Feb 1977.

Cohen, Benjamin J., "Balance-of-Payments Financing: Evolution of a Regime," *International Organization,* 36(2):457-78, Spring 1982.

Cooper, Mary H., "Trade Trouble-Shooting," *Editorial Research Reports,* 64-67, Sept. 5, 1986.

Dunn, J. A., Jr., "Automobiles in International Trade: Regime Change or Persistence?," *International Organization*, 41:225-52, Spring 1987.

Espiell, Hector Gross, "GATT: Accommodating Generalized Preferences," *Journal of World Trade Law*, 6:391-404, July/Aug 1972.

Finger, J. M., "Effects of the Kennedy Round Tariff Concessions on the Exports of Developing Countries," *Economic Journal*, 86:87-95, March 1976.

Finlayson, J., & Zacher, M., "The GATT and the Regulation of Trade Barriers: Regime Dynamics and Functions," *International Organization*, 35:561-602, 1981.

"The GATT and Multilateral Treaty Making: The Tokyo Round," *American Journal of International Law*, 77:51-83, Jan 1983.

Graham, Thomas F., "Global Trade: War and Peace," *Foreign Policy*, 50(50):124-37, Spring 1983.

Haight, F. A., "Customs Unions and Free Trade Areas Under GATT: A Reappraisal," *Journal of World Trade Law*, 6:391-404, July/Aug 1972.

Jackson, John H., "The Changing International Law Framework for Exports: The General Agreement on Tariffs and Trade," *Georgia Journal of International and Comparative Law*, 14(3):505-20, 1984.

Klepper, Gernot, "The Next GATT Round: Bilateralism Versus Multilateralism," *Intereconomics*, 21:232-38, Sept/Oct 1986.

Koekkoek, K. A., "The Integration of Developing Countries in the GATT System," *World Development*, 16:947-57, Aug 1988.

Lipson, Charles, "The Transformation of Trade: The Sources and Effects of Regime Change (Emphasis on the General Agreement on Tariffs and Trade: Based on Conference Paper)," *International Organization*, 36:417-55, Spring 1982.

McRae, D. M., & Thomas, J. C., "GATT and Multilateral Treaty Making: The Tokyo Round," *American Journal of International Law*, 77:51-83, Jan 1983.

O'Leary, James P., "After the Tokyo Round: Protectionism or Collective Economic Security," *Orbis*, 24:129-47, Spring 1980.

Perlow, G. H., "Multilateral Supervision of International Trade: Has the Textiles Experiment Worked?," *American Journal of International Law*, 75:93-133, Jan 1981.

Plank, Rosine, "An Unofficial Description of How a GATT Panel Works and Does Not," *Journal of International Arbitration*, 4:53-102, Dec 1987.

Reuland, James M., "GATT and State-Trading Countries," *Journal of World Trade Law*, 9:318-39, May/June 1975.

Rhodes, C., "Reciprocity in Trade: The Utility of a Bargaining Strategy," *International Organization*, 43:273-99, Sept 1989.

Roessler, Frieder, "The Competence of GATT," *Journal of World Trade Law*, 21:73-83, June 1987.

Sanders, Pieter, "Implementing International Codes of Conduct for Multilateral Enterprises," *American Journal of Comparative Law*, 30(2):241-54, Spring 1982.

Schott, Jeffrey J., & Jacqueline Mazza, "Trade in Services and Developing Countries," *Journal of World Trade Law*, 20:253-73, May/June 1986.

Sevoum, Belaynch, "Export Subsidies Under the MTN (Tokyo Round Multilateral Trade Negotiations): An Analysis with Particular Emphasis on Developing Countries," *Journal of World Trade Law*, 18:512-41, Dec 1984.

Shankar, Saxena, "The Uruguay Round: Expectations of Developing Countries," *International Economics*, 23:268-76, Nov/Dec 1988.

Shelp, R. K., "Trade in Services," *Foreign Policy*, 65:64-84, Winter 1986, 1987.

Story, D., "Trade Politics in the Third World: A Case Study of the Mexican GATT Decision," *International Organization*, 36:767-94, Autumn 1982.

Vernon, Raymond, "International Trade Policy in the 1980s: Prospects and Problems," *International Studies Quarterly*, 26(4):483-510, Dec 1982.

Wells, Sidney, "The Developing Countries, GATT and UNCTAD," *International Affairs*, 45:64-79, Jan 1969.

International Atomic Energy Agency

BOOKS

Fischer, David, & Szasz, Paul. *Stockholm International Peace Research Institute (SIPRI): Safeguarding the Atom: A Critical Appraisal.* New York: Taylor and Francis. 1985.

Scheinman, Lawrence. *The International Atomic Energy Agency and World Nuclear Order.* Washington, DC: Resources for the Future. 1987.

Schiff, Benjamin N. *International Nuclear Technology Transfer: Dilemmas of Dissention and Control.* Lanham, MD: Rowman and Allanheld. 1983.

ARTICLES

Barkenbus, J., "Nuclear Power Safety and the Role of International Organization," *International Organization*, 41:475-90, Summer 1987.

Bechhoefer, Bernhard G., "Negotiating the Status of the International Atomic Energy Agency," *International Organization*, 13:38-59, 1959.

Bechhoefer, Bernhard G., & Stein, Eric, "Atoms for Peace: The New International Atomic Energy Agency," *Michigan Law Review*, 55:747-89, April 1957.

Brewer, Thomas L., "The International Atomic Energy Agency," *Armed Forces and Society*, 4:207-26, Winter 1978.

Daub, William O., & Dukert, Joseph M., "Making Nuclear Energy Safe and Secure," *Foreign Affairs*, 53:756-72, July 1975.

Eklund, Sigvard, "Two Decades of Work with the International Atomic Energy Agency (1961-81 Overview by the Director General Emeritus of the Agency)," *Review of International Affairs*, 33:12-14, Feb 5, 1982.

Hammer, John, "Nuclear Safety," *Editorial Research Reports*, 2:603-24, Aug 22, 1975.

Hasselman, Cord-Georg, "Do We Need New IAEA Safeguards?," *German Yearbook of International Law*, 259-302, 1984.

Imai, Ryukichi, "Safeguards Against Diversion of Nuclear Material: An Overview," *Annals of the American Academy of Political and Social Sciences*, 58-69, March 1977.

Kennedy, Richard T., "IAEA: Unique Member of the UN Family," *Department of State Bulletin*, 85:68-72, July 1985.

Mozlewer, S., "IAEA Safeguards and Non-Proliferation," *Bulletin of the Atomic Scientists*, 37:24-9, Oct 1981.

Pendley, Robert & Scheinman, Lawrence, "International Safeguarding as Institutionalized Collective Behavior," *International Organization*, 29:585-616, Summer 1975.

Quester, George H., "The Nuclear Nonproliferation Treaty and the International Atomic Energy Agency," *International Organization*, 24:163-82, 1970.

Ramberg, Bennett, "Learning from Chernobyl," *Foreign Affairs*, 65(2):304-28, Winter 1986/1987.

Rikicoff, A. A., "Market-Sharing Approach to the World Nuclear Sales Problem," *Foreign Affairs*, 54:763-87, July 1976.

Scheinman, Lawrence, "Nuclear Safeguards, the Peaceful Atom, and IAEA," *International Conciliation*, 572:5-64, March 1969.

Scheinman, Lawrence, "Security in a Transnational System: The Case of Nuclear Energy," *International Organization*, 25:626-49, Summer 1971.

Stanford, Joseph S., "Nuclear Assistance and Cooperation Agreements: Some Problems in the Application of Safeguards," *Journal of International Law and Economics*, 437-51, Aug-Dec 1975.

Stencel, Sandra, "Nuclear Safeguards," *Editorial Research Reports*, 11:867-84, Nov 14, 1974.

Stoessinger, John G., "The International Atomic Energy Agency: The First Phase," *International Organization*, 13:394-411, Summer 1959.

Szasz, Paul C., "The Adequacy of International Nuclear Safeguards (Those of the IAEA Chiefly)," *Journal of International Law and Economics*, 10:423-36, Aug 10, 1975.

International Bank for Reconstruction and Development

BOOKS

Acheson, A. L., et al. (eds.). *Bretton Woods Revisited.* Toronto, Canada: University of Toronto Press. 1972.

Ayres, Robert. *Banking on the Poor: The World Bank and World Poverty.* Cambridge, MA: MIT Press. 1983.

Camps, Miriam, with the collaboration of Catherine Irwin. *Collective Management: The Reform of Global Economic Organizations.* New York: McGraw-Hill. 1981.

King, John A. *Economic Development Projects and Their Appraisal: Cases and Principles from the Experience of the World Bank.* Baltimore, MD: Johns Hopkins. 1967.

Larr, Aart van de. *The World Bank and the Poor.* The Hague Netherlands: Martinus Nijhoff/Kluwer Academic Publishing Group. 1980.

Lewis, John P., & Kapur, Ishan. *The World Bank Group, Multilateral Aid and the 1970s.* San Diego, CA: Lexington Books. 1973.

Mason, Edward S. *The World Bank Since Bretton Woods.* Washington, DC: Brookings Institute. 1973.

McNamara, Robert S. *One Hundred Countries, Two Billion People: The Dimensions of Development.* New York: Praeger. 1973.

Miller, Morris. *Coping is Not Enough: The International Debt Crisis and the Roles of the World Bank and International Monetary Fund.* Homewood, IL: Dow Jones-Irwin. 1985.

Morris, James. *Road to Huddersfield: Story of the World Bank.* New York: Pantheon Books. 1963.

Payer, Cheryl. *The World Bank: A Critical Analysis.* New York: Monthly Review Press. 1982.

Reid, Escott. *Strengthening the World Bank.* Chicago, IL: University of Chicago Press. 1976.

Van Meerhaege, M. A. G. *A Handbook of International Economic Institutions.* (rev. ed.). The Hague, Netherlands: Martinus Nijhoff. 1984.

Vries, Barend A. de: foreward by I. G. Patel. *Remaking the World Bank.* Cabin John, MD: Seven Locks Press. 1987.

ARTICLES

Ascher, W., "New Development Approaches and the Adaptability of International Agencies: The World Bank," *International Organization*, 37:415-40, 1983.

Ayres, Robert L., "Breaking the Bank," *Foreign Policy*, 43:104-20, Summer 1981.

Bacha, E. L., & Feinberg, R. E., "The World Bank and Structural Adjustment in Latin America," bibl., *World Development*, 14:33-46, March 1986.

Baer, Werner, "The World Bank Group and the Process of Socio-Economic Development in the Third World," *World Development*, 2:1-10, June 1974.

Bandow, Doug, "What's Still Wrong with the World Bank?," *Orbis*, 33:73-89, Winter 1989.

Bleicher, Samuel A., "UN v. IBRD," *International Organization*, 24:31-47, Winter 1970.

Clerk, W., "Robert McNamara at the World Bank," *Foreign Affairs*, 60:167-78, Discussion 60:951-53, Spring 1982.

Cohn, Theodore H., "Politics in the World Bank Group: The Question of Loans to the Asian Giants," *International Organization*, 28:561-71, Summer 1974.

Crane, B. B., & Finkle, J. L., "World Bank's Population Program," *World Politics*, 33:516-53, July 1981.

Dell, Edmund, "The Common Fund," *International Affairs (London)*, 63:23-38, Winter 1986, 1987.

Dell, Sidney, "The Question of Cross-Conditionality," *World Development*, 16:557-68, May 1988.

Feinberg, Richard E., "The Changing Relationship Between the World Bank and the International Monetary Fund," *International Organization*, 42:545-60, Summer 1988.

Frev, B. S., "Competing Models of International Lending Activity," *Journal of Development and Economics*, 20:225-45, March 1986.

Gruhn, Iseebill, "The Recolonization of Africa: International Organizations on the March (Roles of the International Monetary Fund and the World Bank)," *Africa Today*, 30:37-48, Fourth Quarter 1983.

Hopkins, Anthony G., "The World Bank in Africa: Historical Reflections on the African Present," *World Development*, 14:1473-87, Dec 1986.

Howe, G., "International Monetary Fund and the World Bank: The British Approach," *International Affairs*, 58:199-209, Spring 1982.

Libby, Ronald, "IDA: A Legal Fiction Designed to Secure an LDC Constituency," *International Organization*, 29:1065-72, Autumn 1975.

Mayer, Otto G., "Development Without Miracles: The World Bank After Forty Years," *Intereconomics*, 18:167-72, July/Aug 1984.

Mingst, Karen A., "Inter-organizational Politics: The World Bank and the African Development Bank," *Review of International Studies*, 13:281-93, Oct 1987.

Nellis, J., & Kikeri, S., "Public Enterprise Reform: Privatization and the World Bank," *World Development*, 17:659-72, May 1989.

Oppenheim, V. H., "Whose World Bank?," *Foreign Policy*, 19:99-108, Summer 1975.

Pave, C., "Is There a Better Way? Development and the World Bank," *Monthly Review*, 34:12-30, Sept 1982.

Reid, Escott, "McNamara's World Bank," *Foreign Affairs*, 51:794-810, July 1973.

Rimmer, Douglas, "Basic Needs and the Origins of the Development of Ethos," *Journal of Developing Areas*, 15(2):215-38, Jan 1981.

Rosenfield, P. L., et al., "Social and Economic Research in the UNDP World Bank/WHO Special Programme for Research and Training in Tropical Diseases," *Social Science and Medicine (Medical Sociology)*, 15A:529-38, Sept 1981.

Rowely, A., "Focus: World Bank/IMF '85," *Far Eastern Economic Review*, 130:47-94, Oct 10, 1985.

Ruggie, John G., "The Politics of Money," *Foreign Policy*, 43:139-54, Summer 1981.

Sanford, J. E., "The World Bank and Poverty: The Plight of the World's Impoverished is Still a Major Concern of the International Agency," *American Journal of Economics and Sociology*, 47:257-75, July 1988.

Sanford, Jonathan, "The World Bank and Poverty: A Review of the Evidence on Whether the Agency has Diminished Emphasis on Aid to the Poor," *American Journal of Economics and Sociology*, 48:151-64, April 1989.

Schweitzer, Pierre-Paul, "A Gradual Reform," *International Development Review*, 22(4):40-45, 1980.

Swedberg, R., "The Doctrine of Economic Neutrality of the IMF and the World Bank," *Journal of Peace Research*, 23(4):377-90, 1986.

Wernert, R. S., "Banks and Bankruptcy," *Foreign Policy*, 50:138-49, Spring 1983.

"World Bank/IMF '86 Focus," *Far Eastern Economic Review*, 134:51-92, 1986.

Zijan, Zhao, "World Bank - IMF: Difficult Tasks Lie Ahead," *Beijing Review*, 30:10-11, Oct 19, 1987.

International Civil Aviation Organization

BOOK

Buergenthal, Thomas. *Law-making in ICAO*. (Procedural Aspects of International Law Series, Vol. 7). Syracuse, NY: Syracuse University Press. 1969.

ARTICLES

Bell, R. G., "U.S. Response to Terrorism Against International Civil Aviation," *Orbis*, Winter 1976.

Kihl, Young W., "Functional Performance and Member State Behavior in International Organizations: Test and Evaluation," *Journal of Politics*, 33:337-39, May 1971.

Kotatite, A., "ICAO: Co-operation for Orderly Development of Air Transport," *Impact of Science on Society*, 31:305-12, July/Sept 1981.

Lowenfield, Andreas F., "A New Takeoff for International Air Transport," *Foreign Affairs*, 54:36-50, Oct 1975.

Miles, E., "Transnationalism in Space: Inner and Outer," *International Organization*, 26:479, 1972.

Sochor, Eugene, "Conflicts in International Civil Aviation: Safeguarding the Air Routes," *Conflict*, 8(4):271-84, 1988.

Sochor, Eugene, "International Civil Aviation and the Third World: How Fair is the System?," *Third World Quarterly*, 10:1300-22, July 1988.

Thayer, Frederick C., "International Air Transport: A Microsystem in Need of New Approaches," *International Organization*, 25:875-98, Autumn 1971.

Thornton, Robert, "Government and Airlines," *International Organization*, 25:541-53, Summer 1971.

Vivian, J., "ICAO Assistance to Civil Aviation in the Developing World," *Impact of Science on Society*, 31:305-12, July/Sep 1981.

International Fund for Agricultural Development

BOOKS

Alexandratos, Nikes. (ed.). *World Agriculture Toward 2000: An FAO Study.* New York: New York University Press. 1990.

Lineberry, William P. *Assessing Participatory Development: Rhetoric Versus Reality.* Boulder, CO: Westview Press. 1989.

ARTICLES

King, John Andrews, "The International Fund for Agricultural Development: The First Six Years," *Development Policy,* 3:3-20, May 1985.

Talbot, R. B., "International Fund for Agricultural Development," *Political Science Quarterly,* 95:261-76, Summer 1980.

International Labor Organization

BOOKS

Alcock, Antony. *History of the International Labor Organization.* Los Angeles, CA: Octagon Books. 1971.

Galenson, Walter. *The International Labor Organization: An American View.* Madison, WI: University of Wisconsin Press. 1981.

Ghebali, Victor Yves, Ago, Roberto, & Valticos, Nicolas. *The International Labour Organization: A Case Study on the Evolution of UN Specialized Agencies.* Dordrecht, Netherlands: Martinus Nijhoff. 1989.

Jenks, Wilfred. *Trade Union Freedom*. Dobbs Ferry, NY: Stevens. 1958.

Jenks, Wilfred C. *Social Justice in the Law of Nations: The ILO Impact After Fifty Years*. Fairlawn, NJ: Oxford University Press. 1970.

Johnston, George A. *The International Labor Organization: Its Work for Social and Economic Progress*. Lanham, MD: Europa. 1970.

Joyce, James Avery. *World Labour Rights and Their Protection*. London: Croom Helm Ltd. 1980.

Kruglak, Gregory Theodore. *The Politics of United States Decision-Making in the United Nations Specialized Agencies: The Case of the International Labor Organization*. Washington, DC: University Press of America. 1980.

Landelius, Torstein. *Workers, Employers and Governments: A Comparative Study of Delegations and Groups at the International Labor Conference 1919-1964*. Stockholm, Sweden: Norstedt & Soner. 1965.

Landy, Ernest A. *The Effectiveness of International Supervision: Thirty Years of ILO Experience*. Dobbs Ferry, NY: Stevens. 1966.

McHugh, Lois. *International Labor Organization: Issues of U.S. Membership*. Washington, DC: Congressional Research Service. 1980.

Morse, David. *The Origin and Evolution of the ILO and Its Role in the World Community*. Ithaca, NY: Cornell University Press. 1969.

Osakwe, Chris. *The Participation of the Soviet Union in Universal International Organizations: A Political Analysis of Soviet Strategies and Aspirations Inside ILO,*

UNESCO and WHO. Atlantic Highlands, NJ: Humanities Press. 1972.

Tipton, J. B. *Participation of the United States in the International Labor Organization.* Urbana, IL: University of Illinois. 1959.

ARTICLES

Alford, William P., "The Prospective Withdrawal of the United States from the International Labor Organization: Rationales and Implications," *Harvard International Law Journal*, 17:623-38, Summer 1976.

Allen, Michael J., "UNESCO and the ILO: A Tale of Two UN Agencies," *Notre Dame Journal of Law Ethics and Public Policy*, 1:391-419, Winter 1985.

Beguin, Bernard, "ILO and the Tripart System," *International Conciliation*, 523:405-48, May 1959.

Cox, Robert W., "Labor and Hegemony," *International Organization*, 31(3):385-424, 1977.

Cox, Robert W., "Labor and Transnational Relations," *International Organization*, 25:554-84, Summer 1971.

Dahl, Karl N., "The Role of ILO Standards in Global Integration Process," *Journal of Peace Research*, 5:309-51, 1968.

Douglas, William A., & Goodson, Roy S., "Labor and Hegemony: A Critique," *International Organization*, 34(1):149-158, 1980.

Dufty, Norman F., "Technical Assistance and the International Labor Office," *Journal of Industrial Relations*, 9:245-57, Nov 1967.

Dufty, Norman F., "Organizational Growth and Goal Structure: The Case of the ILO," *International Organization*, 26:497-98, Summer 1972.

Haas, Ernst B., "System and Process in International Labor Organization," *World Politics*, 14:322-52, 1962.

Haythorne, George V., "The ILO: A Canadian Appraisal After 50 Years," *Canadian Public Administrator*, 14:173-92, Summer 1971.

"The ILO Crisis," *Comparative Labor Law*, 1:2-29, Spring 1976.

"The International Labor Organization and World Poverty," *Canadian Labour*, 16:10-14, June 1971.

Jacobson, Harold K., "The USSR and the ILO," *International Organization*, 14:402-28, 1960.

Jordan, Robert S., "Boycott Diplomacy: The U.S., the UN, and UNESCO (and the International Labor Organization)," *Public Administrative Review*, 44:283-91, July/Aug 1984.

Joyner, Christopher C., "The United States' Withdrawal from the ILO: International Politics in the Labor Arena," *International Lawyer*, 12:721-39, Fall 1978.

McMahon, J. F., "The Legislative Technique in the ILO," *British Yearbook of International Law*, 41:1-102, 1965-1966.

Melanson, Richard A., "Human Rights and the American Withdrawal from ILO (Conference Paper)," *Universal Human Rights*, 1:43-61, Jan/March 1979.

N., M., "International Labor in Crisis," *Foreign Affairs*, 49:519-31, April 1971.

Nafziger, James A. R., "The ILO and Social Change: The Fact Finding and Conciliation Commission of Freedom of Association," *Journal of International Law and Politics*, 2:1-34, 1969.

Osieke, Ebere, "Majority Voting Systems in the International Labour Organization and the International Monetary Fund," *International and Comparative Law Quarterly*, 33:381-408, April 1984.

Pantos, G. J., "United States and the International Labor Organization," *Employee Relations Law Journal*, 3:457-66, 1978.

Partan, Daniel, "The Development of International Law by the ILO," *American Journal of International Law Proceedings*, 139-46, 1965.

Power, P. F., "American Employer Behavior in the ILO," *Midwest Journal of Political Science*, 12:259-78, May 1968.

Schwebel, Stephen M., "U.S. Assaults the ILO," *American Journal of International Law*, 65:136-42, Jan 1971.

Valticas, Nicholas, "The ILO: Its Contribution to the Role of Law and International Protection of Human Rights," *Journal of the International Commission of Jurists*, 9:33-34, Dec 1968.

Windmoller, John P., "U.S. Participation in the ILO: A Political Dimension," *Monthly Labor Review*, 98:35-39, May 1975.

Wolf, Francis, "The ILO Experience in the Implementation of Human Rights," *Employee Relations Law Journal*, 3:457-66, 1978.

International Maritime Organization

BOOKS

Henry, Cleopatra Elmira. *The Carriage of Dangerous Goods by Sea: The Role of the International Maritime Organization in International Legislation.* New York: St. Martin's Press. 1985.

Mankabady, Samir, ed. *The International Maritime Organization.* Baltimore, MD: Croom Helm Ltd. 1984.

Petrow, R. *In the Wake of Torrey Canyon.* New York: David McKay. 1968.

ARTICLES

Dempsey, Paul Stephen, "Compliance and Enforcement in International Law: Oil Pollution of the Marine Environment by Ocean Vessels," *Northwestern Journal of International Law and Business,* 6:459-561, Summer 1984.

Hailbronner, Kay, "Freedom of the Air and the Convention on the Law of the Sea," *American Journal of International Law,* 77:490-520, July 1983.

Halberstam, Malvina, "Terrorism on the High Seas: The Achille Lauro, Piracy and the IMO Convention on Maritime Safety," *American Journal of International Law,* 82:269-310, April 1988.

Lampe, Wilhelm H., "The 'New' International Maritime Organization and its Place in Development of International Maritime Law (Successor to the Inter-governmental Maritime Consultive Organization)," *Journal of Maritime Law and Commerce,* 14:305-29, July 1983.

Wooster, Warren S., "Interactions Between
    Intergovernmental and Scientific Organizations in
    Marine Affairs," *International Organization*, 27:103-13,
    Winter 1973.

International Monetary Fund

BOOKS

Cline, William R. *International Monetary Reform and the
    Developing Countries.* Washington, DC: Brookings
    Institution. 1976.

DeVries, Margaret G. *The IMF, 1966-1971: The System
    Under Stress.* Washington, DC: IMF. 1977.

Ecks, Alfred E., Jr. *A Search for Solvency: Bretton Woods
    and the International Monetary System, 1941-1971.*
    Austin, TX: University of Texas Press. 1975.

Ferguson, Tyrone. *The Third World and Decision Making in
    the International Monetary Fund.* Geneva: Graduate
    Institute of International Studies. 1987.

Ferguson, Tyrone. *The Third World and Decision Making in
    the International Monetary Fund: The Quest for Full and
    Effective Participation.* Albuquerque, NM: Pinter
    Publishers. 1988.

Field, A. N. *The Bretton Woods Plot: The Twin Evils of the
    IMF and the IBRD.* New York: Gordon Press. 1979.

Gardner, Richard. *Sterling-Dollar Diplomacy: The Origins
    and Prospects of Our International Economic Order.*
    New York: McGraw-Hill. 1969.

Grubel, Herbert G. *International Monetary System.* New
    York: Penguin. 1970.

Gwin, Catherine, & Feinberg, Richard E. *Pulling Together the IMF in a Multipolar World*. Washington, DC: Overseas Development Council. 1989.

Hooke, A. W. *The International Monetary Fund, Its Evolution, Organization, and Activities*. Washington, DC: IMF. 1981.

Horrie, Shigeo. *International Monetary Fund: Retrospect and Prospect*. New York: St. Martin's Press. 1964.

Killick, Tony, ed. *The IMF and Stabilization: Developing Country Experiences*. New York: St. Martin's Press. 1984.

Korner, Peter et al. *The IMF and the Debt Crisis: A Guide to the Third World's Dilemma*. East Haven, CT: Zed Books. 1986.

Monroe, Wilbur F. *International Monetary Reconstruction: Problems and Issues*. Lexington, MA: Lexington Books. 1974.

Myers, Robert J., ed. *The Political Morality of the International Monetary Fund*. New Brunswick, NJ: Transaction Books. 1987.

Pastor, Manuel, Jr. *The International Monetary Fund and Latin America: Economic Stabilization and Class Conflict*. Boulder, CO: Westview. 1987.

Payer, Cheryl. *The Debt Trap: The IMF and the Third World*. New York: Monthly Review Press. 1975.

Poniachek, Harvey A. *Monetary Independence Under Flexible Exchange Rates*. Lexington, MA: Lexington Books. 1979.

Solomon, Robert. *The IMF, 1945-1976: An Insider's View*. New York: Harper & Row. 1977.

Steinberg, Eleanor B. *New Means of Financing International Needs.* Washington, DC: Brookings Institution. 1978.

Tew, Brian. *International Monetary Cooperation, 1945-1967.* 9th ed., Amherst, MA: Hutchinson. 1967.

Williamson, John. *The Failure of the World Monetary Reform, 1971-1974.* New York: New York University Press. 1977.

ARTICLES

Altmann, John, "Liquidity Problems of Developing Countries and the International Monetary Fund's System of Facilities," *Economics,* 23:30-51, 1981.

Amuzegar, J., "The IMF Under Fire," *Foreign Policy,* 64:98-119, Fall 1986.

Aronson, Jonathan David, "International Lending and Debt," *Washington Quarterly,* 6(4):62-76, Autumn 1983.

Bacha, E. L., "IMF Conditionality: Conceptual Problems and Policy Alternatives," *World Development,* 15:1457-67, Dec 1987.

Bergsten, C. Fred, "New Urgency for International Monetary Reform," *Foreign Policy,* 19:79-98, Summer 1975.

Bienen, Henry S., & Gersovitz, Mark, "Economic Stabilization, Conditionality, and Political Stability," *International Organization,* 39(4):729-54, Autumn 1985.

Bird, Graham, "The International Monetary Fund and Developing Countries: Retrospect and Prospect," *Economist,* 131(2):161-95, 1983.

Brown, Adlith, "Economic Policy and the IMF in Jamaica," *Social and Economic Studies,* 30:1-51, Dec 1981.

Chand, S., "Toward a Growth-Oriented Model of Financial Programming," *World Development*, 17:473-90, April 1989.

Chandavarkar, A., "Keynes and the International Monetary System Revised (a Contextual and Conjectural Essay)," *World Development*, 15:1395-1405, Dec 1987.

Cohen, B. J., "Balance-of-Payments Financing: Evolution of a Regime," *International Organization*, 36:457-78, Spring 1982.

Cohen, B. J., "International Debt and Linkage Strategies: Some Foreign Policy Implications for the United States," *International Organization*, 39:699-727, Autumn 1985.

Crane, B. B., "Policy Coordination by Major Western Powers in Bargaining with the Third World: Debt Relief and the Common Fund," *International Organization*, 38:399-428, Summer 1984.

Cutler, Tom, "Recycling Petro Dollars to the Third World: A Critique of the IMF Oil Facility," *World Affairs*, 139:189-205, Winter 1976-1977.

De Larosiere, J., "Challenges Facing the World Economy and the Role of the International Monetary Fund," *Atlantic Community Quarterly*, 22:139-47, Summer 1984.

De Larosiere, J., "Role of the International Monetary Fund: The Need for International Economic Adjustment," *Atlantic Community Quarterly*, 20:163-70, Summer 1982.

DeVries, M. G., "The IMF: 40 Years of Challenge and Change," *Finance Development*, 22:7-10, Sept 1985.

DeVries, Tom, "Jamaica, or the Non-Reform of the International Monetary System," *Foreign Affairs*, 54:577-605, April 1976.

Dell, E., "The Common Fund," *International Affairs*, 63:21-38, Winter 1986, 1987.

Dell, S., "The History of the IMF," *World Development*, 14:1203-12, Sept 1986.

Dreyer, J. S., & Schotter, A., "Power Relationships in the International Monetary Fund: The Consequences of Quota Changes," *Review of Economic Statistics*, 62:97-106, Feb 1980.

Eshag, E., "Some Suggestions for Improving the Operation of the IMF Stabilizing Programs," *International Labor Relations*, 128(3):297-320, 1989.

Gerster, Richard, "The IMF (International Monetary Fund) and Basic Needs Conditionality with Special Reference to the United States and the "Basic Needs" Legislation of Congress," *Journal of World Trade Law*, 16:497-517, Nov/Dec 1982.

Girvan, Norman, & Bernal, Richard, "The IMF (International Monetary Fund) and the Foreclosure of Development Options: The Case of Jamaica," *Monetary Review*, 33:34-48, Feb 1982.

Gold, Joseph, "The 'Sanctions' of the IMF," *American Journal of International Law*, 66:737-62, Oct 1972.

Gold, Joseph, "Weighted Voting Power: Some Limits and Some Problems," *American Journal of International Law*, 68:687-708, Oct 1974.

Gold, Joseph, "Political Bodies of the International Monetary Fund," *Journal of International Law and Economics*, 11:237-85, 1977.

Gold, Joseph, "Mexico and the Development of the Practice of the International Monetary Fund," *World Development*, 16:1127-42, Oct 1988.

Gruhn, Iseebill, "The Recolonization of Africa: International Organizations on the March (Roles of the International Monetary Fund and the World Bank)," *Africa Today*, 30:37-48, Fourth Quarter 1983.

Gulati, I. S., "IMF Conditionality and the Low Income Countries (Based on Lecture)," *Economic Bulletin of Asia and the Pacific*, 33(2):1-11, 1983.

Haggard, S., "The Politics of Adjustment: Lessons from the IMF's Extended Fund Facility," *International Organization*, 39:505-34, Summer 1985.

Helleiner, G. K., "Stabilization, Adjustment, and the Poor," bibl., *World Development*, 15:1499-513, Dec 1987.

Horowitz, Irving Louis, "The 'Rashomon' Effect: Ideological Proclivities and Political Dilemmas of the International Monetary Fund," *Journal of Inter-American Studies and World Affairs*, 27(4):37-55, Winter 1985/1986.

Howe, G., "International Monetary Fund and the World Bank: The British Approach," *International Affairs*, 58:199-209, Spring 1982.

Jeker, Rolf M., "Voting Rights of Less Developed Countries in the IMF," *Journal of World Trade Law*, 12:218-227, May/June 1978.

Jones, M., "IMF Surveillance, Policy Coordination, and Time Consistency," bibl., *International Economic Review*, 28:135-58, Feb 1987.

Kenen, P. B., "What Role for IMF Surveillance?," bibl., *World Development*, 15:1445-56, Dec 1987.

Makgelta, N. S., "Theoretical and Practical Implications of IMF Conditionality in Zambia," *Journal of Modern African Studies*, 24:395-422, Sept 1986.

Makhijani, Arjun, & Browne, Robert S., "Restructuring the
    International Monetary System," *World Policy Journal*,
    3(1):59-80, Winter 1985/1986.

Mares, D. R., "Explaining Choice of Development Strategies:
    Suggestions from Mexico, 1970-1982," *International
    Organization*, 39:667-97, Autumn 1985.

Mcleod, A. N., "Reforming the International Monetary
    System (Emphasis on Special Drawing Rights and the
    International Monetary Fund)," *International Journal of
    Social Economics*, 10(2):44-61, 1983.

Mundell, Robert, "The International Monetary Fund," *The
    Journal of World Trade Law*, 3:455-97, Sept/Oct 1967.

Oessler, F. R., "Pressures to Adjust Balance of Payments
    Disequilibria: An Analysis of the Powers of the
    International   Monetary   Fund,"   *International
    Organization*, 30:433-52, Summer 1976.

Officer, Lawrence H., "The Differential Use of IMF Resources
    by Industrial, Other Developed, and Less Developed
    Countries: A Historical Approach," *Finance and
    Development*, 16:401-20, April 1982.

Osieke, Ebere, "Majority Voting Systems in the International
    Labor Organization and the International Monetary
    Fund," *International and Comparative Law Quarterly*,
    33:381-408, April 1984.

Pastor, M., "Latin America, the Debt Crisis, and the
    International Monetary Fund," *Latin American
    Perspective*, 16:79-109, Winter 1989.

Pastor, M., Jr., "The Effects of the IMF Programs in the
    Third World: Debate and Evidence from Latin America,"
    bibl., *World Development*, 15:249-62, Feb 1987.

Paul, Alix-Herard, "The 'Destabilization' Program of the IMF
    in Jamaica (How Attempts to Implement International

Monetary Fund Policies Affected the Country's Economic and Political Situation)," *Inter-American Economic Affairs*, 37:45-61, Autumn 1983.

Remmer, K. L., "The Politics of Economic Stabilization: IMF Standby Programs in Latin America, 1954-1984," *Comparative Politics*, 19:1-24, Oct 20, 1986.

Rowely, A., "Focus: World Bank/IMF '85," *Far Eastern Economic Review*, 130:47-94, Oct 10, 1985.

Russell, Robert O., "Transgovernmental Interaction in the International Monetary System, 1960-1972," *International Organization*, 28(4):431-64, Autumn 1973.

Schoenholtz, A. I., "The IMF in Africa: Unnecessary and Undesirable Western Restraints on Development," *Journal of Modern African Studies*, 25:403-33, Sept 1987.

Schweitzer, P. O., "Political Aspects of Managing the International Monetary System," *International Affairs*, 52:208-18, April 1976.

Seidman, A., "Towards Ending an IMF-ism in Southern Africa: An Alternative Developmental Strategy," *Journal of Modern African Studies*, 221-22, March 1989.

Smith, D., & Knieper, R., "Conditioning of National Policy-Making by International Law: The Stand-by Arrangements of the International Monetary Fund," bibl., *International Journal of Sociological Law*, 11:41-64, Feb 1983.

Steele, D. B., "The Case for Global Economic Management and UN System Reform," *International Organization*, 39:561-78, Summer 1985.

Swedberg, R., "The Doctrine of Economic Neutrality of the IMF and the World Bank," *Journal of Peace Research*, 23(4):377-90, 1986.

"World Bank/IMF '86 Focus," *Far Eastern Economic Review*, 134:51-92, Oct 2, 1986.

Zijan, Zhao, "World Bank — IMF: Difficult Tasks Lie Ahead," *Beijing Review*, 30:10-11, Oct 19, 1987.

International Telecommunications Union

BOOKS

Codding, George. *The International Telecommunications Union*. Dedham, MA: Artech House. 1972.

Codding, George A. *The Future of Satellite Communication*. Boulder, CO: Westview Press. 1990.

Codding, George A., & Rutkowski, Anthony M. *The International Telecommunication Union in a Changing World*. Dedham, MA: Artech House. 1982.

Global Communication in the Space Age: Toward a New ITU. New York: John and Mary Markle Foundation. 1972.

The ITU: Issues and New Steps: A Report. Washington, DC: American Society of International Telecommunication Policy, Carnegie Endowment. 1971.

Leive, David M. *International Telecommunications and International Law: The Regulation of the Radio Spectrum*. Dobbs Ferry, NY: Oceana Publications. 1970.

Savage, James G. *The Politics of International Telecommunication Regulation*. Boulder, CO: Westview Press. 1989.

Smith, Delbert D. *International Telecommunication Control.* Dobbs Ferry, NY: Oceana Publications. 1969.

White, Rita Lauria, & White, Harold M., Jr. *The Law and Regulation of International Space Communication.* Dedham, MA: Artech House. 1988.

ARTICLES

Codding, George A., "Financing Development Assistance in the ITU," *Telecommunication Policy,* 13:13-24, March 1989.

Feketekuty, Geza, "Telecommunications and Trade: Implications for GATT and ITU," *Transnational Data and Communications Report,* 11:16-22, May 1988.

Gregg, Donna C., "Capitalizing on Self-Interest: The Management of International Telecommunication Conflict by the International Telecommunication Union," *Law and Contemporary Problems,* 45:37-52, Winter 1982.

Hudson, Heather, "New Communication Technologies: Policy Issues for the Developing World," *International Political Science Review,* 7(3):332-43, July 1986.

Miles, Edward, "Transnationalism in Space: Inner and Outer," *International Organization,* 25:602-25, Summer 1971.

Rotholatt, Martin A., "ITU Regulation of Satellite Communication (Proposal for Equitable Frequency Allocation by the International Telecommunication Union)," *Stanford Journal of International Law,* 18:1-25, Spring 1982.

Segal, Brian, "Geopolitics of Broadcasting," *Washington Quarterly,* 6(2):140-48, Spring 1983.

Staple, G. C., "The New World Satellite Order: A Report from Geneva," *American Journal of International Law*, 80:699-720, July 1986.

Sussman, Leonard R., & Sussman, David W., "Mass News Media and International Law," *International Political Science Review*, 7(3):344-60, July 1986.

"Telecommunications," *South*, p. 41+, Oct 1987.

"United States Participation in the International Telecommunication Union: A Series of Interviews (the Perceived 'Politicization' of the ITU and U.S. Strategies for Dealing with the Growing Complexities Involved in International Regulation of Communications)," *Fletcher Forum*, 9:37-68, Winter 1985.

United Nations Conference on Trade and Development

BOOKS

Friedeberg, A. S. *The United Nations Conference on Trade and Development of 1964.* Rotterdam: Rotterdam University Press. 1969.

Gosovic, B. *UNCTAD Conflict and Compromise: The Third World's Quest for an Equitable World Economic Order Through the UN.* New York: Heinemann. 1972.

Gosovic, Branislav. *UNCTAD: A Political Analysis.* Washington, DC: Carnegie Endowment. 1968.

Hagras, Kamal M. *The United Nations Conference on Trade and Development: A Case Study in UN Diplomacy.* New York: Praeger. 1965.

Micholak, Stanley. *The United Nations Conference on Trade and Development: An Organization Betraying its Mission.* Washington, DC: Heritage Foundation. 1983.

Rothstein, Robert L. *Global Bargaining: UNCTAD and the Quest for a New International Economic Order.* Princeton, NJ: Princeton University Press. 1979.

Shah, M. *Developing Countries and UNCTAD (United Nations Conference on Trade and Development).* 2nd ed. Bombay, India: Vora. 1969.

Stevenson, Robert L. *Communication, Development, and the Third World: The Global Politics of Information.* White Plains, NY: Longman. 1988.

Weiss, Thomas. *Multilateral Development Diplomacy in UNCTAD.* London: Macmillan. 1986.

Zammit Cutajar, Michael, ed. *UNCTAD and the South-North Dialogue: The First Twenty Years: Essays in Memory of W. R. Malinowski.* Elmsford, NY: Permagon. 1985.

ARTICLES

Bhattacharya, Anindya K., "The Influence of the International Secretariat: UNCTAD and Generalized Tariff Preferences," *International Organization*, 30:75-90, Winter 1976.

Bronfenbrenner, M., "Predatory Poverty on the Offensive: The UNCTAD Record," *Economic Development and Cultural Change*, 24:825-31, July 1976.

Claremont, F. F., "Prebisch and UNCTAD: The Banality of Compromise," *Journal of Contemporary Asia*, 16(4):427-55, 1986.

Cordovez, Diego, "The Making of UNCTAD," *Journal of World Trade Law*, 1:243-328, May/June 1967.

Crane, B. B., "Policy Coordination by Major Western Powers in Bargaining with the Third World Debt Relief and the

Common Fund," *International Organization*, 38:399-428, Summer 1984.

Cutler, R. M., "East-South Relations at UNCTAD: Global Political Economy and the CMEA," *International Organization*, 37:121-42, Winter 1983.

Fawcett, J. E. S., "UNCTAD IV: Another Bill of Rights?," *World Today*, 32:152-59, April 1976.

Frank, Isaiah, "New Perspectives on Trade and Development," *Foreign Affairs*, 45:522-40, April 1967.

Gardner, Richard, "The UN Conference on Trade and Development," *International Organization*, 22:99-130, Winter 1968.

Gonzalex, Heliodoro, "UNCTAD III — Beggar's Opera: The Bureaucratic Overreach," *Inter-American Economic Affairs*, 25(2):51-67, Autumn 1972.

Gosovic, Branislav, "UNCTAD: North-South Encounter," in *The Process of International Organization*, Robert Wood (ed.), Random House, 1971, 468-507.

Juda, L., "World Shipping: UNCTAD and the International Economic Order," *International Organization*, 35:493-516, Summer 1981.

Krishnamurti, R., "UNCTAD as a Negotiating Institution," *Journal of World Trade Law*, 3-40, 1981.

Lipton, M., "UNCTAD Schmunctad?," *Round Table*, 247:297-308, July 1972.

Patel, Surendra J., "Transfer of Technology and Third UNCTAD," *Journal of World Trade Law*, 7:226-39, April 1973.

Ramsay, R., "UNCTAD's Failures: The Rich Get Richer," *International Organization*, 38:387-97, Spring 1984.

Robertson, Charles L., "The Creation of UNCTAD," *International Organization: World Politics, Studies in Economic and Social Agencies,* Robert Cox(ed.), Macmillan, 1969, 258-74.

Roffe, P., "UNCTAD: Code of Conduct for the Transfer of Technology: Progress and Issues Under Negotiation (Particularly on Subjects of Great Concern to Developing Countries)," *Journal of World Trade Law,* 14:160-72, March/April 1980.

Sanders, Ron, "An Assessment of UNCTAD's Effectiveness as an Instrument to Promote the Interests of the Third World," *Round Table,* 272-87, July 1989.

Skelton, James W., Jr., "UNCTAD's Draft Code of Conduct on the Transfer of Technology: A Critique," *Vanderbilt Journal of Transitional Law,* 14:381-96, Spring 1981.

Thompson, Dennis, "The UNCTAD Code on Transfer of Technology," *World Trade Law,* 16:11-37, July/Aug 1982.

Walters, Robert S., "International Organizations and Political Communication: The Use of UNCTAD by Less Developed Countries," *International Organization,* 259(4):818-35, Autumn 1971.

Weiss, Thomas G., "UNCTAD: What Next?," *Journal of World Trade Law,* 19:251-68, May/June 1985.

United Nations Educational, Scientific and Cultural Organization

BOOKS

Besterman, Theodore. *UNESCO, Peace in the Minds of Men.* Portsmouth, NH: Methuen. 1951.

Evans, Luther H. *The United States and UNESCO.* Dobbs Ferry, NY: Oceana. 1971.

Haves, Walter A. C., & Thomson, Charles A. *UNESCO: Purpose, Progress, Prospects.* Bloomington, IN: Indiana University Press. 1957.

Hoggart, Richard. *An Idea & Its Servants: UNESCO from Within.* Fairlawn, NJ: Oxford University Press. 1978.

Huxley, Julian. *UNESCO: Its Purpose and Philosophy.* Washington, DC: Public Affairs Press. 1947.

In the Minds of Men: UNESCO 1946-1971. Lanham, MD: Unipublishers. 1972.

Maheu, Rene. *UNESCO in Perspective.* Lanham, MD: Unipublishers. 1974.

Many Voices, One World: Towards a New, More Just and More Efficient World Information and Communication Order. Paris, France: UNESCO. 1980.

McHugh, Lois. *UNESCO: The U.S. Withdrawal in Perspective.* Washington, DC: Congressional Research Service. 1984.

Preston, William, Jr., et al. *Hope and Folly: The U.S. and UNESCO, 1945-1985.* Minneapolis, MN: Media & Society, University of Minnesota Press. 1989.

Risser, Nancy, Sussman, Leonard, & Wiley, David. *What are the Issues Concerning the Decision of the United States to Withdraw from UNESCO.* Washington, DC: United States National Commission for UNESCO. 1984.

Sathyamurthy, T. V. *The Politics of International Cooperation: Contrasting Conceptions of UNESCO.* Geneva, Switzerland: Droz. 1966.

Sewell, James P. *UNESCO and World Politics: Engaging in International Relations.* Princeton, NJ: Princeton University Press. 1975.

Sharp, Walter. *UNESCO.* New York: Columbia University Press. 1969.

Shuster, George N. *UNESCO: Assessment and Promise.* New York: Harper & Row. 1963.

Smith, Anthony. *The Geopolitics of Information: How Western Culture Dominates the World.* Fairlawn, NJ: Oxford University Press. 1980.

Thomas, Jean. *UNESCO.* Paris, France: Gallimard. 1962.

Wells, Clare. *The UN, UNESCO and the Politics of Knowledge.* London: Macmillan. 1987.

ARTICLES

Allen, Michael J., "UNESCO and the ILO: A Tale of Two UN Agencies," *Notre Dame Journal of Law Ethics and Public Policy,* 1:391-419, Winter 1985.

Argumedo, Alcira, "The New World Information Order and International Power," *Journal of International Affairs,* 35(2):179-88, Fall/Winter 1981/1982.

Belshaw, C. S., "UNESCO's Programme and Priorities," *Current Anthropology,* 17:158-64, March 1976.

Bethell, T., "Lost Civilization of UNESCO," *Political Review,* 24:19-47, Spring 1983.

"Convention on the Means of Prohibiting and Preventing the Illicit Import, Export, and Transfer of Ownership of Cultural Property," *American Journal of International Law,* 65:887-95, Oct 1971.

Diene, D., "UNESCO and Communications in the Modern World," *Journal of International Affairs*, 35:217-24, Fall/Winter 1981/1982.

Evans, Luther H., "Some Management Problems of UNESCO," *International Organization*, 16:76-90, 1963.

Finger, Seymour Maxwell, ed., "Theme Issue: UNESCO's New World Information Order," *Political Communication and Persuasion*, 1(4):317-87, 1982.

Fore, W. F., "A New World Order in Communication," *Christian Century*, 99:442-46, April 14, 1982.

Hocking, Brian, "Words and Deeds: Why America Left UNESCO," *The World Today*, 41:75-78, 1985.

"International Book Year and UNESCO's Role in the Field of Copyright," *Copyright Bulletin*, 69(3):4-11, 1972.

Jordan, R. S., "Boycott Diplomacy: The U.S., the UN, and UNESCO," *Public Administration Review*, 44:283-91, July/Aug 1984.

Krill de Capollo, H. H., "The Creation of the United Nations Educational, Scientific and Cultural Organization," *International Organization*, 24(1):1-30, 1970.

Maheu, Rene, "UNESCO: 1946-1971: UNESCO and Its Programme, Economic and Social Development and the Quality of Life," *UNESCO Chronicle*, 17:397-423, Nov 1971.

Mayor, F., "Bad Act to Follow," *Economist*, 305:50-51, Oct 24, 1987.

Pendergast, W. R., "UNESCO and French Cultural Relations 1945-1970," *International Organization*, 30:453-83, Summer 1976.

Powell, William C., "The New World Information Order," *Political Communication and Persuasion*, 1(4):329-35, 1982.

Sathyamurthy, T. V., "Twenty Years of UNESCO: An Interpretation," *International Organization*, 21:614-33, Summer 1967.

Stevenson, Robert L., "The MacBride Commission Report Reconsidered," *Political Communication and Persuasion*, 2(2):147-57, 1983.

Sussmann, Leonard R., "Independent News Media: The People's Press Cannot be Run by Government," *Journal of International Affairs*, 35(2):199-216, Fall/Winter 1981/1982.

Tocatlian, J., "The Role of UNESCO in International Scientific Communication," *Annals of the American Academy of Political and Social Sciences*, 495:84-94, Jan 1988.

Tripp, Brenda M. H., "UNESCO in Perspective," *International Conciliation*, 497:323-83, March 1954.

Underhill, Evi, "UNESCO and the American Challenge," *Journal of World Trade Law*, 18:381-95, Sept - Oct 1984.

"The United States Withdrawal from UNESCO," (table), *International Legal Materials*, 24:489-530, March 1985.

Universal Postal Union

BOOKS

Codding, George A., Jr. *The Universal Postal Union*. New York: New York University Press. 1964.

Cotreau, James Donald. *Historical Development of the Universal Postal Union and the Question of Membership.* Boston: [s.n.]. 1975.

ARTICLE

Meonon, M. A. K., "Cursus Publicus," *International Conciliation*, 552:3-64, March 1965.

World Health Organization

BOOKS

Berkov, Robert. *The World Health Organization: A Study in Decentralized International Administration.* Geneva, Switzerland: Libraire E. Droz. 1957.

Berkov, Robert. *The First Ten Years of the World Health Organization.* Albany, NY: WHO. 1958.

Berkov, Robert. *The Second Ten Years.* Albany, NY: WHO. 1968.

Brockington, Fraser. *World Health.* 3rd ed. White Plains, NY: Longman. 1975.

Chisholm, Brock. *Prescription for Survival.* Irvington, NY: Columbia University Press. 1957.

Goodman, Neville. *International Health Organizations and Their Work.* White Plains, NY: Longman. 1971.

Hoole, Francis W. *Politics and Budgeting in the World Health Organization.* Bloomington, IN: Indiana University Press. (International Development Research Center, Studies in Development: No. 11). 1976.

Morgan, Murray C. *Doctors to the World.* New York: Viking Press. 1958.

ARTICLES

Andrews, Alice C., "Worldwide Disease Eradication: Malaria and Smallpox (Efforts of the World Health Organization)," *Virginia Social Science Journal*, 17:42-51, April 1982.

Ascher, Charles S., "Current Problems in the World Health Organization's Program," *International Organization*, 6:27-50, Feb 1952.

Codding, George, "Contributions of the WHO and ICAO to the Development of International Law," *American Journal of International Law Proceedings*, 147-52, 1965.

Finkle, Jason L., "The World Health Organization and the Population Issue: Organizational Values in the United Nations," *Population and Development Review*, 2:367-93, 1976.

Gunning-Schepers, Louise J., "Health for All by the Year 2000: A Mere Slogan or a Workable Formula?," *Health Policy*, 6(3): 227-37, 1986.

Kaplan, M., "Science's Role in the WHO," *Science*, 180:1028-32, June 9, 1973.

Navarro, V., "A Critique of the Ideological and Political Positions of the Willy Brandt Report and the WHO Alma Ata Declaration," *Social Science Medicine 18*, 6:467-74, 1984.

Sikkink, K., "Codes of Conduct for Transnational Corporations: The Base of the WHO/UNICEF Code," *International Organization*, 40:815-40, Autumn 1986.

World Intellectual Property Organization

ARTICLES

Braderman, Eugene M., "New Directions in International Production and Intellectual Property," *Department of State Bulletin*, 64:772-77, June 14, 1971.

Kaplinsky, R., "Industrial and Intellectual Property Rights in the Uruguay Round," *Journal of Development Studies*, 25:373-400, April 1989.

Sviridov, Felix A., "International Patent Information: The Role of the World Intellectual Property Organization," *UNESCO Bulletin for Libraries*, 32:315-21, Sept/Oct 1978.

World Meteorological Organization

BOOK

WMO: One Hundred Years of International Cooperation in Meteorology: An Historical Review, 1873-1973. Lanham, MD: Unipublishers. 1973.

ARTICLES

Bailey, H. P., "Reflections on the World Weather Program," *Geographical Review*, 61:303-06, 1971.

Corbridge, James N., Jr., & Moss, Ralph, "Weather Modification: Law and Administration," *National Resources Journal*, 8:207-35, April 1965.

Davies, David Arthur, "The Role of WMO in Environmental Issues," *International Organization*, 26(2):327-36, Spring 1972.

Taubenfeld, Rita F. & Howard J., "Some International Implications of Weather Modification Activities," *International Organization*, 23:808-33, 1969.

Weiss, Edith Brown, "International Responses to Weather Modification," *International Organization*, 29(3):805-26, Summer 1975.

INDEX